Helping Young Children Learn Language and Literacy

CAROL VUKELICH
University of Delaware

JAMES CHRISTIE
Arizona State University

BILLIE ENZ
Arizona State University

With Special Features by
SARAH HUDELSON
IRENE ALICIA SERNA

Allyn and Bacon

Boston ■ London ■ Toronto ■ Sydney ■ Tokyo ■ Singapore

Series Editor: *Aurora Martínez Ramos*
Editorial Assistant: *Beth Slater*
Executive Marketing Manager: *Amy Cronin*
Editorial Production Administrator: *Bryan Woodhouse*
Editorial Production Service: *Chestnut Hill Enterprises, Inc.*
Composition and Prepress Buyer: *Linda Cox*
Manufacturing Buyer: *Julie McNeill*
Cover Administrator: *Kristina Mose-Libon*
Electronic Composition: *Omegatype Typography, Inc.*

Library of Congress Cataloging-in-Publication Data

Vukelich, Carol.
   Helping young children learn language and literacy / Carol Vukelich, James Christie, Billie Enz; with special features by Sarah Hudelson, Irene Alicia Serna.
      p.   cm.
   Includes bibliographical references and index.
   ISBN 0-205-34233-7
      1. Language arts (Preschool)   2. Children—Language.   I. Christie, James F.   II. Enz, Billie.   III. Title.

LB1140.5.L3 V85 2002
372.6—dc21

2001046378

Contents

chapter **3**   **Facilitating Oral Language Learning**   **40**

chapter 9 **Organizing the Curriculum
and Classroom Environment** **195**

chapter **10** **Helping Families Facilitate Language and Literacy Development**   **219**

Preface

This book is about teaching the language arts—about facilitating reading, writing, speaking, and listening development for children between the ages of two and five. The language arts are essential to everyday life and central to all learning. Through reading, listening, writing, and talking, children come to understand the world. This book explains how young children's language and literacy develop and how early childhood teachers can help children become fluent, flexible, effective users of oral and written language.

Themes

Children are at the center of all good language and literacy teaching. This principle underlies the three themes that run throughout this book: a constructivist perspective on learning, respect for diversity, and instruction-based assessment.

Our first theme emphasizes that children construct their own knowledge about oral and written language by engaging in integrated, meaningful, and functional activities with other people. Children do not first study speaking, then listening, then reading, then writing. Children learn by engaging in activities in which language and literacy are embedded. We begin this book with a discussion of these basic assumptions about learning and then show how these principles translate into practice in teaching the language arts at the preschool and kindergarten levels. The book describes how children acquire language and literacy knowledge in many different contexts and how teachers can design authentic classroom reasons for using oral and written language.

Our second theme is respect for diversity. The constructivist view of learning maintains that children build knowledge by combining new information with what they already know. Thus, children's personal experiences, both at home and at school, are important factors in learning. In our diverse society, children come to school with vastly different backgrounds, both in terms of life experiences and language. This diversity needs to be taken into account when designing instructional activities for children and in evaluating children's responses to these activities. Illustrations of how teachers can work effectively with diverse learners can be found throughout this book. Special emphasis is given to linguistic diversity. In a series of Special Features, Sarah Hudelson and Irene Serna describe how teachers can help second-language learners become bilingual and biliterate.

Every child comes to school with a wealth of information about how written and spoken language works in the real world. Teachers must discover what each student already knows in order to build on that student's knowledge through appropriate classroom activities. Because we recognize that assessment cannot be separated from good teaching, instructionally linked assessment is our third major theme. We introduce the principles of instruction-based assessment in Chapter 1. Many subsequent chapters contain information on strategies that teachers can use to understand children's language and literacy knowledge in the context of specific learning and teaching events.

Organization

Chapter 1 provides the foundation for the book by discussing three basic assumptions about language and literacy learning: constructivism, respect for diversity, and instruction-based assessment. These three themes run throughout the book and underlie all of the teaching strategies that we recommend in subsequent chapters.

The next two chapters deal with oral language development. Chapter 2 describes the phenomenal growth of oral language that occurs between birth and age five and discusses the major theories that help us understand language acquisition. Special emphasis is placed on the new biological view of development, which is an outcome of recent advances in brain research. Chapter 3 presents strategies for facilitating oral language learning both at home and at school. Special attention is given to strategies that use play to promote language growth.

Chapter 4 presents the emergent literacy perspective. It describes what children learn about print during the early years and the home experiences that promote this learning. The next three chapters describe instructional strategies for promoting early literacy learning. Chapter 5 discusses sharing books with young children; Chapter 6 covers functional literacy, linking literacy and play, and language experience/shared writing; and Chapter 7 presents developmentally appropriate forms of reading and instruction.

Chapter 8 focuses on ongoing, instructionally linked assessment and explains how to use portfolios to demonstrate growth over time in children's language and literacy learning. In addition, this chapter contains suggestions on how to adapt instruction to meet the needs of bilingual and second-language learners and children with developmental variations and disabilities.

Chapter 9 is aimed at helping teachers pull it all together and organize an effective language arts program. This chapter contains suggestions for integrating the curriculum, designing an effective classroom environment, and organizing the daily schedule.

Finally, Chapter 10 describes how teachers can establish effective home–school links and help parents become effective "first teachers" of language and literacy. Suggestions are given for home visits, workshops, phone calls, and written communication. In addition, examples are given of how teachers and schools can supply resources to promote home language and literacy learning.

Key Features

In order to give concrete illustrations of language and literacy learning, this book contains several detailed case studies. Chapter 2 contains the story of two children's oral language acquisition: a neuro-biological account of Joel's language learning during first two years of life; and a social-interactionist view of Dawn's language development from infancy through kindergarten. Chapter 3 describes the early literacy development of Tiffany, a monolingual English speaker, and Alicia, a Spanish-speaking kindergartner who is just beginning to learn oral English. These case studies bring to life many of the key concepts about language and literacy learning that are stressed in this book.

Special Feature boxes are interspersed throughout the book to provide in-depth information about topics relating to language and literacy learning and to teaching the language arts. Most notable are those by Sarah Hudelson and Irene Serna mentioned earlier that provide information about how teachers can adjust instruction to meet the needs of second-language and bilingual learners and the Special Feature by Karen Burstein and Tanis Bryan in Chapter 8 that describes how to adapt instruction for children with special needs.

The book also contains a number of Trade Secrets boxes in which veteran teachers describe in their own words how they provide children with effective language arts instruction. The Trade Secrets illustrate how teaching strategies can be applied in specific situations and reveal how teachers deal with practical problems that arise in the classroom.

Acknowledgments

Many outstanding educators helped us write this book. Our very special thanks to Sarah Hudelson and Irene Serna for their Special Features on second-language and bilingual learners. Like us, they sat before their computers for many days. From them, we learned how our ideas about teaching the language arts are appropriate for use with children whose primary language is a language other than English. We are also greatly indebted to Karen Burstein and Tanis Bryan for their feature on children with special needs.

Many classroom teachers shared their secrets, showing how theory and research link with quality classroom practice. We are grateful to Doreen Bardsley, Grace and Dan Bass, Chris Boyd, Lynn Cohen, Beth Conway, JoAnne Deshon, Nancy Edwards, Kathy Eustace, Colleen R. Fierro, Dawn Foley, Debhra Handley, Phoebe Bell Ingraham, Maureen Jobe, Donna Manz, Tere Pelaez, Cyndy Schmidt, and Bernadette Watson. From these teachers and others like them, we have seen how exciting language and literacy learning can be when teachers and children are engaged in purposeful language arts activities. From them and their students, we have learned much.

Several of our colleagues played a role in the construction of this book through their willingness to engage us in many conversations about children's language and literacy learning. Never unwilling to hear our ideas and to share their own, colleagues like Kathy Roskos, John Carroll University; Susan B. Neuman, US Dept. of Education; Mary Roe, University of Oregon; Peggy Dillner, University of Delaware; Lyn Searfoss, Jill Stamm, and Chari Woodward, Arizona State University; Sandy Stone, Northern Arizona University; and Cookie Bolig and Mike Kelley, Delaware Department of Public Instruction, have greatly helped us frame our arguments. Our other university colleagues, graduate students like Bonnie Albertson, Luisa Araujo, Gaysha Beard, JoAnne Deshon, Chris Evans, and Tere Pelaez of the University of Delaware; and Maureen Gerard, Myae Han, and Cory Hansen of Arizona State University have been helpful in similar ways.

The students we have nurtured and taught, both young children and college students, also have influenced the development of our ideas. Their questions, their talk, their play, their responses, their enthusiasm—each one of them has taught us about the importance of the language arts in our lives. Their positive response to our ideas fueled our eagerness to share those ideas more broadly. What better honor than to learn that a "black market" of photocopies of the early drafts of the chapters of this book had developed on our campuses.

The final draft of this book is much better because of the feedback we received during our writing. Our students came to us with questions and suggestions. We revised. Alice Shepard, office specialist, read drafts of chapters numerous times and offered valuable suggestions. The "official" reviewers of this manuscript—Judith S. Amatangelo, University of Texas at San Antonio; Susan Gomez, California State University, Sacramento; Delmi B. Gunawardena, Kent State University; Margaret R. Hawkins, University of Wisconsin-Madison; Jann Hunter, New Mexico State University; Judith H. Skyllingstad, Sinclair Community College; Susan Trostle, University of Rhode Island; and Kathleen Pullan Watkins, Community College of Pennsylvania—provided just the right amount of thoughtful praise, suggestions, and criticisms. We revised.

Finally, our families have helped us write this book. Tiffany and Dawn Enz have provided wonderful examples of their use and enjoyment of oral and written language. The story of their journey to being competent language users brings life to the research and theory discussed in our book. Mary Christie, Don (Skip) Enz, and Ron Vukelich gave us time to write but also pulled us from our computers to experience antique shows, museums, trips, home repairs, life. And then, of course, there is our extended family—our parents, David and Dorothy Palm, Art and Emma Larson, Bill and Jeannine Fullerton, John and Florence Christie—who provided our early reading, writing, speaking, and listening experiences and helped us know firsthand the joys of learning and teaching the language arts.

Foundations of Language and Literacy

1

Tiffany and Dawn are shopping with their mother. Two-year-old Tiffany is sitting in the grocery cart as her five-year-old sister Dawn picks up a box of Cheerios.® "No, Dawn," says Tiffany as she vigorously shakes her head. Dawn replies, "Well then, what?" Tiffany points to a brightly colored box containing her favorite cereal, Trix.® "Dat." Dawn places the box in the cart as Tiffany nods in approval.

In the past two decades we have learned much about children's early literacy development. This new knowledge of how children learn language, reading, and writing has resulted in a major shift in our beliefs about how to teach and assess young children's literacy development. While we once thought that learning to read began in first grade, we now know that the process of learning to read begins long before children come to school. Like learning to speak and to listen, learning about print begins in the home at birth, as soon as children's parents begin to read stories to them or when children begin to notice the print that surrounds them.

In the mid-1970s, cognitive psychologists, child psychologists, and anthropologists confirmed that children become aware of print at very early ages (Teale & Sulzby, 1989). The vignette of Dawn and Tiffany shopping for cereal provides an illustration of young children's early awareness of print. As this interaction demonstrates, children as young as two years old can identify signs, labels, and logos they see in their homes and communities (Goodman, 1986; Hiebert, 1981). Similarly, home-based case studies of children under the age of three reveal that children have extensive knowledge of the practical functions of print—of writing lists to aid memory, of writing signs to control other people's behavior, and of writing letters to communicate (Bissex, 1980; Heath, 1983; Taylor, 1983; Taylor & Strickland, 1986).

The term *emergent literacy* is often used to refer to children's early understanding of reading and writing. This somewhat new line of investigation has significantly changed educators' view about two aspects of literacy: (1) how and when children begin to construct knowledge about reading and writing, and (2) how parents and early childhood teachers can most effectively support young children's ongoing literacy development (Morrow, 2001).

The emergent literacy perspective provides a clear and powerful example of how the *constructivist theory of learning* works. Drawing on a synthesis of current research in cognitive psychology, anthropology, and philosophy, the theory defines learning as the result of many "self-motivated interactions, a process of resolving inner cognitive conflicts that often become apparent through concrete experience, collaborative discourse, and self-reflection" (Fosnot, cited in Brooks & Brooks, 1993, p. vii). Although the constructivist theory is relatively new, it offers far-reaching implications for schools, for teachers, and for instruction. This theory reflects our beliefs about learning and provides the framework supporting the views about language and literacy presented in this book.

Before reading this chapter, think about. . .

- your beliefs about how young children first learn to read and write. At what age do children begin to learn about literacy? Is knowledge about reading and writing transmitted from adults to young children, or do children construct this knowledge on their own?

BOX 1.1

Definition of Terms

constructivist theory of learning: the view that children actively construct meaning by making connections between new experiences and their prior knowledge, by making and testing their own hypotheses, and by interacting with peers and more knowledgeable others.

emergent literacy: children's early understandings about reading and writing.

scaffolding: temporary assistance and support that enable young children to do things that they could not do on their own.

schemas: the mental structures that store and organize knowledge.

zone of proximal development: a stage at which a child has partially mastered a skill but can use this skill only with the help of others.

- your beliefs about effective language and literacy instruction. How can teachers best help young children become skilled speakers, listeners, readers, and writers?
- your memories about how you learned to talk, read, and write. Do you recall, for example, reading cereal labels at an early age? Do you recall writing messages to loved ones?

Focus Questions

- How do young children learn about language and literacy?
- Why is it crucial for teachers to respect children's diversity when teaching language and literacy?
- How should young children's literacy learning be assessed?
- What are the best practices in teaching language and literacy to young children?

Language and Literacy: Definitions and Interrelationships

The terms *language* and *literacy* can be defined in many ways. *Language* can be defined very broadly as any system of symbols that is used to transmit meaning (Bromley, 1988). These symbols can consist of sounds, finger movements, print, and so on. *Literacy* also has several different meanings. It can refer to the ability to create meaning through different media (e.g., *visual literacy*), knowledge of key concepts and ideas (e.g., *cultural literacy*), and the ability to deal effectively with different subject areas and technologies (e.g., *mathematical literacy, computer literacy*).

Because the topic of this book is early childhood language arts—the part of the school curriculum that deals with helping children learn to speak, listen, read, and write—we use school-based definitions of these terms. *Language* refers to oral language, (communicating via speaking and listening), and *literacy* refers to reading and writing (communicating through print). However, as we describe how children grow in both these areas, it will become obvious that language and literacy acquisition are closely tied to the total development of the child— learning to think, to make sense of the world, to get along with others, and so on.

While we have organized this book into separate chapters on oral language and literacy, it is important to note that the two types of language are integrally connected and related to each other. Oral language provides the base and foundation for literacy. Oral language involves first-order symbolism, with spoken words representing meaning. Written language, on the other hand, involves second-order symbolism that builds on the first-order symbolism of oral language. Printed symbols represent spoken words that, in turn, represent meaning. Do you see the connections between language and literacy?

One obvious connection between oral and written language is vocabulary. In order for a reader to recognize and get meaning from text, most of the words represented by the text must already be in the reader's oral vocabulary. If the reader can recognize most of the words in the text, context cues might be used to figure out the meaning of a few totally unfamiliar words. Similarly, a writer's choice of words is restricted by his or her oral vocabulary.

Catherine Snow and her colleagues (1991) point out a less obvious, but equally important, link between oral language and literacy. She points out that oral language is actually an array of skills related to different functions. One set of skills is relevant to the negotiation of inter-personal relationships and involves the child's ability to engage in face-to-face conversations (contextualized language). Another involves the ability to use language to convey information to audiences who are not physically present (decontextualized language). Decontextualized language has a vital role in literacy because it is the type of language that is typically used in written texts.

Children gain experience in these different aspects of language through different activities. They become skilled at contextualized language by engaging in conversations with others, whereas they gain skill at decontextualized language by listening to stories and by engaging in explanations and personal narratives and by creating fantasy worlds (Snow, 1991). It not surprising, therefore, that research has shown that children with rich oral language experiences at home tend to become early readers (Dickinson & Tabors, 2000) and have high levels of reading achievement during the elementary grades (Wells, 1986).

The relationship between literacy and oral language becomes reciprocal once children become proficient readers. Extensive reading begins to build children's oral language capabilities, particularly their vocabulary knowledge. Cunningham and Stanovich (1998) present evidence that people are much more likely to encounter "rare" unfamiliar words in printed texts than in adult speech, and Swanborn and de Glopper's (1999) meta-analysis of studies on incidental word learning revealed that, during normal reading, students learn about 15 percent of the unknown words they encounter. The more children read, the larger their vocabularies become.

Because this book deals with the early stages of literacy development, the relationship between oral language and literacy is primarily one-way. Anything teachers can do to build children's oral language skills, particularly their vocabulary knowledge and ability to deal with decontextualized language, will also benefit children's literacy development. So even if a school's primary mission is to boost young children's literacy skills, attention also needs to given to building children's oral language abilities.

The Way Children Learn

A restless Hannah is standing next to her mother in the dance studio, eating a piece of chocolate. As she begins to take another bite, she runs her finger over the raised letters imprinted on the candy. Hannah asks her mother, "What does this say?" Her mother replies, "HER-SHEY, it says HER-SHEY." In a very puzzled voice, with a perplexed look, Hannah repeats "Her-she" several times. Then she asks, "Mommy, is this a girl candy bar?"

Close observations of very young children can provide interesting and sometimes humorous insights about how they construct hypotheses about print through everyday interactions (Holdaway, 1979; Teale, 1986a). As young as she is, 32-month-old Hannah demonstrates a delightful understanding of language and literacy. She knows that the symbols on the candy bar have meaning. She is also aware that the pronouns *her* and *she* are equivalents to the word *girl*. However, Hannah's confusion indicates that this new information did not make sense; nothing in her prior experiences had led her to believe that candy bars had a particular gender.

Supporters of the constructivist perspective on learning would assert that learners like Hannah actively construct their own knowledge by connecting new experiences with what they have previously come to expect and understand (Brooks & Brooks, 1993). Children learn by (1) making a connection between new information and prior known information and then (2) organizing that information into structures called *schemas*. Lea McGee and Don Richgels (1996, p. 5) explain that a schema is a "mental structure in which we store all the information we know about people, places, objects, or activities."

To illustrate this point, please take a few moments to think about vanilla. Do you remember the first time you smelled vanilla extract? (If you have never smelled it, buy a bottle and try it.)

- How would you describe the aroma? (sweet)
- How did you expect it to taste? (good)
- What were your reactions when you finally tasted it? (surprise—because it tasted bitter)

In daily living, we frequently encounter materials (such as vanilla extract), ideas, or words that do not make sense or fit into the way we presently organize our knowledge. For example, how vanilla smells (appealing) does not fit with how it tastes (bitter). When initially confronted with such a contradiction, we either

- interpret what we experience by incorporating new information into our present rules for explaining our world (anything that smells as good as vanilla must also taste good, so this must be a pleasant taste, and the initial judgment of bitter must be wrong), or
- hypothesize a new rule or a new set of rules that better accounts for what we perceive to be occurring (perhaps some things, like vanilla, that smell appealing may have an unappealing taste).

In either case, we are learning through a continual process of perceiving, interpreting our perceptions, confirming our predictions, and adapting our prior knowledge to make sense of new information. Therefore, our schemas about our world are expanding and changing daily as we constantly engage in the learning process.

According to constructivist theory, learning is basically a social process that takes place through the interactions between and among children and others in their environment (Vygotsky, 1978). It is through social interactions that children learn new things. "Working with others and talking about what they are doing is the way in which children learn because the roots of language and thought are social" (Galda, Cullinan, & Strickland, 1993, p. 10). This tenet is clearly illustrated by the following vignette:

> "I can do it, Mom," said three-year-old Zach as he watched his mother breast-feed his newborn sister. "Thank you, Zach, but only mommies make milk," replies his mother. Thinking for a minute, Zach ran to his bedroom and brought out his monkey doll. As he raised his shirt and brought the doll to his chest, Zach proudly announced "Zach makes apple juice! "

As Zach watches his mother feed and take care of his baby sister, he constructs a great deal of knowledge about his sister; about babies in general; and about the language, rituals, and complex routines that accompany child care. In fact, Zach is continually learning as he engages in activities and casual conversation with his parents. For instance, while shopping with his parents, he may learn about the functions and qualities of specific brands of diapers, baby cereal, and baby powder. As Zach reaches to retrieve these items in the store, his parents casually and immediately confirm the predictions he has made about the print on the baby-product labels. Zach is growing into literacy in much the same way as he learned to speak, by engaging in everyday activities with other people.

As the Zach vignette illustrates, it is the verbal interaction between the young child and someone more knowledgeable (parent, sibling) that helps children build new knowledge. Vygotsky referred to this as operating within the child's "zone of proximal development." A more knowledgeable other (parent, older sibling, other adult) supports a young child's completion of a task, allowing the child to succeed and eventually to complete the task independently. Often the adult or older child completes a part of the task (the part of the task the child cannot do on his or her own), and the young child completes another part of the task (the part the child can do independently). The adult or older child talks, as well as offers physical support, while the task is completed. In this way, the more knowledgeable other *scaffolds* the child's learning. Just as in constructing a building, this scaffold builds a support structure to help the child build a richer knowledge base, to create and extend held schema.

Auntie Carol's reading of one of her favorite books to two-and-a-half-year-old Lauren illustrates how an adult might scaffold a young child's learning. The book is *Caps for Sale* (Slobodkina, 1947).

> *Carol (reads):* Once there was a peddlar who sold [pauses] . . .
> *Lauren:* Caps.
> *Carol (reads):* He walked up the street and he walked down the street, holding himself very straight so as not to upset his caps, and as he walked along he called . . .
> *Lauren:* Caps! Caps!
> *Carol:* Ah! You're such a good reader, Lauren.

Lauren has heard this story numerous times. Her aunt "turns over" some of the reading to Lauren. Through her voice and her pausing, Carol signals Lauren that it is her turn to read. Carol scaffolds Lauren's reading of the book, supporting Lauren when Carol thinks Lauren needs help and encouraging her to "read" those parts Carol thinks Lauren can "read."

In sum, then, there are two features central to the constructivist learning theory. First, learners make connections between new experiences and their prior knowledge, constructing and testing hypotheses to make meaning. They revise existing schema or create new schema daily. Secondly, learners learn through social interaction with more knowledgeable others in their environment, in which they assume the role of the apprentice. Children watch and mimic the more knowledgeable others as these experts talk and engage in behaviors. With the appropriate support from these experts, young children's learning is scaffolded, creating a richer knowledge base.

Respect for Diversity

Zach, like most children, is growing up in a family or home setting. Further, his family exists within a community (maybe rural, maybe inner city, maybe suburban). Zach's social, cultural, and economic background will have a profound effect on his oral language and on his home reading and writing experiences. "We come to every situation with stories: patterns and sequences of events which are built into us. Our learning happens within the experience of what important others did" (Bateson, 1979, p. 13). In other words, the ways in which we make meaning and use words are dependent on the practices shared by the members of our community—the words chosen; the sentence structures used; the decision to talk after, or over, another's comment; and so on. As Allan Luke and Joan Kale (1997, p. 13) point out, "different cultures make meaning in different ways, with different patterns of exchange and interaction, text conventions and beliefs about reading and writing."

Given our increasingly diverse communities composed of many different cultures, teachers are more challenged than ever before to understand what this diversity means for their teaching and for their children's learning. Young children cannot be asked to leave their family and cultural backgrounds at the classroom door and enter into a "hybrid culture" (Au & Kawakami, 1991). Teachers must teach in ways that allow their young children to work to their strengths—and these strengths are going to be related to children's cultural backgrounds.

Some children will come to school having learned how to talk in ways that are consistent with their teachers' expectations; other children will not. Luke and Kale (1997, p. 11) provide an illustration of how disparate a child's language might be from school expectations. They share a story told by a young child, Elsey.

> *Tell you 'baut the crocodile first.*
> *Well, this crocodile 'e small tha/watnau? the chicken smell.*
> *It's a raw one.*
> *It's not a cook one*
> *but they eat raw one.*
> *So . . . This first big crocodile where they wanna send them away*
> *well, 'e smell/'e's/ take the smell of it*
> *so 'e went down an' just' stop . . .*

Luke and Kale ask readers to pause and try to "hear" Elsey's contribution. They ask readers to consider the judgments they would make about the child. They ask readers to think about what Elsey *can* do, not what she cannot do.

Unfortunately, we know far less about young children like Elsey's early language and literacy learning than we know about mainstream children's home experiences. In fact, it is only since the 1980s that researchers have investigated early literacy learning in nonmainstream homes and communities. In a pioneering study, Shirley Brice Heath (1983) described how children growing up in one working-class community learn that reading is sitting still and sounding out words, following the rules; whereas children in another working-class community learn that being able to tell a story well orally is more important than being able to read written texts. These conceptions of literacy were quite different from those found in children from middle-class families. The important question is: Should these types of cultural differences be viewed as deficits that must be "fixed" in order for children to succeed in school, or should these differences be viewed as positive characteristics that teachers can take advantage of when helping children learn language and literacy?

In the early 1960s, the "deficit" theory was in favor. For example, researchers and educators viewed use of a different language dialect as an explanation for why some children, particularly those from poverty environments, did not achieve in school. Programs like Head Start and Follow Through were funded to "fix" low-socioeconomic children's language. Specific language programs, like DISTAR, were designed to ameliorate the disadvantaged children's language deficiencies. DISTAR developers believed that if disadvantaged children repeated the structural patterns common to Standard English, the mainstream school dialect, these children would be ready to learn better and achieve more.

Today we know that this "deficit" view of some young children's language learning is based on incorrect language learning assumptions. Linguistically, dialects are just as rich and complex as Standard English. Children who use a dialect like Black English are equally as capable of encoding complex thoughts as those who use Standard English. These dialects need to be respected by teachers and viewed as a difference rather than a deficit.

When children who speak a dialect come to an educational institution outside the home (school, day care center, preschool program), they are faced with the challenge of learning English as it is spoken by the mainstream culture. For example, Elsey, an English-dialect speaker, had to learn which auxiliaries (might, have) to select; the rules for posing a question; how to use English pronouns; the rules governing what can be said to an adult; how to get and hold the floor; a sense of the social purposes for literacy and the interaction patterns around text; the form and content of conventional children's literature stories; and how to use English appropriately in a variety of different settings.

Will children like Elsey meet teachers who have engaged in the study of the children's community's ways with words and texts? Will their teachers provide scaffolded language activities and instruction that will enable these children to be successful in their efforts to learn mainstream English? Will they meet teachers who have redesigned early reading lessons so the lessons better fit the speech events the children are accustomed to at home and in their community (Au & Jordan, 1981)? Will their teachers understand and value the patterns of teaching and learning evidenced in their homes, and build on these patterns so that these children are drawn into the school world (Tharp & Gallimore, 1988)? Will their teachers understand that these children might be quiet in school because their parents have taught them to show respect by being quiet and deferential (Volk, 1997)? Throughout this book, we give pointers on providing culturally sensitive language and literacy instruction.

Another significant and growing group of diverse learners are second language learners. The population of children who speak English as a second language was estimated at 3.5 million in the year 2000 and is projected to grow to 6 million by 2020 (Faltis, 2001). Of this group, those children who speak little or no English are referred to as limited English proficient (LEP). Other children are bilingual and can speak both English and their native language with varying degrees of proficiency. These children's native language might be Spanish, Portuguese, Japanese, or some other world language. When they come to school or the day care center, young second-language learners are typically competent users of their native language. Their native language competence is a strength to be exploited by sensitive teachers.

We have included several Special Feature sections in subsequent chapters of this book that focus on second-language and bilingual learners' literacy development. From these features, readers will learn which strategies presented in this book are appropriate for use with children whose primary language is a language other than mainstream English and which strategies need to be adapted to meet the needs of these children.

Assessing Children's Literacy Learning

How do we know what children are learning? Changes in what we know about literacy learning have necessitated changes in our ways of measuring young children's knowledge about reading and writing. One of the central tenets of the emergent literacy perspective is that assessment should be embedded in instruction. This is one of the underlying themes of this book. We provide illustrations of instructionally linked assessment in many subsequent chapters.

Because literacy learning is no longer viewed as a transmitted process of adding the discrete parts in order to form the whole, it makes more sense to base assessment on new theories of emergent reading and the constructive nature of reading and writing processes. From this new perspective, assessment is viewed as an ongoing process in which the teacher uses a variety of techniques to gather information about what children know and can do. This information is then used to form a portrait that reveals a child's literacy development. The success of the constructivist approach, then, rests with classroom teachers. In fact, Karen Wixson (1992) says that "the teacher is the most important assessment instrument."

Several elements have been identified by various experts as critical components of this new approach to literacy assessment. These elements are summarized in the following points.

1. Assessment is embedded in instruction. While children are engaged in learning, the teacher is simultaneously assessing the children's literacy learning. Hence, the teacher does not take time away from teaching, and the children do not take time away from learning for their teacher to assess them. A result is that curriculum, instruction, and assessment are all closely connected.

2. Teachers use assessment to improve instruction. Teachers gather information, analyze the information, and use what they learn to inform their instruction. In fact, this should be the main purpose of assessment. Using this approach, teachers observe and listen to their students' responses, simultaneously assessing their students' knowledge and process. Based on these on-the-spot assessments, teachers might change their questions or change the activities they had planned. The link between assessment and instruction enables teachers to adapt instruction to meet the needs of specific children.

3. Multiple sources are used to gather evidence to support different perspectives of the child's literacy abilities. When multiple sources of data ("observations made in different situations, . . . by different people at different times, or [using] different assessment instruments") are used, then the likelihood of an accurate understanding of children's literacy knowledge and learning is increased (IRA/NCTE, 1994, p. 30).

4. Assessment should be a chronology of each child's development based on data collected over time. The goal is to compare each child's progress over time. A child's current performance should be compared against that child's previous performance rather than against the performance of others in the classroom.

5. The children's knowledge and learning are assessed while the children are engaged in authentic literacy events. Assessment is considered to be authentic when it is connected with real literacy events (Valencia, 1990). Children must be involved in the performance of tasks that are valued in their own right, rather than in tasks that are merely predictive of children's ability to read or write (Archbald & Newman, 1988).

6. Students should engage in self-reflection and self-evaluation. Students become more interested in and responsible for their own learning when they participate in assessing their own progress. "Self-evaluation leads to the establishment of goals. That is what evaluation is for. We evaluate in order to find out what we have learned so we will know what to study next" (Hansen, 1994, pp. 36–37). In this way, learning is advanced.

Many of the assessment techniques described above will be discussed at length in later chapters of this book. In addition, Chapter 8 features an in-depth discussion on how teachers can maintain and manage multiple sources of data and how these data can be organized into portfolios and used to analyze each child's literacy development over time.

Teaching Language and Literacy to Young Children

The authors of this book share several beliefs that form the foundation of our approach to teaching language and literacy. We believe that

- children learn by constructing and testing their hypotheses about language and literacy;
- children make sense of their world by integrating new experiences into what they understand, making connections between new information and previously known information and then organizing that information;
- learning is a social process that takes place through interactions between and among children and more knowledgeable others (e.g., parents, teachers, older siblings, other children);
- learning is a social act—children learn by watching, practicing, mimicking, and absorbing what those around them do;
- to support children's learning, teachers must "fit the child's needs at the moment" and operate within the child's zone of proximal development (the range of activities that children can do with help from others);
- teachers should study the cultures of the children in their classrooms in order to teach in ways that allow their young students to work to their strengths.

Given these beliefs, what teaching principles should be evidenced by teachers aimed at guiding children's spoken and written language learning in early childhood classrooms?

Knowledgeable Early Childhood Teachers Provide Children with a Print-Rich Classroom Environment

High-quality literacy programs require a literacy-rich environment with many materials to support children's learning. As Susan Neuman and Kathy Roskos (1993, pp. 20–21) explain, a print-rich classroom can help children to learn about language and literacy:

The quality of the physical environment is a powerful factor in language learning. The objects and opportunities it provides are the stuff out of which basic concepts are spun. What is available to label and to talk about, how accessible it is to touch and explore, and how it is organized influence both spoken and written language development.

Rich physical environments do not just happen; the creation of a classroom environment that supports children's learning, teacher's teaching, and the curriculum requires forethought. Some characteristics of this type of classroom environment include a well-stocked library corner and writing center, lots of functional print, theme-related literacy props in play areas, displays of children's writing, and so on. This type of environment offers children opportunities to talk, listen, read, and write to one another for real-life purposes.

Knowledgeable Early Childhood Teachers Demonstrate and Model Literacy Events

Children will try to do what others do. Therefore, demonstrating and modeling literacy events will lead to children imitating these events. When a teacher reads books to young children, children independently pick up the books and say words in ways that would lead a listener to think they are reading. The children sound as though they are reading words, yet their eyes are focused on the illustrations. When children see parents and teachers using print for various purposes—writing shopping lists, looking up information in a book, and writing notes—they begin to learn about the practical uses of language and to understand why reading and writing are activities worth doing.

Deborah Rowe (1994) provides an example of a preschool teacher's demonstration of the use of exclamation points. The teacher is sitting in the writing center with a small group of children. She writes a get-well card to a sick colleague. She writes: "Dear Carol, We hope you get well SOON!!! " She explains, "exclamation mark, exclamation mark, exclamation mark. Because I want her to get well *soon.*" Moments later, Kira and Hana talk about exclamation marks.

> *Kira:*   And this is [pause] extamotion [sic] point. How come?
>
> *Hana:*   Put three cause it's big letters.

Still later, Hana and Christina include exclamation marks in their writing. Christina writes the letters COI over and over inside one band of a rainbow and exclamation marks inside another band, and Hana writes her name and fills the bottom of the page with upside-down exclamation marks (Rowe, 1994, pp. 168–169). This preschool teacher probably did not set out to teach her young students about exclamation points. In the act of writing and talking about her writing, she demonstrated to three curious, observant preschool apprentices the purpose of using an exclamation mark. Notice how she showed her student "observers" what is done during reading and writing. She acted as a writer; not as teacher of reading and writing. In this way, she shared with the children how a reader or a writer thinks as well as acts.

Knowledgeable Early Childhood Teachers Provide Opportunities for Children to Work and Play Together in Literacy-Enriched Environments

Of course, teachers are not the only people in the classroom environment who offer demonstrations of literacy. "Knowledgeable teachers understand that the social, collaborative nature of learning to read and respond to books goes beyond the relationship between adult and child, teacher and student, and includes peers" (Galda, Cullinan, & Strickland, 1993). This statement about learning to read is equally applicable to learning to write. Creating a "community of literacy learners" is often suggested in the professional literature. Children select books to "read" because their peers have selected the book. Children talk to each other about books they are reading or have had read to them. Children turn to each other for information and help in decoding or spelling words. "How do you spell *morning*?" "What's this word say?"

Several researchers have documented what happens when teachers create an environment where children can demonstrate for, or coach, each other. For example, the following exchange illustrates how one preschooler demonstrates for a second preschooler (Lamme & Childer, 1983, p. 47).

> *Laurel:*   Look at my "L."
>
> *Terry:*   It's a "V," you silly.
>
> *Laurel:*   That's a "V."

Researchers (e.g., Christie & Stone, 1999; Vukelich, 1993) also have studied how play in literacy-enriched play settings provides children with opportunities to teach each other. Carol Vukelich (1993), for example, studied how children teach each other about the functions, features, and meaning of print in play. The following peer-to-peer interaction illustrates how one child coaches another child about how to spell his name.

> Jessie is the forest ranger. She is seated at the entrance to the camp site, directing potential campers to get a sticker from her before entering the campground, and *then* she'll tell them which tent they can use.

> *Jessie:*   Ronald, how do you spell your name?
>
> *Ronald:*   R. [Jessie writes *r.*] No, it's the big kind.
>
> [Ronald forms the letter with his finger on the table. Jessie writes *R.*] Good!
>
> *Jessie:*   What else?
>
> [Jessie writes as Ronald dictates each letter of his name, looking up at him after each one. When finished, she gives Ronald the sticker with his name on it.] (p. 390)

When teachers value children's contributions and celebrate what they know, children see the strengths in each other. Within such a supportive climate, children practice what they know and take the risks necessary for learning to occur. This kind of environment encourages young children to learn from themselves, from each other, and from the teacher.

Knowledgeable Early Childhood Teachers Link Literacy and Play

The example above of children's teaching each other how to spell occurred in literacy-enriched play settings in Karen Valentine's kindergarten classroom. The play setting was a park. Karen and the children generated ideas for the dramatic play setting. There needed to be a place to fish, so the water table became the fishing pond labeled "Lum's Pond" after the nearby pond. Fish and fishing poles were made in the art center. Paper clips were attached to the fish and magnets to the end of the string attached to the fishing pole. Soon children were reeling in fish. But to fish, you need a fishing license. A form was created and placed in the writing center. Park rangers ensured that no one fished who did not have a license. Soon the children needed clipboards with paper; tickets had to be issued to children caught fishing without a license.

A beach (blue water) with beach chairs (brought from homes) grew in another section of the play center. Soon, books found their way into beach bags, and sunglasses were needed to shade reading eyes. Samatha insisted that people on vacation write postcards. Karen, the teacher, provided models of several postcards in the writing center; the children used magic markers to draw postcard pictures on one side of 4 × 6-inch index cards. Pens found their way into the beach bags so the writing of postcards could occur while sitting at the beach.

And so the setting developed. By making the tools of literacy available to the children, the children began to incorporate print in very natural and real-world ways into the dramatic play theme. They wrote for many purposes (e.g., to control others' behavior, to share stories of vacation experiences, to reserve a tent). They read books and each other's writing. They talked "park" talk, negotiating their various "camping/park" schema to create a new shared schema. Within this play setting, they had the opportunity to practice the literacy events they had witnessed in the world outside the classroom and to add to their knowledge about literacy. Enriching play settings with appropriate literacy materials provides young children with important opportunities for literacy learning and for practicing literacy.

Knowledgeable Early Childhood Teachers Encourage Children to Experiment with Emergent Forms of Reading and Writing

Years ago, young children were not considered to be writing until they were writing conventionally, that is, correctly forming the letters and spelling the words. They were not considered to be reading until they could correctly recognize numerous printed words. In the 1970s, Marie Clay (1975) and Charles Read (1971) helped us understand emergent forms of writing and reading. We learned that children construct, test, and perfect hypotheses about written language. Their research lead to Elizabeth Sulzby's and her colleagues' (Sulzby, 1985a, 1985b; Sulzby, Barnhart, & Hieshima, 1989) creation of developmental sequences that children pass through on their way to becoming conventional readers and writers.

Today outstanding early childhood teachers do not expect young children's notions of writing and reading to conform to adult models of correctness. They expect children to experiment with print: to scribble, to make marks that look something like letters, to write strings of letters, and so forth. They expect children to look at pictures and "read" a story with an oral telling voice, to look at pictures and "read" a story with a written story voice, to attend to print and "read" in a written story voice, and so forth. As children experiment, these teachers compliment the children on their reading and writing expertise (e.g., "What good readers you are! " "What a wonderful story you have written! " "And you wrote all this?"). Through such explorations, children create meaning and communicate. Their teachers support their explorations with materials and with comments. Their teachers confirm when their hypotheses about print are correct.

Knowledgeable Early Childhood Teachers Provide Opportunities for Children to Use Language and Literacy for Real Purposes and Audiences

Most research on learning supports the proposition that knowing the reason for a learning situation and seeing a purpose in a task helps children learn. By the time children come to school or the child care center, many have experienced a wide variety of purposes for writing to various audiences. If children are allowed to experiment with paper and pencils, these purposes will begin to show up in their early attempts at writing. They will write letters and messages to others, jot down lists of things they need to do, and make signs for their doors warning intruders to stay out.

Similarly, by the time children come to school or to the child care center, many have experienced many opportunities to read for real purposes. They have shopped in grocery stores—and sometimes screamed when their mothers refused to purchase the cereal box they "read" and wanted. They have told the car driver who slowed but didn't come to a full stop at the stop sign that "dat means stop! " They have enjoyed their personal "reading" of a book read and reread many times to them by an adult. They have pointed to the sign written in linear scribble and hung, just like their teenage sibling's sign, on their door and shouted, "Can't you read? It says, 'Keep out! ' " They have "read" the address on an envelope collected at the mailbox and said, "You won't like this one. It's a bill! "

Notice how many of these reading and writing opportunities are literacy events woven into the events of daily life. The event defines the purpose of the literacy activity. Knowledgeable teachers make use of the everyday activities to demonstrate the many purposes of reading and writing. Are they cooking tomorrow? They read the recipe today with the children, and together they make a list to help them remember the food items that need to be purchased at the grocery store. Did a parent or community person volunteer in the classroom? Together they write a thank you note. The teacher might add special paper to the writing center so that individual children might write individual thank you notes or letters. Effective teachers can provide young children with numerous opportunities to engage in purposeful reading and writing activities.

Knowledgeable Early Childhood Teachers Read to Children Daily and Encourage Them to Read Familiar Books on Their Own

Living in a print-rich world provides children with many opportunities to read *contextualized* print. That is, children form hypotheses about what words say because of the context in which the words are embedded. As described in other sections of the chapter, children learn to read cereal boxes, stop signs, and the McDonald's sign early in life. While making such connections with print is important, young children also need multiple experiences with decontextualized print. Susan Neuman and Kathy Roskos (1993, p. 36) explain the meaning of decontextualized print:

> Essentially, this means that unlike contextualized print experiences, written language has meaning apart from the particular situation or context of its use. The meaning of decontextualized print is derived from the language itself and from the conventions of the literary genre. . . . Over time, [children] develop a frame, or sense of story, . . . a mental model of basic elements of a story."

Reading stories to children is one of the best ways to familiarize them with decontextualized print. Effective early childhood teachers plan numerous opportunities for storybook reading experiences. These teachers read aloud daily to individual children, small groups of children, and the whole class. Sometimes the books are regular-sized books, like the ones obtained from the public or school library. Other times, the books are big books, enlarged (about 24 × 26 inch) versions of regular-sized books.

But hearing stories read aloud is not enough. Case studies of children who read early tell us of the importance of talk about the books read (Heath, 1983; Yaden, Smolken, & Conlon, 1989). Therefore, knowing teachers often begin their read-alouds by engaging children in a discussion related to the story about to be read. A teacher might read the title and ask the children what they think the story might be about, or the teacher might ask a question related to the book's content. For example, while reading *Caps for Sale* (Slobodkin, 1947), the teacher might ask the children if they had ever tried to sell anything. While reading, the teacher might invite the children to make comments, to share reactions, or to ask brief questions. After reading, the teacher likely will engage the children in a discussion aimed at extending their understanding of the story. Such a framework for read-alouds was proposed by Marie Clay (1991); she called this structure a "grand conversation." In this way, teachers help children learn how to process the decontextualized text found in books both in terms of the story's structure and by making connections between the context and the children's experiences.

It is also important to provide opportunities for children to independently read books by themselves and to one another. Through such occasions, children have the opportunity to practice what they have learned during the interactive storybook readings. That is, they can engage in "emergent storybook reading" behaviors (Sulzby, 1985a). Children who have heard the same book read to them a number of times (called repeated readings) will attempt to read the book to themselves and to others. They act as if they are readers. As noted above, opportunities to engage in emergent reading behaviors are important to children's development as conventional readers.

Knowledgeable Early Childhood Teachers Use Authentic Forms of Assessment to Find Out What Children Know and Can Do

Is the child's development following the expected stages? Is the child learning? We know that standardized group paper-and-pencil tests do not reveal useful information about individual children's literacy development. Rather than testing children, teachers need to assess children's performance in a variety of contexts under many different conditions. Teachers assess to learn about children's strengths and weaknesses in order to plan the best instruction possible for every child in the classroom.

The 1998 joint International Reading Association and National Association for the Education of Young Children position statement on developmentally appropriate practices for young children suggests the following:

> **Accurate assessment** of children's knowledge, skills, and dispositions in reading and writing will help teachers better match instruction with how and what children are learning. However, early reading and writing cannot simply be measured as a set of narrowly-defined skills on standardized tests. These measures often are not reliable or valid indicators of what children can do in typical practice, nor are they sensitive to language variations, culture, or experiences of young children. Rather, a sound assessment should be anchored in real-life writing and reading tasks and continuously chronicle a wide range of children's literacy activities in different situations. Good assessment is essential to help teachers tailor appropriate instruction to young children and to know when and how much intensive instruction on any particular skill or strategy might be needed. (p. 38)

The joint statement advises teachers of young children to use multiple indicators (observations of children engaged in reading, writing, and speaking events; evaluations of such children's products as writing samples; children's performance during reading and writing) to assess and monitor children's development and learning.

Knowledgeable Early Childhood Teachers Respect and Make Accommodations for Children's Developmental, Cultural, and Linguistic Diversity

Children arrive in the classroom with different individual language and literacy needs. Our challenge is to offer good fits between each child's strengths and needs and what we try to give the child. The instruction we provide needs to dovetail with where children are developmentally and with their language and culture.

In the previous section about diversity, we wondered about the *how* of connecting children's classroom learning with their home cultural and linguistic experiences. We challenge readers to

- engage in the study of their children's community's ways with words and texts;
- carefully consider how to scaffold the classroom language activities and instruction so that all their children will experience success in their efforts to learn mainstream English;
- consider how to teach their young children about print in ways that better fit the speech events their children are accustomed to from their home and community;
- connect with their children's parents so that they can learn from each other how to best serve these children's needs; and
- look for ways to bring the community into the classroom and to connect children's outside learning experiences with their school and child care center learning experiences.

We have challenged ourselves to provide readers with information on what is known about ways to meet all children's needs.

Summary

One basic theory, called the constructivist theory of learning, underlies this book: Language and literacy learning is an active, constructive process. Children listen to and observe the oral and written language that surrounds them in everyday life, and they try to make sense of that language. In this chapter, we briefly explained this constructivist view of learning and discussed its implications for teaching language and literacy. How did the information match up with your own beliefs about literacy learning and instruction?

In subsequent chapters, we provide many explanations of how to implement constructivist teaching strategies aimed at promoting different aspects of language and literacy development. In addition, the themes of respect for student diversity and instructionally linked assessment appear throughout the book. When appropriate, Special Features about the special needs of second-language learners are included. Further, a section titled "Assessment: Discovering What Children Know and Can Do" is included in several of the chapters.

To summarize the key points about the foundations of language and literacy learning, we return to the focus questions at the beginning of this chapter:

- *How do young children learn about language and literacy?*

Children learn about language and literacy by observing, exploring, and interacting with others. Children assume the role of apprentice—mimicking, absorbing, and adapting the words and literacy activities used by more knowledgeable others. As they engage in these social interactions, children integrate new experiences with prior knowledge, constructing and testing hypotheses to make meaning. They store this newly constructed knowledge in mental structures called schemas.

- *Why is it crucial for teachers to respect children's diversity when teaching language and literacy?*

Children's oral language, the way they make meaning, and their early literacy experiences all are dependent on the practices shared by the members of their cultural community. Language-minority children—children who speak nonmainstream English dialects or whose native language is not English—represent a significant and growing group of diverse learners. When these children come to school or the day care center, they will come as competent users of their home language. Teachers must teach in ways that allow their young children to work to their strengths and use their existing language competence as stepping-stones toward learning mainstream English and literacy skills that are so crucial for success in school and adult life.

■ *How should young children's literacy learning be assessed?*

Assessment—discovering what children know and can do with respect to reading and writing—should be ongoing and spread over time and should involve multiple sources of information. It should also be closely embedded with instruction, so that while children are engaged in learning, the teacher is simultaneously assessing the children's literacy learning. The main purpose of assessment should be to improve instruction. Teachers should use information gained from assessment to plan future learning activities that meet the needs of each child in the classroom.

■ *What are the best practices in teaching language and literacy to young children?*
Knowledgeable early childhood teachers

- create print-rich classroom environments;
- demonstrate and model of literacy events for children;
- offer opportunities for children to work and play together;
- link play and literacy;
- provide opportunities for children to experiment with print connected with real purposes;
- establish daily read-alouds and opportunities for children to read books independently; and
- accept and take advantage of children's diversity.

Linking Knowledge to Practice

1. Observe a young child interacting with print in a store, restaurant, or the like. Describe the setting in which the observation was made and the participants who were involved in the event. Describe the event exactly as it occurred. What does it indicate about the child's understanding of literacy?

2. Observe a teacher in a nearby preschool or kindergarten classroom. How does this teacher's language and literacy instruction match up with the teaching principles described in this chapter?

3. Interview a parent or an older sibling about your early language and literacy development. What does this person recall about how you learned to talk, read, and write?

Oral Language Development

2

Perched in the shopping cart, nine-month-old Dawn babbles away to her mother. As they approach the checkout register, the clerk greets her mother. Dawn smiles, loudly says "Hi!" and waves her hand. The startled clerk smiles at Dawn and begins to talk to her. Dawn, obviously pleased with this attention, now babbles back to the clerk.

As this scenario reveals, the power of language is evident to even its youngest users. Dawn demonstrates that she knows how to use language to express—and realize—her desire to become a significant, communicating member in her world. By age 18 months, Dawn will have a vocabulary of dozens of words, and she will begin speaking in rule-governed, two-word sentences. By age 36 months, her vocabulary will number in the hundreds of words, and she will be using fully formed, five- and six-word sentences.

Children's oral language development is remarkable. Lindfors (1987, p. 90) outlines the typical accomplishments of young language learners:

> Virtually every child, without special training, exposed to surface structures of language in many interaction contexts, builds for himself—in a short period of time and at an early stage in his cognitive development—a deep-level, abstract, and highly complex system of linguist structure.

How does Dawn—and every other human child, for that matter—learn to communicate? How does this development occur so rapidly and without any seeming effort on the part of children or their parents? This question has fascinated scholars and parents for hundreds of years and is the subject of this chapter.

Before reading this chapter, think about. . .

- What were your first words? Although you probably do not recall uttering those words, maybe your parents or older siblings recollect your having spoken to them. Were your first words recorded someplace, or does your family rely on an oral tradition, telling the family stories orally?
- How do you think children acquire language? Is language development primarily a matter of genetics (an inborn ability to learn languages), the types of experiences and support children receive from their parents and other people, or a combination of these factors?
- When do children begin to express their thoughts orally? Why do some children develop language early while others experience language delays?
- Have you ever been in a situation where everyone around you used a language you don't know? How did you feel? How did you communicate with these speakers?

Focus Questions

- What are the major views on how children's language develops? Which aspects of language development does each view adequately explain?
- What are the major components of language?

BOX 2.1

Definition of Terms

behaviorist perspective: the view that language acquisition is a result of imitation and reinforcement.

cerebral cortex: the largest part of the brain, composed of two hemispheres that are responsible for higher brain functions, including thought and language.

myelineation: a process in which the neurons of the brain become coated with a white substance known as myelin, which facilitates the transmission of sensory information and promotes learning.

morphemes: the small unit of meaning in oral language. The word *cats* contains two morphemes: *cat* (name of a type of animal) and *s* (plural).

nativist perspective: the view that language development is a result of an inborn capacity to learn language.

neuro-biological perspective: the view that language acquisition can be explained by studying the structural development of the brain.

neurons: the impulse-conducting cells that make up the brain.

otitis media: an inflammation of the inner part of the ear that can retard language acquisition.

phoneme: the smallest unit of sound in a language. There are approximately 44 phonemes in English.

pragmatics: rules that affect how language is used in different social contexts.

semantics: the part of language that assigns meaning to words and sentences.

synapses: connections between the neurons of the brain.

syntax: rules for arranging words into sentences.

social-interactionist perspective: the view that language development is a result of both genetics and adult support.

- How does the structure of an infant's brain develop? How does this structural development affect language acquisition?
- What factors affect children's rate of language acquisition?
- How does children's acquisition of a second language compare with their first language acquisition? What should adults do to make it easier for children to learn English as a second language?

Perspectives on Children's Language Acquisition

There are four views on how children learn language: behaviorism, linguistic nativism, social interactionism, and the neuro-biological perspective. We present a brief description of each perspective in this chapter. Our experiences as parents, teachers, and researchers lead us to believe that the social-interactionism perspective most realistically accounts for similarities and differences in young children's language development. Therefore, we present a more detailed description of what is presently known about children's language acquisition from this perspective. However, we also acknowledge the importance of the new neuro-biological information provided by neuroscientists to help us understand the biology of language acquisition. Together, the social-interactionist and the neuro-biological perspectives provide important insights for teachers and future teachers on how children acquire language.

Behaviorist Perspective

The behaviorist view suggests that nurture—the way a child is taught or molded by parents and the environment—plays a dominant role in children's language development. Through the first half of the 20th century, this was the prevalent view. Researchers and teachers believed that all learning (language included) is the result of two basic processes—classical and operant conditioning (Skinner, 1957). Behaviorists attribute receptive language to associations that result from classical conditioning. For example, every time the baby is offered a bottle, the mother names the object, "Here's the bottle." After numerous repetitions with the adult presenting the action/object and phrase, the baby learns that the clear cylinder filled with food is called a bottle.

Behaviorists suggest that through operant conditioning, infants gradually learn expressive language by being rewarded for imitating the sounds and speech they hear. For instance, a baby spontaneously babbles and accidentally says or repeats the sound "mama." The mother responds joyfully, hugging and kissing the baby, saying "Yes, Mama!" The baby, given this reward, is reinforced and attempts to repeat the behavior. Once the behavior is repeated and rewarded often enough, the child connects the word sound to the object or event.

Nativist Perspective

The nativist view of learning and development, with its emphasis on nature, is at the opposite end of the continuum from the behaviorist perspective. According to the nativist view, a person's behavior and capabilities are largely predetermined. Nativists believe every child has an inborn capacity to learn language. If these theorists were using computer terminology, they would say that humans are hardwired for language. Noam Chomsky (1965) called this innate capacity a language acquisition device (LAD). Nativists posit that the LAD allows children to interpret phoneme patterns, word meanings, and the rules that govern language. For example, when children first begin to use past tenses, they often overgeneralize certain words, such as *goed* for *went*, or *thinked* for *thought*. Since *goed* and *thinked* are not words that children would hear adults say, these examples illustrate that children are using some type of internal rule system, not simple imitation, to govern their acquisition of language.

Nativists also believe that this innate language structure facilitates the child's own attempts to communicate, much the same way as the computer's wiring facilitates the use of a number of software programs. Nativists believe that language learning differs from all other human learning in that a child learns to communicate even without support from parents or caregivers. They view the environment's role in language acquisition as largely a function of activating the innate, physiologically based system. Environment, these theorists believe, is not the major force shaping a child's language development.

Social-Interactionist Perspective

Social interactionists do not come down on either side of the nature versus nurture debate; rather, they acknowledge the influence of genetics and parental teaching. They share with behaviorists the belief that environment plays a central role in children's language development. Likewise, along with nativists, they believe that children possess an innate predisposition to learn language. In addition, social interactionists stress the child's own intentional participation in language learning and the construction of meaning. The social interactionist's point of view emphasizes the importance of the infant's verbal negotiations or "verbal bouts" (Golinkoff, 1983) with caregivers. These negotiations occur partly because mothers or other caretakers treat children's attempts at speech as meaningful and intentional (Piper, 1993). An example is shown by 11-month-old Dawn, standing by the garage door. Dawn is patting the door.

Dawn: "Bice!"

Mom: "Do you want ice?"

Dawn: (shaking her head) "Biiisse."

Mom: (opening the garage door) "Bise?"

Dawn: (pointing at the bike) "Bise."

Mom: "You want to go for a bike ride?"

Dawn: (raising her arms, nodding her head vigorously) "Bice!"

As Dawn's mother (and most mothers) begins to make sense of her child's speech, she also begins to understand her child's meaning and/or intent. Lev Vygotsky (1962) described this type of adult support, or scaffolding, as facilitating the child's language growth within the zone of proximal development, the distance between a child's current level of development and the level at which the child can function with adult assistance. In the preceding example, the mother's questions enable Dawn to successfully communicate using a one-word sentence, something she could not have done on her own. Parents also support children's efforts to learn language by focusing the child's attention on objects in the immediate environment and labeling each object and its action.

A Neuro-Biological Perspective

The psychologists, linguists, and anthropologists who developed the three preceding perspectives of language acquisition had to infer the origins of language and brain activity from careful, long-term observations of external behavior. Over the past two decades, technological innovations have enabled neuroscientists to study the brain at a cellular level. Brain imaging techniques are noninvasive procedures that allow researchers to graphically record and simultaneously display three-dimensional, color-enhanced images of a living brain as it processes information (Sochurek, 1987). These data provide researchers with a better way to understand the organization and functional operations of the brain.

According to this new perspective, the capacity to learn language begins with brain cells called neurons. Neurons emerge during the early phases of fetal development, growing at the fantastic rate of 250,000 per minute (Edelman, 1995). As neurons multiply, they follow a complex genetic blueprint that causes the brain to develop distinct but interdependent systems—brain stem and limbic system, cerebellum and cerebral cortex (MacLean, 1978). New brain-imaging technology has allowed scientists to locate specific areas in the brain that are dedicated to hearing, speaking, and interpreting language. Thus, the nativist linguistic theory of language acquisition is, in part, correct—the human brain has dedicated structures for language, and infant brains are born capable of speaking any of the 3000-plus human languages (Kuhl, 1993). However, infants are not disposed to speak any particular language, nor are they born language proficient. The language that a child learns is dependent on the language that the child hears spoken in the home (Sylwester, 1995).

In fact, the recent discoveries in neuro-biology support elements of the nativist, behaviorist, and social-interactionist views of language development. These biological findings reveal that language learning is a reciprocal dialogue between genetics (nature) and environment (nurture). Clearly, infants are born with key brain areas genetically dedicated to language functions. Yet, for children to learn the language of their culture, it is necessary that they have consistent, frequent opportunities to interact with a persistent caregiver who models the language with the child. Likewise, neuroscientists agree that a child's language capacity is dependent on the quality of language input. Parents and caregivers who consistently engage in conversation with their infants actually help their children develop neural networks that lead to language fluency and proficiency (Healy, 1994; 1997; Kotulak, 1997; Sprenger, 1999). In Figure 2.1, we summarize the major concepts of these four perspectives of language acquisition.

Linguistic Vocabulary Lesson

Linguistics is the study of language. To better understand the complexities of linguistic acquisition, we provide a brief discussion of the components of linguistic structure, of phonology, morphology, syntax, semantics, and pragmatics.

Phonology

The sound system of a particular language is its phonology, and the distinctive units of sound in a language are its phonemes. Individual phonemes are described according to how speakers modify the airstream they exhale to produce the particular sounds.

Phonological development begins when sounds of speech activate neural networks in the infant's brain. This process begins during the last two months of prenatal development as babies are able to hear intonation patterns from their mother's voice (Shore, 1997).

Although the mechanical aspects of the auditory system are in place at birth, the neural network that supports language acquisition is just beginning to develop. Verbal interactions with caregivers allow babies to clearly hear sounds of their native language(s) and observe how the

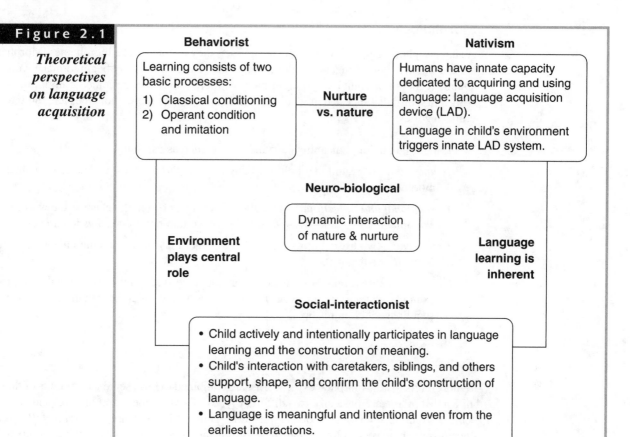

Figure 2.1

Theoretical perspectives on language acquisition

Behaviorist

Learning consists of two basic processes:
1) Classical conditioning
2) Operant condition and imitation

Nurture vs. nature

Nativism

Humans have innate capacity dedicated to acquiring and using language: language acquisition device (LAD).

Language in child's environment triggers innate LAD system.

Neuro-biological

Dynamic interaction of nature & nurture

Environment plays central role

Language learning is inherent

Social-interactionist

- Child actively and intentionally participates in language learning and the construction of meaning.
- Child's interaction with caretakers, siblings, and others support, shape, and confirm the child's construction of language.
- Language is meaningful and intentional even from the earliest interactions.

mouth and tongue work to create these unique sounds. Simultaneously, as babies babble, they gain motor control of their vocal and breathing apparatus. Interactions with caregivers allow babies an opportunity to listen, observe, and attempt to mimic sounds they hear and the mouth and tongue movements they see. Through this process, babies begin to specialize in the sounds of their native language(s). The developmental window of opportunity (sometimes called the critical period) for mastering sound discrimination occurs within the first six months of an infant's life. By this time, babies' brains are already pruning out sensitivity to sounds that are not heard in their environment (Kuhl, 1993). This pruning is so efficient that children actually lose the ability to hear phonemes that are not used in their mother-tongue. Children who consistently hear more than one language during this time may become native bi- or trilinguals, as they retain the ability to hear the subtle and discrete sounds.

Another important aspect of the English phonology is its prosody, or the stress and intonation patterns of the language. Stress refers to the force with which phonemes are articulated. Where the stress is placed may distinguish otherwise identical words (RECord [noun] versus reCORD [verb]). Intonation, on the other hand, refers to the pattern of stress and of rising and falling pitch that occurs within a sentence. These changes in intonation may shift the meaning of otherwise identical sentences:

IS she coming? (Is she or is she not coming?)

Is SHE coming? (Her, not anyone else)

Is she COMING? (Hurry up; it's about time)

Babies as young as four and five months begin to experiment with the pitch, tone, and volume of the sounds they make and often produce sounds that mimic the tonal and stress qualities of their parents' speech.

Morphology

As babies' phonological development progresses, they begin to make morphemes. Morphemes are the smallest unit of meaning in oral language. While babies may begin to make word-like sounds (echolalia) around six to eight months, morphemes will not emerge until around the baby's first birthday. These real words are made up of one or more phonemes and fall into several categories:

Lexical—individual meaning carrying words, such as *cat, baby.*

Bound—units of sound that hold meaning (like *re, un*) but must be attached to other morphemes (*reorder, unbend*).

Derivational and inflectional—usually suffixes that change the class of the word; for example: noun to adjective—*dust* to *dusty;* verb to noun—*teaches* to *teacher.*

Compound—two lexical morphemes that together may form a unique meaning, such as *football* or *cowboy.*

Idiom—an expression whose meaning cannot be derived from its individual parts; for example, *Put your foot in your mouth* carries a very different meaning from the visual image it conjures up.

Syntax

Syntax refers to how morphemes, or words, are combined to form sentences or units of thought. In English, there are basically two different types of order: linear and hierarchical structure. Linear structure refers to the object-verb arrangement. For example, *Building falls on man* means something very different than *Man falls on building.* Hierarchical structure refers to how words are grouped together within a sentence to reveal the speaker's intent. However, different languages have unique and inherent rules that govern syntax. A speaker of English might say: *The long, sleek, black cat chased the frightened tiny, gray mouse.* A language with syntactical rules that differ from English could state it this way: *Chasing the gray mouse, tiny and frightened, was the cat, long, sleek, and black.*

Shortly after their first birthdays, most children are able to convey their intentions with single words. Have you ever heard a young child use the powerful words *no* and *mine*? More complex, rule-driven communication usually emerges between the ages of two and three, when children are able to construct sentences of two or more words.

Though children have prewired capacity for language rules (such as past-tense), adult scaffolding or support plays a significant role in extending and expanding a child's language development. For instance, when Joe says *deenk,* his day care teacher can extend and clarify Joe's intentions: *Joe, do you want to drink milk or juice?* If Joe says *I drinked all the milk,* his teacher might tactfully expand his statement. *Yes, Joe, you drank all of your milk.* This type of subtle modeling is usually the most appropriate way to support children as they learn the conventional forms and complexities of their language. However, even when adults expand a child's speech, the child's own internal rule-governing system may resist modification until the child is developmentally ready to make the change. The following interaction between a four-year-old and an interested adult illustrates this phenomenon (Gleason, 1967):

Child: My teacher holded the baby rabbits and we patted them.

Adult: Did you say your teacher held the baby rabbit?

Child: Yes.

Adult: What did you say that she did?

Child: She holded the baby rabbits and we patted them.

Adult: Did you say she held them tightly?

Child: No. She holded them loose.

Semantics

"How would you differentiate among the following words that a blender manufacturer has printed under the row of buttons: stir, beat, puree, cream, chop, whip, crumb, mix, mince, grate, crush, blend, shred, grind, frappe, liquify?" (Lindfors, 1987; p. 47). Semantics deals with the subtle shades of meaning that language can convey. Variations in language meanings generally reflect the values and concerns of the culture. For instance, dozens of Arabic words may be dedicated to describing the camel's range of moods and behaviors. The Polynesian language has many words that define variations in the wind; likewise, Eskimo languages include many words for snow.

Knowledge of word meaning is stored throughout the brain in a vast biological forest of interconnected neurons, dendrites, and synapses. Beyond culture, children's ongoing personal experience allows them to connect words and meaning. Since words are symbolic labels for objects, events, actions, and feelings, a child may initially call all four-legged animals *kittie*. However, after several firsthand encounters with kitties (with the support of adults who can help label and describe the event) a child will likely develop the concepts and vocabulary to discriminate kitties from doggies, kittens from cats, and eventually Persians from Siamese.

Pragmatics

Sitting in his bouncer, two-month-old Marcus studies his mother's face as she talks to him. In a high-pitched voice, she exaggerates her words in a singsong manner: *Lookeee at Mommeeee. I see baabee Marceee looking at Mommeee.* Baby Marcus appears to mimic her mouth movements and responds to her conversations with smiles, wiggles, and very loud coos. After Marcus quiets, his mother knowingly responds to her baby's comments, *Yes, you're right, Mommeee does love her Marceee-Boy.*

When parent and child engage in singsong conversation of "parentese" and baby vocalizations, the basic conventions of turn-taking are learned, but rarely does the teacher or student realize that a lesson was being taught. Pragmatics deals with the conventions of becoming a competent language user. These include rules on how to engage successfully in conversation with others, such as how to initiate and sustain conversation, how to take turns, when and how to interrupt, how to use cues for indicating subject interest, and how to tactfully change subjects.

Pragmatics also refers to the uses of language (spoken and body) to communicate one's intent in real life. The message of a speaker's actual words may be heightened or may even convey the opposite meaning depending on the manner in which the words are delivered. This delivery may include inflection, facial expressions, or body gestures. Take, for example, this statement: *I'm having such a great time.* Imagine that the person who is saying this phrase is smiling easily and widely, with eyes making direct contact with the person with whom she is sharing her time. Now, picture the person saying *I'm having such a great time* while sneering and rolling her eyes (see Figure 2.2). Though the words are identical, the intent of the two speakers is obviously completely different. Further, pragmatics deals with an increasing conscious awareness of being able to accomplish goals through the use of language.

As children mature, they are able to use social registers—or the ability to adapt their speech and mannerisms to accommodate different social situations. This level of communicative competence can be observed in children as young as five as they engage in pretend play. During dramatic play children may easily switch roles—baby to parent, student to teacher, customer to waiter—by using the vocabulary, mannerisms, and attitudes that convey the role they wish to play.

In reviewing these linguistic structures—phonology, morphology, syntax, semantic, and pragmatics—it seems amazing that children acquire these components naturally. Parents rarely teach these intricate conventions directly. Instead, children acquire these intricate communication skills by listening, imitating, practicing, observing, and interacting with supportive caregivers and peers.

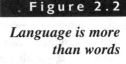

Language is more than words

Observing the Development of Children's Language

"One of the most remarkable cognitive achievements of early childhood is the acquisition of language" (Black, Puckett, & Bell, 1992, p. 179). By the time they enter school, most children have mastered the basic structures of language and are fairly accomplished communicators. Though individual variations do occur, this rapid acquisition of language tends to follow a predictable sequence.

This progression will be illustrated in two ways, first with a neuro-biological focus on Joel's first two years of life, and then with a social-interactionist perspective that follows Dawn from infancy through kindergarten. Joel and Dawn are the children of educational researchers. Their development is like that of almost every other normal child throughout the world, except that it was documented by their researcher-parents. Dawn and Joel's parents used a simple calendar-notation procedure to collect information about their children's language development. When Joel's and Dawn's parents reviewed the calendar each morning, new words were recorded. Thus, it became quite easy to document Joel's and Dawn's growth over time. When these busy parents had a moment, they recorded their recollections (vignettes) of an event and dated it. Often, at family celebrations, a video camera was used to record the events of Joel's and Dawn's use of language in great detail. Occasionally, videotapes also documented storytimes. By using the calendar vignettes and the videotapes, Dawn's and Joel's parents were able to marvel at their children's growth and development.

A Biological View of Development

Brain-scanning technology, such as positron emission-tomography (PET) and functional magnetic resonance imagining (MRI), have allowed scientists to observe and gain a better understanding of how infants' brains mature. This section reviews brain growth during the first two years of life. This information will be brought to life by observing Joel from birth through his second birthday. It is important to note that Joel's skills do not automatically develop at a certain point in brain maturation, but without a particular level of neural-growth, Joel would not be able to accomplish his goals. Joel's development is a dynamic interaction of his intentions, muscle tone and coordination, and neural readiness. The information about brain development comes from several sources, including Shore (1997), Lock (1993), Cowley (1997), Sporns and Tononi (1994), and Bradshaw and Rogers (1993).

At birth, the human brain is remarkably unfinished. Most of the 100 billion neurons, or brain cells, are not yet connected. In fact, there are only four regions of the brain that are fully functional at birth, including the brain stem (which controls respiration, reflexes, and heartbeat) and the cerebellum (which controls the newborn's balance and muscle tone). Likewise, infants' sensory skills are rudimentary; for instance, newborns can see objects only within 12 to 18 inches of their faces. Still, newborns are able to distinguish between faces and other objects, and they recognize the sound of their parents' voices. Grace and Dan Bass have contributed Joel's case study to our text.

> Right from the start, Joel was physically active. He spent his waking time swinging his arms, kicking his legs, practicing tongue movement, and strengthening his lungs by crying. There were subtle differences in his cries which his Mommy and Daddy learned to recognize. There were cries associated with anger or frustration, such as when he hiccuped uncontrollably or couldn't find his thumb to suck. Coos of contentment were often heard when he cuddled with his parents and "ahs," which were sighs when he seemed particularly comfortable.

During the first month of life, the number of neural synapses or connections increase 20 times to more than 1000 trillion. These neural connections are developed through daily verbal and physical interactions that the infant shares with parents, siblings, and other caregivers. Daily routines such as feeding and bathing reinforce and strengthen particular synapses, while neural networks that are not stimulated will eventually wither away in a process called neural pruning.

> Joel began to socialize with people other than his parents as soon as he was born. There were always new faces peering down at him in his bassinet, new arms cuddling him, and new fingers for him to grasp. Joel seemed to scrutinize everything around him and each new person he met commented on his alertness.

As the neuromuscular and sensory systems of the brain mature, babies begin to gain some control over their bodies. Motor control begins at the head and works downward (cephalocaudal) and from the center of body outward (proximodistal). At this time, babies are likely to reach their hands and kick their feet toward close objects.

Babies carefully observe parents, siblings, and other caregivers and often mimic the tongue and mouth movements they see. Babies also experiment with the range of new sounds they can make. These trills and coos are also bids for attention, as most babies have begun to make simple cause-and-effect associations, such as crying equals Mom's attention.

> Throughout his infancy, Joel's parents sang to him. They played lullabies for him while he slept, and talked to him during bath time. Joel kicked his feet and smiled to let them know that this pleased him.
>
> During the second month, Joel's vocalizations grew, as his tongue became more adept and flexible. He frequently sought his parents' attention by adding stress to his "ehs." Multi-syllable sounds, such as "eh-ah," "ey-ere" and "eh-um-mum" began. The "mmm" sound was especially dominant.

The cerebral cortex represents 70 percent of the brain and is divided into two hemispheres. Each hemisphere has four lobes—the parietal, occipital, temporal, and frontal. Each of these lobes has numerous folds, which mature at different rates as the chemicals that foster brain development are released in waves. This sequential development explains, in part, why there are optimum times for physical and cognitive development. For instance, at approximately three months, neural connections within the parietal lobe (object recognition and eye-hand coordination), the temporal lobe (hearing and language), and the visual cortex have begun to strengthen and fine-tune. This development allows babies' eyes to focus on objects that are more than two feet away from their faces. This new ability allows babies to recognize themselves in a mirror and begin to visually discern who's who.

During his third and fourth months, Joel consistently responded to his parents with smiles and a face full of expression and recognition. His eyes widened and almost glowed when he was happy and his laughing became more defined. Joel often greeted his parents with new and unique sounds that he created when he played with the shape of his mouth. Joel could deliberately alter his voice to become terse and choppy and now made raspberry sounds—an interesting combination of lips, tongue, drool and exhaled breath.

The human brain triples its birth weight within the first three years of a child's life. This change is caused as neurons are stimulated and synapse connections increase, as the message-receiving dendrite branches grow larger and heavier. In addition, the long axons over which sensory messages travel gradually develops a protective coating of a white, fatty substance called myelin. Myelin insulates the axons and makes the transmission of sensory information more efficient. Myelineation occurs at different times in different parts of the brain. This process seems to coincide with the emergence of various physical skills and cognitive abilities. For instance, the neuromuscular development during the first four months of life is dramatic. Within the first four months, helpless infants develop the muscle tone and coordination that allows them to turn over at will. Babies develop a sense of balance and better eye–hand coordination as neural connections in the cerebellum and parietal lobe strengthen. This allows most six-month-old babies to sit upright with adult support and to successfully grasp objects within their reach. The ability to hold and inspect interesting items gives babies a lot to "talk" about.

During his fifth and sixth months, Joel's laughter was more exuberant and he responded to pleasurable situations with squeals of delight. A new sound, "hmmm, hmmmm," uttered with some intensity, let his parents know that he wanted something. Joel chuckled when he played on his tummy and rolled over at will. These new physical achievements allowed him to observe and explore more of his world. During these activities, he made singsong noises and produced an extended "ahhhh" in a rattling growl. Other sounds at this time included loud screams, shrills, "ummmmm," "uh-uh-uh" and rasping his voice while breathing. Joel also began to use non-verbal actions as he shook his head from side-to-side in a negative fashion, as a response to spoken questions.

Between six to seven months, the brain has already created permanent neural networks that recognize the sounds of a child's native language(s) or dialect. Next, babies begin to distinguish syllables, which soon enables them to detect word boundaries. Prior to this, *doyouwantyourbottle?* was a pleasant tune, but was not explicit communication. After auditory boundaries become apparent, babies will hear distinct words: *Do / you / want / your / BOTTLE?*

Joel plays with busy box

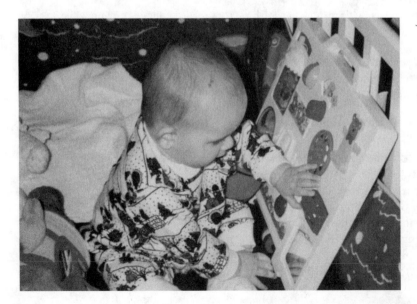

As sounds become words that are frequently used in context to label a specific object, the acquisition of word meaning begins. At this stage of development, babies usually recognize and have cognitive meaning for words such as bottle, mama, and daddy. Their receptive or listening vocabulary grows rapidly, though it will take a few more months before their expressive or oral language catches up.

It is interesting to note that Joel's parents speak with wonderful southern accents. These sounds became a part of Joel's language development. "Bwatuh, bwatuh, bwatuh . . . " was Joel's first echolalia or word-like sound. Joel uttered this often in a singsong conversation like manner. In addition Joel made streams of sound "dadadada," "undat, undat," "um wah wah," "Ba bow bow" and followed these multi-syllable sounds with screams and high squeals.

Joel also observed social conventions, for instance when his picture was taken, he made waving motions and occasionally exaggerated his smile into an extreme grimace. To seek his parents' attention, he began to produce a fake coughing sound. Joel's increased eye–hand coordination and manual dexterity allowed him to put everything he could reach into his mouth.

From about the eighth to the ninth month, the hippocampus becomes fully functional. Located in the center of the brain, the hippocampus is part of the limbic system. The hippocampus helps to index and file memories, and as it matures, babies are able to form memories. For instance, babies can now remember that when they push the button on the busy box it will squeak. At this point, babies' ability to determine cause and effect and remember words greatly increases.

By nine months, Joel was able to pull himself up to a standing position in his crib, crawled everywhere and climbed on anything in his path. Joel enjoyed looking at himself in mirrors and always kissed his reflections. During bath time he splashed a lot, practically drenching his parents and anything next to the tub. Joel was proud of all his accomplishments, particularly the splashing!

At ten months, Joel could pull himself up to a standing position while holding onto the coffee table, but just as soon as he was standing, he would ease himself down to the floor. He practiced this up and down feat repeatedly. Joel developed a great fascination for toys with wheels. He pushed a large plastic fire truck about the house, making engine sounds as he went. Between "furniture cruising" and crawling, Joel was mobile enough to get into things that warranted extra attention, like daddy's coffee, mommy's purse, electrical cords and outlets. He also began to open and close doors, including the glass stereo doors and mommy's jewelry box. For Joel's safety, the house now had to be childproofed. During all this exploration, Joel jabbered continuously "yayayayaya."

Joel developed an intense interest in books, he enjoyed picking them up and looking at them alone, as well as with others. He made happy, loud noises as he worked to turn the thick pages by himself. At this time, Joel's favorite book was *Pat the Bunny* and he liked to interact with each page. As he "read" this book with his mommy or daddy, he called out, "rar rar rar."

At the end of the first year, the prefrontal cortex, the seat of forethought and logic, forms synapses at a rapid rate. In fact, at age one, the full cortex consumes twice as much energy as an adult brain. This incredible pace continues during the child's first decade of life. The increased cognitive capacity and physical dexterity stimulates curiosity and exploration and a deep desire to understand how things work. Neural readiness, in combination with countless hours of sound play and verbal exchanges with loving caregivers, allows most children to begin speaking their first words.

Joel's first birthday marked other firsts—his first two teeth and his first steps. Joel loved squeezing into hidden crevices playing a version of hide and seek. He enjoyed his dolls and stuffed animals and squealed with happiness when he hugged them. His oral language was developing slowly but surely.

At 13 months "blahdee" was the word/sound Joel used for daddy and he used this word frequently. He continued to hide in small, tucked away places, particularly under the computer desk. He also produced new strings of sounds, such as "ooh-blad-day-day-doo" and consistently responded to the request "come here" with "day-bah." During this time, Joel displayed vocables when he became fascinated with the telephone. He chattered and chattered on his play phone for long periods of time, even laughing during each conversation as if he had heard something funny. His vocalizations were conversation-like sounds and phrases, except for an initial greeting of "Heeey!" and the final "Bye." His relatives were aware of Joel's phone passion so they sent him more play phones for various holidays. All of these phones were very important to Joel and he always knew where they were. Sometimes he gave his phone to mom or dad, so they could talk. These pretend conversations were fun for both Joel and his parents. His parents noted, however, that when his grandparent called and wanted to speak to Joel, he held the phone and listened in complete silence.

During his 14th and 15th months, Joel became much more interested in simple mechanics, such as swinging doors open and shut, rolling toys across the floor, and fitting belt buckles together. Balls, tractors, trucks were great toys, but it was the remote controls for the television and satellite receiver that replaced phones as Joel's new play obsession. He began screeching when he wanted something and he wanted the remote controls quite often. His serious devotion to the remotes became quite a nuisance for his parents as he delighted in turning the TV off and on and changing channels. Often, when he worked the TV controls, he would say "yah dad-dey." As he became more and more occupied with control buttons on all electronic devices in his home, he developed a preference for grown-up controls over baby electronic toys. Joel also began some teasing behaviors. He would pretend to hand something to his parents then snatch his hand back as they reached for it.

One of the most interesting features of Joel's language development from one year to 18 months was that it was inconsistent and unpredictable. At about 16 months, Joel began saying, with perfect enunciation, the word "everyday." He accentuated each syllable of this word and used it correctly in response to some statement or question. However, Joel only used this word for two weeks. Another instance of his verbal command occurred one evening as Joel and his daddy were playing. Joel picked up a book, handed it to his daddy and said, "Read this." His daddy almost fainted and his mommy was very excited and optimistic about this phrase that held meaning for his parents. However, it was the last time he used this phrase for several months. Another clearly spoken, context appropriate, but one-time-only sentence emerged, "It's hot in here, let's go outside." Between 15 and 16 months Joel brought book after book to his parents. As they read, he poured over each detail. He wanted everything on the page to be named and discussed. When they stopped reading, he cried and fussed and sometimes he threw the books if they tried to distract him. His parents wisely purchased baby books with the thick indestructible cardboard pages.

By 18 months neural synapses have increased and strengthened and are beginning to transmit information quite efficiently; hence most toddlers begin to experience a language "explosion." Brain-imaging technology clearly reveals that the full cortex is involved in processing language. During this time children are able to learn as many as 12 words a day. Linguists call this phenomenon *fast mapping*.

Increased neural activity, plus verbal expression and physical skill, also gives rise to greater independence. At this time parents may hear "No!" quite often.

Though Joel could say mommy and daddy, he began to call his parents by their given names. Friends suggested that if Dan and Grace would call each other mommy and daddy, then Joel would too. However, this plan did not work. Joel's babysitter, friends at church and school, and the neighborhood children called Joel's parents Dan and Grace, so Joel chose to do this also.

Joel's love of books continued. But now, instead of his parents pointing to and labeling everything on each page, they would ask Joel to point to specific characters or objects. Joel also read books to himself. He would sit on the couch with his books beside him, turn the pages and "read" or "baby talk" about each page.

By 19 months Joel had developed a stubborn streak. He became uncooperative at times and did not want to take a bath or sit in the shopping cart. He asserted his independence by pretending not to hear what his parents said to him. Sometimes, he closed his eyes and turned his head away. Other times, he flung himself on the floor and yelled, "NOOOOOO." His oral language continued to develop. If his mommy asked him if he was ready to go to bed, he would reply "nuht nuht," when he fell, he muttered, "dab uh oh," and when he saw a baby, he would say "uhh baby." Long strings of baby talk words began to flow from his lips such as "dat ah kay, dat ah oh ee yah aye ah bladla beel cuh cuh a ta ah yel bloo day go go ich ah!"

During the next month, Joel speech became much clearer. If he needed something, he muttered, "ah nee" and if he wanted something, he said, "ah ownt." A passing tractor would immediately cause Joel to exclaim, "Dat tractor!" If he wanted to know what something was he inquired "ah is?" When he knew something his parents were telling him, he would interject, "ah no." Joel also became quite adapt at following simple requests, for example, when his parents asked him to get his favorite book *Jamberry* (by Bruce Degen), Joel could go to the bookshelf, find the book and bring it to them.

Though he loved changing channels, Joel did not seem interested in watching television. When he was about 21 months old, Joel's babysitter casually remarked that Joel had started to watch episodes of "Rugrats" and "Blues Clues" with her four-year-old daughter. The babysitter mentioned that Joel would sometimes watch "Blue Clues" for up to 20 minutes at a time. As a result of this conversation, Joel's mommy began to turn on "Barney" and "Captain Kangaroo" to see what would happen. Indeed, Joel watched these programs but in an active way. Instead of sitting, he was up pointing and naming objects and characters on the screen, sometimes with real words and often with baby talk.

At 22 months, Joel pointed to each of the figures in his book, asking, "ah is?" which meant that he wanted his parents to name the objects. His parents were amazed at the minute details that caught Joel's eye, especially when he noticed something new after looking at the same books hundreds of times. For example, Joel noticed a little lighthouse in the top corner of a seascape or a ladybug walking on a small leaf at the bottom of a page.

At two years of age, most children have nimble fingers and are sturdy on their feet. Though they are generally aware of cause and effect, they are still unable to foresee potential problems. In other words, children's physical abilities may exceed their common sense. By this time, most children are able to use language to communicate their needs and accomplish their goals.

Though he did not take his first step until his first birthday, at age two, Joel was coordinated and independent. He could go up and down steps with ease, jump from high places, run very fast without falling, climb, and get whatever he wanted by pushing furniture, using it as a ladder. Joel liked to mimic his parents; he worked on the computer and was able to turn it on and use the mouse; help fold clothes and unload the dishwasher; and when he sat down at the dinner table, he immediately held out his hands so that the blessing could be given.

At age two, Joel experienced an oral language explosion. He said many new words every day and attempted more words that still weren't perfected. Joel used sentences frequently, including "Mama, that a truck"; "That a big, big, truck"; "Are you sure?" "Are you sure you sure?" "I want juice (chips, truck, etc.)."

Joel's development is a wonderful example of the interaction of how the body and brain stimulate interactive development.

A Social-Interactionist View of Language Development

Dawn's development is viewed from a social-interactionist perspective. Her development is described in linguistic terminology. In her five-year case study, we observe how her parents and caregivers stimulate and support her efforts and how she uses language to gain attention and to accomplish her goals at a young age.

During the first month of Dawn's life, most of her oral communication consisted of crying, crying, crying. The greatest challenge her parents faced was perceiving and interpreting the variations in her cries. It took about three weeks for them to understand that Dawn's intense, high-pitched cry meant she was hungry. Dawn's short, throaty, almost shouting cries indicated a change of diaper was necessary, while the whining, fussy cry, which occurred daily at about dinner time, meant she was tired.

During the second to third months after Dawn's birth, she began to respond to her parents' voices. When spoken to, Dawn turned her head, focused her eyes on her mother or father, and appeared to listen and watch intensely. Her parents and grandparents also instinctively began using an exaggerated speech pattern called parentese (often called baby talk). Until recently, parents were cautioned against using baby talk or parentese with their infants because it was believed to foster immature forms of speech. However, recent studies have demonstrated that this slowed-down, high-pitched, exaggerated, repetitious speech actually seems to facilitate a child's language development. Current research suggests that this exaggerated speech allows babies many opportunities to observe how sounds are made and thus learn how to control their own vocal apparatus (Cowley, 1997; Field, Woodson, Greenberg, & Cohen, 1982; Healy, 1994; Shore, 1997). During these baby talk conversations, Dawn would often move her mouth, lips, and eyes mimicking the facial movements of her parents. At the beginning of the fourth month, Dawn discovered her own voice. She delighted in the range of sounds she could make and sometimes chuckled at herself. At this point, Dawn (and most normally developing infants) could make almost all of the vowel and consonant sounds. She cooed and gurgled endlessly, joyfully experimenting with phonemic variations, pitch, and volume. When spoken to, she often began her own stream of conversation, called "sound play," which would parallel the adult speaker. At age six months, Dawn was also becoming an expert at imitating tone and inflection. For example, when her mother yelled at the cat for scratching the furniture Dawn used her own vocal skills to yell at the poor animal, too.

During her sixth month, Dawn's muscle strength, balance and coordination allowed her to have greater independent control over her environment as she mastered the fine art of crawling and stumble-walking around furniture. These physical accomplishments stimulated further cognitive development, as she now had the ability to explore the world under her own power.

At seven months, Dawn's babbling increased dramatically. However, the sounds she produced now began to sound like words, which she would repeat over and over. This type of vocalizing is called "echolalia." Though "MmmmaaaMmmmaaa" and "Dddaaaddaaa" sounded like "Mama" and "DaDa," they were still not words with a cognitive connection or meaning.

In her eighth month, Dawn's babbling began to exhibit conversation-like tones and behaviors. This pattern of speech is called "vocables." While there were still no real words in her babble, Dawn's vocalizations were beginning to take on some of the conventions of adult conversations, such as turn taking, eye contact, and recognizable gestures. These forms of prelanguage are play-like in nature, being done for their own sake rather than a deliberate use of language to communicate a need or accomplish a goal.

At approximately nine months, Dawn first used real, goal-oriented language. As her father came home from work, she ran to him shouting in an excited voice, "Dada, Dada," and held her arms up to him. Dawn's accurate labeling of her father and her desire to be picked up were deliberate actions that revealed that Dawn was using language to accomplish her objectives.

Between age nine months and her first birthday, Dawn's expressive (speaking) and receptive (listening and comprehending) vocabulary grew rapidly. She could understand and comply with dozens of simple requests, such as "Bring Mommy your shoes" or the ever favorite label-the-body game, "Where is Daddy's nose?" In addition, Dawn's command of nonverbal gestures and facial expressions were expanding from waving "bye-bye" to scowling and saying "no-no" when taking her medicine. In addition, holophrases words began to emerge, in which one word carried the semantic burden for a whole sentence or phrase. Such as, "Keeths," while holding her plastic keys, purse and sunglasses meant, "I want to go for a ride," or "iith" meant, "I want some ice." Dawn also used over generalized speech, in which each word embraced many meanings. For instance, "doll" referred not only to her favorite baby doll but to everything in her toy box, and "jooth" stood for any type of liquid she drank.

From one year to 18 months, Dawn's vocabulary expanded quickly. Most of her words identified or labeled the people, pets, and objects that were familiar and meaningful to her. Clark's (1983) research suggests that young children between one and six will learn and remember approximately nine new words a day. This ability to relate new words to pre-existing internalized concepts, then remember and use them after only one exposure, is called fast mapping (Carey, 1979).

Because chronological age is not a reliable indicator of language progression, linguists typically describe language development by noting the number of words used in a sentence, which is called "mean length of utterance" (MLU). At this point, Dawn was beginning to use two-word sentences such as "Kitty juuth." Linguists call these two- and three-word sentences "telegraphic speech," as they contain only the most necessary of words to convey meaning. However, these first sentences may have many interpretations; for instance, Dawn's sentence "Kitty, juuth" might mean "The kitty wants some milk," or "The kitty drank the milk," or even "The kitty stuck her head in my cup and drank my milk." Obviously the context in which the sentence was spoken helped her parents to better understand the intent or meaning of her communication.

Around age 18 months to two years, as Dawn began using sentences more frequently, the use of syntax became apparent. "No shoes" with a shoulder shrug meant she couldn't find her shoes, but "Shoes, no!" said with a shaking head, meant Dawn did not want to put on her shoes.

Though Dawn's vocabulary grew, her phonemic competence did not always reflect adult standards. Many of her words were clearly pronounced (kitty, baby), while others were interesting phonemetic attempts or approximations (bise for bike, Papa for Grandpa, bawble for bottle); yet others were her own construction (NaNe for Grandma). At this age, most children are unable to articulate perfectly the sounds of adult speech. Rather, they simplify the adult sounds to ones they can produce. Sometimes this means they pronounce the initial sound or syllable of a word (whee for wheel), and at other times, they pronounce only the final sound or syllable (ees for cheese). Another common feature is temporary regression, meaning that they may pronounce a word or phrase quite clearly, then later produce a shortened, less mature version. This, too, is a normal language developmental phase for all children. Thus, it is important that parents accept their child's language and not become overly concerned with correcting their pronunciation.

Likewise, children's early attempts to use sentences need thoughtful support, not critical correction. Parents can best support their child's attempts to communicate through extensions and expansions. Extensions include responses that incorporate the essence of a child's sentence but transform it into a well-formed sentence. For example, when Dawn said, "ree stor-ee," her father responded, "Do you want me to read the story book to you?" When parents and caregivers use extensions they model appropriate grammar and fluent speech, and actually help to extend a child's vocabulary.

When parents use expansions, they gently reshape the child's efforts to reflect grammatical appropriate content. For example, when Dawn said, "We goed to Diseelan," instead of correcting her ("We don't say goed we say went"), her mother expanded Dawn's language by initially confirming the intent of Dawn's statement while modeling the correct form, "Yes, we went to Disneyland."

The adaptations parents make when talking to young children—such as slowing the rate of speech, using age appropriate vocabulary, questioning and clarifying the child's statements, and extensions and expansions occurs in all cultures. These early interactions with children and the gradual and building support is called parentese—or more gender specifically motherese and fatherese. When parents use this form of support they are actually helping their

Figure 2.3

Parental expansion of telegraphic speech

children gain communicative competence and confidence (Vygotsky, 1962; White, 1985). Between the ages of two and three years, Dawn's language had developed to the point where she could express her needs and describe her world to others quite well. In addition to using pronouns, she also began to produce grammatical inflections "-ing," plurals, past tense, and possessive inflections.

Statements	*Age*
"I lub you, Mama."	2.0*
"Boot's crywing."	2.1
"Dawn's baby dawl."	2.2
"My books."	2.4
"Grover droppted the radio."	2.6
"Cookie monster shutted the door."	2.8
"She's not nice to me."	2.9
"Daddy's face got stickers, they scratch."	3.0

* Indicates age by years and months.

Dawn also loved finger plays such as the "Itsy, Bitsy, Spider" and "Grandma's Glasses"; poems such as "This Little Pig" and songs such as "Jingle Bells," "Yankee Doodle," and the "Alphabet Song." She was also beginning to count and echo-read with her parents when they read her favorite stories, like the "Three Little Pigs." Dawn would "huff and puff and blow your house down" as many times as her parents would read the story.

From ages three years to five years, Dawn had become a proficient language user. She could make requests, "Please, may I have some more cake?" and demands, "I need this, now!" depending on her mood and motivation. She could seek assistance, "Can you tell me where the toys are?" and demonstrate concern, "What's the matter, Mama?" She sought information about her world, "Why is the moon round one time and just a grin sometimes?"

Dawn's language development, though completely normal, is also a human miracle. Language plays a central role in learning, and a child's success in school depends to very large degree on his or her ability to speak and listen. Dawn's case study also confirms the critical role social interaction plays in language development. Thus, in the following section, we provide more information about ways parents and caregivers may support a child's language acquisition.

What Is Normal Language Development?

While the process of learning to talk follows a predictable sequence, the age at which children say their first word may vary widely from one child to another. Developmental guidelines provide descriptions of specific behaviors and delineate the age at which most children demonstrate this physical or cognitive skill. This type of information helps parents and physicians anticipate normal physical and cognitive growth. While physical maturation is easy to observe, cognitive development is less obvious. Fortunately, children's language development provides one indication that their cognitive abilities are developing normally. In Table 2.1, we present the average ages for language acquisition and review Dawn's and Joel's development from birth to age two. In comparing their progress, it is clear that both children followed the same sequence of language acquisition, but at different rates. Though the age they displayed specific skills differed, their language abilities matured within the age range offered for normal language development. While most children demonstrate language skills well within the normal age range, some do not. If a child's language is delayed more than two months past the upper age limits, caregivers should seek medical guidance, as delays may indicate problems (Copeland & Gleason, 1993; Vines & Rosenthal-Tanzer, 1988; Weiss, Lilly-White, & Gordon, 1980). Early identification of problems leads to appropriate intervention.

Table 2.1	About 90 percent of children will develop the following language skills by the ages indicated. If a child does not demonstrate these behaviors by these ages, it is important for parents to seek medical guidance.

Normal Language Development

Age	Language Skill
2 months	Make sounds in response to stimulus
3 months	Make cooing sounds
7 months	Make sounds such as "giving a raspberry"
10 months	Single-syllable babbling ("ma," "pa," "ba," "da")
11 months	Multiple-syllable babbling ("mama," "dada," "baba")
14 months	Uses *mama* and *dada* (or similar sounds) to call parents
16 months	Uses some words besides *mama* and *dada*
22 months	Has a vocabulary of four to six words Can express some wants Can be understood by strangers about half the time
23 months	Can form two-word sentences
26 months	Has a 50-word vocabulary
29 months	Uses "me," "you," and "my"
34 months	Uses prepositions Can carry on a conversation Can identify and use "cup," "spoon"
37 months	Can be understood by strangers about three quarters of the time
47 months	Can be understood by strangers most of the time

Source: Copeland & Gleason (1993).

While helpful, developmental guidelines are not perfect. To determine norms, data must be collected on specific populations. In most cases these data were collected on middle-income Caucasian children born in modern industrial-technological societies. Since this sample does not represent the world's population, the upper and lower age limits of these "universal" norms must be interpreted carefully.

Factors Contributing to Variations in Rate of Language Acquisition

Since the critical period for language development occurs within the first 36 months of a child's life, significant language delay may indicate specific medical or cognitive problems. Beyond medical problems, there are several factors that could modify the rate of normal language production. We review these factors in the following discussion.

Gender Differences

Are there differences in the rate and ways that boys and girls develop language fluency and proficiency? This question reflects another facet of the ongoing nature versus nurture debate. Observational research consistently reveals that a majority of girls talk earlier and talk more than the majority of boys. It is also true that the majority of late talkers are young boys (Healy, 1997; Kalb & Namuth, 1997). However, it is difficult to determine whether differences in the rate of language acquisition are biological or if biological differences are exaggerated by social influences. There is evidence for both views. For example, neural-biological research offers graphic images that illustrate how men's and women's brains process language somewhat differently (Corballis, 1991; Moir & Jessel, 1991). Though this research appears to support nature as the dominant factor in language differences, it is also important to consider how powerful a role nurture plays. Experimental research consistently documents differential treatment of infants based on gender. In other words, men and women tend to cuddle, coo at, and engage in lengthy face-to-face conversations with baby girls. Yet, with baby boys, adults are likely to exhibit "jiggling and bouncing" behaviors but are not as likely to engage in sustained face-to-face verbal interactions. Perhaps girls talk earlier and talk more because they receive more language stimulation (Huttenlocher, 1991).

Socioeconomic Level

Numerous studies have long documented the differences in the rate of language acquisition and the level of language proficiency between low and middle socioeconomic families (Hart & Risley, 1995; Morisset, 1995; Walker, Greenwood, Hart, & Carta, 1994). These studies found that children, especially males, from low-income homes were usually somewhat slower to use expressive language than children from middle-income homes. These findings likely reflect social-class differences both in language use in general and in parent–child interaction patterns. For example, Betty Hart and Todd Risley (1995) estimate that, by age four, children from professional families have had a cumulative total of 50 million words addressed to them, whereas as children from welfare families have been exposed to only 13 million words. The children from professional families have had more than three times the linguistic input than welfare families' children; this gives them a tremendous advantage in language acquisition.

Results of long-term observations of middle-income and lower-income families concluded that all mothers spent a great deal of time nurturing their infants (e.g., touching, hugging, kissing, and holding), but that there were differences in the way mothers verbally interacted with their children. Middle-income mothers spent a great deal more time initiating verbal interactions and usually responded to and praised their infants' vocal efforts. Middle-income mothers were also more likely to imitate their infants' vocalizations. These verbal interactions stimulate neural-synapse networks that foster expressive and receptive language. It is still unclear why lower-income mothers do not engage their children in verbal interactions at the same level as middle-income mothers. The authors of these studies speculate that this may be a reflection of social-class differences in language use in general.

Cultural Influences

The rate of language acquisition may be somewhat different for children of different cultures. Since spoken language is a reflection of the culture from which it emerges, it is necessary to consider the needs verbal language serves in the culture. Communication may be accomplished in other meaningful ways (Bhavnagri & Gonzalez-Mena, 1997). Janet Gonzalez-Mena (1997, p. 70) offers this example:

> The emphasizing or de-emphasizing the verbal starts from the beginning with the way babies are treated. Babies carried around much of the time get good at sending messages nonverbally—through changing body positions or tensing up or relaxing muscles. They are encouraged to communicate this way when their caregivers pick up the messages they send. They don't need to depend on words at an early age. Babies who are physically apart from their caregivers learn the benefits of verbal communication. If the babies are on the floor in the infant playpen or in the other room at home, they need to learn to use their voices to get attention. Changing position or tensing muscles goes unperceived by the distant adult.

Likewise, some cultures do not view babies' vocal attempts as meaningful communication. Shirley Brice Heath (1983) describes a community in which infants' early vocalizations are virtually ignored and adults do not generally address much of their talk directly to infants. Many cultures emphasize receptive language, and children listen as adults speak.

Medical Concerns

Beyond gender, socioeconomic, and culture differences, other reasons that children's language may be delayed include temporary medical problems and congenital complications. In Special Feature 2.1, "She Just Stopped Talking," we provide an example of one the most common childhood problems—otitis media—that, left unattended, could cause significant language delays and speech distortion and ultimately difficulty in learning to read and write.

Special Feature 2.1

She Just Stopped Talking

On her first birthday, Tiffany mimic-sang "Hap Birffaay meee" over and over. She said "Sank oo" when she received her birthday gifts and "Bye, seeoo" when her guests left. Later that summer, after a bad bout with an ear infection, Tiffany's mother noticed she was turning up the volume on the television when she watched *Sesame Street*. A few days later, after several restless nights, Tiffany became very fussy and irritable and began tugging on her ear. Her parents again took her to the doctor, who diagnosed another ear infection. After a ten-day treatment of antibiotics, Tiffany appeared to be fine, except that she seemed to talk less and less.

About a month later, the situation worsened. Tiffany would not respond to her mother's speech unless she was looking directly at her mother. At that point Tiffany had, for the most part, stopped talking.

Tiffany's story is all too common. She was suffering from otitis media, an inflammation of the middle part of the ear. The symptoms of otitis media usually appear during or after a cold or respiratory infection. Because fluid can collect in the middle ear (behind the eardrum) without causing pain, children with otitis media may not complain. The following is a list of possible symptoms; any one of these symptoms could indicate that a child has otitis media:

- earaches or draining of the ears
- fever
- changes in sleeping or eating habits
- irritability
- rubbing or pulling at the ears
- cessation of babbling and singing
- urning up the television or radio volume much louder than usual
- frequently need to have directions and information repeated
- unclear speech
- use of gestures rather than speech
- delayed speech and language development.

From 12 months through four years of age, language development is at its peak. Even a temporary hearing loss during this time interferes with speech articulation and language learning. Otitis media causes temporary loss of hearing when the fluid pushes against the eardrum. The pressure prevents the eardrum from vibrating, so sound waves cannot move to the inner ear and the child's hearing is greatly distorted or muffled. Consequently, final consonant sounds and word endings are often unheard, and words blend into one another. Because one of the main reasons people talk is to communicate, a child who cannot understand what is said becomes frustrated and easily distracted. This type of hearing loss may continue for up to six weeks after the ear infection has healed.

Though hearing loss caused by otitis media is described as "mild and fluctuating," it is a major cause of speech distortion and language delay in the preschool years. If left untreated, young children with recurrent and persistent otitis media may develop permanent hearing loss, speech distortions, language delays, and problems with focusing attention (Vines & Rosenthal-Tanzer, 1988).

When Tiffany's parents realized that she had stopped speaking, their pediatrician referred them to an otolaryngologist (ear, nose, and throat specialist). The doctor was pleased that Tiffany's parents had written down new words she used on the family calendar. As the doctor reviewed the calendar, it became apparent that Tiffany's normal language development had virtually stopped. He did not seem surprised when her parents mentioned that she had also stopped babbling and singing and that she no longer danced when music was played. Because Tiffany's pediatrician had already tried three months of antibiotics to control the infection with no success, the specialist suggested surgically placing bilateral vent tubes in the eardrum to drain the fluid from the middle ear. When the fluid is drained, the eardrum can then vibrate freely once again and normal hearing may be restored.

After a brief operation (approximately 30 minutes), 18-month-old Tiffany began to speak once again. Though her hearing was restored, the doctor suggested that Tiffany and her parents visit a speech therapist to help her fully regain her language.

Within a year, Tiffany's development was progressing normally, and by age three, the surgically implanted tubes naturally fell out of her eardrums. Since that time, Tiffany has not had a recurrence of otitis media.

Congenital Language Disorders

For most children, learning to communicate is a natural, predictable developmental progression. Unfortunately, some children have congenital language disorders that impair their ability to learn language or use it effectively. The origin of these disorders may be physical or neurological. Examples of physical problems include malformation of the structures in the inner ear or a poorly formed palate. Neurological problems could include dysfunction in the brain's ability to perceive or interpret the sounds of language.

Though the symptoms of various language disorders may appear similar, effective treatment may differ significantly, depending on the cause of the problem. For example, articulation problems caused by a physical malformation of the palate might require reconstructive surgery, while articulation problems caused by hearing impairment might require a combination of auditory amplification and speech therapy. Two of the most common symptoms of congenital language disorders are disfluency and pronunciation.

DISFLUENCY.   Children with fluency disorders have difficulty speaking rapidly and continuously. They may speak with an abnormal rate—too fast or too slow; in either case, their speech is often incomprehensible and unclearly articulated. The rhythm of their speech may also be severely affected. Stuttering is the most common form of this disorder. Many children may have temporary fluency disruptions or stuttering problems as they are learning to express themselves in sentences. Children who are making a transition to a second language may also experience brief stuttering episodes. It is important for parents or teachers to be patient and supportive, as it may take time to distinguish normal developmental or temporary lapses in fluency from a true pathology. Stuttering may have multiple origins and may vary from child to child. Regardless of cause, recently developed treatment protocols have been effective in helping stutterers.

PRONUNCIATION.   Articulation disorders comprise a wide range of problems and may have an equally broad array of causes. Minor misarticulations in the preschool years are usually developmental and will generally improve as the child matures. Occasionally, as children lose their baby teeth, they may experience temporary challenges in articulation. However, articulation problems that seriously impede a child's ability to communicate needs and intentions must be diagnosed. Causes of such problems may include malformation of the mouth, tongue, or palate; partial loss of hearing due to a disorder in the inner ear; serious brain trauma; or a temporary hearing loss due to an ear infection (Copeland & Gleason, 1993).

It is important to remember that some children may simply show delayed language development; this may mean that a child is gaining control over speaking mechanisms at a slower rate than same-age peers or has had limited opportunity to hear speech or interact with others. Children who are learning a second language may also appear to have articulation difficulties when they attempt to use their second language. As we explain in Special Feature 2.2, anyone learning a new phonemic system will experience some difficulty in expressing new sound combinations. "Bilingual children should be assessed in their native language and referred for therapy only if an articulation disorder is present in that language" (Piper, 1993, p. 193). Caregivers and teachers need to be careful not to confuse the normal course of second-language acquisition with speech disorders.

Summary

Children's acquisition of oral language is truly remarkable. By the time they enter kindergarten, most children have mastered the basic structures and components of their native language, all without much stress or effort. How did the information contained in this chapter compare with what you were able to discover about your own first words and early language learning? Which of the four perspectives described above comes closest to your view about children's language development?

Special Feature 2.2

Young Children's Second-Language Development

Sarah Hudelson and Irene Serna

Have you ever been in a situation where everyone around you is using a language that you don't know? How did you feel when the language around you sounded like gibberish? How did you respond? Were there some strategies that you used to cope? Think about yourself in this kind of situation as you read about young children learning a second language.

In Chapter 2 you have learned about how children acquire their native language. Joel and Dawn's language acquisition is typical for a child brought up in a monolingual home—that is, a home where one language is spoken. However, a growing number of children in the United States are raised in homes where two languages are used regularly, and where two languages are addressed to young children. Children raised in such bilingual environments have not one but two native languages, what Swain (1972) refers to as bilingualism as a native language.

Years ago there was concern that young children would be cognitively damaged by such early exposure to two languages, that there would be considerable confusion on the child's part and that normal language development would be delayed (Hakuta, 1986). Recent investigations, however, have made it clear that this is not the case. There is now ample evidence that young children raised from birth with two languages develop language at rates comparable to monolingual children. They begin to use single words and multilingual word combinations at the same time as monolingual children. Young bilingual children develop separate language systems and use them appropriately (Hakuta, 1986). Depending on the frequency of use, one language may develop more fully than the other. It is also common for young bilinguals to borrow words from one language and use them in speaking the other language in order to communicate their intentions. But fluency in two languages is a common occurrence among young children (see Goodz, 1994, for a recent review of research on preschool bilingualism). It is certainly possible that some of the young children in your prekindergarten or primary grade classrooms will be bilingual in English and another language.

It is even more probable, however, that your classroom will contain some children whose native language is other than English—Spanish, French, Russian, Polish, Croatian, Arabic, Vietnamese, Chinese, Khmer, Japanese, Urdu, Navajo, Hopi, Apache, to name a few. There are currently millions of young children in this country who are being raised in households where a language other than English is spoken (Waggoner, 1992). Cultural and linguistic diversity is increasing in our schools. Like monolingual English speakers, non-English speaking children have learned their native languages by living in and being socialized into particular speech communities. Non-English speaking children come to school having acquired the structural systems (phonological, syntactic, morphological, semantic) of one language as well as the pragmatics of what is appropriate language use—in terms of social and cultural norms—of their native language speech community. Thus, these learners bring to school understandings of what language is, what language can do, what language is for, and how to use language appropriately in their own communities (Lindfors, 1987).

Often, appropriate ways of using language in these diverse communities are significantly different from the ways of mainstream English-speaking children. For example, Delgado-Gaitan and Trueba (1991), studying the language socialization of Mexican immigrant children in a California town, discovered that young children were socialized to talk with their siblings and other children, yet to be quiet around adults.

When young speakers of languages other than English enter school, they may be fortunate enough to be placed in bilingual classrooms, where children and adults make use of the native language for learning and where the English language and academic instruction through English are introduced gradually. Or they may find themselves in settings where English is the basic language of the class and of instruction. In either case, children find themselves in the position of acquiring English as a second or additional language (ESL). What this means is that children must develop new ways of expressing themselves, new ways of talking about their experiences, new ways of asking questions, new ways of using language to help them learn. They must also learn to behave appropriately in settings, including school, where the new language is used. This is hard work that involves them in striving both to understand the language around them and to use that language for themselves and with others (Lindfors, 1987; Tabors & Snow, 1994).

The perspective on child second-language acquisition that most researchers and educators take is similar to the social-interactionist perspective articulated in Chapter 2. That is, in learning a new language children engage in the creative construction of the rules of the new language, and this creative construction occurs within the context of multiple social interactions as children use the new language with others (Allen, 1991). The discussion that follows summarizes some essential points about children's ESL acquisition. Most of the understandings presented have been formulated through careful observation of children and teachers in prekindergarten and primary grade settings.

As discussed in Chapter 1, creative construction means that the ESL learner is not simply an empty jar into which the new language is poured. Rather, the learner is an active participant in the development of abilities in the new language. Learners use language from the environment and from specific others to make predictions about how English works and then to try out these predictions

(continued on next page)

in the form of English utterances. Sometimes learners predict that the second language works like the first one, and sounds, lexical items and morpho-syntactic patterns from the native language may influence English. Always, creative construction involves making mistakes, but mistakes need to be seen as the learner's attempt to make sense of the new language, to figure out how that language is put together (Allen, 1991).

Nora, a first-grade, Spanish-speaking child whose acquisition of English was studied by respected researcher Lily Wong Fillmore (1976), provides a good demonstration of the child as creative constructor. Early in first grade, Nora memorized such phrases as "Do you wanna play?" and used them to initiate contact with English-speaking children. Soon she began to use the phrase "How do you do dese?" as a general formula to ask for information and help. After a while she added elements to the formula so that she could ask such questions as: "How do you do dese little tortillas? How do you do dese in English?" Gradually she was able to vary the sentence after the word you to produce: "How do you like to be cookie cutter? How do you make the flower? How do you gonna make these?" She was also able to use *did* as in "How did you lost it?" Later still she was able to use *how* in sentences very different from the original formula; for example, "Because when I call him, how I put the number?" (pp. 246–247) These efforts illustrate how Nora, over time, constructed and reconstructed her English to convey her meanings and accomplish her purposes.

Tabors and Snow (1994) have documented a general sequence in young children's ESL acquisition that appears to be fairly common. When they first encounter the new language, many young learners will continue to use their native language when speaking to English speakers. This behavior is often followed by a period when they do not talk at all but instead attempt to communicate nonverbally through gestures, mimes, and cries or whimpers to attract attention. Young ESL learners also have been observed to engage in spectating—paying close attention to the actions and utterances of English speakers (so that they can connect words to activities)—and rehearsing—practicing the new language to, by, and for themselves, repeating words, phrases, and sounds in English at a very low volume. Following the nonverbal period, children begin to use formulaic expressions in English (e.g.: "What's that?" "Wanna play?" "I want that." "I don't know." "Gimme!"), which may get them into the action with other children. From formulas, as Nora demonstrated, children gradually begin productive language use, moving beyond memorized utterances and formulaic expressions to creative construction. Although this sequence has been described as if it were discrete and unidirectional, this is not necessarily so for all learners.

There are tremendous individual differences in children's second-language learning. Learners differ in the rate at which they learn the second language. They differ in their willingness to learn English and in their avoidance

or nonavoidance of the new language. They differ in the language-learning strategies they use. They differ in whether their stance is more participator or observer. The least successful English learners seem to be those who avoid contact with English speakers and who do not engage with what is going on around them in English (Fillmore, 1976; Saville-Troike, 1988). Some research has suggested that the best ESL learners are those children who are most eager to interact with English speakers, who are most willing to participate and use whatever English they have at a particular point in time, who are risk takers and are not afraid to make mistakes, and who identify with English speakers (Fillmore, 1976; Strong, 1983). However, researchers also have discovered that quiet children who pay close attention to what is going on around them (the careful observer stance) may also be quite effective language learners (Fillmore, 1983; Flanigan, 1988). So not all young children learn a second language in exactly the same way.

What is crucial to children's successful second-language acquisition is the learner's choosing to work at communicating with people who speak the new language. Young ESL learners find themselves in environments where English is used. But they must choose to work at learning the new language; they must want to interact with others in English if acquisition is to occur. Interaction is critical in two ways: (1) it gives learners opportunities to try out the new language to see if they can make themselves understood; and (2) fluent English speakers respond to the learner's efforts, providing both additional language input and a gauge on how well the learner is communicating. This language give and take is critical to continued learning (Ellis, 1985; Tabors & Snow, 1994).

In the ESL setting both adults and other children may act as language teachers for children. Adults tend to modify or adapt their ways of speaking to what they think the ESL learner will understand and respond to. Studies of primary teachers working with ESL learners have reached the following conclusions: As with "baby talk" in native language settings, effective teachers tend to speak more slowly, using clear enunciation, somewhat simplified sentences, and exaggerated intonation. They often use repetitions or restatements of sentences. They also contextualize their speech by using objects and physical gestures so that learners may use nonlinguistic cues to figure out what has been said. Finally, adults make concerted efforts both to encourage the ESL child to talk and to understand what the learner is saying. In their efforts to understand children, adults frequently expand children's incomplete sentences or extend what they have said (Enright, 1986; Fillmore, 1982, 1983; Washington, 1982). Through all of these provisions of "comprehensible input" (Krashen, 1982), adults are responsive persons with whom to try out the new language.

Fluent English-speaking children are also important language models and teachers for their ESL counterparts.

(continued on next page)

During interactions, English-speaking children may assist their non-English speaking peers by gesturing, correcting, giving feedback, engaging in language play, and encouraging the second-language learner to talk (Ventriglia, 1982). But children do not make the consistently concerted efforts that adults do to be understood by and to understand ESL learners unless they have been coached to do so (see Tabors & Snow, 1994). They may tire of the teacher role and move away from it more quickly than an adult would. And children do not tend to focus as exclusively on understanding the ESL child as adults do; what is often most important is carrying out whatever activity they happen to be engaged in (Fillmore, 1976; Peck, 1978). But given that children often (but not always) are more interested in interacting with other children than they are with adults, other children provide strong incentives for ESL children to use their developing English and to make themselves understood. The desire to communicate is at the heart of young children's second-language learning.

Earlier we distinguished bilingual from ESL classrooms. In spite of research evidence that speaks to the efficacy of teaching children through their native language, a major issue with regard to non-English-speaking learners has been the role that languages other than English play in children's learning. The common-sense belief that the most efficient way to encourage English language proficiency is to use only English is still adhered to by numbers of early childhood educators (see Fillmore, 1991). This has meant that numbers of Head Start and kindergarten programs have embraced the idea of an early school introduction of, and sometimes school immersion in, English—with the understanding that parents will continue to use their native languages at home so that young children continue to develop linguistic abilities and communicative competence in their home tongues while acquiring English (Tabors & Snow, 1994). Theoretically, this situation should result in young children becoming bilingual, but using their two languages in different settings.

Unfortunately, the reality is that early introduction to English in school has often meant that non-English-speaking children refuse to communicate in their native languages and try to use English exclusively. In a study of the home language practices of more than 300 immigrant preschoolers, Fillmore (1991) discovered that these young learners, whether they were enrolled in bilingual or English-only classrooms, were particularly vulnerable to language loss. The longer they stayed in school, the more they relied on English for communication, even at home. This jeopardized non-English-speaking parents' abilities to interact verbally with their children and socialize them.

Fillmore raises the issue of whether English-language acquisition has to come at the expense of other languages. Her data point out the potentially devastating consequences of children's refusal to speak their native languages. Parents anguish over how to communicate with their children, how to pass on family and community histories, how to transmit cultural expectations, how to discipline them, and so on if they are unable to communicate with them. We believe that not only early childhood educators but all educators, whether bilingual or not, must wrestle with the reality of how to respect and value children's home languages and cultures.

In many important ways, second-language acquisition in young children is quite similar to first-language acquisition. This general statement means that adults working with second-language learners need to focus both on making themselves understood by children and on understanding children and encouraging them to use their new language. Adults need to focus on the learners' communicative intentions, not on the conventionality of their utterances. Adults also need to be sensitive to individual differences in children's rates of second-language learning and accepting of these differences. Children should be encouraged but not forced to use the new language, and children should not be belittled for hesitancy in trying out English. Adults need to recognize that children are learning English even if they are not responding verbally. Adults need to encourage other children who are native speakers of English to have patience with ESL learners and to assist them in their learning. Finally, adults should value the native languages that children bring to school with them and encourage them to continue to use their native languages.

To summarize the key points about oral language development, we return to the guiding questions at the beginning of this chapter:

■ *What are the major views on how children's language develops? Which aspects of language development does each view adequately explain?*

Four competing perspectives have been used to explain how children acquire language. The behaviorist perspective emphasizes the important role of reinforcement in helping children learn the sounds, words, and rules of language. This view handily explains the imitative aspects of initial language learning. Nativists stress the importance of children's inborn capacity to learn language and suggest that a portion of the brain is dedicated to language learning. Nativist theory explains how children "invent" their own two- and three-word grammars and overgeneralize rules for past tense ("He goed to the store") and plural ("I saw two mouses today!"). The social-interactionist perspective emphasizes the importance of both environmental factors and children's innate predisposition to make sense out of language and use it for practical purposes. According to this view, children learn about language by using it in social situations. The social-interactionist view highlights the role of parental support in language acquisition. Finally, new technology has allowed scientists to observe how the brain perceives, interprets, and expresses language. These developments have lead to a new perspective of children's language learning, the neuro-biological view, which complements the three earlier views on language development. This perspective explains how the structural development of the brain is related to language acquisition. It helps explain why children's experiences during infancy have such a crucial effect on later language learning.

■ *What are the major components of language?*

The major components of language are (1) phonology—the sounds that make up a language; (2) morphology—the meaning bearing units of language, including words and affixes; (3) syntax—the rules for ordering words into sentences; (4) semantics—the shades of meaning that words convey; and (5) pragmatics—the social rules that enable language to accomplish real-life purposes.

■ *How does the structure of an infant's brain develop? How does this structural development affect language acquisition?*

At birth, the human brain is remarkably unfinished. Most of the 100 billions neurons or brain cells are not yet connected. During the first month of life, the number of neural synapses or connections increase 20 times to more than 1000 trillion. As a child matures, the actual number of neurons remains stable; however, the number of synapse connections increase, and the message-receiving dendrite branches grow larger and heavier. At age one, the full cortex consumes twice as much energy as an adult brain. This neural readiness, in combination with countless hours of sound play and verbal exchanges with loving caregivers, allows most children to begin speaking their first words at this age.

By 18 months, neural synapses have increased and strengthened and are beginning to transmit information efficiently. Hence most toddlers begin to experience a language explosion, particularly in the areas of vocabulary and syntax. During this time, children are able to learn as many as 12 words a day. Thus, the neuro-biological perspective reveals how the rapid development of the brain during the first few years of life makes it possible for children to acquire language so quickly and efficiently. This perspective also explains why the first 36 months are a critical period for language development.

■ *What factors affect children's rate of language acquisition?*

While language development follows a predictable sequence, the rate at which children acquire language varies tremendously. Gender, socioeconomic level, and cultural influences all can affect the rate of language acquisition. A child's language learning can also be impeded by illnesses, such as otitis media, and by a variety of congenital problems of a physical and/or neurological nature. Parents and caregivers are cautioned to seek a medical diagnosis if language development is significantly delayed, as early identification and treatment can often avoid irreparable disruption of the language acquisition process.

■ *How does children's acquisition of a second language compare with their first language acquisition? What should adults do to make it easier for children to learn English as a second language?*

In many ways, second-language acquisition in young children is similar to their acquisition of their first language. In learning a new language, children engage in the creative construction of the rules of the new language, and this creative construction occurs within the context of multiple social interactions as children use the new language with others.

Adults working with second-language learners need to focus both on making themselves understood by children and encouraging these children to use their new language. Adults need to focus on the learners' communicative intentions, not on the conventionality of their utterances. Children should be encouraged but not forced to use the new language, and children should not be belittled for hesitancy in trying it. Adults need to recognize that children are learning English even if they are not responding verbally. Adults need to encourage other children who are native speakers of English to have patience with ESL learners and to assist them in their learning. Finally, adults should value the native languages that children bring to school with them and encourage them to continue to use their native languages.

Linking Knowledge to Practice

1. Interview two parents and two early childhood teachers regarding how they believe children learn language. Consider which theory of language acquisition best matches each interviewee's beliefs.
2. Interview a school nurse or health care aide about the numbers of children she or he sees who are affected by illnesses and congenital problems. From the health care worker's perspective, what effect do these medical problems have on children? How often should children be screened for auditory acuity? If a family has limited financial recourses, what agencies can provide medical services?
3. Observe a second-language learner in a preschool or day care setting. Does the second-language learner comprehend some of the talk that is going on in the classroom? How does the child communicate with other children? How does the teacher support the child's second-language acquisition? Are other children helping? Does the second-language learner have any opportunities to use his or her native language?

Facilitating Oral Language Learning

Four-year old Evan, from Arizona, was visiting his grandmother in Vermont during the Christmas holiday. Upon opening the drapes one morning, he viewed snow-covered trees and fields. Evan gasped, "Grammie, who spilled all the sugar?" His grandmother responded, "Evan, that's very clever. It sure looks like sugar. Actually, it's snow."

Clearly, Evan's unfamiliarity with snow didn't prevent him from drawing a clever comparison. His grandmother responded by first showing appreciation for Evan's deduction and then providing the correct word, *snow*. Evan had a great opportunity to learn about the qualities of snow through conversations with his parents, grandparents, and older sister as they played together in the snow. During these adventures, they offered appropriate words for and information about all the new sights, sounds, tastes, smells, and feelings. By the end of the week, Evan knew the difference between wet and powder snow. He made snow angels, helped build a snowman and snow fort, engaged in a snowball war, and had an exhilarating ride on a sled. The new experiences he shared with older and more snow-experienced language users allowed Evan to build new vocabulary and cognitive understandings.

Chapter 2 discussed how infants and toddlers learn their native language through complex social interactions with parents, siblings, and other caregivers. These individuals are essentially a child's first and most important teachers. Throughout the preschool years, the family plays a significant role in helping children become accomplished language users. In this chapter, we examine the talk that goes on in homes and describe ways parents can support and enrich language development. Next, we discuss the many ways teachers can create learning environments that invite the types of rich oral interactions that promote language acquisition and enhance learning in all areas of the curriculum.

Before reading this chapter, think about. . .

- Your home language environment when you were a young child. Did you engage in lengthy conversations with your parents and siblings? Did you have an appreciative audience when you told stories about your own experiences? Did your family discuss the TV shows that you watched?
- The conversations that took place in your classroom when you were in school. Were these mainly teacher-centered exchanges in which you and your classmates responded to questions asked by the teacher, or did you have the opportunity to engage in two-way conversations with the teacher and other students?
- Sharing or show-and-tell. What did you like about this activity? Was there anything that you did not like about it?
- The make-believe play you engaged in when you were a child. What were some of the favorite roles and themes that you acted out during this play?

BOX 3.1

Definition of Terms

active listening: the listener combines the information provided by the speaker with his or her own prior knowledge to construct personal meaning.

anecdotal record: a brief note describing a child's behavior.

checklist: a observation tool that specifies which behaviors to look for and provides a convenient system of checking off when these behaviors are observed.

dramatic play: an advanced form of play in which children take on roles and act out make-believe stories and situations.

initiation, response, evaluation (IRE): a pattern of classroom talk in which the teacher asks a question, a student answers, and the teacher either accepts or rejects that answer and then goes on to ask another question.

metalinguistic awareness: the ability to attend to language forms in and of themselves. For example, a child may notice that two words rhyme with each other.

metaplay language: comments about play itself ("I'll be the mommy, and you be the baby.").

personal narrative: a story told in the first person about a personal experience.

pretend language: comments that are appropriate for the roles that children have taken in dramatic play. For example, a child pretending to be a baby might say "Waah! Waah!"

rubric: a scoring tool with a list of criteria that describe the characteristics of children's performance at various proficiency levels.

scaffolding: temporary assistance that parents and teachers give to children to enable them to do things that they cannot do on their own.

Focus Questions

- How can parents best facilitate their children's oral language development?
- What is the initiation, response, evaluation (IRE) pattern of class talk? What problems are associated with this type of discourse? How can teachers provide children with more stimulating conversations in the classroom?
- How do group activities, learning centers, and dramatic play promote oral language acquisition?
- What can teachers do to promote language-rich dramatic play?
- How can sharing or show-and-tell be turned into a valuable oral language activity?
- How can teachers effectively assess children's oral language development?
- What can teachers do to optimize oral language experiences for bilingual and second-language learners?

Home Talk: A Natural Context for Learning and Using Language

Evan's family helped him understand and label his new experience with snow. Their language support was natural and was guided by Evan's constant questions "Why doesn't this snow make a snowball? Why can't I make an angel on this snow?" Evan's learning while he played was nothing new or extraordinary; he has received language support from his parents and sibling from the moment he was born. His parents and older sister intuitively supported his attempts to communicate. When Evan was an infant his parents, like most parents, naturally used parentese. That is, they talked to him in higher pitched tones, at slower rate of speech, and with exaggerated pronunciation and lots of repetition of phrases. Parentese helped Evan hear the sounds and words of his native language. Between the age of 18 months and three years, as Evan's communicative competence grew, his family intuitively adjusted their verbal responses so that he could easily learn new vocabulary and grammatical structures.

In Special Feature 3.1, we describe the types of verbal scaffolding Evan's family and most adults automatically use to support children's language development. This type of scaffolding is a prime example of Vygotsky's (1978) zone of proximal development in which adults help children engage in activities that they could not do on their own. Through ongoing interactions with his parents, sister, and other caregivers, Evan (and most children) quickly learn basic conversation skills (Danst, Lowe, & Bartholomew, 1990; Manning-Kratcoski & Bobkoff-Katz, 1998;

Special Feature 3.1

Caregivers' Strategies for Supporting Children's Language Development

In almost all cases, caregivers intuitively scaffold children's language development. These communication strategies have been observed across all cultures.

Expansions—Adult recasts the child's efforts to reflect appropriate grammar. When adults use expansions they help introduce and build new vocabulary.

> **Child:** Kitty eat.
> **Adult:** Yes, the kitty is eating.

Extensions—Adult restates the child's telegraphic speech into a complete thought and may add new information in response to the child's comments.

> **Child:** Kitty eat.
> **Adult:** Kitty is eating his food.
> **Child:** Kitty eat.
> **Adult:** The kitty is hungry.

Repetitions—Adult facilitates the development of new sentence structure by repeating all or part of the child's comment.

> **Child:** Kitty eat.
> **Adult:** Time for kitty to eat. Time for kitty to eat.

Parallel talk—Adult describes the child's actions. Parallel talk is an effective way to model new vocabulary and grammatical structure.

> **Child:** Kitty eat.
> **Adult:** Jimmy is watching the kitty eat.

Self-talk—Adult describes their actions. Like parallel talk, self-talk effectively models new vocabulary and grammatical structures.

> **Adult:** I'm feeding the kitty.

Vertical structuring—Adult uses questions to encourage the child to produce longer or more complex sentences.

> **Child:** Kitty eat.
> **Adult:** What is the kitty eating?
> **Child:** Kitty eat cat food.

Fill-ins—Adult structures the conversation so that the child must provide a word or phrase to complete the statement.

> **Adult:** The kitty is eating because she is—
> **Child:** Hungry!

Manning-Kratcoski, A., & Bobkoff-Katz, M. (1998). Conversing with young language learners in the classroom. *Young Children*, 53(3): 30–33.

Norris & Hoffman, 1990). By age three, Evan, like most children, had learned to take turns, backchannel (use fillers like "uh-huh" to keep conversations going), be polite, and make appropriate responses (Menyuk, 1988). He knew how to engage in conversations with adults and his peers.

Encouraging Personal Narratives

Evan's family played a vital role in helping him interpret, label, and recall his new experiences with snow. Back in Arizona, Evan had many stories to tell his teacher and playmates at preschool. For the next several months, each time he spoke with his grandparents, he relived his snow-day tales. The stories, or personal narratives, that Evan told helped him make sense of this new experience, broadened his vocabulary, and reinforced his expressive language skills. Likewise, each time Evan told the story about how the snow ball he threw at his sister knocked off the snowman's nose and made his dad laugh, he deepened his memory of the event.

Children's personal narratives are a window into their thinking. Their language also reveals how they use current knowledge to interpret new experiences. Evan's first interpretation of a snowy field was to relate it to a recent incident with a broken sugar bowl. These verbal expressions of new mental constructions can be both fascinating and humorous. Likewise children's personal narratives offer insight into their language development and overall intellectual, social, and emotional growth.

Though children instinctively know how to put experiences, feelings, and ideas into story form, parents and caregivers can encourage their children's language development by offering many storytelling opportunities and attentively listening while children share their accounts of events (Canizares, 1997). Though nothing can replace quiet and private time to listen to children, many working parents report that they use the time in the car, bus, or subway going to and from day care and/or errands to listen carefully to their children.

Children often share what they know or have learned in story form. This is because the human brain functions narratively—for most of us it is much easier to understand and remember concepts when we are given information in story form rather than as a collection of facts. Since the human brain retains information more efficiently in story form, parents can explain new information using stories. For example, when five-year-old Tiffany wanted to know how to tie her shoelaces, her daddy told her the following story:

> Once upon a time, there were two silly snakes [the shoelaces] who decided to wrestle. They twisted around each other and tied themselves together very tightly [first tie]. The snakes became scared and tried to curl away from each other [the loops]. But the snakes tripped and fell over each other and tied themselves in a knot.

Reading Storybooks

Research reveals a connection between the amount of time adults spend reading storybooks to children and the level of children's oral language development. The stories, pictures, and accompanying adult-to-child interactions facilitate language use and increase expressive and receptive vocabulary. Further, children who have been read to frequently are better able to retell stories than children who have had few opportunities to engage in storytime (Barrentine, 1996; Durkin, 1966). Caregivers may also encourage discussion and comprehension by asking open-ended questions about the story. Children often relate to the characters and story lines, and, when encouraged, they reveal interesting views. The following conversation occurred when Dominique was four-years-old, after a reading of *Goldilocks and the Three Bears*.

Mom:	What part of the story did you like the best?
Dominique:	When Goldilocks kept messing up baby bear's stuff.
Mom:	Who did you like best in the story?
Dominique:	Baby bear.
Mom:	Why?
Dominique:	'Cause baby bear is like me. All of his stuff is wrecked up by Goldilocks, like Sheritta [her 18-month-old sister] messes up mine.

Notice that Dominique's mother asked open-ended opinion questions and accepted her child's responses. This type of question encourages oral responses and children's personal interpretation of the story. Adults should refrain from asking interrogation or detail questions, such as "What did Goldilock's say when she tasted the second bowl of porridge?" Detail questions tend to make storytime avoidable, not enjoyable.

As children snuggle in a parent's lap or beside their parent in a chair or bed, storytime creates a comforting, private time to talk together. In addition to providing wonderful language opportunities, storytime also establishes a foundation for children to become successful readers (See Chapters 4 and 5).

In today's culturally, linguistically, and socioeconomically diverse society, teachers may find that some of their students' parents may not have the ability to read to their children or the financial means to purchase storybooks. Even more parents are unsure how to successfully engage their children in storytime. Teachers may need to help parents by serving as a resource. In Chapter 10, readers will discover a number of concrete suggestions for ways to help teachers provide a range of supports families may need.

Television as a Language Tool

Television has been a major influence in family life in almost all U.S. households since the 1950s. In the 1980s the availability of video rentals and inexpensive video players, video movies, and video storybooks, cartoons, and games have added yet another dimension to television watching. During the 1990s, it was estimated that 99 percent of U.S. homes had at least one television set. In addition, the TV is usually in the part of the home where most family interactions occur (Miller, 1997). Sadly, the average child between two and five years of age will spend 27 hours a week viewing television programming (Lemish, 1987). Anything that occupies children for so many hours a week deserves careful consideration.

TIME. Research regarding the amount of time young children watch TV and the effect of viewing on later academic success is inconclusive, though the data clearly suggest that watching for many hours per day or week has a negative effect on children's academic performance. Susan Neuman (1988) suggests that more than four hours of TV viewing a day has a negative effect on children's reading achievement. Likewise, Angela Clarke's and Beth Kurtz-Costes' (1997) study of low-socioeconomic African American preschool children shows that children who watched the most television (between 30 and 55 hours per week) exhibited poorer academic skills than their peers who watched fewer than 25 hours per week. On the other hand, moderate amounts of TV viewing may be beneficial. The Center for the Study of Reading landmark report, "Becoming a Nation of Readers," suggests that there is actually a positive link between watching up to 10 hours of television a week and reading achievement (Rice, Huston, Truglio, & Wright, 1990). Clarke and Kurtz-Costes (1997) suggest that the variation in researchers' findings may be due in part to the home climate. They suggest that **who** watches TV with young children and **how** TV is watched may have a greater effect on children's learning than simply the **amount** of TV viewing.

CHOOSING PROGRAMMING FOR YOUNG CHILDREN. Selecting appropriate children's programming has become more challenging in recent years. In addition to regular public access, cable service may offer as many as 100 options to choose from each hour of the day. And while there are a number of proven classics—such as *Sesame Street, Reading Rainbow,* and *Mister Rogers*—children's programs change from year to year. One way parents can determine the quality of children's programming is through considering children's needs. Diane Levin and Nancy Carlsson-Paige (1994) created a list of children's developmental needs and suggested program criteria to accommodate these concerns. Figure 3.1 presents A Developmental Guide for Assessing Television Programming adapted from their work.

ACTIVE VIEWING. Young children are extremely impressionable, and television's visual imagery is a powerful force in their lives. Therefore, it is important for parents to help guide and mediate the viewing process. Susan Miller (1997) suggests a number of ways parents and caregivers may interact with children as they view television.

- *Watch television together*—Help children interpret what is seen on the screen.
- *Talk about the programs*—Conversations initiated by television programming offer opportunities to discuss a wide variety of issues.
- *Observe children's reactions*—Ask children to label or describe their feelings.
- *Foster critical thinking*—Ask children what they think about a program. Would they have handled the problem differently? Did they agree with the character's actions?
- *Extend viewing activities*—Children are often motivated to learn more about a topic or activity once television has sparked their interests.

In short, while the television can be a powerful tool in children's learning, careful consideration of how much, what, and how children view TV programs is needed.

School Talk: A Structured Context for Learning and Using Language

By the time most children enter preschool, they are capable of conversing with both adults and their peers. Language learning, however, is far from complete. Research has revealed that the semantic, syntactic, and pragmatic aspects of oral language continue to develop throughout the

Figure 3.1	To help children develop:	Programming qualities to promote:
A developmental guide for assessing television programming	A sense of trust and safety	A world where people can be trusted and help each other, where safety and predictability can be achieved, where fears can be overcome
	A sense of autonomy with connectedness	A wide range of models of independence within meaningful relationships and of autonomous people helping each other
	A sense of empowerment and efficacy	Many examples of people having a positive effect on their world without violence
	Gender identity	Complex characters with wide-ranging behaviors, interests, and skills; commonalities between the sexes in what each can do
	An appreciation of diversity among people	Diverse peoples with varied talents, skills, and needs who treat each other with respect, work out problems non–violently, and enrich each others' lives
	The foundations of morality and social responsibility	Complex characters who act responsibly and morally toward others—showing kindness and respect, working out moral problems, taking other people's points of view
	Imagination and opportunities for meaningful play	Meaningful content to use in play, which resonates deeply with developmental needs; shows not linked to realistic toys so that children can create their own unique play

Levin, D. & Carlsson-Paige, N. (1994). Developmentally appropriate television: Putting children first. *Young Children, 49,* 38–44.

elementary school years (Chomsky, 1969; Karmiloff-Smith, 1979; Menyuk, 1988). Teachers, therefore, have the responsibility to promote language learning by engaging in conversations with students and by encouraging children to converse with each other (Roser, 1998).

Language Opportunities in School

Day care, preschool, and kindergarten teachers must work to enhance children's language development. Fortunately, the school day offers numerous opportunities for oral interactions. Ellen Booth Church (1998) highlights how every aspect of the typical school day can be used to facilitate language and accommodate children's developmental needs. For instance:

- *Morning greeting*—Provides time for the teacher to share one-to-one conversations with the children. These brief conversations engender a sense of belonging and help children transition from home to school.
- *Group time*—Demonstrates how to listen to others, take turns, share ideas, and learn to value others' ideas.
- *Activity time*—Offers opportunities to share and solve problems as children interact with each other and experiment with materials. Teachers can stimulate children's thinking and ability to explain their perspectives by asking open-ended questions.
- *Snack time*—Allows children to learn about the give and take of social language conventions. Teachers can model these subtle social exchanges by engaging in conversation with children during snack time.
- *Storytime*—Offers children an opportunity to hear the drama of story and develop broader vocabulary. Children also learn to listen and respond to all types of questions from simple recall to opinion and inference.
- *Outdoor play*—Fosters challenge talk, like "I can run faster" or "climb higher." Challenge talk is exciting, but sometimes it leads to conflicts. Children may then learn how to use words to convey their feelings and resolve problems.

Teacher Discourse

Over every school day, there are dozens of possibilities for verbal interactions (Smith & Dickinson, 1994). Unfortunately, research indicates that this opportunity is often overlooked in traditional transmission-oriented classrooms. Studies have shown that in many classrooms the teacher dominates the language environment; this does little to promote the children's oral language growth (Cazden, 1988; Howard, Shaughnessy, Sanger, & Hux, 1998; Wells, 1986). For example, these studies suggests that in some classrooms:

- teachers spend most of the time talking to rather than talking with children.
- teachers dominate discussions by controlling how a topic is developed and who gets to talk.
- children spend most of their time listening to teachers.
- when children do talk, it is usually to give a response to a question posed by the teacher.
- teachers tend to ask test-like, closed-ended questions that have one right answer (that the teacher already knows).

The typical pattern of classroom discourse is characterized by teacher initiation, student response, and teacher evaluation. In the IRE pattern, the teacher asks a question, a student answers, and the teacher either accepts or rejects that answer and goes on to ask another question (Galda, Cullinan, & Strickland, 1993). For example, before the following discussion, the kindergarten children had listened to *The Three Little Pigs*.

Teacher: What material did the pigs use to build their first house?

Bobbie: They used sticks.

Teacher: Yes. That is correct, the pigs used sticks for the first house. What did the pigs use to build the third house?

Manuel: They used cement.

Teacher: No. Who remembers what the book says? Jon?

Jon: Bricks.

Teacher: Yes. The pigs used bricks.

Notice how the teacher's questions are not real questions; rather they test whether the children recalled specific details of the story. Note also that children have no opportunity construct their own meaning of the story by combining text information with their prior knowledge. For example, Manuel's answer, *cement,* suggests that Manuel was making inferences based on prior experience. The teacher's negative response to Manuel's comment probably communicates to him that it is incorrect to make inferences when reading. This sends a message to children that one should recall exactly what is said in the text. Finally, notice that there is absolutely no interaction from child to child. The turn-taking pattern is teacher–child–teacher–child.

These types of IRE interactions are sometimes appropriate because teachers do need to get specific points across to students (Dyson & Genishi, 1983). However, problems ensue if this is the only type of talk that is taking place in the classroom. IRE discussions do not provide the type of language input and feedback that "advance children's knowledge of language structure and use" (Menyuk, 1988, p. 105). In addition, these teacher-dominated exchanges do not allow children to negotiate and build meaning through dialogue (Hansen, 1998).

What can early childhood teachers do to provide children with more stimulating experiences with language? We offer three recommendations:

1. Engage children in reciprocal discussions and conversations.
2. Provide ample opportunities for activity-centered language that invite (and, at times, require) children to use language to get things done.
3. Provide language-centered activities that focus children's attention on specific aspects of language.

In the sections that follow, we present guidelines for implementing each of these recommendations.

Reciprocal Discussions and Conversations

Teachers' verbal interaction styles set the general tone for classroom language environments. The worst-case scenario occurs when a teacher insists on absolute silence except during teacher-led initiation, response, evaluation discussions. Such environments definitely limit continued oral language development. Other teachers provide ideal language environments by engaging students in genuine conversations, conducting stimulating reciprocal discussions, and allowing children to converse with each other at a moderate volume during classroom learning activities, using "inside voices" (soft voices that do not disrupt classroom learning).

Teachers have many opportunities to talk with children throughout the school day, ranging from one-to-one conversations to whole-group discussions. Following is an example of an effective conversation between Ms. E., a preschool teacher, and Roberto, age four:

Roberto: See my new backpack, Teacher?

Ms. E: What a neat backpack, Roberto. Show it to me.

Roberto: It has six zippers. See? The pouches hold different stuff. Isn't it neat?

Ms. E: I like the different size pouches. Look, this one is just right for a water bottle.

Roberto: Yeah. The arm straps are great too. See, I can make 'em longer.

Ms. E: Yes [nods and smiles]. It fits your arms perfectly. Where did you get this nifty backpack?

Roberto: We got it at the mall.

Ms. E: What store in the mall?

Roberto: The one that has all the camping stuff.

Ms. E: The Camping Plus store?

Roberto: Yeah. That's the one.

Notice how Ms. E. allowed Roberto to take the lead by listening carefully to what Roberto said and by responding to his previous statements. She let him do most of talking, using back-channeling (nodding and smiling) to keep the conversation going. Ms. E. asked only three questions, and they were genuine—she wanted to know where Roberto purchased the backpack.

Reciprocal conversations are not restricted to one-to-one situations. Teachers can also engage children in genuine discussions pertaining to ongoing instructional activities. Cory Hansen (1998) gives an example of group discussion of George MacDonald's 1872 classic, *The Princess and the Goblin* (Puffin Books). The chapter book is being discussed by a group of kindergarten students in Chris Boyd's classroom.

Previously in the story, the grandmother had given the princess a gift of a glowing ring from which a thread would lead her to comfort if she were frightened. The princess assumed it would lead her to her grandmother, but one night it led her deep into a cave and stopped at a heap of stones. The chapter ("Irene's Clue") ends with the princess bursting into tears at the foot of the rocks. Curdie, the fearless miner's son, was missing.

Joseph: I think that Curdie's on the other side of the rocks.

Mrs. B.: Where'd you get the clue for that?

Anna: Because the strings led her to the mountain. That means it was close to Curdie because Curdie lived by the mountain.

Kim: Maybe Curdie's on the other side of the stones!

Jamal: I think her grandmother was a goblin since she could have went through the rocks.

Jordan: I know. Maybe—when she was falling asleep on the other side—but how could the goblins be that fast?

Anna: Because they're magic.

Richard: I know how Curdie got to the other side . . . .

Chorus: Children begin to talk in small groups simultaneously.

Joseph:	Maybe Curdie's in the heap of stones.
Mrs. B.:	What makes you say that?
Joseph:	Because in the last chapter—Curdie's Clue—it said they piled the rock—a big stone in the mouth of the cave.
Kim:	The grandmother said the ring always led to the grandmother's bedroom so she . . .
Anna:	No it didn't. It said, "This will take me to you—wherever it takes you, you go." And the grandmother said, "Wherever it takes you, you will go."
Mrs. B.:	Can you think of any reason why the princess should go to the cave?
Joseph:	Because it said, "You must not doubt the string."
Adam:	The grandmother said the thread would lead to her but it ended up leading her to Curdie.
Alondra:	I think the grandmother knows about Curdie.
Kim:	It's because her grandmother wanted her to save Curdie!
Anna:	That was the clue.
Jamal:	To get Curdie out cuz she know about him.
Joseph:	Yeah. (Hansen, 1998, pp. 172–173)

Here, Mrs. B. let the students take the lead by listening closely to what they said and responding to their comments. Her questions were genuine (she did not know what the children's responses would be) and were open-ended in nature ("What makes you say that?"). By welcoming the children's viewpoints, she encouraged them to bring their personal interpretations to the story. Also note that the children talked to each other; they engaged in real conversations. The teacher facilitated this child–child turn-taking pattern by encouraging the students to respond to each other's ideas.

Ms. E.'s and Mrs. B.'s effective use of reciprocal questions allowed children to engage in authentic discussion with the teacher and each other. Obviously, the way a teacher interacts with young children influences the way children communicate. Therefore, it is important for teachers to reflect on the quality of their conversations and discussions with young children.

Contexts for Encouraging Language

We know that what children say and do is greatly influenced by where they are and what is around them For example as Evan played in the snow, he learned snow-related vocabulary with his family. Teachers must create dynamic learning environments that are contexts for language development. In other words the curriculum must give children something to talk about. In the following section, we describe how teachers might use group activities, learning centers, and dramatic play to expand children's learning and opportunities to use language.

GROUP ACTIVITIES. Teachers can support language by involving children with group activities that encourage, and at times necessitate, verbal interaction. What sort of activities would require children to talk? As Celia Genishi (1987) points out, "almost every object or activity presents an opportunity for talk when teachers allow it to" (p. 99). In the following vignette, we provide an illustration of a whole-group activity that required a rather large group of multilingual, four-year-old children to reveal and assert needs and wants and connect with themselves and others.

The children have been learning about manners and balanced meals. As part of a culminating activity, the entire room has been transformed into a restaurant. Twelve little tables are draped with tablecloths, and each table has a vase of flowers. Today, the teachers are waitresses, and a few parents have volunteered to cook real food. The children must choose between the Panda Café (spaghetti, meatballs, garlic toast, juice or milk) or the Café Mexico (burrito, chips, salsa, juice or milk). Each café has a menu with words and pictures. The children must select the specific items they wish to eat and give their orders to the waitress. The waitress takes the children's orders on an order form and gives the order form to the cooks. The cooks fill the orders exactly as the children request. Then, the waitress returns with the food and the order form and asks the children to review the order.

Teacher: What café would you like, sir?

Roberto: [Points to menu.]

Teacher: Which café? You must tell me.

Roberto: The Café Mexico.

Teacher: Right this way, sir. Here is your menu. Take a moment to decide what you want to eat. I'll be right back to take your order.

Roberto: [Looks over the menu and shares his choices with his friend by pointing to the items he wants.]

Teacher: OK, sir. What would you like?

Roberto: [Points to the items on the menu.]

Teacher: Please, sir. You will have to tell me.

Roberto: [Hesitates for a few seconds.] I want the burro and chips and juice.

Teacher: Do you want salsa? [She leans over so he can see her mark the items on the order form.]

Roberto: No. [Firmly.]

Notice how the teachers organized this activity so that the children had to verbally express their needs multiple times throughout the restaurant adventure. In addition, the children had many opportunities to see how print is used in real life. However, teachers are not the only valuable source of language input. Children can also gain valuable oral language practice from talking with peers who are not as skilled as adults in initiating and maintaining conversations. To encourage peer-to-peer interactions, these teachers also created a miniature version of the restaurant in a dramatic play learning center. In this center, Roberto and his classmates will be able to play restaurant together for a few weeks.

LEARNING CENTERS. Since children's learning and language is greatly influenced by their environment, good teachers guide children's language development through the deliberate structuring of the classroom environment. For example, the teachers in the previous vignette created a restaurant to encourage talk about food, ordering meals, taking orders, cooking meals, and the like. Later, as the children interacted together in the restaurant dramatic play center, they continued to help each other build and reinforce their knowledge of restaurants. In learning center classrooms, the teacher's role is to set up the environment, observe as children interact with the materials, supply help and guidance when needed, and engage in conversations with the children around the materials and the children's use in their learning. A good deal of the teacher's effort is expended on the setting-up or preparation phase. Centers are created when the teacher carves the classroom space into defined areas. (See Chapter 9 for ideas on how to carve the classroom space into learning centers.)

Readers seeking more information on establishing centers will find *The Creative Curriculum for Early Childhood Education* (Dodge & Colker, 1992) to be a useful resource. This book presents detailed, easy-to-follow instructions for setting up popular interest areas (centers). It also contains practical tips on schedules, routines, and other aspects of classroom management, plus good suggestions for encouraging parental involvement.

DRAMATIC PLAY. Another context for activity-centered language is dramatic play. Dramatic play occurs when children take on roles and use make-believe transformations to act out situations and play episodes. For example, several children might adopt the roles of family members and pretend to prepare dinner, or they may become superheroes who are engaged in fantastic adventures. This type of play—also called sociodramatic, make-believe, pretend, or imaginative play—reaches its peak between the ages of four and seven.

Although to some dramatic play appears simple and frivolous at first glance, close inspection reveals that it is quite complex and places heavy linguistic demands on children (Fessler, 1998). In fact, Jerome Bruner (1983, p. 65) reported that "the most complicated grammatical and pragmatic forms of language appear first in play activity." When children work together to act out stories, they face formidable language challenges. They not only need to use language to act out their dramas, they must also use language to organize the play and keep it going. Before starting, they must recruit other players, assign roles, decide on the make-believe identities of objects (e.g., that a block of wood will be used as if it were a telephone), and plan the story line. Once started, language must be used to act out the story, keep the dramatization heading in the right direction (e.g., be sure that everyone is doing things appropriate to their role), and re-energize the play if it is becoming repetitive and boring.

To accomplish these tasks, children must use two different types of language: (1) pretend language that is appropriate for their roles, and (2) metaplay language about the play itself. Children switch between their pretend roles and their real identities when making these two types of comments. This linguistic complexity is illustrated in the following example.

Three preschoolers are enacting a domestic scene in their classroom's housekeeping corner. John has taken the role of the father; Wendy is the mother; and George, the youngest of the three, has reluctantly agreed to be the baby.

Wendy:	Baby looks hungry. Let's cook him some food. [Pretend.]
John:	Okay. [Pretend.]
Wendy:	[Addressing George.] Cry and say that you're hungry. [Metalanguage.]
George:	But I'm not hungry. [Metalanguage.]
Wendy:	Pretend that you are! [Metalanguage.]
George:	[Using a babyish voice.] I'm hungry. [Pretend.]
Wendy:	[Addressing John.] Father, what should we have for dinner? [Pretend.]
John:	How about eggs. [Pretend.]
Wendy:	I'll go get some eggs from the 'frigerator. [She goes to a wall shelf and takes several cube-shaped blocks.] [Pretend.]
George:	Aah! I'm hungry! [Pretend.]
Wendy:	[Pretending to scold George.] Be quiet! [She puts the blocks in a toy pan and places the pan on the toy stove.] The eggs are cooking. Father, you'd better set the table.
John:	Okay. [Pretend.]
George:	Let me help, Daddy. [Pretend.]
John:	No! Babies don't set tables! You're just supposed to sit there and cry. [Metalanguage.] (Johnson, Christie, & Yawkey, 1999, p. 1)

In this example, Wendy is in her role as mother when she makes her initial comment about the baby. She reverts to real-life identity when she tells George what to say next and to pretend to be hungry. Then she shifts back to the role of mother when she asks father what he wants for dinner.

In order to take full advantage of dramatic play's potential as a medium for language development, attention needs to be given to three factors: (1) the settings in which play occurs, (2) the amount of time allocated for play activities, and (3) the type of teacher involvement in play episodes.

Play Settings. It is important to remember that children play best at what they already know. Therefore, dramatic play settings need to be familiar to children and consistent with their culture (Neuman, 1995). For example, the domestic play themes, such as parents caring for a baby or a family eating a meal, are very popular with young children because these are the roles and activities with which they are most familiar. For this reason, we recommend that preschool and kindergarten classrooms contain a housekeeping dramatic play center equipped with props that

Dramatic play is an ideal medium for promoting oral language development.

remind children of their own homes. Not only do such centers encourage dramatic play, but they also provide a context in which children can display the types of literacy activities they have observed at home.

The range of children's play themes and related literacy activities can be greatly expanded by the addition of a theme center to the classroom. These centers have props and furniture that suggest specific settings that are familiar to children, such as a veterinarian's office, restaurant, bank, post office, ice cream parlor, fast-food restaurant, and grocery store (Table 6.1 contains lists of literacy materials that can be used in a variety of theme centers). For example, a veterinarian's office might be divided into two areas: (1) a waiting room with a table for a receptionist and chairs for patients, and (2) an examination room with another table, chairs, and a variety of medical props (doctor's kit, scales, etc.). Stuffed animals can be provided as patients. Theme-related literacy materials—appointment book, patient folders, prescription forms, wall signs, and so on—should also be included to encourage children to re-enact the literacy activities that they have observed in these settings. Children will use their knowledge of visits to the doctor to engage in play with their peers. The following scenario illustrates how three preschoolers verbalize their knowledge of what occurs at the animal hospital.

Sergio: [The vet is looking at the clipboard.] It says here that Ruffy is sick with worms.

Marie: [Owner of a toy kitty named Ruffy.] Yep, uh huh. I think she ate bad worms.

Sergio: That means we gotta operate and give Ruffy big horse pills for those worms.

Joy: [The nurse.] OK, sign here. [Hands Marie a big stack of papers.] Sign 'em all. Then we'll operate. But you gotta stay out in the people room. You could faint if you stay in here.

Chari Woodard (1984), a teacher who has had considerable success with theme centers in her university's laboratory preschool, recommends that one theme center be introduced at a time and left for several weeks. Then the center can be transformed into another theme. She also advises locating these centers near the permanent housekeeping center so that children can integrate the theme center activities with their domestic play. Children acting as parents for dolls, pets, or peers in the housekeeping area might, for example, take a sick baby to the doctor theme center for an examination. Or, children might weld or examine cars in the classroom garage (Hall & Robinson, 1995). Woodard found that children, particularly boys, began engaging in more dramatic play when the theme corners were introduced.

Time.   Dramatic play requires providing a considerable amount of time for children to plan and initiate. If play periods are short, children have to stop their dramatizations right after they have started. When this happens frequently, children tend to switch to less advanced forms of play, such as functional (motor) play or simple construction activity, which can be completed in brief sessions.

Research has shown that preschoolers are much more likely to engage in rich, sustained dramatic play during 30-minute play periods than during shorter 15-minute sessions (Christie, Johnsen, & Peckover, 1988). Our experience indicates that even longer periods are needed. For example, Billie Enz and Jim Christie (1997) spent a semester observing a preschool classroom that had 40-minute play periods. Very often, the four-year-olds had just finished preparing for a dramatization when it was time to clean up. Fortunately, the teachers were flexible and often let the children have an extra 10 to 15 minutes to act out their dramas. We recommend that, whenever possible, center time last for at least 60 minutes.

Teacher Involvement.   For many years, it was believed that teachers should just set the stage and not get directly involved in children's play activities. This hands-off stance toward play has been seriously challenged by a growing body of research that suggests that classroom play can be enriched through teacher participation. Teacher involvement has been found to assist nonplayers to begin to engage in dramatic play, to help more proficient players enrich and extend their dramatizations, and to encourage children to incorporate literacy into their play episodes (Enz & Christie, 1997; Roskos & Neuman, 1993). However, teachers need to use caution because overzealous or inappropriate forms of involvement can interfere with ongoing play and sometimes cause children to quit playing altogether (Enz & Christie, 1997).

The simplest and least intrusive type of teacher involvement in play is observation. By watching children as they play, teachers demonstrate that they are interested in the children's play and that play is a valuable, worthwhile activity. Observation alone can lead to more sustained play. Bruner (1980) reported that preschoolers' play episodes lasted roughly twice as long when a teacher was nearby and observing than when children played completely on their own. In addition, the children were more likely to move toward more elaborate forms of play when an adult was looking on.

Observation can also provide clues about when more direct forms of teacher involvement in play are appropriate. A teacher may find that, in spite of conducive play settings, some children rarely engage in dramatic play. As we explain in Special Feature 3.2, this pattern of play behavior is atypical for four- and five-year-old children. Or the teacher may notice that there is an opportunity to extend or enrich an ongoing play episode, perhaps by introducing some new element or problem for children solve (Hall, 1999). Both situations call for active teacher involvement.

Chapter 6 describes three roles that are ideal for initiating and extending dramatic play: the stage manager role, in which the teacher supplies props and offers ideas to enrich play; the co-player role, in which the teacher actually takes on a role and joins in the children's play; and the play leader who stimulates play by introducing, in a role, some type of problem to be resolved. For more information about these roles and other roles that teachers can adopt during play, see Jones and Reynolds (1992).

In addition to promoting language acquisition, dramatic play encourages children to help each other learn academic skills and content (Hansen, 1998; Christie & Stone, 1999), make friends, and develop important social skills (Garvey, 1977). Peer-to-peer interaction is particularly important for the growing numbers of students who are learning English as a second language and need help with more basic aspects of oral language (Fessler, 1998). For these reasons, dramatic play centers need to be a prominent feature in early childhood classrooms.

Special Feature 3.2

Age Trends in Children's Play

Researchers have been very interested in how children's play changes with age. Typically, they have used cross-sectional research methods, observing children of different ages during indoor free-choice periods. The children's behavior was systematically observed and categorized, often with Smilansky's (1968) play categories:

1. *Functional play*—Repetitive movement with or without objects. Examples include (a) running and jumping, (b) stacking and knocking down blocks, (c) digging in a sand box, and (d) bouncing a ball against a wall.
2. *Constructive play*—Using objects (blocks, Legos,™ Tinkertoys™) or materials (sand, playdough, clay) to build something.
3. *Dramatic play*—Taking on a role and using make-believe transformations to act out a situation or a story.
4. *Games with rules*—Engaging in games that require the recognition of, acceptance of, and conformity with preestablished rules.

Kenneth Rubin, Greta Fein, and Brian Vandenberg (1983) summarized the results of this observational research and identified several major age trends with respect to these cognitive play categories. Functional play is the most prevalent form of play during the first 3 years of life. Starting at around 18 months of age, both constructive and dramatic play appear and begin to increase. Between the ages of 4 and 6 years, constructive play is the modal form of play activity, accounting for almost half of the play observed in preschool and kindergarten classrooms (due, in part, to the abundance of constructive materials in school settings). During this same period, dramatic play continues to increase at the expense of functional play, rising to approximately 20 to 30 percent of all play by age 6 years. As children enter the primary grades, dramatic play declines in frequency. Dramatic play thus appears to follow an inverted-U developmental progression, first appearing between the ages of 1 and 2 years, increasing during the preschool years, peaking at about age 6 years, and then declining during middle childhood.

Several aspects of dramatic play change during the preschool period:

- Dramatic play becomes more social with age (Fenson, 1984). Because of limited social skills, children's first attempts at pretending are usually solitary. By age 3 or 4 years, many children have learned to share, compromise, and cooperate with others, and they soon begin to engage in group dramatizations with other children.
- The story lines children enact in their pretend play become more complex with age (Fenson, 1984), changing from isolated events (e.g., feeding a doll) to complex, interrelated episodes (e.g., cooking a make-believe meal, serving it to guests, and then eating the meal while conducting polite conversation).
- The roles and themes children enact change with age, becoming more creative and unusual (Garvey, 1977). Initially, children adopt highly familiar roles, such as family members, and act out very routine types of domestic activity, such as preparing dinner or going shopping. As they mature, children begin taking on less familiar roles, such as occupations (e.g., mail carrier) and fictional characters (e.g., Batman), and they begin to introduce unusual elements into their dramatizations (e.g., an earthquake may occur during a shopping trip).

As a result of this research, teachers now have a clearer picture of how dramatic play changes with age. Dramatic play begins at around age 2 years and is marked by solitary make-believe, isolated actions, and familiar roles. By the time dramatic play reaches its peak at around age 6 years, it has evolved into a complex endeavor that involves groups of children, interrelated action sequences, and highly imaginative roles and themes.

These age trends can help teachers interpret the play they observe in the classroom. While the beginnings of dramatic play begin to appear by 2 years of age, most children do not engage in fully elaborated group dramatic play until age 4 years or beyond. Therefore, teachers should not worry when 2- and 3-year-olds rarely engage in dramatic play. Teachers should also not be concerned when children of this age engage in dramatic play by themselves or if their dramatizations are limited to simple, isolated actions. However, if these characteristics persist at ages 4 or 5 years, teachers may want to take steps to facilitate children's play development.

Language-Centered Activities

Beyond creating contexts that encourage language and facilitate verbal interactions, teachers can also provide activities that focus specifically on language. Read-alouds, sharing, storytelling, and language play all fall into this category. The first of these, teacher read-alouds, is the subject of an entire section of Chapter 5. Storybook reading can be an ideal context for promoting attentive listening and oral discussion skills. We discuss the remaining four language-centered activities below.

SHARING. Sharing, or show-and-tell, is a strategy designed to promote students' speaking and listening abilities. Traditionally, sharing has been a whole-class activity in which one child after another gets up, takes center stage, and talks about something of her or his own choosing—often some object brought from home (Gallas, 1992). Children in the audience are expected to quietly listen and not participate.

In this traditional format, sharing is not a very productive language experience for the child who is speaking or for those who are listening. The large group size can intimidate the speaker and reduce participation—only a small percentage of students get to share on a given day. Or if many students share, it becomes a very drawn-out, boring affair. The lack of participation on the part of the audience leads to poor listening behavior. Listening is an active, constructive process in which listeners combine information provided by a speaker with their own prior knowledge to build personal meaning. Mary Jalongo (1995) relates a teacher's definition of listening that captures the essences of active listening: "it is hearing and making and shaping what you heard—along with your own ideas—into usable pieces of knowledge" (p. 14). The passive role of the audience in traditional sharing works against this process.

With two modifications, sharing can be transformed into a very worthwhile language activity. First, group size should be "small enough to reduce shyness, encourage interaction, permit listeners to examine the object, and afford everyone a long enough turn without tiring the group" (Moffett & Wagner, 1983, p. 84). Groups of three to six students are ideal for this purpose. Second, listeners should be encouraged to participate by asking questions of the child who is sharing. "Let the sharer/teller begin as she will. When she has said all that initially occurs to her, encourage the audience by solicitation and example to ask natural questions" (Moffett and Wagner, 1983, p. 84). The teacher's role is to model questioning that encourages elaboration and clarification ("When did you get . . . ?" "What happened next?" "What's that for?"). After asking one or two questions, teachers should pause and encourage the audience to participate. Prompts, such as "Does anyone have questions for Suzy?" may sometimes be needed to get the process started. Once children realize that it is acceptable for them to participate, prompting will no longer be necessary.

This peer questioning stimulates active listening by giving the audience a reason to listen to the child who is sharing. Children know that, in order to ask relevant questions, they are going to have to listen very carefully to what the sharer has to say. The child who is sharing benefits as well. Children can be encouraged to elaborate their brief utterances or to organize their content more effectively and to state it more clearly (Moffett & Wagner, 1983).

Teachers can add variety to sharing by occasionally giving it a special focus, such as by asking children to bring something that

1. has a good story behind it, which encourages narrative discourse,
2. they made or grew, which facilitates explanation or description, or
3. works in a funny or interesting way, which fosters expositive communication.

STORYTELLING. Chapter 5 discusses many of the values of reading stories to children. Telling stories to children is also very worthwhile. The direct connection between the teller and audience promotes enjoyment and active listening. Marie Clay (1989) describes some of the values of storytelling:

> Storytelling is more direct than story reading. Facial expressions, gestures, intonations, the length of pauses, and the interactions with the children's responses create a more direct contact with the audience, dramatic in effect. The meaning can be closer to the children's own experiences because the teller can change the words, add a little explanation, or translate loosely into a local experience. (p. 24)

Because of the literate and technological nature of our culture, many teachers lack experience with storytelling. This, in turn, can lead to avoidance of telling stories. For this reason, we include tips for getting off to a good start with storytelling in Chapter 5. Here we focus on children as storytellers.

The first stories that children tell usually involve real-life experiences—they relate something that has happened to them. Sharing, discussed in the previous section, can be an ideal context to allow children to tell these types of stories in the classroom. Small-group, interactive sharing provides feedback that enables children to tell clearer, better-organized stories about personal experiences (Canizares, 1997).

Some children need assistance in broadening the range of their storytelling to imaginative, fictional stories. The following suggestions can help with this task:

- Open up the sharing period to include fantasy stories. Once teachers begin permitting their children to tell "fictitional" stories, the children may begin sharing imaginative, creative stories that feature language that is much richer than that used in their show-and-tell sharing (Gallas, 1992).

- Encourage children to retell the stories contained in their favorite storybooks. Books remove the burden of creating an original story to tell. Story retelling has other benefits for children, including enhanced oral fluency and expression and improved story comprehension (Morrow, 1985).

- Have children make up words for the stories in wordless picture books, such as *Pancakes for Breakfast* by Tomie dePaola (1978). Here again, the book is providing the content for the child's story. See Appendix A, Quality Literature for Young Children (page 249) for a list of other exemplary wordless picture books.

- Link storytelling with play and writing. Vivian Paley (1990) has developed a strategy in which children come to a story table and dictate a story that the teacher writes down. During this dictation, the teacher asks the children to clarify any parts of the story that are unclear or difficult to understand. The teacher reads the story plays to the class. Finally, children serve as directors and invite classmates to join in acting out their stories. Children enjoy watching their stories dramatized, motivating them to create additional imaginative stories.

LANGUAGE PLAY. In addition to using language in their dramatic play, children also play with language. This intentional "messing around" with language begins as soon as children have passed through the babbling stage and have begun to make words (Garvey, 1977). This play involves the phonological, syntactic, and semantic aspects of language. By age two, language play becomes quite sophisticated. Ruth Weir (1962) placed a tape recorder in her two-and-a-half-year-old son Anthony's crib and turned it on after he had been placed in his crib for the evening. During this presleep time, Anthony engaged in an extensive amount of systematic language play. He experimented with speech sounds ("Babette . . . Back here . . . Wet"), substituted words of the same grammatical category ("What color. What color blanket. What color mop. What color glass"), and replaced nouns with appropriate pronouns ("Take the monkey. Take it." and "Stop it. Stop the ball. Stop it"). These monologues constituted play because language was being manipulated for its own sake rather than being used to communicate.

Young children also make attempts at humor, playing with semantic aspects of language. Kornei Chukovsky (1976) explains that "Hardly has the child comprehended with certainty which objects go together and which do not, when he begins to listen happily to verses of absurdity" (p. 601). This, in turn, leads children to make up their own nonsense. Chukovsky uses his two-year-old daughter as an example. Shortly after she had learned that dogs say "bow wow" and cats say "miaow," she approached him and said, "Daddy, 'oggie—miaow!" and laughed. It was his daughter's first joke!

Children gain valuable practice while engaging in these types of language play. They also begin to acquire metalinguistic awareness, the ability to attend to language forms as objects in and of themselves. Courtney Cazden (1976) explains that when language is used for its normal function—to communicate meaning—language forms become transparent. We "hear through them" to get the intended message (p. 603). When children play with language, the situation is reversed. The focus is on the language—the grammatical rules and semantic relationships they are manipulating.

The type of language play children engage in is also age related (Geller, 1982). At age three, children like to repeat traditional rhymes ("Mary Had a Little Lamb"). They eventually begin to make up their own nonsense rhymes, playing with sound patterns ("Shama sheema / Mash day n' pash day . . ."). By ages five and six, children delight in verbal nonsense ("I saw Superman flying out there! ") and chanting games ("Cinderella, dressed in yellow / Went upstairs to kiss her fellow / How many kissess did she get? / 1, 2, 3, 4, 5, . . .")—forms themselves rather than meaning. Children become aware of the sounds (Cinderella dressed in yellow, went upstairs to kiss her fellow./ How many kisses did she get?/ 1, 2, 3, 4, 5 . . .").

The obvious educational implication is that language play should be encouraged and supported at school (Cazden, 1976). Judith Schwartz (1983) recommends that teachers try three things to stimulate their students to play with language.

1. Create a climate that allows play to flourish—a classroom atmosphere in which "children and teacher laugh easily and often."
2. Serve as a model by sharing humorous anecdotes, word play, folk literature, jokes, and stories with children and by using gentle humor in interpersonal relationships with children.
3. Value each child's contributions by allowing many opportunities for sharing oral and written language play.

SONGS AND FINGER PLAYS. Sitting on the floor with a small group of preschoolers, Ms. K. begins:

> *Where is Thumbkin?*
> *Where is Thumbkin?*
> *Here I am! Here I am!*
> *How are you today, sir?*
> *Very well, I thank you.*
> *Run away, Run away.*

The three- and four-year-old children quickly join in and immediately start the finger movements that accompany this familiar song. Very young children love to sing. The human fondness for a catchy tune and a snappy, clever rhyme begins early. Beginning in infancy and continuing on throughout their childhood, they are experimenting with their voices and the sounds that they can make. In Special Feature 3.3, we describe children's musical development

---

Special Feature 3.3

Musical Development from Infancy through Kindergarten

Age 0 to 9 months

- Begins to listen attentively to musical sounds; is calmed by human voices. Starts vocalization, appearing to imitate what he or she hears.

Age 9 months to 2 years

- Begins to respond to music with clear repetitive movements. Interested in every kind of sound; begins to discriminate among sounds and may begin to approximate pitches. Most attracted to music that is strongly rhythmic.

Age 2 to 3 years

- Creates spontaneous songs, sings parts of familiar songs; recognizes instruments and responds more

enthusiastically to certain songs. Strong physical response to music.

Age 3 to 4 years

- Continues to gain voice control; likes songs that play with language; and enjoys making music with a group as well as alone. Concepts such as high and low, loud and soft are beginning to be formed. Likes physical activity with music.

Age 4 to 6 years

- Sings complete songs from memory, is gaining pitch control and rhythmic accuracy. Loves language play and rhyming words. Attention span increases for listening to tapes and compact discs.

Adapted from Collins, M. (1997). Children and music. In B. Farber (Ed.), *The parents' and teachers' guide to helping young children learn,* Cutchogue, NY: Preschool Publication, Inc.

from infancy through kindergarten. Singing encourages risk-free language play, especially for children who are learning a second language (Freeman & Freeman, 1994; Jackman, 1997). Singing songs in a new language allows children to make safe mistakes as they experiment with the new phonemic system—similar to the way toddlers may begin to sing jingles they hear on the television long before they can actually speak in full sentences. As noted in a recent report by Catherine Snow and her colleagues (1998), singing songs is an important literacy activity.

Therefore, teachers of young children would be wise to build in singing as part of their language arts curriculum (Collins, 1997). In particular, children enjoy songs that

- offer repetition and chorus, such as "Polly Put the Kettle On," "Mary Had A Little Lamb," or "Here We Go Round the Mulberry Bush";
- provide repeated words or phrases that can be treated like an echo, such as "Miss Mary Mack" or "She'll Be Comin' Round the Mountain";
- require sound effects or animal noises, such as "If You're Happy and You Know It" or "Old MacDonald Had a Farm";
- tell a story, such as "Hush, Little Baby," "Humpty Dumpty," or "Little Bo Peep"; and
- ask questions, such as "Where Is Thumbkin?" or "Do You Know the Muffin Man?"

In addition to singing, many songs or poems include finger plays. Do you recall the "Itsy-Bitsy Spider" and how your fingers became the spider who climbed up the waterspout? Children's minds are fully engaged when they act out the words of a song or poem with their fingers (Collins, 1997).

Many preschool and kindergarten teachers write the songs the children love to sing on chart paper or purchase the big book format of these beloved songs. As the children sing, the teacher uses a pointer to underline each word. The follow-the-bouncing-ball approach to teaching reading is quite effective with some children (Segal & Adcock, 1986). Singing is a wonderful way for children to play with and enjoy language.

Children who are learning a second language need many opportunities to practice their new language in a safe classroom environment. Special Feature 3.4 offers classroom teachers suggestions on how to encourage language learning in their classrooms.

Special Feature 3.4

Optimizing Oral-Language Learning Experiences for Bilingual and Second-Language Learners

Sarah Hudelson and Irene Alicia Serna

In Chapter 2, several general points were made about young children's second-language acquisition. Second-language development was discussed from the perspective of creative construction, suggesting that learners, at their individual rates and using their individual styles, engage in figuring out how their new language works, much as they had to figure out how their native language works. The focus was on the social-interactionist perspective on language acquisition, noting that children learn a second language as they interact with others (adults and other children) in that language. This means that teachers and English-speaking children in classrooms are all language teachers. Also, as noted earlier, there is evidence that teachers of second-language learners use language in ways that are similar to the talk parents use with their young children. This observation suggests that the attrib-

utes of parental talk discussed at the beginning of Chapter 3 also would apply to adults working with second-language learners.

With this general perspective in mind, the specific recommendations for promoting oral language articulated in this chapter are discussed as they relate to educators who work in bilingual and second-language settings.

The Use of Reciprocal Discussions and Conversations with Bilingual and Second-Language Learners

Environments that promote genuine conversations and discussions—both among children themselves and between children and adults—are critical to the language growth of bilingual and second-language learners. Teachers' understandings and attitudes are central to the establishment of these linguistic contexts. In bilingual education settings, where the philosophy is to use both the children's native language and English as vehicles for learning, teachers provide non-native-English-speaking children with

(continued on next page)

Special Feature 3.4 (continued)

opportunities to extend both native and English language ability by using both languages in academic settings. As they provide these opportunities, bilingual teachers must decide how to allocate the use of the two languages in the classroom. Such allocation often depends on program design and goals, and on the language abilities of specific teachers and children (Lessow-Hurley, 1990).

Bilingual teachers may use one language for certain content or activities (such as language arts and mathematics) and the other language for other content and activities (such as science and art). Instead, one language may be used for part of the day and the other language for the rest of the time. Alternatively, the teacher and the children may use both languages freely, alternating between them in the ways that bilingual people often do (Jacobson & Faltis, 1990). In some settings, more of the native language is used in conversations and discussions when children are less comfortable in English. As the children gradually become more fluent in English, more time is spent in English. In other settings, teaming occurs, with one teacher using only a language other than English for instruction and the other educator using only English. Across these settings, the message that teachers send to children is that of valuing and using both languages and that it is possible to learn English without sacrificing their home language. In many classrooms, teachers also encourage English speakers to try to learn some of the non-English language, just as they encourage non-English speakers to use English (Reyes, Laliberty, & Orbansky, 1993; Turner, 1994).

Many elementary school teachers, however, are not bilingual and will therefore use only English in their teaching, even though several of their students may use languages other than English. In these settings, it is necessary for teachers to make adjustments in their ways of talking and presenting content, in order for children who are still learning English to participate more fully. These adjustments are also the case for bilingual teachers when they are working in the learners' second language. Teachers need to make adjustments in the following ways:

- Teachers need to provide contextual, extralinguistic support for their spoken language in the form of gestures, acting out, facial expressions, and use of visual aids (e.g., objects, pictures, diagrams, or films), so that visual information makes clear what is being said. Early in their language acquisition, second-language learners need more than the spoken language to understand what is going on in the classroom (Enright, 1986; Freeman & Freeman, 1994b). Their reliance on extralinguistic cues and modified input diminishes over time as they learn more English (Willett, 1995).
- Teachers need to organize class environments that are rich with materials and that provide opportunities for collaborative, hands-on experiences (Enright, 1986; Enright & McCloskey, 1988).

- Teachers need to adjust their own speech when speaking with and responding to second-language learners—focusing on the here and now, slowing down their delivery, simplifying their syntax and repeating and rephrasing, attending carefully to children's understandings or confusion, focusing on the child's meaning over correctness, and extending and expanding the second-language learner's language (Enright, 1986; Freeman & Freeman, 1994b; Lindfors, 1987).
- Teachers need to structure opportunities for second-language learners to experiment with English and need to encourage learners to do so (Ernst, 1994). Early on, second-language learners may do better in situations where teachers are involved directly. As these children become more fluent, they need to interact with their peers in English and to use the new language for academic content (Willett, 1995).
- Teachers need to acknowledge that mistakes are a natural and necessary part of language learning and to set up environments that encourage risk taking and allow mistakes (Freeman & Freeman, 1994b).
- Teachers need to provide learners with feedback on their efforts within the context of their engagement with content. The focus needs to be on the learners' ability to communicate, not simply on the accuracy of grammatical forms (Freeman & Freeman, 1994b).
- Teachers need to allow children to use languages other than English as a way to negotiate content before expressing their understandings in English (Freeman & Freeman, 1994b; TESOL, 1996).
- Teachers may need to sensitize native or fluent English-speaking children to the struggles of children who are working both to learn English and to use English to learn. This may be done, for example, through using a language other than English to teach a lesson or to read a story to English-speaking children and then discussing how the children felt, what problems they had in understanding, and how they could help others in similar situations (Rudnick, 1995).

Keeping the factors just mentioned in mind should mean that children who are learning English as a second language have more opportunities to participate in classroom activities, conversations, and discussions.

The Use of Contexts for Activity-Centered Language with Bilingual and Second Language Learners

Children, including English-language learners, learn a lot of language from each other and often prefer to interact with peers instead of with adults. English learners will

(continued on next page)

learn the new language most naturally when they need to use it to engage with others, at least with some others who are more proficient in English than they are (TESOL, 1999). In a school setting, such engagement logically springs from interesting and meaningful content that children examine in collaboration with others in thematic units, in centers, and in paired and group projects. One challenge many teachers may face is how to structure activities to promote collaboration, including verbal interactions. An added challenge is how to structure groups to maximize the participation of children who are learning English.

Teachers whose classes include second-language learners need to give serious consideration to the linguistic abilities of children as they form groups. There are times when children organize their own groups. There is evidence that ESL learners who choose to work with others still learning the language can be successful at negotiating content and using English to learn, especially if the learners come from different native language backgrounds and are in the numerical minority in a classroom (Willett, 1995). At other times, however, teachers may assign children to work or play with others. At these times, particularly if the teachers have an agenda of language development along with academic learning, teachers may group heterogeneously in terms of language ability, making sure that groups contain more- and less-able users of English. In this way, the less proficient speakers learn from those with more proficiency. However, factors other than language proficiency may also need to be taken into account when organizing groups. Jerri Willett, for example, has reported that a teacher grouped two English speakers with a Spanish speaker, thinking that the English speakers would work with the other child and thus facilitate his English development (1995). However, the two English speakers were girls, and they resisted collaborating with the Spanish-speaking boy, refusing to interact with him. Collaboration became a reality only when this young child worked (and played) with other boys.

In settings where many of the learners come from one home language (e.g., Spanish), groups may be formed that include at least one native English speaker, one child who is bilingual, and one child who speaks Spanish fluently but is not yet fluent in English. In these groupings, the bilingual learner often acts as a language broker, assisting the other children in communicating with each other (Fournier, Lansdowne, Pastenes, Steen, & Hudelson, 1992). This assumes that children are free to use languages other than English in the classroom, even if children ultimately share their work in English.

The Use of Language-Centered Activities with Bilingual and Second-Language Learners

In bilingual and second-language classrooms, many activities that teachers organize focus specifically on language. This chapter discusses the language-centered practices

of read-aloud experiences, sharing, storytelling, and language play, all of which need to be considered for bilingual and ESL learners. Each language-centered practice is discussed in turn.

Read-Aloud Experiences

Reading aloud is a central component of instruction, not a frill. It is central to both first- and second-language development. Reading aloud should be done in children's home languages, as well as in English, even if there is not a formal bilingual program in place. In some Spanish-English bilingual classrooms, teachers group children by language for one read-aloud experience daily, so that the Spanish-dominant children listen and respond to Spanish-language literature and the English-dominant children do the same in English. At other times, the children are mixed, and both languages are used to negotiate story content.

Read-aloud experiences need to be chosen carefully. Ms. Espinosa and Ms. Moore chose some books, particularly those read early in the children's second-language development, on the basis of predictability, to ensure that the children would understand the stories. Other books should be chosen for the quality of the story, the potential for discussion by children and teacher, and cultural relevance and authenticity (Espinosa & Fournier, 1995; Hudelson, Fournier, Espinosa, & Bachman, 1994). It is important to choose some books that reflect the experiences of the children (Barrera, Ligouri & Salas, 1992).

Sharing

Sharing is a practice employed by many teachers because it gives children an opportunity to talk about aspects of their own lives and encourages them to listen to each other. There is evidence that successful participation in such classroom activities is important for ESL learners' linguistic development and for their ability to negotiate in mainstream classrooms (Ernst, 1994). However, children who are just learning English may be much less confident in using the new language than their English-speaking peers. They may speak more slowly, with more hesitations. They may not articulate as native speakers do. Their verbalizations may be incomplete or unconventional syntactically. This may make it more difficult for them to share their experiences and to get and maintain the attention of their peers. Given these realities, teachers may need to take an active role in facilitating the participation of ESL children. This role may include negotiating with others opportunities for ESL learners to talk, assisting children in articulating what they want to contribute, and sensitizing other children to their struggles to express themselves (Ernst, 1994; Rudnick, 1995).

Storytelling

It has been our experience working with bilingual and second-language learners from many different backgrounds that many of them come from cultures where

(continued on next page)

oral stories abound and storytelling traditions are strong (Au, 1993). Therefore, storytelling should occupy a prominent place in classrooms that are populated by numbers of culturally and linguistically diverse students. When teachers are telling stories, they need to incorporate stories that reflect the heritages of the children with whom they work (see, for example, Bishop, 1994; Bosma, 1994; Harris, 1992; and Miller-Lachman, 1995, for animal stories, fables, folktales, legends, and myths that might be used). Children need to be encouraged to tell stories from their cultural backgrounds. Parents may also be invited to classrooms to participate in storytelling. Storytelling opens up multiple possibilities for understanding diverse world views.

Language Play

Across cultures, children engage in language play (Lindfors, 1987). One of the oral traditions of many cultures is the sharing of rhymes, songs, riddles, games, tonguetwisters, jokes, and so on across generations and among children. Teachers should make deliberate plans to use these forms, both to foster appreciation for other lan-

guages and cultures and to provide children with opportunities to manipulate the sounds of familiar and new languages. For example, teachers can make written records of these rhymes, songs, and finger plays in Spanish and English and can use them repeatedly in daily routines such as opening exercises, transitions between activities, introduction to read-aloud time, and school closing. Because children usually chant these forms in chorus, practice with the sounds of the new language takes place in a risk-free environment.

There are many collections of such traditional lore in Spanish readily available in the United States (e.g., Bravo-Villasante, 1980; Delacre, 1989; Jaramillo, 1994; Schon, 1994). Shen's Books and Supplies (8221 South First Avenue, Arcadia, CA 91006) has collections of traditional poetry available in Japanese, Chinese, Korean, and Vietnamese, as well as in English translations. In languages where material is not available commercially, teachers might invite parents to share traditional forms. The use of material from the oral tradition is strongly recommended.

Assessment: Finding Out What Children Know and Can Do

By the time most children are preschoolers, their oral language is quite rich and complex. This complexity makes assessment difficult. The only way to truly capture the full richness of children's language is to tape record their conversations and then make a verbatim transcription of what is said, along with a detailed description of the context in which the language occurred. The transcript can then be analyzed to determine the mean length of sentences used, which forms of language the child used, the pragmatic rules followed, and so forth (see Genishi & Dyson, 1984). Unfortunately, such endeavors are very time-consuming and not practical in most teaching situations.

A number of more practical options are available for assessing children's oral language abilities. To illustrate these options, we use an incident recently observed by two of the authors in a university preschool. Julie is a four-year-old Korean girl who has been in the United States for about eight months. She participates in classroom activities, especially dramatic play, but rarely speaks either in Korean (she is the only child from Korea in the class) or in English. Chari, Julia's teacher, is playing with several other children at the time of the incident. Chari takes on the role of a customer and asks to use the toy phone in a post office theme center. She picks up the phone and makes a pretend phone call to Buddy, whose behavior is becoming very raucous. Chari says, "Ring, ring, ring . . . Buddy, there's a package waiting here for you in the post office." This is successful in redirecting Buddy away from the rough-and-tumble play that he had been engaging in.

Julia is playing by herself in the housekeeping center, pretending to be a parent taking care of a baby (a doll). Julia overhears Chari's pretend phone call to Buddy, but she continues with her solitary play. A few minutes later, Julia picks up a toy phone in the housekeeping center, and says: "Ring, ring . . . Miss Chari, will you come over to my house?" This is Julia's first complete sentence used in the classroom!

Chari has several options for recalling Julia's language breakthrough. She might use a checklist. Figure 3.2 is a checklist used in a multilingual classroom. This checklist focuses on Michael Halliday's (1975) functional uses of language (see Table 2.1, page 31). Such checklists are easy to use and require little time. This checklist can be easily modified to fit other

Figure 3.2

Oral language checklist

Child's Name	English	Spanish	Other	Child	Several Children	Adult	Library	Writing	Listening	Housekeeping	Theme (play)	Blocks	Math/Sci	Art	Instrumental	Regulatory	Interaction	Personal	Heuristic	Imaginative	Informative
	Language			Partner(s)			Location								Function						
Julia	✓									✓										✓	

situations (for example, for a monolingual classroom, the language columns could be eliminated) or to focus on other aspects of language (grammatical forms could replace Halliday's functional uses of language). Such instruments provide a broad view of the language that children use in the classroom. However, much of the richness of the children's actual language is lost.

Chari might use a less-structured observation recording form, such as the one illustrated in Figure 3.3. Forms like this allow teachers to record more detailed information about children's language behaviors. Typically such forms have columns for children's names, samples of their speech, and other variables that might be of interest to the teacher. Chari is interested in knowing the context within which her children's language samples are collected and the language forms illustrated. Hence, she added two columns to the observation recording form she uses in her classroom. Notice that she does not put lines on her observation recording form. This is intentional. No lines means that Chari can record as much information about each incident as necessary for her to recall each language event. Compare the information on this form to that recorded on the checklist. Notice how the observation recording form captured much more of the essence of Julia's language accomplishment than did the checklist.

Chari might use an anecdotal record. Anecdotal records are even less structured than an observation recording form (Figure 3.4). Here, the teacher writes a brief description of the language incident on a piece of paper, index card, or Post-it-Note™. Later, Chari can file these anecdotes in individual folders for each of her children. This unstructured format allows Chari to make the most detailed description of Julia's language exchange with her. Of course, anecdotal records require more time and effort on the part of the teacher than do the two previous methods.

Child's Name	Context	What Was Said	Language Forms
Julia	Playing role of mother in housekeeping center.	Ring, ring... Miss Chari... Will you come to my house?	Complete sentence!

Julia   4/6/95

Julia observed me making a prentend phone call to Buddy from the post office center. Several minutes later she picked up the toy phone in the housekeeping center and said "Ring, ring .. Miss Chari, will you come to my house?" It was her first complete English sentence!

As suggested earlier, teachers may elect to make audio or video recordings of children's language activity. Genishi and Dyson (1984) have developed guidelines for making audio recordings. These are adapted to include video recordings:

- Select an activity setting that encourages language interaction. (Dramatic play areas are a good place to start.)
- If you are using a tape recorder, place it in the target setting and turn it on, checking first to make sure that the equipment is working. If using a video camcorder, place the camera on a tripod and adjust the zoom lens so that it covers the main area where children will be interacting. Turn the camera on, and check it occasionally to make sure that the camera angle is capturing the significant action.
- Do a trial recording to make sure that the equipment is working correctly and that the children's language is being clearly recorded. This trial will also help desensitize the children to the equipment.
- Listen or view the recordings as soon as possible so that your memory can help fill in the gaps in unintelligible parts of the recordings.

An effective way to analyze the data contained in audio and video recordings is to use a rubric to judge the quality of individual's oral language behavior. A rubric is a set of criteria that describe student performance in terms of proficiency levels (O'Neil 1994). Special Feature 3.5 presents an adaptation of part of the rubric used to assess students' oral language proficiency in the Wichita Public Schools. Originally, the rubric was intended for use with older children; we adjusted the criteria for each proficiency level to allow use at the preschool and kindergarten levels.

Special Feature 3.5

A Rubric to Assess Students' Oral Language Proficiency

Adapted from work of Bryan Fillion, Philip Rhea, Linda Douglas, and Mary Beasley

Oral language proficiency is defined in speech situations, such as conversations with adults, sharing views in group or circle, casual interactions with peers, and sharing ideas in collaborative group work. The child who is proficient in oral language

1. participates actively
2. speaks with clarity
3. takes turns speaking
4. listens when others speak
5. responds appropriately to questions
6. is confident when expressing ideas/views
7. converses coherently and makes sense.

Each trait is scored on a scale of 1 to 5.

- A score of 1 or 2 implies a problem that interferes with communication. If more than two traits are scored below 3, the child may need to be referred to a speech therapist for further evaluation.
- A score of 3 or 4 indicates an absence of obvious problems and some positive characteristics related to the specific trait.

- A score of 5 suggests that the child is consistently proficient with this trait.

For each trait, scores of 1, 3, and 5 are described, and sample behaviors are listed. The behaviors listed after each description are intended as aids to scoring, and as illustrations of the particular behaviors students might work on to improve their performance and proficiency. The following is the rubric for Trait 2.

Speaks with Clarity

5 Child uses word choice and voice to make meanings understandable and convey intended messages effectively. Uses words and voice consciously and deliberately to achieve clarity and intended effects.

Chooses words with precision to convey intended meanings accurately and economically; does not overwhelm the message by saying too much.

Effectively rewords previous messages when necessary for clarity or effect.

Enunciates clearly, neither mumbling nor slurring nor mispronouncing words.

Uses rate and volume effectively to convey stress and emphasis that support intended meanings.

Avoids actions and verbal behaviors that may distract audience from meanings (e.g., interrupters such as "Y'know" or large words to impress rather than mean).

(continued on next page)

Special Feature 3.5 *(continued)*

Phrases ideas in language that is clear, forceful, effective; avoids nonstandard forms that may distract listeners.

3 Child's word choice and voice (rate, tone, volume) are unobtrusive and do not interfere with meaning.
Expresses concisely, in understandable language. Avoids inexact terms (e.g., "all that stuff") where precision is possible and appropriate.
Attempts to correct or clarify his or her own expressions where necessary, or to check understanding of others' expressions, demonstrating some awareness of the importance of clarity and understanding.
Enunciates clearly, and uses appropriate rate, tone, and loudness of speech, not interfering with meaning.
Avoids or uses few interrupters such as "Y'know" and similar repetitive phrases.

Phrases ideas and information in acceptable, unobtrusive form, avoiding excessive slang or nonstandard forms.

1 Child's word choice and/or voice interfere with meanings or confuse the intended message.
Uses inexact wording of ideas or information.
Fails to rephrase or repeat when needed for clarity.
Enunciates poorly; mumbles or slurs words or phrases.
Speaks too rapidly or slowly, or too loudly or softly to be easily understood.
Frequently uses interrupters or verbal fillers such as "Y'know" and "I mean".
Phrases ideas in excessively nonstandard or slangy form that may distract audience.

Copyright Pending. Bryan Fillion, Philip Rhea, Wichita Public Schools. Used by permission.

Summary

This chapter began with a review of the many ways parents can support their child's language development within the home. The remainder of the chapter described ways that teachers can provide young children with stimulating oral language experiences that promote active listening and more precise, sophisticated speech. How did your own experiences at home and at school compare with those described in this chapter? Did you recall other types of beneficial oral language activities that were not covered?

To summarize the key points about facilitating oral language learning, we return to the guiding questions at the beginning of this chapter:

■ *How can parents best facilitate their children's oral language development?*

Parents can promote their children's oral language by scaffolding their language, encouraging them to tell personal narratives about their experiences, reading stories to them on a regular basis, and monitoring their children's TV viewing and encouraging active viewing.

■ *What is the initiation, response, evaluation (IRE) pattern of class talk? What problems are associated with this type of discourse? How can teachers provide children with more stimulating conversations in the classroom?*

The IRE pattern of discourse occurs when the teacher asks a question, a student answers, and the teacher either accepts or rejects that answer and goes on to ask another question. These types of question-and-answer exchanges do not provide the type of language input and feedback needed to advance children's language skills. Teachers can provide richer oral language experiences for children by engaging them in reciprocal conversations and discussions—listening closely and responding to their comments; asking genuine, open-ended questions; welcoming the interjection of personal experiences; and encouraging child–child turn-taking.

■ *How do group activities, learning centers, and dramatic play promote oral language acquisition?*

These types of activities create language content (i.e., give children something to talk about). In addition, children must use language to participate successfully in these types of activity.

■ *What can teachers do to promote language-rich dramatic play?*

Teachers can promote language-rich play by providing (1) settings equipped with theme-related, culturally-relevant props; (2) scheduling lengthy play periods; and (3) being actively involved in children's play activities.

■ *How can sharing or show-and-tell be turned into a valuable oral language activity?*

Traditional sharing involves having one child speak to the entire class. This activity can be transformed into a valuable oral language activity by limiting group size and encouraging children in the audience to actively participate by ask questions and making comments.

■ *How can teachers effectively assess children's oral language development?*

Teachers should observe children interacting during regular classroom activities and use checklists, observation sheets, and/or anecdotal records to document significant milestones in their oral language acquisition.

■ *What can teachers do to optimize oral language experiences for bilingual and second-language learners?*

The same strategies recommended for native English speakers are also appropriate for use with bilingual and second-language learners. The major adaptations that are needed are (1) exposing children to books and other print in child's native language, and (2) allowing children lots of opportunity to speak, listen, read, and write in their native language.

Linking Knowledge to Practice

1. Visit an early childhood classroom and observe children interacting in a dramatic play center. Note the theme that the children are acting out and the roles that they are playing. Record examples of both metaplay language and pretend language.

2. Observe children engaging in a sharing (show-and-tell) activity. Describe the teacher's role and the children's behavior (both the speaker and the audience). Did this sharing time involve most of the students in active listening?

3. Make an observation recording form similar to the one in Figure 3.3. Visit an early childhood classroom and observe a small group of children interacting at a learning center. Use the observation recording form to record several significant utterances from each child. What do these behaviors indicate about each child's language development?

chapter 4

The Beginnings of Reading and Writing

Snuggled next to her mother, one-year-old Tiffany is listening to one of her best-loved bedtime stories, Goodnight Moon, *by Margaret Wise Brown (1947, Scholastic). Her mother reads:*

> And two little kittens
> And a pair of mittens
> And a little toy house
> And a young mouse.

Pointing to the picture, Tiffany says, "Mamma, da mousey."
"That's right, Tiffany," says her mother, who resumes reading:

> And a comb and a brush and a bowl full of mush
> And a quiet old lady who was whispering Hush.

Tiffany, touching the pictures of the bunny mother sitting in the rocking chair, says, "Dat's like Nane Gammaw."
Her mother replies, "Yes, Tiffany, she looks like Grandma."
Throughout the story, Tiffany comments on the illustrations. As her mother finishes the last line,

> Goodnight stars, goodnight air, goodnight noises everywhere.

a very sleepy Tiffany yawns, "Ganight, Mamma."

As children sit in their parents' or other caregivers' laps, surrounded with love and attention, the storybook is a wonderful introduction to the world of print. Are you surprised to learn that *Goodnight Moon* was the first book Tiffany read to her teacher in first grade?

For children living in a culture that values literacy, the process of learning to read and write begins very early, often before their first birthdays. In recent years, researchers have made great progress in expanding our understanding of early literacy development. We now know that children acquire written language in much the same way that they learn oral language. Both are social, constructive processes. With oral language, children listen to the language that surrounds them, detect patterns and regularities, and make up their own rules for speech. Children then try out and refine these rules as they engage in everyday activities with others. With written language, children observe the print that surrounds them and watch their parents and others use reading and writing to get things done in daily life. They then construct their own concepts and rules about literacy, and they try out those ideas in social situations. With experience, these child-constructed versions of reading and writing become increasingly similar to conventional adult forms. Yet, as noted in Chapter 1, children need more instruction from adults to become readers and writers than they do to become speakers.

Social interaction plays a key role in early literacy learning. Susan Neuman (1998, p. 68) explains:

> Especially in these early years, literacy is a profoundly social process that enters children's lives through their interactions in a variety of activities and relationships with other people. Close observations suggest that children often become interested in writing and reading because it

can be useful for them in their social relationships; it can give them power, help them to better understand the world around them, and enable them to express their feelings of friendship or frustration. As they learn about written language and how to use it in contexts and activities that are personally meaningful, children will even seek help from others who are more competent and who can serve as spontaneous apprentices.

To place this current view of early literacy development in historical perspective, we begin by describing its predecessors. These traditional ways of looking at beginning reading and writing are commonly known as the readiness and earlier-is-better views. Next, we discuss the new view of early literacy learning and the research on which this perspective is based. Finally, two case studies are used to illustrate two children's early literacy development: Tiffany, a native English speaker, and Alicia, a Spanish-speaking kindergartner.

Before reading this chapter, think about. . .

- your early experiences with storybooks. Do you recall snuggling into an adult's lap and sharing a storybook? Did this happen regularly, at bedtime? In line at the supermarket? on the bus? What were your favorite books as a young child?
- how you learned to read and write. Do you remember reading and writing at home before going to school? Do you remember having lots of books in your home? Do you remember having access to paper and pencils? Were you an early reader—that is, did you learn to read without any formal instruction from an adult?

Focus Questions

- How does the early literacy view of young children's literacy development compare with the readiness and earlier-is-better views?
- What knowledge about written language do young children exhibit when adults watch them closely?
- What is the relationship among oral language, phonemic awareness, and phonics?
- What are emergent writing and emergent reading?
- What home factors affect young children's literacy development?
- What does early literacy look like in a language other than English?

BOX 4.1

Definitions of Terms

alphabetic principle: knowing that there is a systematic relationship between the letters of written language and the sounds of oral language.

conventions of print: social rules (left-to-right and top-to-bottom sequence, spaces between words) and terminology (letter, word, page) of written language.

early literacy: the new view of literacy development suggesting that children learn literacy by constructing, testing, and refining their own hypotheses about print.

emergent reading: forms of reading young children use as they move toward conventional reading.

emergent writing: forms of writing young children use as they move toward conventional writing.

graphic awareness: visually recognizing environmental print, letters, and words.

logographic reading: using environmental print's entire context to give meaning to the print, to read the word.

phonemes: speech phonological units that make a difference in meaning. For example, toad has three phonemes: /t/, /o/, /d/.

phonemic awareness: understanding that words consist of a sequence of phonemes.

phonics: making connections between letters in written words and sounds (phonemes) in speech.

Traditional Views of Literacy Development

Some years ago, it was assumed that written language is acquired in a totally different manner than is speech. According to this view, literacy development starts much later than oral-language acquisition, and it involves totally different learning processes. Children were not considered to be ready to begin learning to read and write until about age six, and this learning was not believed to occur naturally (Durkin, 1987). Children needed to be taught, using basal readers, worksheets, handwriting practice, spelling workbooks, and grammar exercises. Literacy instruction was serious business, best left in the hands of specially trained teachers. Parents were cautioned not to try to encourage early reading or writing for fear that children might learn incorrect concepts and skills, which would later have to be untaught by teachers.

This traditional view of literacy development can be traced to the maturational theories of the mid-1920s (Gesell, 1928). It was believed that children had to reach a certain level of intelligence and physical maturity before they could learn to read and write. During this same period, the concept of readiness skills took hold. According to this view, children needed to master a number of visual, auditory, and motor skills before they could learn to read. Reading readiness tests were developed to measure children's mastery of these skills, and readiness workbooks designed to promote perceptual-motor growth soon became a standard component of the beginning levels of basal reading programs (Stallman & Pearson, 1990).

The merger of the maturation and readiness orientations led to the persistent belief that early childhood was a time during which readiness skills should be taught as a prelude to real reading and writing (Teale & Sulzby, 1986). As a result, kindergarten and beginning first-grade students did lots of readiness activities that had little to do with actual reading. Figure 4.1 illustrates a typical reading readiness worksheet item. This visual discrimination exercise requires students to find the house that matches the one on the far left. Children usually did not have access to books until the middle part of first grade. Writing instruction was postponed even later, after handwriting, spelling, and phonics skills had been mastered.

Sparked by the launching of the Soviet satellite *Sputnik* in 1957 and the resulting uproar that American education needed to catch up with Soviet education, attitudes about delaying reading instruction finally started to change. This event, combined with a growing awareness of the importance of early learning and a concern about the education of children from low-income families, led to a movement to begin academic instruction at a much younger age (Elkind, 1990). The result of this earlier-is-better orientation was to shift the timing of traditional practices downward. Reading readiness workbooks and worksheets, which had been used in kindergarten and first grade, now began appearing in preschools. Basal preprimers and worksheets providing isolated drill on letter recognition and phonics became common in kindergartens.

This earlier-is-better phenomenon was hardly an improvement over the traditional readiness approach. Both had serious shortcomings. The traditional approach withheld reading and writing activities from many faster-developing children who were ready and eager to begin mastering written language. In contrast, the earlier-is-better movement required slower-developing children to engage in structured instructional activities (phonics worksheets, lengthy teacher-led lessons, basal preprimers) for which they were not developmentally ready. The resulting mismatch between the instructional demands and children's capabilities often caused slower-developing children to fail in their initial school-literacy experiences. This failure, in turn, fostered negative attitudes about reading and writing that were very difficult to reverse later on.

Figure 4.1

Visual discrimination worksheet

New Perspectives on Early Literacy

Fortunately, at the same time that the earlier-is-better movement was taking hold, several new areas of research emerged, which were eventually to lead to a radically different conception of early literacy development. According to this new perspective, which has come to be commonly known as emergent literacy (Clay, 1966), written language acquisition has much in common with oral language development. Children begin learning about reading and writing at a very early age by observing and interacting with readers and writers and through their attempts to read and write (Sulzby & Teale, 1991). Each reading and writing attempt teaches children, as they test out what they believe about how written language works. Based on others' responses, their beliefs are modified. The next time they read or write, they test out their new knowledge. The term *emergent* conveys the evolving nature of children's concepts as they move from personalized, idiosyncratic notions about the function, structure, and conventions of print toward conventional reading and writing. As Catherine Snow and her colleagues (1998, p. 45) note, "growing up to be a reader [and writer] is a lengthy process. . . ."

Susan Neuman and Kathy Roskos (1998) point out several problems associated with the terms *emergent* and *conventional*. *Emergent* implies that there is a distinct point at which literacy acquisition begins, and *conventional* implies that there is a point at which acquisition suddenly ends with the appearance of fully mature reading and writing. Neuman and Roskos (1998, p. 2) argue, to the contrary:

> It is now recognized that there is no beginning point. Even at a young age, children are legitimate writers and readers. Similarly, there can be no end point, no single boundary denoting conventionalized practices. Rather, literacy development begins early, is ongoing, and is continuous throughout a lifetime.

We are going to follow Neuman and Roskos' lead and use the term *early literacy* throughout this book to refer to the new perspective on literacy acquisition.

Interest in early literacy began with studies of early readers, children who learned to read before they entered kindergarten. This research led to investigations of what preschool-age children typically learn about print. At the same time, researchers began to investigate children's home literacy experiences, seeking to discover the factors that promote early literacy acquisition.

The following sections review major findings of four strands of research on early literacy: early readers, children's concepts about print, early forms of reading and writing, and home literacy experiences. Many of these research studies link acquisition of knowledge or skills with specific ages. It is important to note that there are large individual differences in literacy development and that the ages at which particular knowledge or skills appear will vary widely for specific children. In fact, it is not unusual to find up to a five-year range in children's literacy development within a kindergarten classroom (IRA/NAEYC, 1998).

Part of this variation in the rate of literacy acquisition is due to differences in children's innate intelligence and aptitude. Considerable diversity also exists in children's experiences with oral and written language during the early years (IRA/NAEYC, 1998). That is, some children live in homes with adults who provide the kind of resources and support that optimize literacy acquisition, and others do not. In addition, variations exist in how essential written language is for communicating in different cultures (Neuman & Roskos, 1993). In cultures with a strong oral tradition, the motivation for acquiring literacy may not be as strong as in cultures emphasizing the importance of written language.

Early Readers

Early readers are children who learn to read during the preschool years without receiving formal instruction from their parents or teachers. Teachers who subscribed to the traditional readiness view were well aware that such children existed. These children created problems because their needs did not match with the reading readiness curriculum (Hall, 1987). The general consensus was that these early readers were intellectually gifted and that their high IQ was responsible for their early acquisition of literacy.

In the mid-1960s and early 1970s, researchers in the United States and Great Britain began to study these children (Clark, 1976; Durkin, 1966). Results showed that many early readers were of normal intelligence, contradicting the commonly assumed link between early reading and giftedness. Parental interviews revealed that these children shared several characteristics:

1. They were curious about written language at a very young age, asking many questions about letters, words, and print.
2. They showed an early interest in writing and liked to scribble, write their names, send notes, and so forth.
3. They loved to have favorite stories read to them over and over again.
4. They had a parent, older sibling, or other adult who answered their questions about written language and who read to them on a regular basis.

These findings suggested that home experiences had an important role in promoting early reading.

Concepts about Print

Research on early readers in turn stimulated interest in what typical children were learning about literacy during the preschool years. The earliest studies on this topic were conducted in laboratory settings and had rather negative results, reporting that preschool-age children had only vague conceptions about reading and writing (Downing & Oliver, 1973–1974). In these studies, children were typically taken out of their classrooms and interviewed by a researcher; the adult, the setting, and the situation were not familiar to the children.

More recent studies have shifted the focus to the knowledge about literacy that young children exhibit in everyday situations at home or in school classrooms. This shift in perspective has resulted in an entirely different picture of preschool-age children's print awareness.

One of the first concepts about literacy that children learn is the distinction between print and pictures. Most children discover the print–picture distinction quite early, often by age three. Ask three-year-olds to draw a picture and to write their names. Their markings when asked to draw a picture likely will be quite different from those made when asked to write their names. This distinction is important because it establishes a separate identity for print and allows children to begin learning about its functions and structure.

Research indicates that children's knowledge about print follows a loose developmental sequence (Lomax & McGee, 1987):

1. general concepts about the purpose and functions of print;
2. graphic awareness—the ability to visually recognize environmental print, letters, and words;
3. phonemic awareness—the concept that words consist of a sequence of spoken sounds (phonemes); and
4. letter–sound relationships (phonics).

PURPOSE AND FUNCTIONS OF PRINT. One of the earliest discoveries that children make about written language is that print has meaning. Jerry Harste, Virginia Woodward, and Carolyn Burke (1984) found that many three-year-olds expect print to be meaningful. This understanding becomes evident when children point to words on signs, cereal boxes, or menus and ask, "What does that say?" Alternatively, after making marks on a piece of paper, children make comments such as, "What did I write?" or "This says . . . "

A related discovery is that print is functional; it can be used to get things done in daily life. Children's knowledge of the practical uses of print grows substantially during the preschool years. Elfrieda Heibert (1981) found that three-year-olds demonstrated limited knowledge of the purposes of several types of print, such as labels on Christmas presents, street signs, and store signs, but five-year-olds showed much greater knowledge of these functions.

Children's knowledge of the functional uses of literacy frequently shows up in their make-believe play. For example, Marcia Baghban (1984) recounts how she took her 28-month-old daughter Giti out to eat at a restaurant. On returning home, Giti promptly acted out the role of a waitress, making marks on a pad of paper while recording her mother's food orders. Other researchers have reported numerous incidents of preschoolers' engaging in a variety of functional literacy activities while engaging in dramatic play, including jotting down phone messages, writing checks to pay for purchases, looking up recipes in cookbooks, and making shopping lists (Neuman & Roskos, 1991b, 1997; Vukelich, 1992).

GRAPHIC AWARENESS.   Children begin to recognize environmental print—print that occurs in real-life contexts—at a very early age. Several researchers (e.g., Goodman, 1986; Lomax & McGee, 1987; Mason, 1980) have shown that many three- and four-year-olds can recognize and know the meanings of product labels (Colgate, Cheerios, Pepsi), restaurant signs (McDonald's, Pizza Hut), and street signs (Stop). Even if children do not say the correct word when attempting to read such print, they usually will come up with a related term. For example, when presented with a Coke can, the child might say "Pepsi."

In recognizing environmental print, children attend to the entire context rather than just the print (Masonheimer, Drum, & Ehri, 1984). This *logographic reading* begins quite early. Yetta Goodman (1986) found that 80 percent of the four-year-olds in her study could recognize environmental print in full context—they knew that a can of Pepsi Cola said *Pepsi*. Typically, by mid-kindergarten, many children learn to recognize a limited set of whole words without environmental context clues, using incidental cues such as shape, length, and pictures (Ehri, 1991).

Children often begin to recognize the letters of the alphabet at about the same time as they "read" environmental print. This ability varies considerably among children, with some children recognizing one third of the alphabet by age three (Heibert, 1981), and others not learning any letters until they enter kindergarten (Morgan, 1987). As is explained later in this chapter, variations in children's home literacy experiences appear to be responsible for some of these differences.

Interest appears to be a key factor in determining the specific letters that children learn first (McGee & Richgels, 1989). Children's own names and highly salient environmental print are often the source of initial letter learning. Marcia Baghban (1984), for example, describes how K (K-Mart), M (McDonald's), and G (Giti) were among the first letters recognized by her two-year-old daughter Giti.

The ability to recognize letters is an important step in early literacy development. Children must realize that words are made up of individual letters in order to grasp the *alphabetic principle* that underlies written English. As explained in the next section, this principle is an important prerequisite to invented spelling, decoding, and independent reading. Children's letter recognition ability has been repeatedly shown to be a powerful predictor of later reading achievement (Adams, 1990). We present strategies for helping children learn the alphabet in Chapter 7.

PHONEMIC AWARENESS.   In order to become fluent readers and writers, children need to move beyond *logographic* reading (recognition of environmental print and whole words) and understand that sentences are composed of individual words, that words are composed of combinations of individual letters, and that these letters have a relationship to the phonemes (smallest units of sound) of speech. Understanding this *alphabetic principle*—that there is a systematic relationship between the letters of written language and the sounds of oral language—requires more than letter recognition. Children must also become aware that the words in speech are composed of sequences of individual sounds or phonemes. This conscious awareness of phonemes sets the stage for children to discover the relationship between letters and sounds that will, in turn, facilitate the recognition of words that are in their oral vocabulary but are not familiar in print (Stanovich, 1986). In addition, children need to be able to isolate sounds in words in order to use invented spellings in their writing (Richgels, Poremba, & McGee, 1996).

Most children come to understand the phonological structure of speech gradually during their preschool years. Adults report observing children as young as two or three years of age playing with sounds. For example, young children rhyme words, (e.g., bunny, sunny, funny), or they mix words (e.g., pancake, canpake). These children are exhibiting phonological awareness.

According to Catherine Snow and her colleagues (1998), for most children phonemic awareness begins when they appreciate alliteration. That is, they understand that two words begin with the same sound (e.g., baby and boy begin with /b/). This is a challenging task for young children. It is not until children are five or six that the majority of them can identify words that begin with particular phonemes. Those children whose oral language is the most proficient are the children whose phonemic awareness is the most developed.

On entering school, children's level of phonemic awareness is one of the strongest predictors of success in learning to read (Adams, 1990). In fact, phonemic awareness has been shown to account for 50 percent of the variance in children's reading proficiency at the end of first grade (Adams, Foorman, Lundberg, & Beeler, 1998).

Unfortunately, phonemic awareness is difficult for many young children to acquire. Marilyn Adams and her colleagues (1998, p. 19) report that

> Phonemic awareness eludes roughly 25 percent of middle-class first graders and substantially more of those who come from less literacy-rich backgrounds. Furthermore, these children evidence serious difficulty in learning to read and write.

One reason that phonemic awareness is difficult to learn is that there are few clues in speech to signal the separate phonemes that make up words (Ehri, 1997). Instead, phonemes overlap with each other and fuse together into syllabic units. Adams and her colleagues (1998) give the example of *bark*. They point out that this word is not pronounced /b/, /a/, /r/, /k/. Instead, the pronunciation of the medial vowel *a* is influenced by the consonants that precede and follow it. Because phonemes are not discrete units of sound, they are very abstract and are difficult for children to recognize and manipulate (Yopp, 1992).

Ample evidence exists that phonemic awareness can be developed through instruction (Adams et al., 1998). However, there is considerable controversy over how this important skill should be taught. A variety of strategies are available, ranging from direct instruction using isolated words to activities involving rhymes and games. As will become apparent in Chapter 7, we favor approaches that make this difficult concept enjoyable and interesting for young children to learn.

LETTER–SOUND RELATIONSHIPS (PHONICS). Once children have acquired phonemic awareness, they can begin to make connections between letters in written words and the phonemes in speech. Young children's knowledge of letter–sound relationships becomes evident when they begin using invented spellings in their early writing. Figure 4.2 illustrates young Sareena's invented spelling. Note how she used letter–sound relationships in choosing the one or two letters used to represent each word: *g* for going, *pz* for pizza, *ht* for hut, and so on. In Chapter 7, we present developmentally appropriate strategies for promoting children's phonics learning.

CONVENTIONS OF PRINT. Conventions of print refer to the social rules (left-to-right and top-to-bottom sequence, spaces between words, capitalizing the first letter of each sentence) and terminology (letter, word, page) that surround written language. Knowledge of these conventions tends to grow slowly. For example, knowledge of the left-to-right and top-to-bottom sequence of print is often not acquired until age five or six, and metalinguistic terms such as *letter* and *word* continue to confuse many children during the primary grades (Clay, 1972).

Figure 4.2

Sareena's invented spelling: "I am going to Pizza Hut today"

Early Forms of Reading and Writing

Traditionally, strict criteria have been used to define the onset of reading and writing. Children were not considered to be reading until they could correctly recognize numerous printed words, and they were not considered to be writing until they had mastered correct letter formation and could spell words conventionally. Children's early attempts at reading (labeling illustrations or making up a story to go along with the pictures in a book) and their early tries at writing (scribbles or random groups of letters) were dismissed as insignificant and inconsequential.

As interest in early literacy increased during the 1970s, some researchers began focusing attention on these initial attempts at reading and writing (Clay, 1975; Read, 1971). It soon became clear that these early forms appeared to be purposeful and rule governed. Children appeared to construct, test, and perfect hypotheses about written language. Research began to reveal general developmental sequences, with the early forms of reading and writing gradually becoming more conventional with age and experience (Ferreiro & Teberosky, 1982; Sulzby, Barnhart, & Hieshima, 1989).

EMERGENT WRITING. Building on the earlier work of Marie Clay (1975) and of Emilia Ferreiro and Ana Teberosky (1982), Elizabeth Sulzby asked preschool children to write stories and to read what they had written (Sulzby, 1985b, 1990). Based on this research, Sulzby (1990) has identified seven broad categories of early writing: drawing as writing, scribble writing, letter-like units, nonphonetic letter strings, copying from environmental print, invented spelling, and conventional writing (see Figure 4.3).

Figure 4.3

Sulzby's categories of emergent writing

Drawing as writing—Pictures represent writing.

Context: Angela (age 4), who is playing in the housekeeping center, makes a shopping list for a trip to the supermarket.

Text: "Hamburgers [the two bottom circles] and chocolate chip cookies [the two top circles]"

Scribble writing—Continuous lines represent writing.

Context: Rimmert Jr. (age 6) writes a thank-you letter to a family friend.

Text: "Thank you for your letter from America."

(continued on next page)

Figure 4.3

Continued

Letter-like units—The child makes a series of separate marks that have some letter-like characteristics

Context: Lauren (age 4) writes a story about a recent experience.
Text: "I buy the food at the store. I baked it, and I washed it and ate it."

Nonphonetic letter strings—The child writes strings of letters that show no evidence of letter–sound relationships. These can be random groups of letters or repeated clusters of letters.

Context: Debbie (age 4) writes in her journal about a recent school experience.
Text: "We play together, and Bobby fought with us. We fight with him, then we play again."

Copying from environmental print—The child copies print found in the environment.

Context: Pierce (age 4), in the role of a veterinarian, writes a prescription for a sick teddy bear. He copies the words *apple juice* from a can he has retrieved from a nearby garbage can.
Text: "Penicillin" [invented spelling]
           "Apple juice" [copying]

(continued on next page)

Figure 4.3

Continued

Invented spelling—The child creates his own spelling using letter–sound relationships. This can range from using one letter per word to using a letter for every sound in each word (as in the example below).

Context: Chris (age 5) writes in his journal.
Text: "I like dinosaurs. They are neat."

Conventional—The child uses correct spelling for most of the words.

Context: Johnny (age 5) writes in his journal.
Text: "This is a dog jumping over a box."

Sulzby believes that these categories do not form a strict developmental hierarchy. While there is a general movement from less mature forms toward conventional forms, children move back and forth across these forms when composing texts, and they often combine several different types in the same composition. Several of the examples in Figure 4.3 show this type of form mixing. Angela's shopping list contains drawings to represent cookies and a hamburger, while a scribble stands for the word *and*. Pierce used both invented spelling and copying from environmental print to write his prescription for the sick teddy bear. Children also appear to adjust their form of writing to the task at hand. Kindergartners tend to use invented or conventional spellings when writing single words. When writing longer pieces of text, they often shift to less mature forms, such as nonphonetic letter strings or scribbles, which require less time and effort (Sulzby & Teale, 1991).

Sulzby cautions teachers against having unrealistic expectations of children's emergent writing capabilities. Case studies of early readers (Baghban, 1984; Bissex, 1980) might lead teachers to expect that invented spelling is a common occurrence among four- and five-year-olds. However, Sulzby's longitudinal research has revealed that children's writing development is typically much slower, with invented spelling not arriving until late kindergarten for some and not until the end of first grade for others (Sulzby & Teale, 1991). Both groups of children (the early and the late spellers) are normal.

EMERGENT READING.   Sulzby has also investigated the patterns in children's early attempts at reading familiar storybooks (Sulzby, 1985a). She found that children's storybook-reading behaviors appeared to follow a developmental pattern, with their attention gradually shifting from the pictures to the text and their vocalizations changing from sounding like oral storytelling to sounding like reading. The following is a condensed list of Sulzby's storybook-reading categories (Sulzby & Barnhart, 1990):

1. *Attending to pictures, not forming stories*—The child looks at the pictures in the book, labeling or making comments about them.
2. *Attending to pictures, forming oral stories*—The child looks at the book's pictures and weaves a story across the pages. However, the child's intonation sounds like she or he is telling an oral story. The listener must be able to see the pictures to follow the story.
3. *Attending to pictures, forming written stories*—The child reads by looking at the book's pictures, and the child's wording and intonation sound like reading. The listener does not usually have to see the pictures to follow the story.
4. *Attending to print*—The child attends to the print rather than to the pictures when attempting to read the story. The child may refuse to read because of print awareness, may use only selected aspects of print (e.g., letter–sound relationships), or may read conventionally.

Allison's (age five) emergent reading of "The Hare and the Tortoise" is illustrated in Special Feature 4.1. Her reading is representative of Sulzby's category, "attending to pictures, forming written stories." Notice how Allison has memorized parts of the story and paraphrases the rest of the text, using her own words to reconstruct its meaning.

Other studies by Sulzby revealed that children's reading of their own emergent writing follows roughly the same pattern (Sulzby, Barnhart, & Hieshima, 1989). First, children refuse to read or claim that they did not write. Next, they label or describe what they have written. This is followed by making up stories to go along with their writing, with their voice shifting gradually from sounding like oral language to sounding like reading. Finally, children begin to actually attend to the print that they have written, reading "aspectually" (just attending to letter–sound relationships or to selected whole words that can be recognized by sight) at first and then conventionally.

Research has shown that young children's emergent readings can be influenced by the number of times a child has heard a book read (Pappas & Brown, 1987) and how many times the child has read the book independently (Pappas, 1993). Repeated readings of a book, either by the child or adult, increases the degree to which children's subsequent emergent reading approximates the actual text of the book. In addition, text features, such as pictures and grammatical subordination, and narrative structure have been found to affect children's emergent reading, as measured by the Sulzby scale (Elster, 1998). Thus, children's emergent reading levels should be expected to vary, depending on the features and familiarity of the texts being read.

Allison's Emergent Reading of "The Hare and The Tortoise"

Text

Once upon a time, a hare and a tortoise lived near a large. . . . They lived in a large open field.

Every day, the hare went zigzagging across the field, with a *hippity-hop, hoppity-hop.* His long hind legs made it easy for him to move quickly. If danger was near, off he would scamper, quick as a flash.

The tortoise, on the other hand, was not very fast. He plodded along slowly, without a care in the world.

It so happened that the hare loved to make fun of how slowly the tortoise moved. The tortoise tried not to let it bother him, but he did not like it. One day the hare began teasing the tortoise in front of other animals.

"You are so slow." said the hare, "that I get tired just watching you! Why, if you were any slower, you would be standing still."

Re-enactment

Once upon a time there lived a hare and a tortoise.

Every day the hare goes zigzagging across the field, with a *hippity-hop, hoppity hop.* When danger was near, he would scamper off in the quick of the night.

The tortoise and the hare were slow. He didn't care if the tortoise—the hare made fun of him. He plodded along slowly, without a care in the world.

One day the hare decided to tease the tortoise. When the tortoise passed by the hare started teasing the tortoise. You are so slow, I'll bet I could even beat you in a race.

You are so slow, so slow. You are like a statue.

Emergent reading of familiar story books has an important role in early literacy development.

Interestingly, children's level of early reading does not always correspond to their early writing (Sulzby, Barnhart, & Hieshima, 1989). For example, a child might be able to write with invented spelling, using letter–sound relationships to encode words. However, the same child might not use letter–sound relationships when decoding words during reading. So children who begin to use invented spelling are not automatically able to read their own writing. The pattern of relationships between the emergent forms of literacy are far from simple!

Home Literacy Experiences

The fourth and final strand of research has focused on young children's home environments in an attempt to discover factors that promote early literacy development. Whereas the first three groups of studies are concerned with what children learn about written language, home literacy research is concerned with how this learning takes place.

Early studies in this area focused on umbrella characteristics such as family income and parents' levels of education (Sulzby & Teale, 1991). Results revealed positive relationships between these variables and reading achievement in the early grades. For example, children from middle-income families tend to be better readers than those from low-income families. Unfortunately, such findings do little to explain how these variables directly affect children's literacy growth.

More recent studies have narrowed their focus and have attempted to describe the actual literacy-related experiences that children have at home. These home literacy studies have identified several factors that appear to have important roles in early literacy acquisition. These factors are described in the sections that follow.

ACCESS TO PRINT AND BOOKS. In order to learn about literacy, young children must have opportunities to see lots of print and must have easy access to books. Plentiful home supplies of children's books have been found to be associated with early reading (Durkin, 1966), interest in literature (Morrow, 1983), and positive orientation toward schooling (Feitelson & Goldstein, 1986).

Because of the literate nature of our society, all children are surrounded by large amounts of environmental print. For example, they see print on product containers (Cheerios, Pepsi) street signs (Stop), and store signs (McDonald's, Pizza Hut). Differences do occur, however, in children's exposure to books and other forms of reading materials. Bill Teale's (1986b) descriptive study of the home environments of 24 low-income preschoolers revealed that, while some of the homes had ample supplies of children's books, other homes contained none. This is not to suggest that all children from low-income families lack exposure to reading materials at home (see Taylor & Dorsey-Gaines, 1988). However, those children who do not have access to books at home are at a great disadvantage in acquiring literacy.

ADULT DEMONSTRATIONS OF LITERACY BEHAVIOR. Children also need to observe their parents, other adults, or older siblings using literacy in everyday situations (Smith, 1988). When children see their family members use print for various purposes—writing shopping lists, paying bills, looking up programs in the television listings, and writing notes to each other—they begin to learn about the practical uses of written language and to understand why reading and writing are activities worth doing. If their parents happen to model reading for pleasure, so much the better. These children see literature as a source of entertainment. Children's exposure to these types of functional and recreational literacy demonstrations has been found to vary greatly.

SUPPORTIVE ADULTS. Early readers tend to have parents who are very supportive of their early attempts at literacy (Morrow, 1983). While these parents rarely attempt to directly teach their children how to read and write, they do support literacy growth by doing such things as (1) answering their children's questions about print; (2) pointing out letters and words in the environment; (3) reading storybooks frequently; (4) making regular visits to the local library; (5) providing children with a wide variety of experiences such as trips to stores, parks, and museums; and (6) initiating functional literacy activities (such as suggesting that a child write a letter to grandmother or help make a shopping list).

The amount of such support that children receive during the preschool years varies greatly from family to family, and these differences have been found to have a considerable effect on children's literacy learning during kindergarten and the elementary grades (Christian, Morrison, & Bryant, 1998; Leseman & de Jong, 1998).

INDEPENDENT ENGAGEMENTS WITH LITERACY. Young children need to get their hands on literacy materials and to have opportunities to engage in early forms of reading and writing. This exploration and experimentation allows children to try out and perfect their growing concepts about the functions, forms, and conventions of written language.

Independent engagements with literacy often take place in connection with play. Don Holdaway (1979) has described how, as soon as young children become familiar with a storybook through repetitive read-aloud experiences, they will begin to play with the books and pretend to read them. He believes that this type of reading-like play is one of the most important factors promoting early literacy acquisition.

Young children also incorporate writing into their play. Sometimes this play writing is exploratory in nature, with children experimenting with different letter forms and shapes. At other times, emergent writing occurs in the context of make-believe play. Figure 4.4 is an example of this type of play-related writing. Four-year-old Ben was engaging in dramatic play in the housekeeping center. He wrote a Post-it™ Note message to another child, who was acting out the role of his mother, informing her that he was at soccer practice.

Sulzby (1985b) has described how children's early writing follows a loose developmental sequence, becoming more conventional over time (see Figure 4.3). Play provides children with highly pleasurable and meaningful opportunities to experiment with these early forms of writing. In addition, social interaction during play (such as when other players cannot read a shopping list written in scribble writing) may provide motivation for children to develop more conventional forms of script.

Young children also use literacy in functional, nonplay situations. An excellent example is Glenda Bissex's (1980) account of how her four-year-old son Paul, after failing to get her attention by verbal means, used a stamp set to write "RUDF" (Are you deaf?). He also attempted to secure his privacy by putting the sign "DO NOT DSTRB GNYS AT WRK" (Do not disturb . . . Genius at work) on his door.

Figure 4.4

Ben's Post-it™ Note message: "My sister and dad took me to soccer practice. Be back at 4"

Opportunities to engage in these types of independent engagements with literacy depend on access to books and writing materials. As mentioned previously, research on children's home environments indicates that there are wide discrepancies in the availability of children's books and other reading materials. Similar differences also exist in the availability of writing materials. Teale's (1986b) descriptive study of the home environments of low-income preschoolers revealed that only 4 of 24 children had easy access to paper and writing instruments. He noted that these particular children engaged in far more emergent writing than did the other subjects in the study.

STORYBOOK READING. Storybook reading is undoubtedly the most studied aspect of home literacy. Quantitative studies have attempted to establish the importance and value of parents' reading to their children. A recent meta-analysis of 29 studies spanning more than three decades indicated that parent–preschooler storybook reading was positively related to outcomes such as language growth, early literacy, and reading achievement (Bus, van Ijzendoorn, & Pellegrini, 1995).

Other studies have attempted to describe and analyze what actually takes place during storybook-reading episodes and to identify the mechanisms through which storybook reading facilitates literacy growth (e.g., Altwerger, Diehl-Faxon, & Dockstader-Anderson, 1985; Heath, 1982; Holdaway, 1979; Snow & Ninio, 1986; Taylor, 1986; Yaden, Smolkin, & Conlon, 1989). These studies have shown that parent–child storybook reading is an ideal context for children to receive all of the previously mentioned factors that promote literacy acquisition:

1. Storybook reading provides children with access to enjoyable children's books, building positive attitudes about books and reading. (We provide a list of books for young children in Appendix A.)
2. During storybook reading, parents present children with a model of skilled reading. Children see how books are handled, and they hear the distinctive intonation patterns that are used in oral reading.
3. Parents provide support that enables young children to take an active part in storybook reading. Early storybook-reading sessions tend to be routinized, with the parent first focusing the child's attention on a picture and then asking the child to label the picture. If the child does so, the parent gives positive or negative feedback about the accuracy of the label. If the child does not volunteer a label, the parent provides the correct label (Snow & Ninio, 1986). As children's abilities grow, parents up the ante, shifting more of the responsibility to the children and expecting them to participate in more advanced ways.
4. Storybook reading encourages independent engagements with literacy by familiarizing children with stories and encouraging them to attempt to read the stories on their own (Holdaway, 1979; Sulzby, 1985a).

Other researchers have studied how cultural factors affect the manner in which parents mediate storybook reading for their children. Shirley Brice Heath (1982) found that middle-class parents tended to help their children link book information with other experiences. For example, John Langstaff's popular predictable book *Oh, A-Hunting We Will Go* (1974, Macmillan) contains the following lines:

> *Oh, a-hunting we will go.*
> *A-hunting we will go.*
> *We'll catch a lamb*
> *And put him in a pram*
> *And then we'll let him go.*

To help the child understand the term *pram,* a middle-class parent might say, "The pram looks just like your sister's baby carriage." Working-class parents, on the other hand, had a tendency to not extend book information beyond its original context and would simply define the word *pram* for the child. Sulzby and Teale (1991) speculate that these differences in story-reading style may have a considerable effect on children's early literacy acquisition.

Case Studies

The following sections present two case studies of early literacy development. Tiffany, a native English-speaking child, is the subject of the first case study. The second study describes Alicia's literacy acquisition. Alicia is a native speaker of Spanish, and English is her second language. There are many interesting similarities and differences in the early literacy acquisition of these two girls.

Tiffany

Tiffany's parents began reading to her soon after birth, and by age one, she was actively participating in storybook-reading sessions. Now, nearly two years later, 30-month-old Tiffany has begun to attempt to read on her own. The story begins in her bedroom, where she was looking at Richard Scarry's *Best Word Book Ever* (1980, Western Publishing Company) with her sister Dawn. Though her house has many children's books, this book was one of her favorites. Tiffany delighted in labeling the pictures and describing the actions of the Bunny family as they engage in familiar, everyday situations. As Tiffany pointed to the pictures of Nicki Bunny going to the doctor for a checkup, both she and Dawn laughed at the animals who are all dressed up in clothing: "Nicki Bunny wears shoes! " While attempting to read this text, Tiffany displayed many aspects of her concepts about print, including book handling and turning pages (starting at the front of the book and progressing to the back), as well as an appreciation of storybook reading.

On the way to the grocery story several months later, Tiffany's family passed a McDonald's sign. Thirty-three-month-old Tiffany shouted with gleeful recognition, "Donald's—ummm, eat burgers." Tiffany, like most children brought up in a literate culture, had already begun to recognize that her world is full of environmental print. Though Tiffany's reading of the McDonald's sign came more from interpreting the color and shape of the logo than from differentiating letters, it demonstrated her understanding that print carries meaning—another important developmental milestone.

Tiffany was also beginning to demonstrate an understanding that writing, as well as oral language, communicates meaning. Waiting with her mother in the bank, 36-month-old Tiffany took a handful of bank forms. While her mother talked to the bank manager, Tiffany occupied herself by using a pen to fill out the many forms. Her writing contained many squiggly lines and some picture-like forms (Figure 4.5). When Tiffany's mother asked her what she had written, Tiffany replied, "I write, 'Tiffy can buy money.' " At this stage, it is typical for children's writing to include both pictographs (pictures that represent writing) and scribble writing. Notice that her scribbling has the appearance of an adult's English cursive writing.

Figure 4.5

Tiffany (age 36 months) writes a note using a drawing and scribbles: "Tiffany can buy money"

Sitting on her father's lap, 42-month-old Tiffany was reading him Maurice Sendak's *Where the Wild Things Are* (1963, Scholastic):

This bad boy in the wolf pajamas is mean to his mommy.
He runs away 'cause he is mad.
He gets in a boat, like "rubba a dub" [Tiffany's bathtub toy boat].
Then he meets some big bad chicken monsters and yells at them.
They make him the King, 'cause he yelled so loud!!!
Then he goed home 'cause he wanted to eat.

The story she told consisted of her interpretations of the text's illustrations, and she used a story-telling tone as she held the book and turned the pages. As explained earlier, this behavior is indicative of Elizabeth Sulzby's category of emergent reading, "attending to pictures, forming oral stories" (Sulzby & Barnhart, 1990). Though Tiffany's oral retelling of the story was fairly accurate, her father noted that she did not include the monster refrain—"and they rolled their terrible eyes, gnashed their terrible teeth, and showed their terrible claws! " Her omission of this salient part of the story was probably caused by the fact that, during this stage of emergent reading, story retelling is guided by the illustrations rather than by the words in the text. As the pictures did not explicitly detail this refrain, Tiffany lacked the visual cues that would have triggered the recitation of this phrase.

At age four years, Tiffany continued to refine her understanding of the many functions of print. Sitting at her child-sized table in her playhouse with her best friend Becca, Tiffany pondered over a piece of paper with her pencil in her mouth.

Tiffany: What do you think the babies will eat?

Becca: Baby food, Tiff.

Tiffany: I know that! What kind of baby food?

Becca: Oh, I think the orange stuff, but not the green.

Tiffany: [Now writing this information down.] Okay. What else?

Becca: You need to write down cat food and take the coupons.

Tiffany: [Pulling out a bunch of coupons from her drawer, she sorts through them until she finds the Purina Cat Chow coupon.] Yeah, that coupon says "free cat food."

Figure 4.6 demonstrates that Tiffany had begun to produce letter-like forms. Though she continued to use pictographs, Tiffany could distinguish print from pictures. Pointing to the drawing she said, "This is a picture of baby food." She went on to describe her letter-like forms with the comment, "This says buy peaches and diapers."

This episode also reveals that Tiffany was continuing to expand her environmental print vocabulary. In fact, she was becoming quite adept at recognizing dozens of product names. This

Figure 4.6

Tiffany (age 48 months) makes a shopping list using a picture of baby food plus "Buy peaches and diapers"

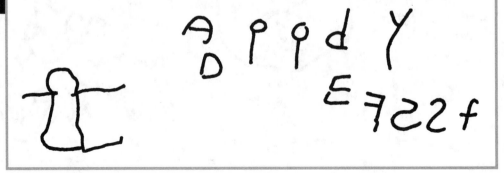

ability was fostered by parental praise and encouragement each time Tiffany joined her parents as a member of the grocery-shopping expedition.

At age four years, Tiffany started preschool. One of the first academic activities her preschool teachers undertook was helping the children recognize and print their own names. As is often the case, Tiffany's first attempts to print her name were somewhat frustrating. Though she was quite accomplished at making letter-like forms, trying to reproduce specific letters in a specified sequence was definitely a challenge. At that time, Tiffany received a chalkboard from her grandparents. The new writing implement seemed to inspire her to practice more frequently, and soon Tiffany had mastered the fine art of printing her name (Figure 4.7).

Along with printing her name, Tiffany, like most of her preschool classmates, was becoming interested in naming and printing the alphabet. This interest was sparked by her teachers through direct, developmentally appropriate instruction. Prior to her preschool experience, Tiffany only casually watched the *Sesame Street* letter segments, paying attention instead to the social drama of the *Sesame Street* characters. However, between the ages of four and five years, Tiffany became an astute alphabet hunter—shouting with great authority the names of the letters as they flashed across the television screen. Tiffany sang the alphabet song, read alphabet books, did alphabet puzzles and alphabet dot-to-dot worksheets, and molded clay letters. She diligently wrote alphabet symbols with every type of writing tool imaginable—markers, pens, pencils, and water paints and paint brushes. She wrote her letters on every surface conceivable, including her bedroom walls! Her all-time favorite alphabet activity was writing her letters with soap crayons on the bathtub wall.

Tiffany's new proficiency with letter formation resulted in the production of many strings of random capital and lowercase letters, or using Sulzby's (1990) terminology, strings of nonphonetic letter strings (see Figure 4.8). Notice that though Tiffany knew many upper- and lowercase letters, she was not yet forming words or clustering her letters in word-like units.

Soon after Tiffany entered preschool, she became interested in joining her sister Dawn (age seven) in playing school. During these dramatic play sessions, Tiffany would listen to Dawn as she read basal texts and their favorite literature. In the role of teacher, Dawn would ask factual questions during and after reading storybooks to Tiffany. For example, after reading Maurice Sendak's *Where the Wild Things Are* (Harper & Row, 1963), Dawn asked, "What did the monsters say to Max? What did Max say to the monsters?" Dawn would model writing letters on the chalkboard and then ask Tiffany to copy what she had written. Tiffany did her best to reproduce the words that Dawn wrote. Every so often, Tiffany would run out to her mother and proclaim, "Look it! What it say?"

Later in the year, when Dawn was at school, Tiffany would play school by herself, only this time she was the teacher. Dressed in a long white pleated skirt, heels, and jacket, she looked like Ms. O'Bannon, her sister's second grade teacher. She would "read" stories to her teddy bear and to rows of doll students, and she would use her ruler to point to alphabet cards posted on the wall. She would ask Teddy to pay attention and ask Annie (a doll) to tell her what the letters said. It is interesting to note that, when Tiffany pretended to be the teacher, her writing became more conventional. She carefully wrote her letters as she practiced saying the phrases

Figure 4.7

Tiffany (age 52 months) writes her own name

Figure 4.8

Tiffany (age 54 months) writes a stream of random letters

that Dawn had used earlier: "Start at the top, draw a flat-hat top, then find the middle and draw a straight line. Now you see, you have a *T*."

Sitting in her miniature rocker holding her beloved baby doll Ramalda, four-and-a-half-year-old Tiffany began reading another favorite story, *Old Hat, New Hat* by Stan and Jan Berenstain (1970, Random House). Pointing to the pictures, Tiffany recited the story line, "new hat, new hat, new hat" and "too feathery, too scratchy," then the rousing finale, "just right, just right, just right! " Tiffany's recitation involved following the pictures and recalling the phrases she had heard and repeated with her parents virtually dozens of times. At this point in her development, her storybook reading was beginning to sound like reading as she imitated the expression and phrasing her parents used when they read this story to her.

When Tiffany began kindergarten at age five, she could recognize most alphabet letters. During her kindergarten year, Tiffany learned that each alphabet letter made a specific sound, but some alphabet letters made two or three sounds. For Tiffany, this phonics knowledge was an exciting step toward literacy. She reveled in baking Big Bird's brown banana bread with butter and studying the scientific qualities of bubbles and bouncing balls billions of times.

Her teacher, Ms. C., also modeled the writing process at the end of each day. She began by asking the children to summarize what they had learned that day, and as the children volunteered ideas, she would write their statements. While Ms. C. wrote, she would ask, "Who knows what letter Baby Bear starts with? What other sounds do you hear?" This type of informal modeling provided the spark that ignited Tiffany's reading–writing connection. This very sensitive teacher also had the kindergarten children write in their journals at their own developmental level. Figure 4.9 illustrates one of Tiffany's first invented-spelling journal entries. At this point, she was beginning to separate her words.

During the latter part of the kindergarten year, Tiffany used sophisticated invented spelling to express her thoughts and feelings. Simultaneously, Tiffany's interest in interpreting written materials of all types was increasing. In addition to reading product labels, she attempted to decode greeting cards, print she saw on television, and billboards. She also insisted that her parents use manuscript printing as opposed to cursive writing. Tiffany was spending a great deal of time reading texts that contained predictable patterned rhythm and rhyme. After these predictable books were read with Tiffany several times, she could begin to read them to herself. Her read-by-myself books included *Oh, A-Hunting We Will Go* by J. Langstaff (1974, Houghton Mifflin) and *Chicken Soup with Rice* by M. Sendak (1962, Harper & Row).

As is the case with most children, Tiffany's writing did not correspond directly to her early reading development. Though her use of invented spelling seemed to suggest that she would be able to decode a great number of words, she refused to attempt to decode the text in literature books that had not been read to her previously. Tiffany needed to have a sense of context, or an understanding of what the print was about, before she felt comfortable attempting to read the material. Notice that the items she was decoding earlier—grocery products, greeting cards, and the print used in TV or magazine advertisements—provided strong contextual clues that indicated what the script might be saying.

When six-year-old Tiffany entered first grade, she had made tremendous progress in acquiring literacy. She was able to write and instantly recognize all the upper- and lowercase alphabet symbols. She was also able to distinguish and label all single consonant and vowel sounds. She was able to express her thoughts in written form by using invented spelling, and she could read some familiar predictable books. Tiffany had a strong foundation for more formal reading instruction that would follow in first grade.

Alicia

In Special Feature 4.2, Irene Serna and Sarah Hudelson present a second case study of early literacy. This case study features, Alicia, who came from a home in which Spanish was the primary language. When she entered kindergarten, Alicia was speaking perfect Spanish but was only partially proficient in oral English. She was fortunate to attend a bilingual kindergarten in which she was allowed to learn to read and write in Spanish and then transfer what she had learned to English literacy. It is interesting to compare Alicia's acquisition of reading and writing in Spanish with Tiffany's literacy development in English. As you will see, there are many interesting parallels.

Special Feature 4.2

Alicia's Early Literacy Development in Spanish

Irene Serna and Sarah Hudelson

As Tiffany's case study illustrates, young children begin to read and write English by engaging in daily literacy activities with family members and teachers. These adults support early literacy by creating opportunities for reading and writing and by responding to children's requests for assistance. What does early literacy look like in a language other than English? Alicia, a Spanish-speaking kindergartner we came to know through our research, provides a good example of how children construct their literacy in Spanish (Serna & Hudelson, 1993).

Alicia's Home Language and Literacy

Spanish was the dominant language in Alicia's home. Her mother reported that Alicia had requested that books be read to her since she was four years old. In addition, Alicia had been eager to engage in writing within family activities. At home, Alicia helped produce shopping lists, notes, and cards sent to family members. Of course, these were written in Spanish. Clearly, Alicia came from a very literate home environment that featured frequent storybook reading, many opportunities to write in connection with daily activities, and adults who supported her early attempts at reading and writing. In this regard, Alicia's early literacy development was quite similar to Tiffany's and that of other English-speaking children who come from supportive home environments. There was one significant difference—Alicia reported that her mother and grandmother frequently told her *cuentos* (folk tales) and family stories. Thus, storytelling (oral literacy) was also a strong part of Alicia's home literacy experiences.

Alicia's Literacy Development in Kindergarten

Though Alicia participated in a bilingual Head Start program as a four-year-old, when she entered kindergarten, her score on an oral language proficiency test identified her as limited-English proficient. Two-thirds of the children in her bilingual kindergarten program spoke English, and one-third spoke Spanish. Alicia used both languages to socialize with her peers. However, she primarily used

(continued on next page)

Special Feature 4.2 (continued)

Spanish to explain her thinking, to narrate stories, and to express herself personally. At the beginning of kindergarten, Alicia only discussed books that were read aloud in Spanish. By the latter half of the year, she was discussing books read in both languages. This was particularly helpful to the monolingual children because Alicia could interpret books and communications in English or Spanish. Alicia's role in the classroom became that of translator. Thus, while her one year of Head Start was not sufficient time for Alicia to develop oral proficiency in English, the second year of bilingual programming in kindergarten did allow her to develop bilingual abilities.

Writing

Beginning in October of her kindergarten year, Alicia was asked to write in a journal for 45 minutes daily. Throughout the year, she also drew and wrote in learning logs to record information from study in thematic units. She contributed to group language experience charts, which summarized findings from the children's thematic studies. In her earliest journal entries, Alicia wrote a patterned and familiar phrase in English, "I love my mom." A November entry demonstrated that Alicia had moved from producing a patterned phrase to creating a label for her picture: *"Mi papalote"* (my kite). In November, Alicia also wrote her first sentence describing a picture, *"Yo ciro mi babe Martinsito"* (I love my baby Martincito), using both invented (*ciro* for *quiero*) and conventional spelling. She also wrote additional patterned sentences, *"Mi Nana bonita come sopa Mi mami bonita come sopa"* (My pretty grandmother eats soup. My pretty mother eats soup). In December, Alicia repeated phrases to write two lines of text describing her picture, *"Los colores del arco iris son bonitos Colores del arco ids"* (The colors of the rainbow are pretty. The colors of the rainbow). Her writing did not become more expressive until February when she wrote about playing in the pile of snow that had been trucked to the school (see Figure 4.10).

Figure 4.10

Alicia's February writing sample

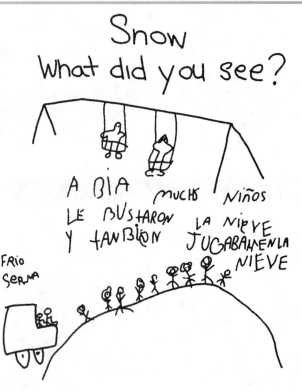

Alicia's Spelling	Conventional Spanish Spelling	English Translation
A bia muchs niños	Había muchos niños	There were many children
le bustaron la nieve	Les gustaron la nieve	They like the snow
y tanbien	Y también	And also
jugaban en la nieve	jugaban en la nieve	they played in the snow

(continued on next page)

Special Feature 4.2 (continued)

This February sample demonstrates that Alicia's invented spellings included most sounds in each syllable, that the vowels were standardized, and that she confused some of the consonants. Though she put spaces between most words, conventional word separation was not used consistently.

In April, Alicia wrote a personal narrative about her little cousin Martincito, primarily describing how she cared for and played with him. Figure 4.11 contains two of the ten sentences she wrote in this personal narrative. Written over a three-week period, Alicia's personal narrative illustrates that her invented spellings were very close approximations of standard Spanish spellings. Alicia also

separated words more consistently. Syntactically, all of her sentences were complete, and all grammatical inflections were correct. By the end of kindergarten, Alicia was the classroom's most fluent writer in Spanish. As a result, other children often asked her to write their personal narratives.

Reading

From September through February, Alicia retold stories from familiar, predictable picture books using some of the story language in Spanish and some in English. In March, her first story was typed for publication (in Spanish). Alicia read this text for the first time using

Figure 4.11

Alicia's April writing sample

Yo LueGo
coN mi
PRimi+o
A LAS   ESooNaipns
CUANDo
Yo   AGo
UNA MA RoMA
   E Me
   COPeA

Alicia's Spelling	Conventional Spanish Spelling	English Translation
Yo juego	Yo juego	I play
con mi	con mi	with my
primito	primita	little cousin
alas escondidas	a las escondidas	hide-and-seek
Cuando	Cuando	When
Yo ago	yo hago	I make
una ma roma	una moroma	a somersault
e me copea	el me copea	he copies me

(continued on next page)

Special Feature 4.2 (continued)

letter–sound cues and a phonetic decoding strategy (i.e., she tried to sound out the words). While this initial reading was not very smooth, Alicia practiced reading the words until she could reread her own story fluently. From March to the end of the year, Alicia used this same strategy with familiar, predictable books in Spanish. Initially, each book was read utilizing the phonetic decoding strategy, focusing on sounding out unfamiliar words. Subsequently, she reread the text until she could read it fluently. Alicia chose to read books that had plain print, with only one or two lines of text per page. She rejected books with too many words or italic print. By the end of May, Alicia read the Spanish versions of Maurice Sendak's *Where the Wild Things Are* (1963, Harper & Row) and Robert Kraus's *Herman the Helper* (1974, Windmill), familiar and unfamiliar texts, respectively. She made a few mistakes, primarily grammatical. She did

not correct these mistakes, but they were rather minor and did not change the meaning of the story. Alicia read more effectively, using multiple cues (letter–sound, meaning, and grammatical) as well as illustrations to decode unfamiliar words. Alicia also demonstrated that she was reading to construct the meaning of each text because she was able to retell each story accurately. By the end of kindergarten, Alicia had become a fluent writer and reader in Spanish. She was able to use sophisticated invented spellings that were very close approximations of standard Spanish spellings, and she could compose coherent narrative stories. Alicia learned to read in Spanish through reading both her own writing and familiar, predictable books. By April, Alicia was reading picture books fluently and independently. She was able to use multiple cueing systems and reading strategies in Spanish.

Summary

The four research strands reviewed in this chapter have joined to provide a picture of the new early literacy perspective. How does what you read in this chapter compare with how you learned to read and write? Were the supportive factors described in the section "Home Literacy Experiences" present in your home?

Here, we return to the questions posed at the beginning of the chapter, and briefly summarize the information presented.

■ *How does the early literacy view of young children's literacy development compare with the readiness and earlier-is-better views?*

According to the early literacy view, the literacy learning process shares much in common with the oral language development process. Literacy acquisition, like oral language development, begins early. For many children, literacy development begins in infancy when caregivers read storybooks to children and children begin to notice print in the environment. Literacy learning is an active, constructive process. By observing print and having stories read to them, young children discover patterns and create their own early versions of reading and writing that initially have little resemblance to conventional forms; the story they read may be quite different from the one in the book, and their writing may look like drawing or scribbles. As children have opportunities to use these early forms of literacy in meaningful social situations and as they interact with adults who draw their attention to the features and functions of print, their constructions become increasingly similar to conventional reading and writing.

According to the readiness view, literacy development begins much later (at about age six). The process through which children acquire literacy is unlike the oral language acquisition process. Rather than constructing knowledge about literacy by experimenting with forms of literacy in supportive environments, supporters of this view believed that children must be directly taught by specially trained teachers who guided children's acquisition of literacy concepts and skills, known as reading readiness skills, which had little to do with actual reading. Children did not meet real reading materials, like books, until the middle of first grade. Children did not write to communicate until much later, after they knew how to form letters and spell words.

The earlier-is-better view borrowed the practices of the readiness view and moved them to earlier grades. What children had been guided to do in first grade now was moved to the kindergarten and preschool years.

■ *What knowledge about written language do young children exhibit when adults watch them closely?*
Watch children and you will see the following:

> Children as young as three years of age know the difference between drawing and writing, expect print to be meaningful (to say something), and know something about the purposes of print.
>
> Two- and three-year-olds play with sounds, thus exhibiting their phonological awareness knowledge.
>
> Three- and four-year-olds read product labels, restaurant signs, and street signs.
>
> Three-year-olds can name about one-third of the letters of the alphabet.
>
> Five- and six-year-olds identify words that begin with the same phoneme, thus exhibiting their phonemic awareness knowledge.
>
> Young children write /m/ for man, thus exhibiting their knowledge of phonics.
>
> Young children show that they know such concepts as print moves from left-to-right and top-to-bottom across the page and that words have spaces between them.
>
> Young children use early forms of writing and of reading, becoming more conventional with age and experience.

■ *What is the relationship among oral language, phonemic awareness, and phonics?*
Research data suggest that those children whose oral language is the most proficient typically are the same children whose phonemic awareness is the most developed. That is, these tend to be the children who best understand that words in speech are composed of sequences of individual sounds or phonemes. Once children have acquired this critically important concept, they are then able to make connections between letters in written words and the phonemes in speech.

■ *What are emergent writing and emergent reading?*
On their way toward reading and writing conventionally, young children construct, test, and perfect hypotheses about written language. Research has shown general developmental sequences, with children's early forms of reading and writing gradually becoming more conventional with age and experience. These early reading and writing forms are known as emergent. Children using all forms of reading and writing are legitimate writers and readers.

■ *What home factors affect young children's literacy development?*
Several factors have been identified as having important roles in early literacy acquisition. These include

> opportunities to see lots of print and have easy access to books;
>
> opportunities to observe adults using literacy in everyday situations;
>
> adults who support children's literacy development by answering children's questions, pointing to letters, taking the children to the library, providing children with a wide variety of experiences, and initiating functional literacy activities;
>
> literacy materials that support children's engagement in early forms of reading and writing; and
>
> experiences with adults who share books with children.

■ *What does early literacy look like in a language other than English?*
Children learn the dominant language of their home. When these homes—be they English-speaking, Spanish-speaking, or Arabic-speaking—provide a literate model, typically the young children who live in them are eager to engage in talking, writing, and reading in the home's dominant language. So early literacy across languages looks quite similar. Some cultures and families place emphasis on oral storytelling in addition to reading and writing. Adults in these homes share stories with their young literacy learners and with each other. Of course, children from families whose dominant language is a language other than English will enter school using the language that works for them in their home environment. A quality program that supports these children's emergence as readers and writers is important.

Linking Knowledge to Practice

1. With a group of colleagues, talk about an early childhood classroom you have seen. Which view of literacy was evidenced in this classroom? Provide specific descriptions of what you observed (like the vignette at the beginning of this chapter) to support your decision of the view evidenced.

2. Read a storybook with a child three years or older. Ask the child to point to where you should begin reading. Does the child know that you will read the print, not the pictures? After you have read the story to the child, ask the child to read the story to you. What form does the child use to read the story (e.g., attending to pictures, forming oral stories; attending to pictures, forming written stories; attending to print)? When you have finished reading the book, select an important word from the story. Can the child tell you the name of the letters in this word? Say a word that rhymes with this word. Now, it's the child's turn. Can the child say another word that rhymes with this word? Say a word that begins with the same sound. Can the child say a word that begins with the same sound? Point to each letter. Can the child say the sound of each letter? Can the child blend the letter sounds to form the word? Compare your findings with those gathered by your colleagues.

3. Observe young children at play in a literacy-enriched dramatic play setting (for example, a home center equipped with paper, pencils, telephone books, television guides, cookbooks, junk mail, cereal boxes, etc.) Watch two or three children while they play in this setting. What do they talk about? What do they write? For example, do they make grocery lists? What does their writing tell you about what they know about the kinds of written language (lists, letter writing, check writing) and forms of written language (scribbles, nonphonetic letter strings, invented spellings)? Do they expect their writing to say something? How do they use the reading materials in the setting? Can they read the cereal boxes? What form of reading do they use to construct meaning from the print? What does your observation tell you about these children's development as readers and writers? If possible, complete this activity with a colleague who watches other children in the play setting. Compare the children's literacy behaviors in the same play setting.

4. Mem Fox (1993, p. 29) describes how she brings buckets of water into her college classroom and plunges naked dolls into the water saying, "If the water is Italian, will this child learn English? . . . If the water is a home without books, will this child be an avid reader? . . . If the water is a classroom in which the teacher bathes this child in good literature by reading aloud everyday, will the child's reading and writing develop in leaps and bounds?" Explain the point Mem Fox is making with this demonstration. Add three similar ideas to her "crassly obvious" points.

chapter 5

Sharing Good Books with Young Children

The four-year-olds in Ms. Jensen's class sit expectantly in a semicircle on the floor, waiting for one of their favorite activities—storytime. They know that every day at this time their teacher will read them an interesting and entertaining story. "Today, I'm going to read you one of my all-time favorites, Where the Wild Things Are *by Maurice Sendak. Look at the strange creatures on the cover! What do you think this story will be about?" After fielding several predictions and comments from the children, Ms. Jensen reads this classic story with expression and a sense of drama. The children listen raptly to each page as Max, the main character, takes a fantastic journey to an island populated with fierce monsters. The children like the way Max manages to take control of the huge beasts (symbols for adults?) and becomes king of the island, but they are also relieved when Max decides to give up his newly found power and return to the comforts of home. When the story is finished, Ms. Jensen invites the children to discuss the parts that they liked best and to tell what they would have done if they were in Max's place. She then shows the children some stick puppets that represent Max, his mother, and some of the monsters. She invites the children to re-enact the story during free-choice activity time.*

As early as 1908, Edmond Huey wrote about children's acquisition of reading and noted that "the key to it all lies in the parent's reading aloud to and with the child" (p. 332). Today, after decades of research on the teaching of reading, we continue to agree with Huey. More recently Marilyn Adams (1990) summarized what many educators believe and research supports: "The single most important activity for building the knowledge and skills eventually required for reading appears to be reading aloud to children" (p. 46). This single act—parents' and teachers' reading aloud to children—has received more research attention than any other aspect of young children's literacy development. Yet, data suggest that only about 45 percent of children below the age of three and 56 percent of three- to five-year-olds are read to daily by their parents (National Education Goals Panel, 1997).

What do we know about the benefits of parents' or other adults' reading aloud to young children? Come peek in on one of Joseph's storybook reading events with his father, Mike (Mowery, 1993). The reading begins with Mike inviting 18-month-old Joseph to pick "one [a book] that Daddy hasn't read in a while"—and Joseph eagerly climbing up into his father's lap. Already *Joseph knows that books are enjoyable;* he even has favorites. Dad waits for Joseph to snuggle in and turn the book so it is ready to be opened. Already *Joseph knows how to hold the book and that it needs to be held in a certain way to open*—skills Marie Clay (1985) would call important concepts about print. Joseph quickly moves beyond the title page; *he knows the story begins on the page with more print*—another concept about print. He looks up at Mike, perhaps signaling "ready." *He knows what his father will do (read), and he knows what he should do (listen)*—though at this age, Mike doesn't always read, and Joseph doesn't always listen. Sometimes Mike says, "What's this?" as he points to a picture in the book. Joseph does his best to label the picture. And Mike says, "Hey, it's a _____! And this is a _____." And Joseph says, "Hey! _____!" *Joseph increases his vocabulary as he labels pictures in books* and as he hears words read aloud in the context of a story.

Today Mike reads a story that is one of Joseph's favorites, but one Mike has grown weary of reading. To hurry the reading along, Mike creates a sentence to accompany the picture on a page. Joseph says, "NO! NO! READ!" and he points to the words on the page. *Already Joseph knows about the stability of words in books; they tell the same story each time. He also seems to know that his father reads the words on the page, not the pictures.* This is an atypical skill for an 18-month-old. As soon as Mike finishes reading the book, Joseph looks up at him and says sweetly, "Read it again, Daddy." *Joseph is learning to love books,* one of the most important gifts his family can give him. The National Education Goals Panel (1997) summarizes:

Early, regular reading to children is one of the most important activities parents can do with their children to improve their readiness for school, serve as their child's first teacher, and instill a love of books and reading. Reading to children familiarizes them with story comprehension such as characters, plot, action, and sequence ("Once upon a time . . . ," ". . . and they lived happily ever after"), and helps them associate oral language with printed text. Most important, reading to children builds their vocabularies and background knowledge about the world. (p. 20)

This chapter is about how to share books with young children. We begin by explaining how teachers can set up inviting library centers in their classrooms and how they can effectively read stories to young children. Finally, we discuss how story-reading sessions can be an ideal context for assessing children's literacy growth.

Before reading this chapter, think about. . .

- the favorite books from your childhood. Did you have one or two favorite books that you liked to have your parents, siblings, or other adults read to you or a favorite book that you liked to read on your own?
- when your teachers read stories to you in school. Does any one teacher stand out as being particularly skilled at storybook reading? If so, why?

Focus Questions

- How can teachers set up a well-designed library center?
- What are the characteristics of effective adult storybook reading?
- What are some of the ways children can respond to and extend the stories that they have been read?
- How can teachers use storybook reading sessions to assess children's literacy development?

BOX 5.1

Definition of Terms

author's study: the teacher reads a set of books by one author and invites children to discuss and compare the books.

creative dramatics: children act out a story with no printed script or memorized lines.

performance sampling: teachers set up situations that enable them to gather information about children's literacy abilities.

shared book experience: the teacher reads a big book with enlarged print and encourages the children to read along on parts that they can remember or predict.

Making Books Accessible to Young Children

The careful selection of quality picture storybooks can play an important role in young children's development. According to Charlotte Huck, Susan Hepler, Janet Hickman, and Barbara Kiefer, quality picture storybooks can

> enlarge children's lives, stretch their imaginations, and enhance their living. The phenomenal growth of beautiful picture books for children of all ages is an outstanding accomplishment of the past fifty years of publishing. Children do not always recognize the beauty of these books, but early impressions do exert an influence on the development of permanent tastes for children growing up. (p. 250)

To help teachers with the task of making appropriate selections of quality books, we suggest two resources. First, we suggest readers consider obtaining a copy of Charlotte Huck, Susan Hepler, Janet Hickman, and Barbara Kiefer's (1997) book, *Children's Literature in the Elementary School.* Though the title says "elementary school," the book is a rich resource for teachers of children of all ages. It alerts readers to titles, and titles, and titles of outstanding literature, noting the likely age of children who would enjoy the book most. At the end of each chapter, readers will find pages and pages of recommended titles. The latest edition, the sixth edition, of this book, reproduces many pages from quality picture books and picture storybooks for teachers' examination. This book is a *must* for every teachers' professional library.

There is a second book Billie Enz believes we should encourage readers to discover. This is Frances S. Goforth's (1998) *Literature and the Learner.* Billie describes this book as a "fabulous resource."

To further support readers' efforts to begin the task of selecting quality literature for use with young children, we provide a list of several outstanding children's literature books in Appendix A. Embedded in this list, readers will find suggestions made by Sarah Hudelson of books especially for Hispanic young children.

Certainly, teachers should share tales representative of various cultures. Many resources are available to locate high quality multicultural literature. For example, the National Association for the Education of Young Children (1509 16th Street, N.W., Washington, D.C. 20036-1426) publishes a brochure, *African American Literature for Young Children,* developed by the National Black Child Development Institute. The most up-to-date information on multicultural

Eighteen-month-old Lauren reads her favorite book to her favorite bear.

books can be found on the World Wide Web. A variety of sites can be found using the descriptors "multicultural children's literature" with any of the major search engines (Yahoo, Lycos, Excite, Alta Vista, etc.). For example, a recent search located the site, POWERFUL ASIAN AMERICAN IMAGES REVEALED IN PICTURE BOOKS compiled by Kay Vandergrift (http://www.scils.rutgers.edu/special/kay/asian.html) and a number of similar sites with lists of books about children from different cultures.

Once appropriate selections have been made, the teacher's challenge is to organize the books to make them accessible to their students—to encourage them to voluntarily read, read, read.

Classroom Library Centers

A key feature of a classroom for young children is a well-stocked, well-designed library center. Classroom libraries promote independent reading by providing children with easy access to books and a comfortable place for browsing and reading. Children have been found to read more books in classrooms with libraries than in ones without libraries (Morrow & Weinstein, 1982). As Stephen Krashen (1987, p. 2) has pointed out, this finding supports "the common-sense view that children read more when there are more books around."

However, the mere presence of a classroom library is not enough to ensure heavy use by young children. The library must contain an ample supply of appropriate and interesting books for children to read. Design features are also important. Lesley Morrow and Carol Weinstein (1982) found that children did not choose to use "barren and uninviting" library corners during free-play time. However, when the design features of centers were improved, children's library usage increased dramatically.

Unfortunately, classroom libraries are not a universal feature of early childhood classrooms, and many of the libraries that do exist are not well-designed. Jann Fractor, Marjorie Woodruff, Miriam Martinez, and Bill Teale (1993) collected data on the libraries in 89 kindergarten through second-grade classrooms and found that only 58 percent of classes had a library center. Only 8 percent of these classroom libraries were rated as being good or excellent (having large numbers of books, partitions, ample space, comfortable furnishings, book covers rather than book spines facing out on book shelves, and book-related displays and props). The vast majority of libraries were rated as basic, containing small numbers of books and few desirable design characteristics. These authors collected data in less formal ways on the libraries in day care centers in Delaware and in Arizona and found that many day care center classrooms did not contain a library center—that is, no space was cordoned off from the classroom's wide expanse to cue children that this was the area for reading books. Sadly, many classrooms visited contained very few books. Classroom libraries definitely need to be given a higher priority in many classrooms.

BOOKS. In order to attract and hold children's interest, a classroom library must be stocked with lots of good books to read. Experts recommend that classroom libraries contain 5 to 8 books per child (Fractor et al., 1993; Morrow, 1993). According to these guidelines, a class of 20 children would require 100 to 160 books. These books should be divided into a core collection and one or more revolving collections. The core collection should be made up of high-quality literature that remains constant and available all year. These should be books that appeal to most of the children in class and that most children will enjoy reading on more than one occasion. Lesley Morrow (1993) also recommends that the books be color-coded according to type. For example, all animal books could be identified with blue dots on their spines so they can be clustered together on a shelf marked *Animals*. Each category would be distinguished by a different color. Morrow suggests that color coding "introduces children to the idea that books in libraries are organized so as to be readily accessible" (p. 135).

Revolving collections change every few weeks to match children's current interests and topics being studied in class. For example, if several children become hooked on an author, such as Tomie de Paola or Maurice Sendak, collections of the author's books could be brought into the library to capitalize on this interest. If the class were studying seeds and plants, then picture storybooks and informational books relating to these topics could be added. When student

A well-designed library center invites children to read books.

interest shifts to a new author or when a new topic is under investigation, the old sets of revolving books are replaced with new ones.

Quality and variety are also of utmost importance in selecting books for the classroom library (Fractor et al., 1993). In order to motivate voluntary reading and to instill positive attitudes toward written texts, books must catch children's attention, hold their interest, and captivate their imaginations. Only high-quality literature will achieve these goals.

Physical Characteristics. A number of physical features have been identified that make libraries attractive to children and that promote book reading (Morrow, 1983, 1993):

- *Partitions*—Bookshelves, screens, large plants, or other barriers set the library center apart from the rest of the classroom. This gives children a sense of privacy and provides a cozy, quiet setting for reading.
- *Ample space*—There should be room enough for at least five or six children to use the library at one time.
- *Comfortable furnishings*—The more comfortable the library area, the more likely it is that children will use it. Soft carpeting, chairs, old sofas, bean bags, and a rocking chair all help create a comfortable atmosphere for reading.
- *Open-faced and traditional shelves*—Traditional shelves display books with their spine out, whereas open-faced shelves display the covers of books. Open-faced shelves are very effective in attracting children's attention to specific books. Researchers have found that, when both types of shelves are used, kindergartners chose more than 90 percent of their books from the open-faced displays (Fractor et al., 1993). Traditional shelves are also useful because they can hold many more books than open-faced shelves. Many teachers rotate books between traditional and open-faced shelves, advertising different books each week.
- *Book-related displays and props*—Posters (available from such sources as the Children's Book Council, 67 Irving Place, New York, NY 1003; the American Library Association, 50 East Huron Street, Chicago, Illinois 60611; and the International Reading Association, 800 Barksdale Road, Newark, Delaware 19711), puppets, flannel boards with cutout figures of

story characters, and stuffed animals encourage children to engage in emergent reading and to act out favorite stories. Stuffed animals also are useful as listeners or babies for children to read to.

■ *Label the center*—Like cordoning off the area from the classroom space, symbolic cues help define the space and identify appropriate activities for young children. Using both print, "Library Corner," and symbols associated with the library—book jackets, a photograph of a child looking at a book—helps even the youngest child read the label for the corner.

■ *Writing center*—Some teachers like to place a writing center near the library corner. This accessibility seems to prompt young children to make illustrations and write in their personal script or dictate a sentence to an adult about the stories they are reading. A description of one young writer's behaviors illustrates how children might use the library corner to support their efforts in such a writing center. Allen, a kindergartner, sits looking into space, thinking, in the writing center. He collects a Post-it® Note and writes "dot toht" ("Don't touch"), attaches it to his blank paper, and wanders into the library corner. Shortly, he returns, sits, and instantly begins writing a story about a caterpillar, with one word per line. His teacher surmised that while in the library corner Allen was engaging in prewriting, thinking about his topic and using Eric Carle's (1969) *The Very Hungry Caterpillar* as his writing model (see Figure 5.1).

Remember, the better designed the library corner, the more use children will make of it—that is, more children will choose to participate in book reading and literature-related activities during free-choice periods. Therefore, a classroom library corner that is voluntarily used by few children is suspected to be a poorly designed center. What might an enticing library corner look like? We provide a drawing of a possible library corner for an early childhood classroom in Figure 5.2.

Figure 5.1

Allen's story

Figure 5.2 *Library Center*

Classroom Lending Library

We have already said it once: Reading aloud to young children is the single most important activity for building the knowledge and skills eventually required for their success in learning to read. Therefore, teachers regularly recommend that parents read to their young children. Unfortunately, many parents face great financial hardships and cannot provide high-quality reading materials in their homes (Becker & Epstein, 1982). While many communities house excellent public libraries with quality children's literature sections, these same parents often find it difficult to carve out time from their busy schedules to visit the library; working two or three jobs to meet pressing financial needs understandably takes priority. Therefore, for parents to fulfill their roles as partners in literacy programs, teachers must work with these families to offer easy access to books (Brock & Dodd, 1994).

Many early childhood teachers have attempted to get quality literature into the homes of all their young students through the creation of classroom lending libraries. These libraries allow children to check out a book every day, thus ensuring that all parents have an opportunity to read to their children frequently.

A first step in the creation of a lending library is the acquisition of books. Because the children will exchange a book for a different book each week, a teacher in a 12-month day care program with 20 children in her classroom would need at least 52 books in the classroom lending library. For a new teacher, that is a lot of books, especially when that new teacher is also building the classroom library. It's important for readers to begin *now* to use the tips for acquiring inexpensive children's books suggested in Trade Secrets 5.1.

 Trade Secrets 5.1

How I Developed My Kindergarten Book Backpack Program

Lynn E. Cohen

What are book backpacks?

Backpacks come in different sizes, shapes, and colors and usually contain a child's personal belongings. Backpacks in my classroom contain books that provide children with interesting language and present experiences that have a connection to their lives.

Quality children's literature

Inside the backpacks are five to seven books centered on a theme, author, or genre (poetry, nonfiction, memoirs, and so on). The outside of each backpack is labeled with an oaktag sign. The titles are selected on the basis of thematic units of study in my classroom and the interests of the children. For example, there is a folktales and fairy tales backpack, a post office backpack, a grandparents backpack, an ecology backpack, a birthday backpack, and a travel backpack. One or two books are hardcover, and the rest are paperbacks.

Favorite authors also make a good collection of books for backpacks. Our Parent Teacher Association sponsors cultural arts programs, and occasionally it invites a children's author to make a school visitation. After such a visit, I try to capitalize on the enthusiasm by organizing a backpack of the author's books. And by watching the children's responses while I read aloud books by such authors as Bill Martin, Jr., and Eric Carle, I know that these are authors that must be shared with parents.

A book for parents, too

Including parenting books in the backpacks educates my parents about my philosophy on developmentally appropriate practice. I select topics on early literacy, child development, play, antibias curriculum, discipline, or organizing birthday parties. Sometimes I find a parent book that correlates to a theme.

A response notebook

A composition book is included in each backpack. The children are encouraged to write about the books in the backpack or any favorite book read to them. Writing takes on a variety of different styles, depending on the developmental level of the kindergartners. Some children draw pictures of their favorite characters or scenes; some dictate their reactions for adults to write; and others use approximations and write a few invented words.

I read the comments each week when the backpacks are returned. The first year I did the program, I read every backpack's response notebook weekly. This was time-consuming and tedious. Now I read only two or three notebooks a week. A checklist is kept to ensure that I read every class response notebook within a month.

An inventory card

An inventory card is included as a reminder for parents to return the entire contents of the backpack. A 4 × 6-inch index card lists the title of the backpack, the parent book, and the titles and authors of the five to seven pieces of children's literature.

How can I fund a book backpack program?

I began with five backpacks in 1990, and this year I have assembled 20, one for each of the children in my classroom. A few years ago my school offered teachers minigrants for interesting classroom projects that would enhance the curriculum. I wrote a proposal and was awarded $200 for my book backpack project. I purchased five backpacks and text sets—literature having a common theme—of five books for each bag. The first backpack sets were travel, monster, water, folktales and fairy tales, and health.

To put together 20 book backpacks, I creatively turned to outside resources. I frequented garage and tag sales over summer vacation, asked local libraries for used children's books that they were discarding, and carefully saved all my book-club bonus points. Money isn't expended anymore on backpacks because I have established a recycling system. When my five-year-olds return from summer vacation and enter the first grade, they turn in their kindergarten backpacks.

Although I am a public school kindergarten teacher, teachers in private schools, preschools, child care centers, and Head Start programs could do this. In my building, a first-grade and third-grade teacher are initiating this program, too.

How do I manage the book backpack program?

At the beginning of November a letter is sent home that describes the program. Book backpacks go home with the children every Thursday and are returned the following Thursday, provided the previous week's books were returned. Sending backpacks home on Thursdays gives working families ample time to read with their children.

(continued on next page)

Trade Secrets 5.1 *(continued)*

Letter to Parents about the Book Backpacks

Dear Parents,

Every week you and your child will have an opportunity to share a traveling backpack of books. The traveling backpacks will *usually* go home every Thursday. Each backpack includes five to seven children's books on a theme, a book for parents, a response notebook, and an inventory card that lists the contents of the backpack.

The children's books can bring joy to the entire family. After reading and discussing the books with your child, invite him or her to record impressions and responses in the notebook titled "Comments about Books." The format for written communication in the notebook can be dictation to you, pictures, or inventive spelling—it doesn't matter. You can keep the parenting book as long as necessary; just let me know in the notebook.

This program is designed to foster literacy through reading and writing. Please be sure to check all backpacks against the inventory cards to ensure that everything is being returned. Lastly, please return the backpack no later than Thursday, as other children are eager for their turn.

Happy reading!

On the computer, I made a list with columns for each child's name, the name of the backpack, and the date the backpack is returned. I keep about 30 copies of this form.

	Computer Checklist	
Child	**Backpack**	**Returned?**
Joshua		
Adam		
Neil		
Juleen		
Jessica		
Melanie		
Esther		
Brian		
Andrew		
Yael		
Maxwell		
Michelle		
Sara		
Lauren		
Zachary		
Jake		
Brittany		
Shuaib		

Reprinted by permission of Lynn E. Cohen from *Young Children, 52,* January 1997, pp. 69–71. Lynn E. Cohen is a kindergarten teacher in Great Neck, New York, and an early childhood curriculum consultant. She has written six teacher trade books as well as parenting and assessment articles for *Early Childhood Today.*

(continued on next page)

Trade Secrets 5.1 *(continued)*

During kindergarten orientation, I solicit parent volunteers to assist in my classroom. One assignment is book backpack librarian. The parent volunteer spends an hour a week checking book backpack inventory cards against the contents. If a book is missing, the backpack librarian alerts me, and I send home a form letters with the child. The success rate for returned items is 99 percent.

Reminder to Parents

Dear _____,

After checking through the backpack your child returned, I found that _____

_____ was missing. Please look around your home and return the book as

soon as possible.

Sincerely,

Before the children go home on Thursday, I spread all the book backpacks out in our meeting area. Together we read the oaktag labels, and children select new topics to enjoy with their families. I write the new topics on the computer checklist.

Through the book backpacks, teachers and parents truly share the responsibility and the joy of nurturing the development of children's literacy learning. The classroom library is brought into the home for a shared book opportunity each evening.

Reading aloud does much more than promote readiness for future reading instruction. It is an integral part of the process of learning to make sense of print. Parents who read to their children not only produce children who can read but also children who have acquired a strong disposition for reading and learning.

References

Baskwill, J. (1989). *Parents and teacher: Partners in learning.* New York: Scholastic.

Butler, D., & Clay, M. (1990). *Reading begins at home.* Portsmouth, NH: Heinemann.

Schickendanz, J. A. (1986). *More than the ABCs: The early stages of reading and writing.* Washington, DC: NAEYC.

Strickland, D., & Morrow, L. (1990). Family literacy: Sharing good books. *The Reading Teacher, 43*(7), 518–519.

Vukelich, C. (1984). Parents' role in the reading process: A review of practical suggestions and ways to communicate with parents. *The Reading Teacher, 37*(6), 472–477.

For Further Reading

Brock, D., & Dodd, E. (1994). A family lending library: Promoting early literacy development. *Young Children, 49*(3), 16–21.

Conlon, A. (1992). Giving Mrs. Jones a hand: Making group storytime more pleasurable and meaningful for young children. *Young Children, 47*(3), 14–18.

Lancy, D., & Nattiu, A. (1992). Parents as volunteers: Storybook readers/listeners. *Childhood Education, 68*(4), 208–212.

Strickland, D. S., & Morrow, L. M. (1989). *Emerging literacy: Young children learn to read and write.* Newark, DE: International Reading Association.

Taylor, D. (1983). *Family literacy.* Portsmouth, NH: Heinemann.

Taylor, D., & Strickland, D. (1986). *Family storybook reading.* Portsmouth, NH: Heinemann.

Trelease, J. (1989). *The new read aloud handbook.* New York: Viking Penguin.

The rules that accompany the classroom lending library are simple. A child may borrow one book each week. When the book is returned, the child may check out another book. Teacher Carolyn Lingo puts a book and an activity appropriate for the book in a bag for her young learners. For example, one of her book bags is built around *Mouse Paint* (Walsh, 1989). The materials in the book bag include small vials of paint, a smock, newspaper to cover the table, a paint brush, and mixing cups. First the parent and child read the book together. Then they pretend they are the mice in the book; they are to mix the yellow, blue, and red paints, just like the mice in the book did. What happens? In Trade Secrets 5.1, Lynn Cohen describes how she operates the classroom lending library in her classroom.

Sharing Literature with Children

Teachers can share literature with young children in several ways: by reading stories aloud, by engaging children in shared reading, and by encouraging them to respond to literature in a variety of ways.

Effective Story-Reading Techniques

The verbal interaction between adult and child that occurs during story readings has a major influence on children's literacy development (Cochran-Smith, 1984). Much of the research on effective story-reading techniques reports on the interactions between a parent and his or her child during story reading. We have extrapolated the findings of this research to teacher–children story-reading interactions.

Some of this research discusses the affective benefits of story reading. For example, researchers like David Yaden, Laura Smolkin, and Laurie MacGillivray (1993, p. 60) describe story reading as a pleasurable activity. "Children learn very quickly that bringing a book to a parent or caregiver will begin a certain predictable and, for the most part, pleasurable activity." Bill Teale (1986b) describes the exchange as a dance, a choreographed interaction between adult and child reader (sometimes the adult and sometimes the child) and listener (sometimes the adult and sometimes the child).

ADULT BEHAVIORS WHILE READING. The majority of researchers have concentrated on the human interactions during story reading. From this research, we learn about turn-taking in story reading. Through story reading, very young children are guided into the turn-taking pattern inherent in all conversation: the adult (in this research the adult is usually a parent) talks, then the child talks, then the adult talks, and so forth.

It is within this verbal exchange that the dyad (parent and child) engages in its most significant negotiations: negotiating the meaning of the story. Obviously the adults' understanding exceeds the child's understanding of the text. Through scaffolding, the adult gently moves the child toward the adult's understanding of the text. That is, the adult questions the child about the text's meaning. The child replies, and this reply gives the adult a cue. Based on the child's response, the adult adjusts the kind of support (the scaffold) provided. To aid the child's construction of the meaning, the adult behaves in three ways: (1) as a co-respondent who shares experiences and relates the reading to personal experiences, (2) as an informer who provides information, and (3) as a monitor who questions and sets expectations for the reading session (Roser & Martinez, 1985).

Adults play these roles differently depending on the child's response and age. (See Figure 5.3 for a summary of how adults read to children of different ages.) With a baby or toddler (12 months or younger), the adult tends to do most of the talking. Mostly adults label the pictures. "Look, Licky, a train! Yup, that's a train—choo, choo!" Typically adults point as they label.

Between the ages of 12 and 15 months, adults tend to ask the child rhetorical questions (e.g., DeLoache, 1984): "And that's a kite. Isn't that a kite, Josh?" The questions function to reinforce the picture's label; the adult does not really expect the child to answer. The adult's playing of both roles, asking the question and giving the answer, provides the toddler with experience in the question–answer cycle before the child is required to participate verbally in the exchange.

Beginning around 15 months, the adult's expectations shift, and the child is expected to be a more active participant in the story reading. As the child acquires more facility with language, the adult expects the child to answer more of the questions posed. First, the adult asks the child to provide the label for the picture. The adult says things like "Look!" or "What's that?" or "It's a what?" If the child hesitates, the adult intervenes and provides the answer. When the child seems to be correct (Joseph says, "Pithee" in response to his father's query),

Figure 5.3 *Typical adult behaviors when reading aloud to children of different ages*

12 Months or Younger	12 to 15 Months	15 to 36 Months	36 Months and Older
Adult does most of the talking.	Adult asks rhetorical questions ("Is that a bus, Kareen?")	Adult asks child to label the object ("What's that?")	Adult expects child to attend and listen to larger chunks of the text.
Adult labels the pictures ("Look, a train!") and answers ("Yup, it's a train.")	Adults answer question ("Yup! It's a bus allright!")	If the child does not answer, the adult provides the answer ("It's a peach.") If the child provides the correct answer, the adult repeats and reinforces the child's correct answer ("Peach! Yeah! This is a peach.")	Adult questions child about characters and story meaning ("Who brought the goodies to her grandmother?" "What did the wolf first say when he saw Little Red Riding Hood?") Most questions are literal (the answers are in the text). Adult points to object.
Adult points to object.		As the child's competence increases, the adult asks for more ("What color is that peach?" "When do you eat a peach?")	Adult encourages child to read a section of book with support ("What did the Gingerbread Man say to the Little Old Woman?" "Run, run, as fast as you can. . . .")

the adult typically repeats the label or positively reinforces the toddler's response (Joseph's father says, "Yeah. These are peaches."). When the child shows competence at this task, the adult ups the ante, requesting perhaps a description, like asking for information about the color.

Researchers have discovered that this story-reading sequence (adult question, child response, adult feedback) is just like the typical interaction sequence between teacher and student in many classrooms (Mehan, 1979). Hence, these story readings also begin children's socialization into the response pattern typical of many classrooms.

Researchers like Marilyn Cochran-Smith (1984) and Denny Taylor and Dorothy Strickland (1986) discovered that adults from all socioeconomic levels do the same thing when they introduce a child to a new concept in a book. They try to make the concept meaningful for the child by linking the text to the child's personal experiences. For example, Ann Mowery (1993, p. 46) describes how, when young Joseph and his father read *Wish for a Fish,* Joseph's father made numerous text-to-life connections: "That sure looks like where we go, doesn't it?" "See, that's a can of worms just like what we fish with." "That's a bobber just like ours." "That boy is waiting quietly for a fish. You usually play with the worms and throw rocks, don't you?"

When children approach about three years of age, adult story readers tend to increase the complexity of the questions. Now they question the child about the characters and the story meaning. Before, the adult asked questions to involve the child in the book reading; now the adult expects the child to remain quiet and listen for a much longer period of time. Sometimes the adult and child read the book together. That is, the adult reads a few lines, pauses so the child can contribute a phrase, and then reads on. Of course, this only happens with books the child has heard several times; often these books are predictable books with repeated phrases.

CHILD BEHAVIORS DURING READING.   What do children do when they are being read to by a caring adult? Several researchers (e.g., Baghban, 1984; Morrow, 1989) have studied young children's behavior, often their own children, during adult–child readings. These researchers tell us that even infants focus on the book. They make sounds even before they are speaking, as if they are imitating the reader's voice. They slap at the picture in the book. A little older child with some language facility begins to ask questions about the pictures. They play the "What's that?" game, pointing and asking "What's dat? What's dat? What's dat?" almost without pausing for an answer.

David Yaden, Laura Smolkin, and Mark Conlon's (1989) longitudinal case studies of preschoolers, age three to five, revealed an interesting trend in the questions children ask during reading aloud at home. Initially, most of the children's questions were about the pictures in books. Over time, there was an increase in the number of questions about word meanings and the story being read, and a decrease in picture-related questions. The investigators concluded that "it is possible that after 4 years of age, children begin to pay more attention to the story itself and to the written displays than they do at age 3" (p. 208).

CULTURAL VARIATIONS IN STORY READING.   Do children from nonmainstream families have similar early childhood home reading experiences? Shirley Brice Heath's answer to this question is no. In her book *Way with Words* (1983), Heath provides a rich description of the literacy experiences of working-class African American, working-class Caucasian, and mainstream families in the Piedmont area of the Carolinas. From her research, Heath learned that the parents from mainstream families read to their children well into elementary school; use a wide variety of complex questioning strategies to develop their children's understanding of story, plot event sequence, and characterization; and look for ways to connect the text information to their children's experiences. Parents from the working-class Caucasian families also read to their children, but what they do while they read is different. They stress the sequence of the stories and ask children literal meaning questions ("What did the little boy do then?" "What's the hen's name?"). Further, they make few attempts to connect the events described in the books to their children's experiences. Finally, Heath learned that the African American families tell lots of stories, but reading is strictly for functional purposes. These families read forms, recipes, and the newspaper. They tend not to read books to their children. Of course, Heath's work can not be generalized to all mainstream, Caucasian working class, or African American families. As Teale (1987) notes, there is a great deal of variation among and within social and cultural groups. Teachers need to learn from their students' parents about the experiences their young children have had with books.

We believe that children who have had experiences with books and have experienced dialogic interactions with adults with books are advantaged over children who have no experiences with books and whose parents or early teachers have not shared books with them. Therefore, we strongly encourage teachers and parents of young children to read, read, read to their children.

CLASSROOM READ-ALOUDS.   When a parent and a child read together, they cuddle. Like 18-month-old Joseph, whom readers met at the beginning of this chapter, the child typically sits in the parent's lap or snuggles under the parent's arm. Many parents establish a bedtime reading ritual, cuddling with the child for a quiet reading time before the child goes to bed. Parents report enjoying this ritual as much as the child, and it establishes a mindset that encourages the child to read before going to sleep when the child can read independently. Teachers of the very youngest children, infants, and toddlers should follow parents' lead and apply what is known about how parents read to infants and toddlers to their reading to their young students. The low teacher–child ratio recommended by the National Association for the Education of Young Children for infant (one adult to one infant) and toddler (one adult to four toddlers) programs helps permit this kind of adult–child interaction—though with toddlers, such one-on-one reading together requires some careful arranging (Bredekamp, 1989). We recommend that teachers create a daily reading ritual, perhaps just before naptime. Some day care centers connect with church groups or nearby residential facilities for elderly citizens for the explicit purpose of adults coming to the center just before naptime to read to the children. Now, like at home, every child can have a lap, a cuddle, and a "grandparent" all alone.

We are concerned when we hear infant and toddler teachers say, "Read to the kids in my classroom? You must be kidding!" We are even more concerned when we read that this response about reading to young children is not uncommon (Kupetz & Green, 1997). Barbara Kupetz and Elise Green describe the benefits of reading to infants and toddlers:

- It helps infants' eyes to focus.
- It increases infants' recognition of objects and their ability to label objects and understand basic concepts.
- It enhances infants' listening skills.
- It stimulates their imaginations.
- It builds infants' sensory awareness.
- It extends infants' experiences.
- It establishes the physical closeness so critical to young children's emotional and social development.

These two former early childhood teachers acknowledge that it takes organization and working together to structure the infants' and toddlers' day to include story reading. "Reading to infants and toddlers is certainly not a large-group activity. It can effectively occur only in very small groups or in one-to-one pairing" (p. 23). Like us, they recommend the center attempt to make appropriate extra-adult arrangements in order to ensure the inclusion of this important activity in infants' and toddlers' days.

The older the young child, the larger the permitted-by-law number of children in the group. The typical kindergarten class, for example, is often one teacher and 20 (unfortunately, sometimes even more) children. Teachers of these children are challenged to keep read-alouds enjoyable, pleasurable experiences. Of course, selecting age- and interest-appropriate books is important. Read-aloud experiences are one means to ensure that high-quality literature is accessible to all students, something that is especially important for children who have had few storybook experiences outside school. The *how* of reading is also important. Now there are too many children for everyone to cuddle next to the adult reader. Yet physical comfort is important. Having a special carpeted area for reading to the group is important. Often this area is next to the library center. Nancy asks her young learners to sit in a semicircle. Patty asks her young learners to sit on the X marks she has made using masking tape on the carpet. Lolita asks her three-year-olds to sit or lie wherever they like in the small carpeted area—as long as they can see the pictures. Each day a different child gets to snuggle with her. In each of these classrooms, the teacher sits at the edge of the circle or the carpet on a low chair, holding the picture book about at the children's eye level. The chair the teacher sits in to read from is a special chair, used both for teacher read-alouds and for the children to read their own writing to the class. Each teacher calls this chair *the author's chair*. Nancy, Patty, and Lolita have mastered reading from the side. Thus the children can see the illustrations while the teacher reads.

These teachers know the story they are about to read. They have carefully selected it and read it through, practicing how it will sound when read aloud, in advance. They know how to read it with excitement in their voices. They are careful not to overdramatize, yet they use pitch and stress to make the printed dialogue sound like conversation. They show that they enjoy the story. Each of these teachers recalls how, in her teacher preparation program, she was required to videotape or audiotape herself reading to a group of children. Then she complained; now she realizes how important it is to continually reflect on one's practice. After listening to a tape of her story reading, Nancy, a kindergarten teacher, says, "We all think we are fine readers. But just listen to me! I love this story, but you'd never know it from the way I sound! My intonation is the same on every page. Also, I *meant* to tell them the name of the author and the illustrator. Oops!" There is value in listening to yourself read—even for veteran teachers.

Nancy hints at how to effectively do a read-aloud with young children. The following sequence describes the typical read-aloud strategies recommended by several groups of researchers based on their survey of research studies, reading methods textbooks, and books and articles about reading to children (Teale & Martinez, 1988).

- *Read to students every day*—Research done during the 1980s indicated that only 50 to 60 percent of teachers read aloud to their classes on a regular basis (Lapointe, 1986; Morrow, 1982). A more recent study by James Hoffman, Nancy Roser, and Jennifer Battle (1993) presents a much more positive picture. These researchers found that, on a given day, 84 percent of kindergarten teachers read to their classes.

■ *Select high-quality literature*—A key element to a successful read-aloud experience is the book that is being read. Try to find books that will appeal to the children's interest, evoke humor, stimulate critical thinking, stretch the imagination, and so on. While a good story is always effective, also try to include informational books and poetry written for young audiences. A great source for locating good read-aloud books is Jim Trelease's (1989) *The New Read-Aloud Handbook.*

■ *Show the children the cover of the book*—Draw the children's attention to the illustration on the cover ("Look at the illustration on this book!"). Tell the children the title of the book, the author's name, and the illustrator's name. ("The title of this book is . . . The author is . . . The illustrator is . . . ") Draw your finger under the title, the author's name, and the illustrator's name as you read each. Remind the children that the title, author's name, and illustrator's name are always on the front of the book. Remember that these are new concepts for young children.

■ *Ask the children for their predictions about the story*—("What do you think this story might be about?") Take a few of the children's predictions about the story's content. ("Let's read to see what this story is about.")

■ *Or provide a brief introduction to the story*—This can be accomplished in a number of ways. You might provide background information about the story ("This story is going to be about . . . "), connect the topic or theme of the story to the children's own experiences, draw the children's attention to familiar books written by the same author, draw the children's attention to the book's central characters, clarify vocabulary that might be outside the children's realm of experiences, and so on. Keep the introduction brief so there is ample reading time.

■ *Identify where and what you will read*—Two important concepts about print for young children to learn is that readers read the print on the pages, not the pictures, and where readers begin reading. Begin read-alouds by identifying where you will start reading and what you will read. Repeating this information often ("Now, I'll begin reading the words right here") weaves this important information into the read-aloud. Be sure to point to the first word on the page as you say where you will begin. Eventually the children will be able to tell you where to begin reading. After many exposures to this important concept, you might playfully ask, "Am I going to read the words or the pictures in this book?" "Where should I begin reading?"

■ *Read with expression and at a moderate rate*—When teachers read with enthusiasm and vary their voices to fit different characters and the ongoing dialogue, the story comes alive for children. It is also important to avoid reading too quickly. Jim Trelease (1989), a leading authority, claims that this is the most common mistake that adults make when reading aloud. He recommends reading slowly enough that children can enjoy the pictures and can make mental images of the story.

■ *Consider reading some stories interactively; that is, encourage children to interact verbally with the text, peers, and the teacher during the book reading*—Some teachers pose questions throughout their book reading to enhance the children's meaning construction and to show how one makes sense of text (Barrentine, 1996). They encourage their students to offer spontaneous comments, to ask questions, and to respond to others' questions, to notice the forms and functions of print features (words, punctuation, letters) as the story unfolds. They use the during-reading book discussions to help children understand what to think about as a story unfolds. With a group of colleagues, Jerry Harste (1984) identified the range of information that teachers can demonstrate to children through interactive read-alouds, including the relationship between page turning and moving through the story, how readers read, how readers self-correct while reading and monitor their construction of meaning, and why readers change voice inflections while reading. According to Brian Cambourne (1988), children learn through active engagement with literacy events, not through passive absorption. Interactive storybook reading provides an opportunity for such needed engagement. However, all this talk while reading might interfere with children's ability to appreciate the literature. Perhaps some books lend themselves better to interactive storybook reading experiences while others should be enjoyed and discussed after the reading.

■ *Read favorite books repeatedly*—Not every book you read has to be a book the children have never heard before. In fact, repeated readings of books can lead to enhanced comprehension and better postreading discussions (Martinez & Roser, 1985; Morrow, 1988). In addition, reading a book three or more times increases the likelihood that young children will attempt to select that book during free-choice time and will try to re-enact or read it on their own (Martinez & Teale, 1988). Of course, the benefits of repeated reading need to be balanced against the need to expose children to a wide variety of literature.

■ *Allow time for discussion after reading*—Good books arouse a variety of thoughts and emotions in children. Be sure to follow each read-aloud session with a good conversation, with questions and comments ("What part of the story did you like best?" "How did you feel when . . . ?" "Has anything like that ever happened to you?" "Who has something to say about the story?"). This type of open-ended question invites children to share their responses to the book that was read. After listening to a book read aloud, children want to talk about the events, characters, parts they liked best, and so forth. As children and teacher talk about the book together, they construct a richer, deeper understanding of the book. Reader response theorists, like Louise Rosenblatt (1978), provide theoretical support for the importance of teachers' talking with children about shared books. Rosenblatt believes that as children listen to stories, they are constructing meaning based on the previous experiences they bring to the text and their purpose for listening. Listeners focus on two kinds of information: remembering information (e.g., the story's main idea, the three main events) and connecting through personal images, ideas, feelings, and questions evoked while listening. Through good conversations about books, teachers and children can explore ideas of personal importance and, thus, can analyze and interpret the book. Teachers want to work toward being a member of the book circle, one of the discussants who takes turns talking with the children. When the teacher does ask questions, they are open-ended questions that encourage children to interpret, extend, and connect with the text. In Trade Secret 5.2, Cory Hansen describes how Chris Boyd engages her kindergartners in discussions that help them jointly construct deeper meaning for the stories they are read. Chris' strategy lays the foundation for literature study groups in the primary grades.

When teachers follow the preceding guidelines, they can help ensure that their story reading has the maximum impact on children's literacy learning.

SHARED BOOK EXPERIENCE.   Teachers usually read picture books to their classes by holding the books so that the children can see the illustrations, pausing occasionally to elicit students' reactions to the stories or to ask story-related questions. This traditional whole-class read-aloud experience differs from parent–child storybook reading interactions in a very important way: Most children can see only the pictures, not the print. To remedy this situation, Holdaway (1979) devised the shared book experience, a strategy that uses enlarged print, repeated readings, and increased pupil participation to make whole-class storybook reading sessions similar to parent–child reading experiences. Today, the shared book experience has become an important component of a quality early literacy program.

To use this strategy, the teacher first needs to select an appropriate book. Andrea Butler and Jan Turbill (1984) recommend stories that have (1) an absorbing, predictable story line; (2) a predictable structure, containing elements of rhyme, rhythm, and repetition; and (3) illustrations that enhance and support the text. These features make it easy for children to predict what is upcoming in the story and to read along with the teacher.

Once a book has been selected, an enlarged copy needs to be obtained. This can be done in several ways. The teacher can (1) rewrite the story on chart paper, using 1-inch or 2-inch tall letters and hand-drawn illustrations; (2) make color transparencies of the pages from the original picture book and use an overhead projector; or (3) acquire a commercially published big book (about 24 × 26 inches) version of the story. Commercial big books are becoming increasingly available. Scholastic and McGraw-Hill/The Wright Group, for example, publish

Trade Secrets 5.2

Getting Children to Talk about a Story

Cory Hansen and Chris Boyd

I had the opportunity to observe in Chris Boyd's kindergarten classroom on the day she read De Paola's (1975) *Strega Nona,* a wonderful story of what happens when Big Anthony ignores good advice and overruns his town with pasta from the magic pasta pot. As Chris was reading the book, the carpet in front of her was scattered with children. Some were lying flat on their backs looking up at the ceiling; others were on their sides, only a finger wiggle away from good friends; and others were sitting up, cross-legged, their eyes never leaving the pages of the story. The last page of the story is wordless. Big Anthony's expression tells it all as he sits outside the house, his stomach swollen almost to bursting, with one last strand of pasta lingering on his fork. The children burst into laughter, and as Chris motioned with her index finger, they regrouped, calling out, "I think . . . , I think . . . " on their way to forming a large circle. And for the next half hour, that was what was talked about: what the children thought about the story.

The conversation began with what the children thought was going to happen and comparing it to what really did. Chris asked the children why they thought the way they did, and then the serious business of making meaning together began. She gradually lowered herself down from the reading chair and joined in as one participant in this group talk about story: the one with a copy of the text and the one writing comments into a notebook. The kindergartners called on her only when they needed someone to reread part of the text to settle disputes. Chris did not enter the conversation unless the children lost sight of her one rule for talk about story or unless an opportunity to seize a literary teachable moment emerged.

After the group examined Big Anthony's motives and explored connections from this story to their own lives, Chris and I had an opportunity to talk about how she structured and scaffolded meaningful talk about the story with young children. My first question was why the children were all over the room as she read. She explained that she offered the children the opportunity to "go to wherever they could do their best listening." In this way she felt she respected the children's choices and could hold them accountable if they acted in ways that did not show good listening by moving them to a different part of the room. By respecting their choices, focus was on listening and thinking rather than sitting or being still.

"So why," I was quick to ask, "do they form a sitting circle after the story?"

"Well, first, it is easier to hear what is being said if they are in a circle. I teach them to look at the person who is talking. I think it encourages them to listen carefully and think through what others are saying. As well, when they are all in a circle they begin to watch for nonverbal cues that show that another person has something to add or introduce to the conversation."

I noticed that the kinds of questions Chris asked her kindergartners during the talk were different than those I had heard in other classrooms. When the children were arguing about why Big Anthony didn't know to blow the three kisses, Chris' question to the group was, "Was there any clue that that might have been a problem for him?" Matthew was quick to suggest that Chris should read the part when Strega Nona was singing to the pot again. The children listened very carefully as Chris reread that part of the story and used the information from the book to settle their disagreement. While that particular part of the conversation was going on, Chris was writing hurriedly in her notebook. I asked her why she recorded what the children were saying as they talked about story.

"When I write down what they say, they see and feel the importance of their words. They know I value what they say and what they think is special enough to write down. It makes them realize how important talk about story really is. Also, I can bring the conversation back around to something a child said when everyone gets talking at once or if a soft-spoken or shy child makes a comment that may otherwise go unnoticed. Like when they were arguing about Big Anthony, Sara made a really smart comment about how the pot needed someone to be nice to it. Her comment was lost in the discussion but later on, after the issue was settled, I could bring it up again and then the conversation started anew."

I wondered why Chris didn't just have the children raise their hands when they had something to say. She told me that, even though it takes a long time and lots of patience to teach children to follow her one rule for talk about story—talk one at a time and talk to the whole group—they eventually learn more than just being polite. Chris found that if she had children raise their hands to talk, they just sat there, waving their arms, waiting to say what they wanted without listening to and considering what other people were saying or connecting their ideas to the book or the opinions of others. Even though it is loud and messy at times, the results are worth the effort.

The kindergartners in Chris Boyd's classroom obviously loved the chance to talk about the story with each other. They used talk about the story to learn more about how things worked in the world and, in the process, learned more about the world of story.

DePaola, T. (1975). *Strega Nona.* New York: Prentice Hall.

enlarged versions of a number of high-quality picture books. Initially, only picture storybooks were available in the big book size. Today informational books also can be located in big book size. These ready-made big books have the advantage of saving teachers time by eliminating the need to make enlarged texts. Understandably, they are expensive since they include large versions of the original illustrations.

Unlike when regular-sized books are shared with children, big books permit all children to see the print. Teachers may take advantage of the enlarged print by drawing young children's attention to the print in the same ways that an adult draws a child's attention to the print in a regular-sized book during a read-aloud. Typically, teachers use a pointer to point to the words as they read big books and invite the children to read along, particularly to the words in a familiar text or to the refrain in a book. As children "read" along with the teacher, they internalize the language of the story. They also learn about directionality (reading from left to right with return sweeps), one important convention of print.

Through the use of big books, teachers can introduce children to other conventions of print—to letter–sound relationships (phonics); to the sequence of letter sounds in words (phonemic awareness); to the difference between letters, words, and sentences; to the spaces between words; to where to start reading on the page; to reading left to right; to return sweeps; to punctuation. In addition, through the use of big books, teachers are able to further children's development of important concepts about books (e.g., the front and back of a book, the difference between print and pictures, that pictures on a page are related to what the print says, that readers read the print, where to begin reading, where the title is and what it is, what an author is, what an illustrator is). In essence, using big books teaches skills in context. Read Trade Secrets 5.3 to discover how two kindergarten teachers use big books with their young students. Clearly, children can learn many reading skills and strategies if their teachers conscientiously weave this information into their shared readings.

Extending Literature

Interactive storybook readings and postreading discussions are not the only way children can respond to books. They can use dramatizations, drawing, cooking, puppetry, and more to extend stories' content. In this section, we provide an overview of several possible literature extension activities. We encourage readers to obtain a copy of Betty Coody's *Using Literature with Young Children* (1997) book for many additional suggestions.

CREATIVE DRAMATICS.   Creative dramatics is informal dramatizing with no printed script or memorized lines. Stories that are good for dramatizing need dialogue and action—characters who say and do something. Sometimes props are used; sometimes the children use their imaginations. For example, they can imagine the bears' bowls, chairs, and beds when acting out *The Three Bears* (Galdone, 1979) or the Troll's bridge when dramatizing *The Three Billie Goats Gruff* (Galdone, 1973). Sometimes the teacher reads the story, pausing for the players to pantomime and fill in the dialogue. For example, student teacher Syma reads *Caps for Sale* (Slobodkina, 1947) to her young students. One child is the peddler; the other children, seated in their spots on the rug, are the monkeys. She reads: "Once there was a peddler who sold caps. He walked up the street and he walked down the street [Syma pauses while the child playing role of the peddler walks up the street and down the street] calling [Syma waits for the child to speak], 'Caps! Caps! Who wants a cap?' " The "peddler" does not say exactly what the peddler says in the book; this is acceptable. Syma moves on to the next page. Later, the children delight at shaking their fingers and then their hands at the "peddler" who wants his caps back from the "monkeys." Occasionally the teacher and children or the children alone decide on the scenes to play, and the dialogue and action develops.

Karen Valentine has props stored in large see-through plastic bags in her classroom's library center for various old favorites. During free-choice, Doug coerces three friends into playing *The Three Bears* with him. He puts on the yellow crepe-paper wig and assumes the role of Goldilocks and the narrator. One child puts on the Daddy Bear headgear (made of poster board), another child puts on the Momma Bear headgear, and a third child puts on the Baby Bear headgear. Doug lines up three chairs and gathers three bowls from the dramatic play center.

Shared Book Experiences

Ms. Johnson's Sharing of *Mrs. Wishy-washy*

Ms. Johnson, a kindergarten teacher, prefers to use big books from the Story Box collection published by the Wright Group. One of her favorites is *Mrs. Wishy-washy (Cowley, 1987)*. She begins each shared book experience by placing the book on an easel so that everyone in her class can see the print and illustrations. The easel also frees up her hands and allows her to use a pointer during reading. She introduces the book by discussing the author and title, examining the illustration on the cover, and encouraging the children to make predictions as to what the story might be about. As she reads the text, she uses the pointer to help children follow along and to see the one-to-one relationship between print and oral language. Ms. Johnson pauses frequently to elicit predictions about what will happen next in the story. When finished, she encourages the children to give their reactions to the story. During subsequent rereadings, Ms. Johnson encourages children to read along on parts they remember. She pauses periodically for incidental teaching, commenting on the left-to-right sequence, punctuation, and other conventions of print. She also provides opportunities for the children to engage in a variety of story-related activities. With *Mrs. Wishy-washy*, for example, children write their own versions of the story, draw or paint pictures of their favorite part, and read regular-size versions of the book with a partner.

Ms. Watson's Sharing of *Mrs. Wishy-washy*

Ms. Watson's kindergarten children read together every day. The following describes how she engages in shared reading with her young students. Like Ms. Johnson, she begins the reading with the big book on the special big book easel purchased for her by her school's PTA. The book is closed with the cover showing.

The First Reading

"What do you see on the cover of this book?" she asks the children. Their responses range from "a picture of a lady," to "words," to "a title." With each suggestion, Ms. Watson confirms the response and points to the item on the cover.

"What do you think this story will be about?" With this question, Ms. Watson is attempting to activate the children's prior knowledge, which will help them understand this story. She is modeling what she hopes they will soon do on their own as independent readers. As the children respond, she sometimes writes their predictions on a piece of chart paper, sometimes putting the child's name by each prediction. Today the children are all pretty sure it's going to be about a "mad woman." Mrs. Watson says, "Let's read and see if you are correct." As she reads, Mrs. Watson points to each word using her special big book pointer, a stick with a small stuffed glove tied to the

end with the index finger pointing out and the other fingers folded under. While she reads, she does not pause for questions or comments. She wants to the children to hear the story and to focus on the words.

When she finishes reading, she asks, "So, were you right? Was this a story about a mad lady?"

The children unanimously respond, "YES!"?

Ms. Watson asks them when they first thought their prediction was correct. "Was it this page?" "Was it this page?" As she asks the question, she turns the pages.

The Second Reading

The next day, Ms. Watson reads the story again. This time, she invites the children's comments and questions. She begins by reading the title. (The author is not indicated on the title page or cover. A child asks about the author. She hunts through the small print to learn that the author is Joy Cowley.) She reads the title again and turns to the first page. "What do you think this page will be about?"

Immediately several children respond, "The cow?" "How do you know?"

A child tells her "because of the picture of the cow" and another child says, "I can read cow." Mrs. Watson has him use the pointer to point to the word *cow*.

She reads the words on the first two pages and continues the pattern of "What will this page be about?" and "How do you know?" Once she says, "Right! The picture on the page helps readers know what the words on the page will be. You are so smart!" On several pages, she asks the children if they have any questions or comments about the story. "What are you thinking?" On the next to the last page, she asks, "What do you think the cow, pig, and duck might be thinking?"

Her goal during this reading is for the children to become engaged with the print and the story. She invites talk about each page. She encourages the children's questions and comments. She is modeling that reading is about constructing meaning from the text. Readers think while they read. Readers make sense of stories by connecting what happens in the story with their experiences.

The Third Reading

Mrs. Watson begins, "Today how about if you read *Mrs. Wishy-washy* with me? She points and reads *Mrs. Wishy-washy*. "Oh, lovely mud," said the [she pauses] cow." Some children are "reading" all the words with her as she reads and points. More children join in more loudly. She pauses. She continues this pattern, encouraging the children to use the picture cues to help them decode the word if they can not read or remember it.

"Now, I'm going to cover a word. Let's see if you can figure out what it is." Using a Post-it® Note, she covers *mud* on page 4, "Oh, lovely mud," said the pig." She opens the book to that page and reads, "Oh, lovely blank," said the pig." "What might that word be?" Someone shouts, "Mud." Mrs. Watson asks, "How did you know?" The child

(continued on next page)

Trade Secrets 5.3 *(continued)*

"remembered." "How else could you figure out the word?" Someone says, "Pigs like mud." Mrs. Watson says, "Good. You used what you knew about pigs to make a guess. How else might you know?" She pulls the Post-it® Note back so the *m* is revealed. "What letter is this? What sound does it make? Could this help you figure out the word?" She stretches the sound of *m*, reveals the *u* and says its sound, and reveals the *d* and says its sound. "Looking at the letters and saying their sounds can help you figure out the words. Let's try another mystery word." She does one more. "Remember, this book is in the library corner if any of you would like to read it. Oh, I also have five small copies of the book. If you'd like to take it home to read to your parents, just check it out with Missy, this week's class librarian."

Pointing to the words is very important. The message Mrs. Watson communicates is: You read the words, not the illustrations, when you read. Having all the children read together is important; no one fails, everyone can "read." She also taught (actually retaught since she had used these procedures before—and will over and over again) decoding strategies.

*Cowley, J. (1987). *Mrs. Wishy-washy*. Melbourne, Australia: Rigby Education. Distributed by the Wright Group in the United States.

He tells the story while his friends pantomime and speak. Doug often corrects their language since they are not saying exactly what he thinks they should say.

Such experiences promote many aspects of development by offering children an opportunity to take on the behaviors of others, to try out vocabulary and sentence structure perhaps unfamiliar to them, to play cooperatively with others, and to accept and give criticism.

PUPPETS.   Many young children, particularly shy children, can speak through the mouth of a puppet in ways they can not speak on their own. Puppets provide children with another means—for some children, a safer means—of dramatizing a good story. Again, stories with strong dialogue and distinctive characters who do something are best suited for dramatization with puppets. Betty Coody (1997) recommends old favorite stories, like "The Three Little Pigs," "The Three Bears," "The Three Billy Goats Gruff," "Little Red Riding Hood," and so forth.

Manufactured puppets are available from many sources; for example, most early childhood equipment catalogs and teacher stores include puppets for retelling children's old favorites. Typically these are hand puppets (the kind that fit over the hand of the puppeteer). However teachers can also construct their own puppets (Figure 5.4).

COOKING.   Teachers of young children have long recognized the value of cooking activities as a component of their total program for young learners. In cooking children experience math (e.g., measurement, counting, determining how much is needed so that everyone in the class gets a piece), reading (e.g., the recipe), social skills (e.g., following the recipe together, eating), health and safety habits (e.g., nutrition and preparing food), and eating the food they enjoyed making. As Betty Coody (1997, p. 141) notes, "Cooking makes the book memorable, and in turn, the story serves to make cooking in the classroom even more important."

Some books include a recipe for readers to test. For example, Tomie dePaola's (1978) *The Popcorn Book* suggests two ways popcorn might be made. What better incentive to try two approaches to making popcorn? The content of other books suggests appropriate cooking activities. For example, after hearing Russell Hoban's (1964) *Bread and Jam for Francis,* a natural response is for the children to try their hands at making jam sandwiches, and after hearing Ed Arno's (1970) *The Gingerbread Man,* a natural response is to make a gingerbread man. A rainy day presents a reason for reading at least two books followed by cooking: Listening to Maurice Sendak's (1962) *Chicken Soup with Rice* and making chicken soup with rice or listening to Julian Scheer's (1964) *Rain Makes Applesauce* and making applesauce. Many books can be stretched to connect with a related cooking activity. For example, an extension of Robert McCloskey's (1963) *Blueberries for Sal* might be the making of blueberry pancakes or blueberry

Figure 5.4 *Puppets*

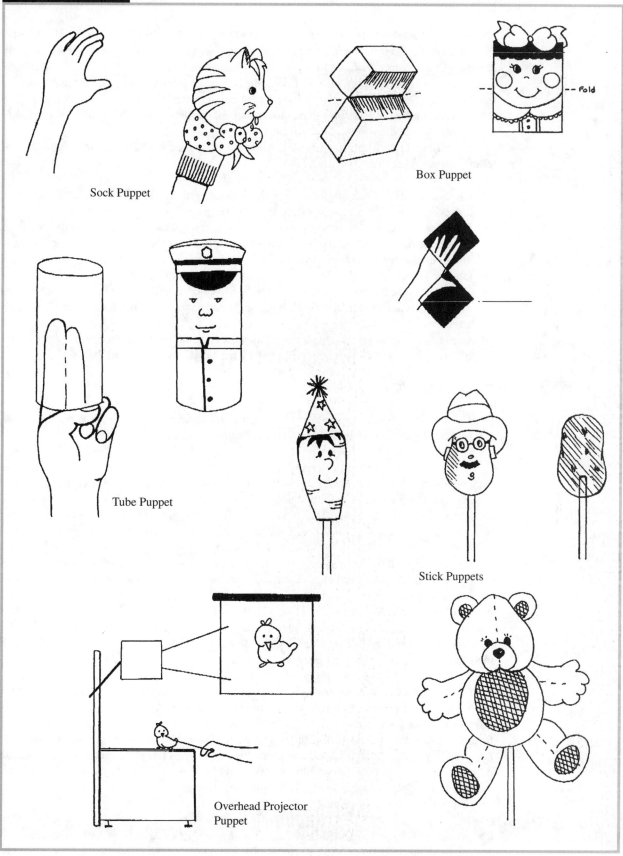

Sock Puppet

Box Puppet

Tube Puppet

Stick Puppets

Overhead Projector Puppet

muffins, and an extension of Ruth Krauss' (1945) *The Carrot Seed* might be the making of buttered carrots, carrot cake, or carrot bread.

FELT OR FLANNEL BOARDS AND CHARACTERS. In Chapter 3, we share information about the importance of providing opportunities for children to tell stories in the early childhood classroom. Our focus here is literature that stimulates storytelling. Typically, this literature is a folktale or a fairy tale. Children are nudged to retell these stories by teachers who tell them first. Sadly, many teachers have yet to be converted to the art of storytelling. Their children are missing much, for a good story can take children into a different world, into another place, and perhaps into another time.

Janet Towell (1998) provides several suggestions for teachers new to selecting stories for telling, instead of reading:

- Choose stories that are simple and relatively short, with a minimum number of characters and events and with no lengthy descriptive passages.
- Look for stories with dialogue and action. This permits the reader to take on the voices of the characters—to sound like a scoundrel or a villain, to sound like the dog or the cat—and to use gestures (though not too many of them) to draw listeners into the story.
- Choose stories with a problem that is resolved in a satisfying way.
- Substitute names in the stories with listeners' names. This makes the story even more memorable for young children, especially those whose names were used, and helps hold their attention.
- Use scribbles or notes to help you remember the structure and sequence of the story. A single word or a symbol will help jog a teller's memory in a momentary lapse.

To this list, Betty Coody would add:

- Do not memorize the whole story; only memorize certain portions, like the opening or introduction, the regularly recurring phrase or verse, and the conclusion.

Teachers can use several different kinds of visual aids to illustrate stories. Some might use stick puppets; some might draw with chalk while telling the story; others prefer to use a felt or flannel board with paper or cutouts made of interfacing fabric for this is the most popular visual aid used in early childhood classrooms. (Interfacing fabric can be purchased in a store that sells materials for sewing. It is typically used to interface garments, to add stiffness to collars and cuffs.)

Books are available to reduce the time it takes for teachers to locate stories appropriate for telling and to make pellon or paper characters. Two of the authors' favorites are *Flannelboard Stories for the Primary Grades* by Paul Anderson (1962), published by T. S. Denison & Co., Inc. of Minneapolis, Minnesota, and Doris Hicks and Sandy Mahaffey's (1997) *Flannelboard Classic Tales,* published by the American Library Association. These books contain the script for stories to tell and the patterns for the characters to accompany each story. For teachers with modest artistic talent, they are a must.

ART PROJECTS. The central purpose of an art program for young children should be free expression. Teachers should offer children opportunities to be creative, to use their imaginations, to produce something original, and to be inventive. How the children do (the process) is far more important than what the children produce. Therefore, teachers of young children do not want to produce models that all children must copy or to tell children to "Draw a picture of your favorite part of the story." Instead, teachers of young children should put materials out for children's exploration and creation. Within these boundaries, literature can serve as a stimulus for many creative art projects.

- *Artist's media*—Many illustrators (e.g., Leo Lionni, Eric Carle, Ezra Jack Keats) use collage to illustrate children's books. Shirley Rigby, a collage artist and a teacher of four-year-olds, follows the reading of *Inch by Inch* (Lionni, 1962) with a brief discussion of Lionni's choice of medium—collage. She tells her young learners, "Lionni used collage to make the pictures in the book." She writes *collage* on large chart paper behind her. "Collage means to make pictures by cutting or tearing shapes from different kinds of materials—newspaper, wallpaper, fabric, aluminum foil, and so forth. I thought you might like to be collage artists, just like Leo Lionni, today. In the art center, you'll find all kinds of different materials. Try cutting or tearing these materials and pasting them on a sheet of colored construction paper. What do you suppose the sign says over the bulletin board at the back of the room?"

Paul reads, "We are collage artists, just like Leo Lionni!"

Shirley adds, "So, if you want to be a collage artist just like Leo Lionni, visit the art center today, and I'll mount your artwork on the bulletin board. Oh, there are several other books by artists who illustrate by using collage to make their pictures on the shelf beneath the bulletin board. You might want to look at them before or after you make your collage. Please remember, no fingers with paste on the books!"

Teachers can invite children to experience the media used by many different picture book artists. What better way for them to understand artists' techniques?

■ *Papier-mâché*—Perhaps the children have a favorite literary character: Curious George? Francis? By inflating a balloon or balloons, the teacher can craft a form for the children's creation of a replica of their literary favorite. By dipping newspaper strips into a bowl of wallpaper paste thinned to about the consistency of cream and applying the strips to the balloons until the balloons have about four layers of paper on them, the children can create the literary animal shape. When the paper is dry, the children can paint the figure with tempera paint. The teacher can add distinquishing features (e.g., eyes, mouth).

■ *Paint-on shapes*—Nadine Herman's three-year-olds love Eric Carle's books, especially *The Very Hungry Caterpillar.* One day, Nadine cut butterfly shapes for the children to paint on at the easel, instead of using the regular-sized easel paper. More children than ever chose to easel paint. The following day the children attached pipe cleaners to the painted butterfly shapes for antennae. Nadine made a paper replica of a *Buddleia* plant (the plant that attracts butterflies) in one corner of the room, and the children hung their butterflies on the plant. Later, when Nadine read *The Very Busy Spider* (Carle, 1984), the children wondered: Could they paint on spider paper? Nadine answered, "How about using chalk on black spider shapes?"

WRITING. *Flat Stanley* (Brown, 1964) is the story of a little boy named Stanley who is squashed flat when his bulletin board falls on him. Being flat permits him to be sent through the mail to his cousin. Kindergarten teacher Gerri Moody used this book as a stimulus for a year-long project with her children. With the help of the children and their parents, Flat Stanley has been mailed on many adventures to one of each child's extended family members. While visiting, it is the host's responsibility to write a description of one of Flat Stanley's adventures. When Flat Stanley is returned, he comes with a written description (and sometimes photographs) of this adventure. The children think that Flat Stanley's best adventure was with the Los Angeles Lakers basketball team. He was returned to the class with a story about his debut as the mascot for one of the team's games, complete with a photograph of him with the team. Flat Stanley also got to surf during this visit to the West Coast. Flat Stanley's adventures are plotted on a classroom map so the children can see the distance he has covered. All written stories of Flat Stanley's adventures are collected into a notebook so the children can read and reread the stories about his visits. Flat Stanley is very popular; there is always a long list of invitations for him to choose among—with the children's help.

Karen Carey-Wilkerson's children often write their own version of books they have read, particularly cumulative tales. For example, after reading *The Great Enormous Turnip* (Tolstoy, 1968), Karen's children wrote *The Great Big Cabbage.* First Tymone tried to pull up the cabbage, but it would not come out. Tymone drew the picture to accompany this text. Then Tymone and William tried to pull up the carrot, but it would not come out. William drew the picture to accompany this page of text. The story proceeded until all the interested children's names were included in the book. Karen photocopied the pages so that all the children could have a complete copy of the book to take home to read to their families.

Figure 5.5	Steps in a Study
Steps in an author study	

1. **Select an author whose books children enjoy, and collect a large sample of his or her work.** Then invite children to help you compile information about the author from the books. If the author has a particular illustration style, you can also get reference books on that technique. Information about authors is also easily found on the Internet.

2. **Read the books with children over the course of a few weeks.** Share the information about the author, including his or her personal history. Talk about each individual book and encourage children to share their responses and think about the characters, illustrations, and writing style. Write children's comments on chart paper, and revisit them as you read more books. After reading each book, remind children of the others they've explored and talk together about the similarities and differences among them.

3. **Based on the author's work and the children's responses, select a focus for the study—** illustrations, characters, themes, text patterns, or a combination of these topics. Then review the books, highlighting that aspect and sharing related information you've collected.

4. **Invite children to create their own work based on the author's.** They might use the same illustration technique, create a story about a character or theme from one of the stories, or write a story that uses the same text patterns. Keep the author's books on display for inspiration.

'Steps in a Study' from "Meet the authors" by Ellen Booth Church published in Scholastic's *Early Childhood Today*. February 1998, p. 39. Copyright © 1998 by Scholastic Inc. Reprinted by permission.

AUTHOR STUDY.　Ellen Booth Church (1998) suggests that an author study is a great way to invite children to take an insider's look at the art and craft of writing and illustrating children's books. Each week or month, a different author holds center stage. Through discussion and careful analysis, the children come to understand the themes, characters, rhythm, story patterns, and structure used by different authors. Invite children to discuss and compare the books written by Ezra Jack Keats or Denise Fleming or Leo Lionni. Ellen describes how a group of kindergarten children discovered that Denise Fleming usually writes about animals and that there are rhythmic similarities between the text and the title of *In the Small, Small Pond* (1993) and *In the Tall, Tall Grass,* (1991). Inspired, the children wrote their own book—*In the Big, Big Kindergarten.* Soon they moved on to comparing two authors. They learned that Leo Lionni usually uses collage (tearing paper into small pieces) and Denise Fleming does not. Both authors usually write about animals. Fleming uses short rhymes and phrases, and Lionni uses detailed stories. In Figure 5.5 readers will find steps for to initiating an author study with young children.

Assessment: Discovering What Children Know and Can Do

In earlier chapters, we suggested that the best, most authentic opportunities for assessing young children's emergent literacy knowledge occurs during normal classroom activities. While children engage in storybook reading and story retelling and while teachers share books—regular-sized and big books—with children, teachers can learn much about what their young students know about the concepts of print, and the conventions of print and about their young learners' comprehension of the story. Watching and recording (primarily using anecdotal notes and checklists), teachers can gather important information about children's literacy knowledge and learning.

How Might Teachers Structure the Day to Include Performance Sampling?

One problem with systematic observation is that teachers have to wait for each child to engage in storybook reading. Teachers sometimes need to hurry things along a bit in order to gain the information they need to plan effective literacy instruction. They can do this using performance sampling—setting up situations that enable teachers to gather data about children's literacy abilities (Teale, 1990).

Earlier in this chapter we suggested that teachers begin their read-aloud and shared reading sessions by showing the children the cover of the book. We advised teachers to begin read-alouds and shared reading sessions by first telling and later asking children to identify the title of the book and the author. We suggested that teachers might ask the children to indicate where they should begin reading (the first line of print) and what they should read (the print or the pictures) and that teachers should consider reading some stories interactively—that is, by encouraging children to offer spontaneous comments as the story unfolds—and allow time for discussing the story after the reading. We recommend that teachers ask children to retell stories. When all of these suggestions are followed, teachers are provided with data-gathering opportunities. What is the focus of the children's questions? Do their questions show they are interested in the story's structure, or in making meaning of the information, or in the print, or in the illustrations?

But how do teachers keep track of which child is providing which information? The teachers at St. Michael's Early Childhood Center found an answer that works for them. Each day, a different child is the "star of the day" in their classrooms. The star has several privileges, including showing the class the title and author of the book the teacher will read and cuddling next to the teacher as she reads. If the book being shared that day is a big book, the teacher might ask the star to show the class a letter, a word, or a sentence after the reading. These teachers borrowed a fly-swatter idea from Patty Buchanan, a teacher in another school who probably borrowed the idea from someone else. Each teacher has a fly swatter with a small hole, about the size of a letter in a big book, and a fly swatter with a slightly larger hole about the size of a word in a big book. The star uses the fly swatters to frame different letters and words in the big book. Then the star decides who will be next to use the fly swatters to frame letters and words. What power the star has! With these kinds of activities, these teachers gather the same kind of information Marie Clay's (1979) *Concepts about Print* test gathered, but in a much more informal way. Ken Goodman (1981) and Bill Teale (1990) suggest that this informal way is better because it uses books that are familiar and highly meaningful to the children. When the reading is completed, the teachers often ask the star to retell the story to the class, with help from the pictures or classmates if needed.

Of course, these teachers know that this procedure is requiring the child to demonstrate knowledge in front of a group, something not all children are comfortable doing. They also realize that there are many book-related behaviors that are important to children's literacy development that cannot be assessed in this context. Therefore, these teachers also watch, read, and converse with individual children as the children interact with books. Again, the St. Michael's teachers use the day the child is the star to focus on the literacy behaviors of that one child. They review what they know about that child the night before. They use this information to help guide their decisions about what they might want to particularly attend to, ask the child to do, or do with the child. Of course, this does not mean that they are not observant of other children's literacy behaviors every day; the star program gives them a means of ensuring that every child receives the special focus of their attention regularly. Not a day slips by without gathering information on at least one child.

What Book-Related Literacy Accomplishments Should Young Children Be Able to Demonstrate by the End of Kindergarten?

Being alert to ways to gather information about children's literacy accomplishments is but a beginning. Knowing what literacy accomplishments are important to note is critically important. A recently published National Research Council report (Snow et al., 1998) on how to prevent literacy problems identifies several book-related developmental accomplishments of literacy acquisition that can guide teachers' observations. Crafted by a committee of experts in the early literacy field chaired by Catherine Snow, this report provides important suggestions to teachers to guide their data gathering. St. Michael's Early Childhood Center used these experts' ideas to make a list of accomplishments for their young children.

Teachers might use the suggested developmental accomplishments of literacy acquisition to guide their creation of checklists. Checklists help make teachers' observations more systematic. Some years ago the teachers at the St. Michael's Early Childhood Center worked together to construct a literacy checklist. They knew that children's book-reading behaviors were important for them to understand, but they were not certain just which book-reading behaviors were important to track as their young learners moved through their center. They agreed to form a study group to read and discuss professional literature on young children's literacy development in order to understand better how they should conduct their read-aloud and shared reading sessions and what they should focus on during their observations of their young learners. One outcome of their study was a checklist. Following the publication of the National Research Center report, they worked together to reconsider their checklist to ensure that they were appropriately following their young children's literacy accomplishments. We reproduce a version of their checklist in Figure 5.5 to guide our readers' consideration of their young learners' literacy accomplishments. Each St. Michael's teacher has a notebook with a checklist for every child in the classroom. On the day that a child is the star, the teacher puts the star's checklist on the top of the notebook. Over the day, she marks those accomplishments she sees the child demonstrating. When the checklist is filled, she removes it, places it in the child's portfolio (more on using portfolios in early childhood classrooms in Chapter 9), and replaces it with a clean checklist.

Certainly, observing a behavior once is insufficient to justify drawing the conclusion that the behavior is a part of the child's permanent repertoire. Teachers will want to look for repeated evidence that the child is habitually exhibiting these accomplishments. We recommend that teachers indicate the dates of their observations on the checklist and make quick notes of the specific behaviors the child exhibited. At St. Michael's, the checklist follows the child from year to year as a part of the child's portfolio. Knowing when each child demonstrated each literacy accomplishment helps teachers and parents understand individual children's patterns of development. Reading each child's checklist informs the teacher of the child's strengths and the instructional program for that child. Collectively reading all children's checklists informs the teacher of the instructional needs of all the children in the class.

Figure 5.6 *Checklist for Assessing Young Children's Book-related Understandings*

_____ can
(Child's name)

Concepts about Books	Date	Comments
look at the picture of an object in a book and realize it is a symbol for the real object	_____	_____
handle a book without attempting to eat or chew it	_____	_____
identify the front, back, top, and bottom of a book	_____	_____
turn the pages of a book correctly	_____	_____
point to the print when asked, "What do people look at when they read?"	_____	_____
show how picture and print connect	_____	_____
point to where a reader begins reading	_____	_____
point to a book's title	_____	_____
point to a book's author	_____	_____
recognize specific books by their covers	_____	_____

(continued on next page)

Figure 5.6 *Continued*

_____ can
        (Child's name)

Concepts about Books	Date	Comments
Conventions of Print		
show that a reader reads left to right with return sweeps	_____	_____
find a requested letter or provide the letter's name	_____	_____
ask questions or make comments about letters	_____	_____
ask questions or make comments about words	_____	_____
read words or phrases	_____	_____
read sentences	_____	_____
read along while adult reads familiar stories	_____	_____
Comprehension of Stories		
answer and ask literal questions about story (provide example)	_____	_____
answer and ask interpretative questions about story (provide example)	_____	_____
answer and ask critical questions about story (provide example)	_____	_____
ask questions about story	_____	_____
retell stories	_____	_____
by relying on pictures and with help to recall details	_____	_____
without book and with knowledge of the details	_____	_____
without book and with knowledge of key story elements	_____	_____
setting	_____	_____
characters	_____	_____
theme (what main character wanted or needed)	_____	_____
episodes (___/___)	_____	_____
ending	_____	_____
sequence	_____	_____
from beginning to middle	_____	_____
from middle to end	_____	_____
connect information in stories to events in his/her life	_____	_____
Attitude Toward Books		
participate in book-sharing routine with caregiver	_____	_____
listen to story	_____	_____
voluntarily look at books	_____	_____
show excitement about books and reading	_____	_____
asks adults to read to him/her	_____	_____
use books as resource for answers to questions	_____	_____

Summary

We hope that readers will set up well-stocked, well-designed library corners in their classrooms, read to their classes on a daily basis, and provide children with a wide variety of means to respond to the literature that they listen to during storybook reading time.

To summarize the key points about selecting and sharing literature with young children, we return to the guiding questions at the beginning of this chapter:

■ *How can teachers set up a well-designed library center?*

A well-stocked and managed classroom library should be a key feature of every early childhood classroom. To encourage young children to engage in book reading in this area, the classroom library must be well-designed with partitions, ample space, comfortable furnishings, open-face and traditional bookshelves, and book-related props and displays. Teachers will know quickly if their classroom library meets the well-designed criteria; inviting classroom libraries are heavily used by the children.

■ *What are the characteristics of effective adult storybook reading?*

What adults say—the verbal interaction between adult (parent or teacher) and child—during story readings has a major influence on children's literacy development. During storybook readings, children learn about the turn-taking inherent in all conversation. The adult helps the child negotiate the meaning of the text, assisting by relating the content to personal experiences, providing information, asking questions, and setting expectations. Who talks the most and the content of the talk varies with the age of the child.

Specific read-aloud strategies have been recommended for use in early childhood classrooms. These include read aloud every day, select high-quality literature, show and discuss the cover of the book before reading, ask children to make predictions about the story, provide a brief introduction, identify where and what you will read, read with expression at a moderate rate, read some stories interactively, read some stories repeatedly, and allow time for discussion after reading.

Shared reading, the reading of big books, is also recognized as a critically important practice in quality early childhood literacy programs because big books permit all children to see the print, something not possible when teachers read aloud a regular-sized book. By using big books, teachers can introduce children to the conventions of print and the concepts about books.

■ *What are some of the ways children can respond to and extend the stories that they have been read?*

Interactive storybook readings and postreading discussions are not the only ways that children can respond to books. Children can also engage in dramatizing a story, in retelling the story using puppets and a felt or flannel board and characters, in participating in a cooking experience, in creating an art project, in writing, or in studying an author's art and craft of writing.

■ *How can teachers use storybook reading sessions to assess children's literacy development?*

When children engage in storybook reading and shared reading, teachers can closely and systematically observe children's book-related behaviors and gather important information about children's literacy knowledge and learning. Teachers can learn about children's understandings of the concepts about books and of the conventions of print, and they can learn about children's comprehension of the stories. To provide a record of children's developing book-related knowledge, many early childhood teachers use checklists such as the one used at St. Michael's.

Linking Knowledge to Practice

1. Visit an early childhood classroom and observe a storybook reading or shared reading activity. What type of book was being read? How did the teacher introduce the book? Did the teacher read with expression and at a moderate rate? After reading, was there a thought-

ful discussion of the book? Did the children have an opportunity to respond to the story through art activities, drama, or writing?

2. Observe a library center in an early childhood classroom and evaluate its book holdings and design features. Are there a large number and wide variety of books available for the children to read? Are any basic types of books missing? Does the library center contain partitions, ample space, comfortable furnishings, open-face and traditional bookshelves, and book-related props and displays? Is there a writing center nearby?

3. Go with a friend or two to a library or bookstore. Plan to treat yourselves to a whole day of reading children's literature. Take your computers or 4 × 6-inch note cards with you. Record the bibliographic information and a brief description of the books you read. Be sure to read books for all age groups, infancy through kindergarten, and all kinds. What a wonderful day you will have!

4. Tape yourself during a read-aloud with a small group of children. Analyze your read-aloud for the strategies suggested in this chapter. What goals would you set for yourself?

Building a Foundation for Literacy Learning

As Isaac enters his kindergarten classroom, he and his classmates collect laminated helper necklaces from their name pockets on the attendance chart. Each necklace has a tag listing a classroom task. Isaac "reads" his tag—Errand Runner. He checks the nearby Helper Board where all the duties for each task have been described in both words and pictures. Today he will run any errands his teacher may have, such as taking the attendance count to the center's office. Yesterday, Isaac was Pencil Sharpener, which involved gathering and sharpening pencils. He hopes to be Pet Feeder tomorrow.

In Chapter 4, we described how most children begin to learn about reading and writing at an early age by engaging in everyday activities with their family and peers. Research has revealed that several types of home experiences stimulate early literacy learning: (1) easy access to print and books; (2) supportive parents or other caregivers who read stories aloud, demonstrate different types of literacy behaviors, answer children's questions about print, and scaffold children's literacy efforts; and (3) opportunities for children to engage in emergent forms of reading and writing. But just as children have varying degrees of verbal interactions with their families (Chapter 2), research also has revealed that children may have vastly different opportunities to interact with print in their homes.

Home literacy experiences help children develop an awareness of the forms and functions of print. Therefore, developmentally appropriate early childhood programs feature literacy activities that mirror the types of literacy experiences found in enriched home environments, such as print-rich settings, storybook reading, demonstrations of various forms of literacy, and lots of opportunities for children to engage in meaningful reading and writing activities. These types of experiences build on what children have already learned about written language, provide a smooth transition between home and school, and help ensure initial success with language arts instruction.

In the sections that follow, we discuss three strategies that form the foundation of developmentally appropriate preschool and kindergarten language arts programs: functional literacy activities, literacy play, and the language experience approach (also known as shared writing). These strategies are particularly valuable because they provide a broad spectrum of learning opportunities that are appropriate for children at different ages and with different prior experience with print. When used with large groups of children, opportunities exist for *all* children to gain valuable knowledge about literacy.

Before reading this chapter, think about . . .

- how you used print as a child. Did you write notes to your family? Did you pretend to write checks? Send a letter to Santa? Write a thank-you card to Grandma?
- advertisement logos you remember from your childhood. Could you spot a McDonald's a mile away? Did your favorite toy or snack food have a special logo or trademark?
- how print controls your actions on a daily basis. How old were you when you first recognized that the red octagonal sign with white letters meant stop the car?
- how you played house as a child. Did you have real cereal boxes and egg cartons for your pretend kitchen? Did an interested adult join in your pretend play?

BOX 6.1

Definition of Terms

broad-spectrum instructional strategy: Strategies that are effective and appropriate for a wide-range of learner abilities.

environmental print (EP): Includes the real-life print children see in the home or community, including print on food containers and other kinds of product boxes, store signs, road signs, advertisements, and the like. Because the situation gives clues to the print's meaning, EP is often the first type of print young children can recognize and understand.

functional literacy activities: Reading and writing activities that accomplish real-life purposes, such as writing lists and reading directions.

functional print: Print that guides everyday classroom activity (e.g., labels, lists, directions, sign-up sheets).

language-experience approach/shared writing: The teacher works with whole groups, small groups, or individual children to write down the children's oral language stories. These highly contextualized stories are easy for children to read.

literacy-enriched dramatic play centers: Sociodramatic play centers that are enhanced with appropriate theme-related literacy materials, such as recipe cards, cookbooks, and food containers for the kitchen center.

Focus Questions

- What are functional literacy activities, and how can teachers use these activities in a preschool or kindergarten classroom?
- How can dramatic play centers be used to encourage young children's literacy development?
- How can teachers help link literacy and play?
- How does the language experience approach (or shared writing) increase a child's understanding of print and facilitate reading development?

Functional Literacy Activities

As we explained earlier in Chapter 4, children's home reading experiences are usually functional in nature. Children watch their parents and older siblings use reading and writing to accomplish real-life purposes. They often join in these activities (e.g., reading food labels and signs in the environment). It is important for teachers to provide opportunities for children to continue to learn about functional qualities of reading and writing.

In the vignette at the opening of this chapter, note how the helper necklaces in Isaac's classroom provide the same type of functional literacy experiences that children have at home. The print on the helper necklaces serves a real purpose and assists with everyday activities (classroom chores). The surrounding context—the chores that are done on a daily basis in the classroom—makes the print on the necklaces easy to recognize and understand.

Functional literacy activity is a broad-spectrum strategy that provides opportunities for children who are at different stages in their literacy development to learn new skills and concepts. For example, if Isaac is just beginning to learn about the meaning and functions of print, the helper necklaces provide an opportunity to learn that print can inform him about his assigned chores and help him remember these chores. If he has already acquired this basic concept, the necklaces provide opportunities to learn about the structure of print. For example, he may eventually learn to recognize some of the printed words on the necklaces (*runner, pencil, pet*), or to figure out some related letter-sound relationships (the letter *p* represents the sound that *pencil* and *pet* begin with).

In the sections that follow, we describe two types of print that can provide children with functional literacy activities: (1) environmental print that exists in everyday life outside of school, and (2) functional print that is connected with classroom activities.

I can read better up high.

Environmental Print

At home and in their neighborhoods, young children are surrounded by print that serves real-life functions: labels on cereal boxes and soft-drink cans, road signs, billboards, and restaurant menus. This type of functional print is referred to as environmental print (EP). Because the situation gives clues to the print's meaning, EP is often the first type of print that young children can recognize and understand. Because EP is so meaningful and easy to read, it should be available in all preschool and kindergarten classrooms.

Unfortunately, EP tends to be rather scarce in school settings (Morrow, 2001). Therefore, teachers must make an extra effort to make this type of print available to their children. Following are several strategies that can be used to bring real-world EP into the classroom:

■ *EP board*—The teacher asks children to bring from home examples of EP that they can read. Selected pieces are displayed on a bulletin board entitled, "Print I Can Read." For example, the board might contain empty, clean product containers (cereal boxes, milk cartons, candy wrappers, toy boxes), menus for local fast-food restaurants, shopping bags with store logos, illustrated store coupons, and so on. Children work in small groups to try to figure out the meaning of all the pieces of EP on the board.[1]

■ *EP alphabet chart*—The teacher places pieces of chart paper around the room for every letter of the alphabet. Each day, children bring to class product labels they can "read." During circle time, these labels are read and attached to the correct chart. For example, the Kix (cereal) label would go on the *K k* page. Then the group reads the labels on all the charts, starting with the *A a* page. After several months, when most of the chart pages are full, the teacher can use the product labels from the charts to make books such as "I Can Read Cereals."

■ *EP folders*—Selected pieces of EP can be attached to file folders to make EP books (Anderson & Markle, 1985). For example, a pizza book could be made by pasting or laminating the product logos from pizza advertisements, coupons, and delivery containers onto the inside surfaces of a file folder (see Figure 6.1). Children can decorate the front cover with pizza-related illustrations. Other book possibilities include toothpaste, cookies, milk, cereal, and soft drinks.

---

[1] The EP board strategy is based on ideas in the September 1994 issue of *Reading between the Lines,* published by the reading and writing specialists of the Paradise Valley School District, Paradise Valley, Arizona.

Source: The EP board and EP walk strategies are based on ideas in the September 1994 issue of *Reading between the Lines,* published by the reading and writing specialists of the Paradise Valley School District, Paradise Valley, Arizona.

Figure 6.1

EP folder

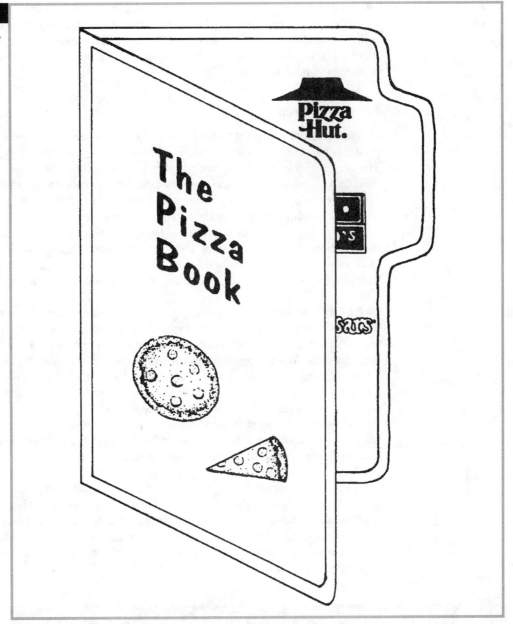

These EP folders should be placed in the classroom library so that children can show off to their friends how well they can read this type of contextualized print.

■ *EP walks*—This strategy involves taking a class for a walk in the neighborhood surrounding the school (Orellana & Hernández, 1999). Before leaving, the children are told to be on the lookout for EP. As examples of EP are encountered during the walk, they are pointed out by the teacher or by the children. After the children return to the classroom, they draw pictures of the print they could read on the walk. The pictures are put into a group book, which the teacher reads aloud to the class. The children can then take turns reading EP items in the book.

■ *Individual EP booklets*—This approach involves using magazine coupons or advertisements that feature products children are familiar with to make personalized "I Can Read" books. Children sort through the ads or coupons, select the products they recognize, and then use glue sticks to secure the coupons to pre-made construction paper booklets. The children can share their booklets with each other and take them home to read to family members.

■ *Sociodramatic play*—As will be explained later in this chapter, environmental print can be used as props in children's dramatic play. For example, empty product boxes such as cereal containers and milk cartons can be used in the kitchen area of housekeeping or home centers. As children act out home-related themes such as making dinner, they will have opportunities to attempt to read the print on the containers.

Functional Print

Unlike environmental print that is found in the world outside of school, functional classroom print is connected with everyday school activities. This print is practical as well as educational. The helper necklace in the opening vignette helps children remember their assigned chores, making the classroom run more smoothly. Simultaneously, the necklaces offer opportunities for children to learn about the functions and structure of print. As with all functional print, the context helps children discover the meaning of the print.

Nancy Taylor and her colleagues (1986) observed the print in a number of preschool classrooms and used qualitative procedures to develop categories of written language displays, many of which involved functional uses. The following are the major types of functional print that they discovered in classrooms: labels, lists, directions, schedules, calendars, and messages.

LABELS. As illustrated by the helper necklaces in the vignette at the beginning of this chapter, labels may be used to delineate tasks that students are assigned to complete, such as line leader, pencil sharpener, pet feeder, or paper passer. Labels can also be used to help organize the classroom. For example, cubbies can be labeled with children's names so that students know where their belongings are stored. Containers can be labeled to designate their contents, and labels can be used on shelves to indicate where materials are to be stored. Labels can also be used for designating different areas of the classroom (library, home center, blocks, games, art), informing children about the types of activities that are supposed to take place in each location. Finally, labels can be used to convey information. For example, teachers often use labels to identify objects in displays (e.g., types of sea shells) and pictures ("This is a . . .").

LISTS. Lists have a variety of practical classroom uses. Attendance charts can be constructed by placing each child's picture and name above a pocket. The children sign in by finding their name card in a box and by matching it with their name on the chart. After the children become familiar with their printed names, the pictures can be removed. In Trade Secrets 6.1, a preschool teacher offers another way of using this approach to take attendance and to document ongoing literacy development.

Trade Secrets 6.1

Connecting Names and Faces

Ms. Martinez uses a visual approach to help her three- and four-year old preschool students recognize their names and document their literacy growth over time. During the first day of school, Ms. Martinez takes an individual picture of each of her students using an instant camera. As the child's image emerges on the photo, she asks each child to write his or her name on a piece of construction paper. (If the child's writing is completely illegible, she writes the child's name conventionally next to the child's personal script and then explains, "This is how I write your name."). She places the child's picture above the name and places the page in a clear plastic page protector. She places the pictures on a child's eye-level bulletin board. She uses the bulletin board to help the children take attendance (as the children enter the room

in the morning they attach a brightly painted clothespin to their pictures).

In a few weeks, Ms. Martinez repeats this process. She takes new pictures of the children and again asks them to print their names on a new piece of construction paper. In addition, she asks them to write anything else they would like to share. She is always amazed at how much the children's ability to print their names and their understanding about print has developed during the first few weeks. Instead of sending the first set of pictures home, she organizes the pages in a book-like fashion and places the "Our Class" book in the library. It is one of the children's favorite library books.

Ms. Martinez repeats this process four to five times during the year. By the end of the year, Mrs. Martinez has a visual record of her students' writing development throughout the school year.

The teacher can use a second set of name tags to post jobs on a helper chart. This chart, which is an alternative to the helper necklaces described at the beginning of this chapter, contains a description of jobs needing to be done and display pockets that hold the children's name cards (see Figure 6.2). When attendance and helper charts are used on a daily basis, children quickly learn to recognize their own names and the names of their classmates.

DIRECTIONS.   Instructions can be posted for using equipment such as tape recorders and computers. Classroom rules (e.g., "We walk in our classroom") can be displayed to remind children of appropriate behavior. In addition, children can create their own personal directives. For example, a child may place a "Look, don't touch!" sign on a newly completed art project or block structure. At first, children will need help from the teacher or from peers in reading these types of directions. Soon, however, they will learn to use the surrounding context to help them remember what the directions say. Teachers can help this process by constantly referring children to these posted directions. For example, if a child is running in the classroom, the teacher could direct the child's attention to the "We walk in our classroom" sign and ask, "What does that sign say?"

Directions can also include recipes for cooking or directions for art activities. The directions can be put on wall charts. Even very young children can follow simple directions that use both words and pictures.

Figure 6.2

Helper chart

SCHEDULES.   A daily schedule can be presented at the beginning of class to prepare children for upcoming activities. Pictures can be used to help children remember the different segments of the day (see Figure 6.3). If children ask what is going to happen next, the teacher can help them use the chart to figure it out.

CALENDARS.   A monthly calendar can be set up at the beginning of each month and used for marking children's birthdays, parties, and other special events (field trips, classroom visitors, when a student's dog had puppies, etc.). The teacher can encourage the children to use the calendar to determine how many more days until a special event takes place and to record events of importance to them.

MESSAGES.   Often, unforeseen events change the day's plans. It's raining, so there can be no outdoor playtime. Instead of just telling children, some teachers write a message. For example,

Circle time will be first thing this morning.

We have a special visitor!

She will share her cookies with us.

Because these messages inform children about activities that directly affect their day, even the youngest children quickly learn to pay close attention to these notices.

Figure 6.3

Daily schedule

SCHEDULE

9:00	Opening
9:10	Free-Choice Time
10:00	Circle Time
10:30	Snack
10:45	Outdoor Play
11:30	Go Home

SIGN-IN AND SIGN-UP LISTS. Children can write their names on lists for a variety of functional purposes. For example, kindergarten teacher Bobbi Fisher (1995) writes the date and day at the top of large 9 × 18-inch piece of drawing paper and has her children write their names on the paper each morning when they first arrive in the classroom. Bobbi and her assistant teacher sign the list also. During circle time, the list is read to the class as a means of taking attendance and to build a sense of community. As the children become familiar with each other's printed names, they take over the activity. She periodically uses this sign-in procedure to assess the children's emerging writing abilities.

Lists can also be used to sign-up for popular classroom centers and playground equipment. Judith Schickedanz (1986) describes how teachers at the Boston University laboratory preschool have children sign up on lists to use popular centers such as the block and dramatic play areas. If children do not get a chance to use the area on a given day, they are first in line to use it the next day. Sign-up sheets are also used to get turns using tricycles on the playground.

Children should be encouraged to use emergent forms of writing. If a child's writing is completely illegible, the teacher may need to write the child's name conventionally next to the child's personal script. The teacher can explain, "This is how I write your name." Once the child's name is recognizable, this scaffold can be discontinued.

INVENTORY LISTS. Lists can also be used to create inventories of the supplies in different classroom areas. Susan Neuman and Kathy Roskos (1993) give an example of a chart that contains an inventory of the supplies in the art area. The list contains a picture and the name of each item, as well as the quantity of each item available. The sign informs children that there are 8 paintbrushes, 12 pairs of scissors, lots of paper, and so on. During cleanup, children can use this information to make sure the center is ready for future use.

Linking Literacy and Play

In Chapter 3, dramatic play is described as an ideal context for developing young children's oral language. Dramatic play can also offer a context in which children can have meaningful, authentic interactions with reading and writing in early childhood classrooms (Christie, 1991). The following vignette, which involves four-year-old preschoolers, illustrates some of the advantages of integrating play and literacy:

> With some teacher assistance, Noah and several friends are getting ready to take a make-believe plane trip to France. The elevated loft in the classroom has been equipped with chairs and has become the plane, and a nearby theme center has been turned into a ticket office. Noah goes into the ticket office, picks up a marker, and begins making scribbles on several small pieces of paper. The teacher passes by with some luggage for the trip. Noah says, "Here Kurt . . . Here are some tickets." The teacher responds, "Oh great. Frequent flyer plan!" Noah then makes one more ticket for himself, using the same scribble-like script. The teacher distributes the tickets to several children, explaining that they will need these tickets to get on board the plane. As Noah leaves the center, he scribbles on a wall sign. When asked what he has written, Noah explains that he wanted to let people know that he would be gone for a while.

The most obvious benefit of linking literacy and play is that play is fun. When children incorporate literacy into their play, they begin to view reading and writing as enjoyable skills that are desirable to master. This is in marked contrast to the negative attitudes that can be perpetuated by dull skill-and-drill lessons and worksheets found in classrooms.

The airplane trip vignette illustrates how the nonliteral nature of play makes literacy activities significant to children. The pieces of paper that Noah produced would be meaningless in most situations. However, within the context of a make-believe plane trip, Noah's scribbles represent writing, and the pieces of paper signify tickets—not just to Noah, but also to the teacher and the other children. This make-believe orientation enabled Noah to demonstrate his growing awareness of the practical functions of print. He showed that he knew that printed tickets can grant access to experiences such as trips and that signs can be used to leave messages for other people.

The low-risk atmosphere of play encourages children to experiment with emergent forms of reading and writing. When children play, their attention is focused on the activity itself rather than on the goals or outcome of the activity. This means-over-ends orientation promotes risk taking. If outcomes are not critical, mistakes are inconsequential. There is little to lose by taking a chance and trying something new or difficult. Noah felt safe using scribble writing to construct tickets and signs. In nonplay situations, the tickets and signs themselves would assume more importance, decreasing the likelihood that Noah would risk using a personal form of script to construct them.

Like functional literacy, linking literacy and play is a broad-spectrum instructional strategy that offers children many opportunities to learn a variety of different skills and concepts (see Figure 6.4). In order to illustrate this feature, we will use literacy-enriched play centers, a strategy described in detail later in this chapter. This strategy involves adding theme-related reading and writing materials to sociodramatic play areas. For example, the following literacy props could be used in the pizza parlor play center:

- Cardboard pizza crusts (large circles)
- Felt pizza ingredients (tomato sauce [large red circles the same size as the cardboard crusts], pepperoni, black olives, onions, etc.)
- Pencils, pens, markers
- Note pads for taking orders
- Menus
- Wall signs ("Place Your Order Here")
- Employee name tags
- Pizza boxes with company name and logo
- Cookbooks
- Bank checks
- Newspaper ads and discount coupons

This literacy-enriched pizza parlor setting provides children with opportunities to learn important concepts about print. At the most basic level, the literacy props illustrate that print has meaning. Children demonstrate this awareness when they point to a menu or wall sign and ask the teacher or peer, "What does that say?" These print props also provide opportunities for children to learn more advanced concepts such as the difference between a letter and a word. Literacy terms, such as *letter* and *word,* are often used by children and adults during play in print-enriched centers.

The pizza parlor setting contains many examples of the functional uses of print. Print is used to convey information on menus and pizza boxes. Signs such as "Place Your Order Here" and "The Line Starts Here" illustrate the regulatory function of print. Pizza parlors also are associated with literacy routines—sets of reading and writing actions that are ordinary practices of a culture (Neuman & Roskos, 1997). These routines demonstrate the instrumental functions of print and present opportunities for children to use emergent forms of writing and reading. Customers can read or pretend to read menus while placing orders. Waiters and counter clerks can use note pads to write down orders that will later be used by the chefs to determine which types of pizzas to bake. Chefs can consult cookbooks for information on how to prepare pizzas. Once the pizzas are baked, customers can use discount coupons from the newspaper to reduce the cost of their meals and pay their bill by writing checks.

As young children have repeated exposure to print props, opportunities arise for developing alphabet and sight word recognition. Some children may learn to recognize the letter *p* because it is the first letter in *pizza.* Others may learn to recognize entire words such as *pepperoni, menu,* and *cheese.* Others may begin to learn about letter–sound relationships.

Opportunities also exist to learn comprehension skills. Neuman and Roskos (1997) have detailed how playing in print-enriched settings can lead children to develop several types of strategic knowledge that have a role in comprehending text. In a pizza parlor setting, children have opportunities to:

- *Seek information*—A child might ask a playmate about the identity of a word on the pizza menu.

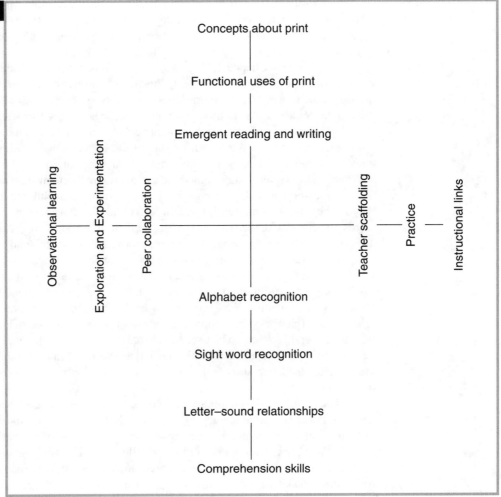

Figure 6.4

Literacy-enriched play centers provide a broad spectrum of learning opportunities

- *Check to see if guesses and hypotheses are correct*—A child might ask the teacher, "Is this how you spell pizza?"
- *Self-correct errors*—While writing the word *pizza* on a sign, a child might exclaim, "Oops, *pizza* has two *z's!*"

Checking and correcting are self-regulatory mechanisms that build a base for cognitive monitoring during reading.

In addition to offering children opportunities to learn a variety of different skills and concepts, the pizza play center can provide multiple ways for children to learn these skills. For example, the pizza parlor center presents many opportunities for observational learning. The center contains different types of print for children to observe and study: signs, menus, name tags, print on pizza boxes, cookbooks, and so on. As players act out the literacy routines associated with pizza parlors—ordering from a menu, writing down orders, paying bills with checks—opportunities are created for other children to observe many functional uses of print.

As children act out restaurant-related literacy routines, opportunities emerge for exploration and experimentation. Children can try out emergent versions of reading and writing and see how they work. Customers can attempt to read menus, using memory, print, and picture cues to come up with their best guesses about the contents. Waiters can write down orders using scribbles, letter-like forms, random letter streams, or invented spelling. The make-believe play frame makes it clearly permissible to use personalized script to represent writing and to pretend to read rather than to accurately recognize every word in a text.

Much of the play in print-enriched centers is social, creating opportunities for peer collaboration. Research has shown that children use a variety of strategies—such as modeling, designating, and coaching—to help each other when they engage in play-related literacy activities (Neuman & Roskos, 1991a; Christie & Stone, 1999).

As explained in Chapter 1, Vygotsky (1978) has described how adult–child interaction can create a zone of proximal development, allowing children to engage in activities that they could not do on their own. Many opportunities for this type of teacher scaffolding can occur naturally in the course of play in literacy-enriched settings (Enz & Christie, 1997; Roskos & Neuman, 1993). For example, the teacher might help children make a sign for their pizza shop, assist with reading words on the menu, or supply the conventional spellings of words when requested by children. This type of play-related teaching tends to be very effective because the skills are of high interest and immediate use to children in their play activities.

Literacy-enriched play settings provide opportunities for children to practice literacy skills they are beginning to master. For example, a child may have begun to recognize some of the words associated with pizza parlors: *pizza, pepperoni, sausage, cheese, olives,* and *mushrooms.* This child will delight in reading these words repeatedly on menus and on orders that other children have written. The sight recognition practice that occurs in play contexts is likely to be much more meaningful than identifying a series of random words on flashcards or on a worksheet.

Finally, opportunities also exist for teachers to make instructional links between play and the academic curriculum. For example, if a teacher were instructing children about letter–sound relationships (phonics), links could be made to important play-related words. For example, the words *pizza* and *Pepsi* could be used to help children discover the relationship between the letter *p* and the sound it represents. This play linkage would create a personal connection between the child and the letter–sound relationship, likely making the rule more meaningful and easier to remember.

When children play in literacy-enriched settings, they are presented with opportunities to learn a variety of different literacy concepts and skills. In addition, children can learn these skills in a variety of ways, including observation, experimentation, collaboration, and instruction. As a result, there are greater opportunities for children at different levels of development to learn new skills and to consolidate newly acquired skills that are only partially mastered. Unlike narrowly focused skill-and-drill activities, opportunities exist for every child in the classroom to advance his or her literacy development.

Literacy-Enriched Play Centers

Nigel Hall (1991) recommends that classroom play areas be subjected to a print flood, an abundance of reading and writing materials that go along with each area's play theme. The goal is to make these play centers resemble the literacy environments that children encounter at home and in their communities. For example, a restaurant center might be equipped with menus, wall signs, pencils, and note pads (for taking food orders). These props would invite children to incorporate familiar restaurant-based literacy routines into their play. Research has shown that this print-prop strategy results in significant increases in the amount of literacy activity during play (Morrow & Rand, 1991; Neuman & Roskos, 1992, 1997).

Different types of literacy materials have been found to stimulate different kinds of literacy play. Lesley Morrow and Muriel Rand (1991) reported that unthematic literacy materials such as pens, pencils, felt-tip markers, and books encouraged children to practice and to experiment with the form and structure of print. For example, children practiced writing letter characters and/or jotted down all the words they knew how to spell. These literacy activities tended to be unconnected with other play activities. In Figure 6.5, we present an example of four-year-old Ryan's unthematic writing. He picked up a piece of paper at the writing center and proceeded to write his name and several random strings of letters and black dots. When asked what he was writing, he responded, "Letters and periods." He had just noticed this punctuation convention (in books or environmental print) and decided to include it in his writing.

In contrast, the thematic literacy props in a veterinarian play center tended to elicit reading and writing activities that were related to the play theme. The thematic literacy play activities appeared to focus on the functional uses of print rather than on its form and structure. For

Figure 6.5

Unthematic play writing—Ryan writes "letters and periods"

example, children acting in the doctor role wrote make-believe prescriptions, jotted down notes on patients' charts, and filled out appointment cards for future checkups. Other children, in the role of pet owners, pretended to read the pamphlets in the waiting room while their pets were examined. Figure 6.6 is an order that four-year-old Adam wrote while working behind the counter in a ice-cream-store play center. Note that he is using invented spelling to stand for the flavors ordered by the customers: *V* for vanilla, *CH* for chocolate, and *S* for strawberry. An obvious instructional implication of this research is that preschool and kindergarten sociodramatic play centers should be well stocked with reading and writing materials. Both thematic and unthematic literacy materials should be included so that children will be encouraged to explore the structural features and practical functions of print.

Figure 6.6

Theme-related play writing—Adam writes down "orders" in an ice cream shop

Beyond writing implements such as pencils, markers, crayons, and pens, we provide examples of thematic and unthematic literacy materials that can be used with a variety of dramatic-play themes in Table 6.1 (Christie & Enz, 1992).

Preparatory Experiences

Matching the classroom settings to children's experiences outside the classroom is important. Children can play only what they know. Nigel Hall and Anne Robinson (1995), for example, used a mechanic's garage as a classroom play setting and as a stimulus for multiple kinds of reading and writing. Prior to initiating the garage play theme, the children were taken on a field trip to visit a neighborhood mechanic's garage. This firsthand, direct experience greatly increased the children's understanding of what goes on in a mechanic's garage, helped them plan and construct a realistic garage play center, and enhanced their subsequent play.

Using Hall and Robinson's book as their guide, a group of undergraduate students at the University of Delaware designed a bakery play setting in their kindergarten field placement classroom. First, they took the kindergartners on a walk to the neighborhood bakery. There the children saw how bread, cookies, cakes, and so forth were made. They watched cakes and cookies being decorated. The children also recorded the kinds of environmental print they saw in the bakery on the clipboards they had carried with them. They watched the bakery's owner serve a customer. They heard about the importance of cleanliness in preparing food and of being certain to get the correct spelling of names for writing on cakes.

On return to the classroom, the undergraduate students talked with the children about setting up a bakery play setting. How could they create a display case? "Put some of that um, um paper you can look through on one side of those shelves [shelves open on both sides]." What should we call our bakery? "McVey Bakery." What do we need in the bakery? "Cakes, cookies, a cash register," and the list grew.

The next day, the undergraduate students had created a bakery. They brought cooking pans from home, posters borrowed from a bakery, Styrofoam ™ circles of various sizes with paper disks of the same size that could be decorated with magic markers to look like cakes, a cash register, play money, checkbooks with blank checks, an order pad, cookbooks, wall signs, brown foam pieces that looked like doughnuts, and two chef hats. Together, the college students and the children set the limit on the number of children who could play at any one time—five. This necessitated a sign-up sheet. The children played and wrote orders, decorated cakes with messages ("Happy Birthday"), made signs advertising specials, wrote checks to pay for ordered cakes, wrote receipts, and so forth. The undergraduate students entered the setting periodically to model various literacy events: placing an order for a cake, writing a check, decorating a cake with writing.

By the third day of play, the undergraduates noticed that the children were not cleaning up the area very well. One undergraduate student pretended to be a health inspector. She wrote a letter to the class suggesting that she had stopped to check on the setting last night and found food on the floor. She threatened to close the bakery unless greater care was taken to keep it clean. It was a health hazard. "What should we do?" asked Sara. Opinions varied. "Tell her never to come again." "Tell her we'll be good." "Get a custodian." "But, who would pay the custodian?" wondered Sara. Soon the children decided that one of them should have the job of making a final check the bakery at the end of playtime and cleaning up what needed tidying.

Later another undergraduate student wrote a letter of complaint about receiving the wrong cake, a wedding cake when she had ordered a birthday cake. After much discussion, the children crafted a group letter to her tell her she could have a free birthday cake and apologizing for their mistake. This letter of protest offered the children an opportunity to use their literacy knowledge to solve meaningful problems.

It is clear that the environment has a powerful coercive effect on the children's literacy behavior. The thematic literacy play activities focuses children's attention on the functional uses of print; the form and structure of the writing is less important. Children easily engage in reading each other's messages and conventional print in the environment because that print is supported by the context.

Table 6.1	**Home Center**	**Business Office**
Literacy Materials Added to Play Settings in the Christie and Enz (1992) Study	Pencils, pens, markers	Pencils, pens, markers
	Note pads	Note pads
	Post-It ® notes	Telephone message forms
	Baby-sitter instruction forms	Calendar
	Telephone book	Typewriter
	Telephone message pads	Order forms
	Message board	Stationery, envelopes, stamps
	Children's books	File folders
	Magazines, newspapers	Wall signs
	Cookbooks, recipe box	
	Product containers from children's homes	
	Junk mail	

Restaurant	**Post Office**
Pencils	Pencils, pens, markers
Note pads	Stationery and envelopes
Menus	Stamps
Wall signs ("Pay Here")	Mailboxes
Bank checks	Address labels
Cookbooks	Wall signs ("Line Starts Here")
Product containers	

Grocery Store	**Veterinarian's Office**
Pencils, pens, markers	Pencils, pens, markers
Note pads	Appointment book
Bank checks	Wall signs ("Receptionist")
Wall signs ("Supermarket")	Labels with pets' names
Shelf labels for store areas ("Meat")	Patient charts
Product containers	Prescription forms
	Magazines (in waiting room)

Airport/Airplane	**Library**
Pencils, pens, markers	Pencils
Tickets	Books
Bank checks	Shelf labels for books
Luggage tags	("ABCs," "Animals")
Magazines (on-board plane)	Wall signs ("Quiet!")
Air sickness bags with printed instructions	Library cards
Maps	Checkout cards for books
Signs ("Baggage Claim Area")	

Notice how easy it was for the undergraduate students to provide the needed preparatory experience (the field trip) and to gather the materials needed to create the bakery. Most were inexpensive, or free. To convert traditional play areas into literacy-enhancing play centers requires a minimum of resources and effort. In return, children's play options are expanded, and the children are presented with opportunities to have meaningful engagements with reading and writing.

Teacher Involvement in Play

Lev Vygotsky (1978) has described how adult interaction can facilitate children's development within the children's zone of proximal development. That is, adults can help children engage in activities that go beyond their current level of mastery, which the children could not do on their own without adult mediation. Many opportunities for this type of adult scaffolding occur when children are engaged in dramatic play in literacy-enriched settings (Roskos & Neuman, 1993). Teachers can encourage children to incorporate literacy activities into ongoing play episodes and can help children with reading and writing activities that the children cannot do independently. This, in turn, can promote literacy growth. Carol Vukelich (1994) found that when adults assumed the role of a more knowledgeable play partner with kindergartners in print-rich play settings, the children's ability to read environmental print was enhanced.

The following vignette illustrates how one teacher used literacy scaffolding to enrich her four-year-olds' pizza parlor dramatization.

Channing and several friends ask their teacher whether they may play pizza parlor. The teacher says "Yes" and brings out a prop box containing felt pizza pieces, pizza boxes, menus, tablecloths, and so on. The children spend about ten minutes separating the pizza ingredients (olives, pepperoni slices, onions, and cheese shavings made out of felt) into bins. When they have finished, the teacher asks which pizza shop they would like to be today. They respond, "Pizza Hut." While the children watch, the teacher makes a sign with the Pizza Hut name and logo. Channing requests, "Make a 'closed for business' sign on the back." The teacher turns over the paper and writes "CLOSED FOR BUSINESS." She then hangs the "CLOSED" sign on the front of the play center. The children spend another ten minutes rearranging furniture and setting up the eating and kitchen areas in their pretend restaurant. When the children have finished their preparations, the teacher asks, "Is it time to open?" Channing responds, "Yeah. Switch the sign now." The teacher turns the "CLOSED" sign over so that the Pizza Hut logo is showing. The teacher then pretends to be a customer, reads a menu, and orders a pizza with pepperoni, green peppers, onions, and lots of cheese. Once the cooks have piled the appropriate ingredients onto the pizza, the teacher carries it over to a table and pretends to eat it. When she finishes eating, she writes a make-believe check to pay for her meal.

The teacher played several important roles in this episode. First, she served as stage manager, supplying the props that made the pizza play possible. She also provided scaffolding, making signs that the children could not make on their own. The "Pizza Hut" and "CLOSED" signs provided environmental print for the children to read and also created an opportunity for the children to demonstrate their growing awareness of the regulatory power of print. The pizza shop could not be open for business until the "CLOSED" sign was taken down.

The teacher also served as a co-player, taking on a role and becoming a play partner with the children. Note that she took the minor role of customer, leaving the more important roles (pizza cooks) to the children. While in the role of customer, the teacher modeled several literacy activities—menu reading and check writing. Several children noticed these behaviors and imitated them in future play episodes.

Research has revealed that teachers assume a variety of roles when interacting with children during play (Enz & Christie, 1997; Roskos & Neuman, 1993). As we illustrate in Figure 6.7, these roles form a continuum from no involvement to complete domination of play. The roles in the center of this continuum have been found to be the most effective for enriching the quality of children's play and encouraging play-related literacy activities:

Figure 6.7 *Teacher's roles in play*

Uninvolved	Interviewer/ Narrator	Stage Manager	Co-Player	Play-Leader	Director
Out of room Engaged in other activities	Asks literal nonplay-related questions Engages in informal conversation, "chatting" Narrates activities	Gathers materials Makes props Constructs costumes Organizes set Script suggestions	Assumes role and within the role: Supports dialogue Guides plot Makes plot suggestions Defines roles and responsibilities of different characters	Introduces conflicts Facilitates dialogue Problem solving	Delegates props Dictates actions Directs dialogue

←——→

Uninvolved	Interviewer/ Narrator	Stage Manager	Co-Player	Play-Leader	Director
Monster/doggie/superhero play Rough-&-tumble play	Literal responses No pretend behaviors Chatting	Theme construction: Organizing play set, assembling costumes, constructing props	Metaplay: Developing screenplay ("Let's pretend that") Discussion of role function & characterization Labeling props	Role-play: Immersion into character/role Intense dialogue Plot development, conflict, & resolution	Repetitive pretend behaviors Sporadic play episodes Pantomime

- *Stage manager*—In the stage manager role, the teacher stays on the sidelines and does not enter into children's play. From this position outside the play frame, the teacher helps children prepare for play and offers assistance once play is underway. Stage managers respond to children's requests for materials, help the children construct costumes and props, and assist in organizing the play set. Stage managers also may make appropriate theme-related script suggestions to extend the children's ongoing play.

- *Co-player*—In the co-player role, the teacher joins in and becomes an active participant in children's play. Co-players function as an equal play partners with children. The teacher usually takes a minor role in the drama, such as a customer in a store or a passenger on a plane, leaving the prime roles (store clerk, pilot) to the children. While enacting this role, the teacher follows the flow of the dramatic action, letting the children take the lead most of time. During the course of play, many opportunities arise for the adult to model sociodramatic play skills (e.g., role-playing and make-believe transformations) and play-related literacy activities (e.g., writing a shopping list, ordering food from a menu).

- *Play leader*—As in the co-player role, play leaders join in and actively participate in the children's play. However, play leaders exert more influence and take deliberate steps to enrich and extend play episodes. They do this by suggesting new play themes and by introducing new props or plot elements to extend existing themes. For example, if the teacher has taken on the role of a family member preparing a meal, she might exclaim, "Oh my goodness, we don't have any meat or vegetables for our soup! What should we do?" This creates a problem for the children to solve and may result in the writing of a shopping list and a trip to a nearby store center. Teachers often adopt this role when children have difficulty getting play started on their own or when an ongoing play episode is beginning to falter.

Other roles tend to be less effective—uninvolved, interviewer (the teacher quizzes children about their play activities), and director, in which the teacher takes over control of the play and tells children what to do. These latter two roles tend to disrupt children's play rather than to enhance it. When adults take over control of children's play and intervene too heavy-handedly, children lose interest and often stop playing.

The key to successful play involvement is for teachers to observe carefully and to choose an interaction style that fits with children's ongoing play interests and activities. Kathy Roskos and Susan Neuman (1993) observed six experienced preschool teachers and found that they used a repertoire of interaction styles to encourage literacy-related play. These veteran teachers switched styles frequently, depending on the children who were playing and the nature of the play. The teachers' ability to switch styles to fit the children's play agenda appeared to be as important as the specific interaction styles the teachers used.

When teachers set up literacy-enriched play settings and become involved in play in appropriate ways, they provide children with opportunities to have meaningful engagements with emergent reading and writing. These playful literacy activities go hand-in-hand with the functional, real-world writing activities such as signing up to use a popular center, making an invitation to class parties or performances, writing a message to custodians ("Plz du nt tch"), and so on. Both types of literacy engagements give children opportunities to form, try out, and perfect their own hypotheses about the function and structure of print.

Shared Enactments

In sociodramatic play, children make up their own stories as the play progresses. In shared enactments, on the other hand, the players enact a written story. This story can be composed by the children in the classroom or by an adult author.

WRITTEN STORY TO DRAMATIZATION. Vivian Paley (1981) has developed a strategy that combines storytelling and play. Children first dictate stories that are tape recorded and later written down by the teacher. The teacher reads the stories aloud to the class, and then the children work together as a group to act out the stories. This strategy promotes children's narrative skills—over time, their stories become better organized and increasingly more complex—and makes contributions to many aspects of their social, oral language, and cognitive development.

In her book, *Boys and Girls: Superheros in the Doll Corner,* Paley (1984, pp. 50–51) gives an example of a story written by one of her kindergarten boys:

Superman, Batman, Spiderman, and Wonderwoman went into the woods and they saw a wicked witch. She gave them poisoned food. Then they died. Then Wonderwoman had magic and they woke up. Everybody didn't wake up. Then they woke up from Wonderwoman's magic. They saw a chimney and the wolf opened his mouth. Superman exploded him.

Note how this story has a rudimentary narrative plot: the main characters encounter a problem (dying as a result of eating poison); an attempt is made to solve the problem (magic); and there is a resolution (waking up). Then a new problem comes along (the wolf), and the narrative cycle continues. Also, notice that this child has incorporated superheroes from popular media with elements from classic fairy tales to build his story: finding a cottage in the woods (*Hansel and*

Gretel), a witch who gives poison food (*Snow White*), and a wolf and a chimney (*The Three Pigs*).

Greta Fein, Alicia Ardila-Rey, and Lois Groth (2000) have developed a version of Paley's strategy that they call *shared enactment*. During free-choice activity time, the teacher sits in the classroom writing center (see Chapter 7), and children are encouraged to tell the teacher stories. The teacher writes down the children's words verbatim. When a child finishes with his or her story, the teacher asks if there is anything else he or she wishes to add. Then the teacher reads the story back to the child to make sure that it matches the child's intentions. The child decides whether to share the story with the group. If the child does, it is put in a special container called the story box.

Later, during shared enactment time, the teacher reads the story to the class, and the story is dramatized. Fein, Ardila-Rey, and Groth (2000, p. 31) describe a typical shared enactment session:

> The children gathered along two sides of a large space used for circle time and the teacher sits among them. The empty space before them became the stage. The teacher summoned the author to sit by her side and read the story out loud to the group. The teacher then asked the author what characters were needed for the enactment. The author identified the characters (often with the eager help of other children) and chose a peer to portray each one. When the actors had been assembled, the teacher read the story slowly as a narrator would, stopping to allow for action and omitting dialogue so that the actors could improvise. The players dramatized the story, following the lead of the author who acts as director. At the completion of the enactment and the applause, another story was selected for dramatization.

Fein and her colleagues used the shared enactment procedure with a class of kindergartners twice a week for 12 weeks and found that it resulted in a substantial increase in narrative activity (story enactment and storytelling) during free play. The investigators noted that this brief intervention appeared to penetrate the daily life of the classroom and promised to make important contributions to the children's narrative development.

DRAMATIZATION TO WRITTEN STORY. Another version of combining play and storytelling for preschool children involves an observant teacher who witnesses an interesting drama emerging from the children's pretend play. At the conclusion of the dramatic play, the teacher privately asks these children if they would like to retell their drama with the class. If the children wish to share their pretend adventure, the teacher quickly writes it down as the entire group listens. This strategy helps the children realize how spoken words and actions can be written down and shared with others. The following is an example of dramatic play-to-written story told by three four-year-old girls.

> There were two mommies who were going to take their babies to the doctor 'cause their babies were sick from a sleeping spell. On the way to the doctor they got lost in the forest. Just then Xena came by on her big white horse. They all got on the horse together and they found Dr. Mary, Medicine Woman. The doctor gave the babies shots and medicine and the babies got better.

Notice how the children's story reflected a traditional plot line—a problem that needed to be solved, a crisis, and two heroines who saved the day. Once again the children had interwoven story elements from classic fairy tales (*Sleeping Beauty*) with current TV heroes.

Language-Experience Approach or Shared Writing

The language-experience approach (LEA), which became popular in the 1970s (Allen, 1976; Veatch et al., 1979), has children read texts composed of their own oral language. Children first dictate a story about a personal experience, and the teacher writes it down. The teacher reads the story back to the children and then gives them the opportunity to read it themselves.

Sometimes the children illustrate their dictated sentences. This strategy is also referred to as shared writing.

The LEA or shared writing strategy is an excellent means for teachers to demonstrate the relationship between speaking, writing, and reading. It can help children realize that (1) what is said can be written down in print, and (2) print can be read back as oral language.

Like functional print and play-based literacy, the language experience or shared writing strategy presents children with a broad array of learning opportunities. At the most basic level, LEA/shared writing helps children learn that the purpose of written language is the same as that of oral language: to communicate meaning. For other children, the strategy enables teachers to demonstrate explicitly the structure and conventions of written language. The children watch as the teacher spells words conventionally, leaves spaces between words, uses left-to-right and top-to-bottom sequences, starts sentences and names with capital letters, ends sentences with periods or other terminal punctuation marks, and so on. This is an ideal means to show children how the mechanical aspects of writing work.

LEA/shared writing has the additional advantage of making conventional writing and reading easier for children. By acting as scribe, the teacher removes mechanical barriers to written composition. The children's compositions are limited only by their experiential backgrounds and oral language. Reading is also made easier because the stories are composed of the children's own oral language and are based on their personal experiences. This close personal connection with the story makes it easy for children to predict the identity of unknown words in the text.

A number of variations of LEA/shared writing have been developed. In the sections that follow, three that are particularly appropriate for use with young children are described: group experience stories, individual experience stories and classroom newspapers.

Group Experience Stories

This strategy begins with the class having some type of shared experience: The class takes a field trip to a farm, to a zoo, across the street to the supermarket, to see a play; the class guinea pig has babies; the class completes a special cooking activity or other project. Whatever the event, the experience should be shared by all members of the group so that everyone can contribute to the story.

The following is a description of how early childhood teachers might engage their children in a group shared story-writing experience. The "make-a-word" and "make-a-sentence" ideas described below are Pat Cunningham's (1995b). Many early childhood teachers have begun to weave activities like these into their children's LEA/shared writing experiences. Many believe their children are much more knowledgeable about print because of their use of Cunningham's ideas.

Teachers need to be selective about which of these activities to use in a single LEA/shared writing. To use all of these activities in one LEA/shared writing might take too much time. It is important to keep the group's attention and to ensure that this reading and writing activity remains enjoyable.

1. The teacher begins by gathering the children on the rug in the whole-group area to record their thoughts about the experiences—to preserve what they recall in print. Teachers often begin with a request to "tell me what you remember about . . . ?"

2. As children share their memories, the teacher records exactly what the children say. The teacher does not rephrase or correct what a child says. The teacher records the children's language, just as they use it. The sentence structure, or syntax, is the child's. The spellings, however, are correct. As the teacher writes the child's comments on a large sheet of chart paper with a magic marker in print large enough for all the children to see, the teacher verbalizes the process used to construct the text. (The teacher might choose to write on the chalkboard, overhead transparency, or chart paper.) The following dialogue (sometimes a bit of a monologue) illustrates what the teacher might say as the child's language is recorded:

Our Trip to the Farm

Lollie: We went on a hayride.

Teacher: *We*—because that word is the first word in Lollie's sentence, it needs to be capitalized.

Teacher: Lollie's next word is *went*. I need to make a space between *We* and *went*. [Teacher reads: "We went."] How many letters are in *went*? Let's count them.

Children: 1–2—3–4

Teacher: *On*. Does anyone know how to spell *on*? No? *O—n*. On is spelled *o—n*. Another space before I write the *o*. Watch while I write a *n*. First I draw a straight line down, from top to bottom. Then I come to the top of the straight line, and I make a curved line like that. That's a *n*. Another space. *A*. Watch while I make an *a*. First make a circle, and then I make a line on the right-hand side of the circle, from top to bottom. *Hayride*. That sounds like two words, doesn't it? What two words, Marcus?

Marcus: Hayride. [He says them together.]

Teacher: That's right. *Hay* and *ride*. That's the end of Lollie's sentence. What do I need to put at the end of this sentence?

Kristol: A period.

Teacher: Right. A period. [She makes a large dot and rereads Lollie's sentence.] [Teacher points and reads the whole sentence.]

Many concepts about the structure and conventions of print are taught during the creation of this single sentence—capitalize the first word of a sentence; put a space between words; form an *n* like this; an *h* and an *n* are formed the same way; letters make up words, and so forth. Every sentence in LEA/shared writing lends itself to exploring how our language conventions work, to introducing and reinforcing young children's knowledge of the mechanics of writing. In addition, by reading each word as it is written, the teacher promotes word recognition and one-to-one matching of speech and print.

Because of the amount of time spent on each sentence, the teacher takes sentences from only a small number of students. Taking sentences from all the children would make the sitting time too long for the young learners.

If a student's contribution is vague or unclear, the teacher might have to ask the child to clarify the point or may have to do some *minor* editing to make the sentence comprehensible to the rest of the class. The teacher must exercise caution when a student's contribution is in a divergent dialect (e.g., "He be funny."). Changing this utterance to so-called standard English may be interpreted as a rejection of the child's language. This, in turn, might cause the child to cease to participate in future experience stories. In such cases it is usually better to accept the child's language and not change it. As Nigel Hall (1987) points out, this dialect sensitivity does not need to extend to differences in pronunciation. If a child pronounces a word in a divergent manner (e.g., *bes* for *best*), the conventional spelling of the word can still be used. The child is still able to pronounce the word as *bes* when reading it.

3. When the whole story is created, the teacher rereads it from beginning to end, carefully pointing to each word and emphasizing the left-to-right and return-sweep progression. Then the class reads the story as a group (a practice called choral reading). Often a child points to the words with a pointer as the class reads.

4. The teacher hangs the story in the writing center, low enough so interested children can copy the story. Because the teacher wrote the story on chart paper (teachers' preferred medium for group stories), the story can be stored on the chart stand and reviewed periodically by the class. Sometimes the teacher rewrites each child's sentence on a piece of paper and asks the originator to illustrate his or her sentence. The pages are then collected into a book, complete with a title page listing a title and the authors' names, and placed in the library corner. These

books are very popular with the children. Other times, the teacher makes individual copies of the story—via photocopying or word processing—for each child.

5. (*Optional.*) With five-year-olds, the teacher may want to add some story-related activities that build word recognition skills. For example, the teacher could engage the children in a make-a-word activity. Sometimes the teacher asks, "How many words are in this story? Let's count them," or the teacher may ask a child to find and read one word from the story. The teacher could then ask the class to say the letters in that word as each letter is written on a 4 × 6-inch card. The teacher shuffles the cards and hands out one card per child. The children with the letter cards come to the front of the group, hold their cards so others can see them, and attempt to arrange themselves in the order needed to spell the word correctly. The children say the letters aloud. They look for the word on the chart. They compare the order of the letters on the cards the children are holding and the order of the letters in the chart to check themselves.

Individual Language Experience Stories

In an individual language experience story, each student meets individually with the teacher and dictates her or his own story. As the child dictates, the teacher writes the story. Because the story is not intended for use with a group audience, editing can be kept to a minimum, and the child's language can be left largely intact. Once the dictation is completed, the teacher reads the story back to the child. This rereading provides a model of fluent oral reading and gives the child an opportunity to revise the story ("Is there anything you would like to change in your story?"). Finally, the child reads the story.

A variety of media can be used to record individual experience stories, each with its own advantages. Lined writing paper makes it easier for teachers to model neat handwriting and proper letter formation. Story paper and unlined drawing paper provide opportunities for children to draw illustrations to go with their stories. Teachers can also use the classroom computer to make individual experience stories. Children enjoy watching the text appear on the monitor as the teacher keys in their story. Word-processing programs make it easy for the teacher to make any changes the children want in their stories. Stories can then be printed to produce a professional-looking text.

Individual experience stories can be used to make child-generated books. One approach is to write children's stories directly into blank books. Blank books are made of sheets of paper stapled between heavy construction paper or bound in hard covers. An alternative approach is to staple completed experience stories between pieces of heavy construction paper. For example, books can be made up of one student's stories ("Joey's Book") or of a compilation of different children's stories ("Our Favorite Stories" or "Our Trip to the Fire Station"). Child-authored texts can be placed in the classroom library for others to read. These books tend to be very popular because children like to read what their friends have written.

Individual experience stories have several important advantages over group stories. The direct personal involvement produces high interest and motivation to read the story. There is a perfect match between the child's experiences and the text, making the story very easy to read. Children also feel a sense of ownership of their stories and begin to think of themselves as authors.

The one drawback to this strategy is that the one-to-one dictation requires a considerable amount of teacher time. Many teachers make use of parent volunteers or older students (buddy writers) to overcome this obstacle. Another strategy is to have a tape recorder available for children to dictate their stories. Teachers can then transcribe the children's compositions when time allows. Of course, children miss out on valuable teacher modeling when tape recordings are used.

Classroom Newspaper

The classroom newspaper strategy (Veatch, 1986) begins with oral sharing in which individual children discuss recent events that have happened to them. For example, Bobby might say, "We went to the lake, and I saw a big fish swimming in the water. I tried to catch it, but I fell in and got all wet." After five or six children have shared their personal experiences, the teacher picks several of the most interesting to put in the classroom newspaper. The teacher then writes these

Trade Secrets 6.2

Daily Time Capsules

Just before class is dismissed each day, Cyndy Schmidt asks her kindergartners what they have learned. As students tell their "significant learnings," she lists them on the chalkboard. Next, Cyndy asks the children to pick the one that they are most likely to remember next year. The item picked by the most children becomes the Time Capsule for that day. The Capsule item can be written, along with the day's date, on a large piece of construction paper and illustrated by student volunteers. These Capsules are permanently displayed on the classroom wall. By the end of the year, several rings of Capsules encircle the entire classrooms! Other teachers prefer to put Capsules into a book that is displayed in the library center. Daily Time Capsules can be reviewed occasionally with children to reinforce learning and to give them additional reading practice. Cyndy has found that these Capsules also make a very favorable impression on parents and others who visit the classroom.

Trade Secrets 6.3

Headline News

Kindergarten teacher Nancy Edwards begins each Monday's class with a group session called Headline News. The children are divided into pairs. They talk to each other about what they did over the weekend. Then each child shares her partner's news. Emma, for example, tells about Jordan's adventure getting new tennis shoes at the mall. When Emma finishes, Nancy says, "What was the most important thing about Jordan's weekend?" The children agree: getting the new shoes. On a strip of paper Nancy writes: "Jordan gets new shoes!" This strip, along with a strip for every other child, is posted on the Headline News bulletin board.

experiences on a piece of chart paper with the date on the top. The teacher rephrases the children's contributions, polishing them up a bit and converting them to the third person. For example, Bobby's contribution might be edited into the following: "Bobby and his family went to the lake. He tried to catch a large fish and fell into the water. He got all wet!" Note that Bobby's thoughts are preserved, but the text is transformed into third-person, newspaper-style writing.

Children then take turns reading the day's news. The charts can be saved and reviewed at the end of the week. Classroom news does not require a shared experience, making it easier to use this technique on a regular basis than to use the group experience story. This technique also can give quite an ego boost to the children whose experiences are reported. For this reason, an effort should be made to ensure that all children get a turn at having their stories included in the news.

The classroom newspaper is an excellent way to help shift children from first-person narrative style used in individual and group stories to the third-person narrative styles used in many magazines and adult-authored children's books. We describe two variations of this strategy—daily time capsules and headline news—in Trade Secrets 6.2 and 6.3.

Summary

When most children enter preschool or kindergarten, they already possess considerable knowledge about reading and writing. Teachers can capitalize on this prior learning by using a number of effective yet remarkably simple broad-spectrum instructional strategies that link home and school literacy learning. In this chapter, we discussed three strategies that, along storybook reading (Chapter 5), form a solid foundation for an effective, developmentally appropriate early childhood language arts program: functional literacy activities, play-based literacy, and language experience or shared writing approach.

- *What are functional literacy activities, and how can teachers use these activities in a preschool or kindergarten classroom?*

Functional print (labels, lists, directions, and schedules) is ideal for beginning readers because the surrounding context helps explain its meaning. This contextualized print is easy for young children to read and helps them view themselves as real readers. In addition, functional literacy activities help develop the concept that reading and writing have practical significance and can be used to get things done in everyday life. This realization makes print more salient to children and provides important motivation for learning to read and write. Functional print also presents opportunities for children to learn to recognize letters and words in a highly meaningful context.

■ *How can dramatic play centers be used to encourage young children's literacy development?*
Dramatic play provides an ideal context for children to have meaningful, authentic interactions with print. Dramatic play offers children of all ages and abilities multiple low-risk opportunities to explore and experiment with reading and writing.

■ *How can teachers help link literacy and play?*
Teachers can encourage such play by
1. stocking dramatic play centers with literacy props that invite children to engage in theme-related reading and writing activities,
2. providing preparatory experiences relating to play themes, and
3. assuming the stage-manager role and supplying resources for play, taking on a minor role and becoming a co-player in the children's play, and using the play leader strategy to introduce theme-related problems for children to solve.

■ *How does the language experience approach (or shared writing) increase a child's understanding of print and facilitate reading development?*
The language experience approach/shared writing strategy involves having the teacher write stories that children dictate. The resulting experience stories are a dynamic means to demonstrate the connections among talking, reading, and writing. As the teacher writes the children's speech, the children immediately see the one-to-one correspondence between spoken and written words. Because the children are the authors of these highly contextualized stories, they can easily read the stories. Experience stories can be composed by either a single child or a group of children. Group stories are more time-efficient, but individual stories are more personalized and ensure a perfect match between reader and text. Classroom newspapers and daily time capsules are current-event variations of the LEA strategy, and provide children the same opportunities to read print in highly contextualized, authentic situations.

Linking Knowledge to Practice

1. Visit a preschool or kindergarten classroom and record the different types and ways functional literacy activities are used in the classroom. How did the children respond to or use functional print within classroom? Did the teacher refer to the functional print?
2. Visit a preschool or kindergarten classroom and observe children playing in a dramatic play center. Note the types of literacy props are available to children in this center. Record how the children use these materials in their dramatic play.
3. With a partner, design plans for a literacy-enriched play center. Select a setting appropriate for a group of children. Describe how this center might be created in a classroom. What literacy props could be placed in the play center? What functional uses of print might be used to convey information? What literacy routines might children use in this center? What roles might children and teacher play? How might you scaffold children's play and literacy knowledge in this play center?
4. Observe a LEA/shared writing activity. Describe how the teacher used this opportunity to teach children about the forms and functions of print.

Teaching Writing and Reading in a Balanced Literacy Program

When Carol was three and four, she lived in California, and her beloved Grammy lived in Minnesota. Whenever her mother wrote home, Carol wrote to her grandmother. When she had completed her letter, her mother always asked, "And what did you tell Grammy?" Carol pointed to the scribbles on the page, every scribble, and eagerly told her mother exactly what the letter said. Her mother listened intently, always ending with, "And you wrote all that?" Later, her clever mother inserted a slip of paper into the envelope telling Grammy the gist of Carol's message. Grammy's response to Carol's letter always arrived within a week or two. Carol and her mother snuggled together on the overstuffed green sofa to read Grammy's letter, over and over. When her daddy came home from work, Carol met him with "It's a Grammy letter day!" Then, she'd "read" Grammy's letter to her Daddy.

Some contend that children learn written language just like oral language. That is, children learn to read and write simply by having opportunities to see print in use and by engaging in activities where literacy is embedded in the task, just like Carol did in the vignette above. These people believe that children learn without ever knowing they are learning. This view supports the implicit teaching of literacy. Others believe that children need to engage in activities that help them focus on the abstract features of our written language, like on letter names and sounds. This perspective supports the explicit teaching of literacy. We believe the truth lies somewhere in the middle: Children do need opportunities to see reading and writing in use and to experience the purposes of literacy. Children also need to be directly taught about the functions and features of print. The key is that the activities and experiences that early childhood teachers offer young children must be appropriate for the children's age and stage.

Some children learn to write simply by engaging in meaningful writing activities. Others need direct instruction.

Chapter 5 and 6 present the core components of a balanced early childhood language arts program:

- daily storybook reading by the teacher (Chapter 5),
- opportunities for children to attempt to read books on their own in the library center (Chapter 5),
- opportunities to respond to books that are read (Chapter 5),
- functional reading and writing activities (Chapter 6),
- literacy activities linked to play (Chapter 6), and
- language experience or shared writing activities (Chapter 6).

This chapter is about two other key components of a balanced early literacy program: writing and reading instruction. The chapter begins with a discussion of several effective means for teaching children about writing: the writing center, writing workshop, interactive writing, and publication. Then, developmentally appropriate forms of reading/decoding instruction are explored. Skill areas include phonological awareness, of which phonemic awareness is a component, letter recognition, letter–sound correspondences (phonics), and sight word recognition.

Before you read this chapter, think about . . .

- how you learned to write. Not handwrite, but write. Do you remember writing messages to special people, maybe messages that were lines and lines of scribble? Do you remember writing on walls, much to someone's dismay?
- how you learned the names of the letters of the alphabet. Did you learn by singing the alphabet song?
- how you learned the sounds letters make. Do you remember phonics workbooks or learning phonics rules (e.g., when two vowels go walking, the first one does the talking)?

Focus Questions

- Why is a writing center an important area in the preschool classroom? How might an adult teach in the writing center?
- How does a teacher teach during a writing workshop?
- Why is it important to publish children's writing?
- What does it mean to offer young children a balanced approach to reading instruction?
- What is the difference between phonological awareness, phonemic awareness, and phonics? In what sequence do young children typically acquire these skills? What does this sequence suggest about classroom instructional strategies?
- How might early childhood teachers introduce young children to the letters of the alphabet?
- How can early childhood teachers reassure the public that they are teaching phonics?

Writing Instruction

Even the youngest of children like to write—-not only on paper, but also on walls and floors. As Pam Oken-Wright notes, "The urge to make one's mark is such a strong one that it is manifest on many a bedroom wall, executed with whatever implement was handy or seemed exciting" (1998, p. 76). Early childhood teachers, then, must take advantage of this natural urge by providing a variety of writing materials to their young writers, learning to ask the right question at the right time, and providing the right instruction at the right time to nudge their young writers' development. In this section, we explore the what and the how of writing instruction in an early childhood classroom.

alphabetic principle: the idea that letters, or groups of letters, represent phonemes.

onsets: the beginning parts of words.

phonemes: the individual sounds that make up spoken words.

phonemic awareness: the awareness that spoken words are composed of individual sounds or phonemes.

phonics: the relationship between sounds and letters in written language.

phonological awareness: awareness of the sound structure of oral language.

rimes: the endings parts of words.

writing center: an area in the classroom that is stocked with materials (lots of kinds of paper, different writing tools) to invite children to write.

writing workshop: a time in the schedule when all children meet to study the art and craft of writing.

The Context for Writing: The Writing Center

A writing center is a special area in the classroom that is stocked with materials that invite children to write. When setting up such a center, teachers need to remember that writing is a social act. Children want to share their writing with peers, to know what their peers are writing, to ask for assistance with the construction of their text. "Morning. How do you spell 'mororornnn-nnninggg'?" Knowing children's need for talk while writing, teachers typically provide a table and chairs in the writing center.

GATHER THE NEEDED MATERIALS. In addition to a table and chairs, teachers stock the writing center with materials that invite children to write, to play with writing materials. Such materials include but are not limited to the following:

- many different kinds of paper (e.g., lined theme paper, typical story paper, discarded computer or office letterhead paper with one side clean, lots of unlined paper, paper cut into different shapes to suggest writing about particular topics, paper folded and made into blank books, stationery and envelopes, cards);
- various writing tools (e.g., pencils, markers—be certain to purchase the kind that can withstand the kind of pressure young children exert as they write—crayons, felt-tip pens, a computer or computers with a word-processing program);
- writing folders for storage of each child's writing efforts; and
- a box or file drawer in which to store the file folders.

Notice that oversized (fat) pencils and special primary-lined paper were not recommended as the only paper and pencils to be provided. For young children, Miriam Martinez and Bill Teale (1987) recommend unlined paper because it does not signal how writing is supposed to be done. Children are freer to use the emergent forms of writing—pictures used as writing, scribble writing, letter-like forms, and so on—that do not fit on the lines of traditional lined writing paper or story paper (e.g., top half blank, bottom half lined).

In addition to these required items, many teachers include the following items in their classroom writing center:

- a bulletin board for displaying such items as samples of the children's writing, examples of different forms of writing (e.g., thank you notes, letters, postcards, stories), writing-related messages (e.g., "Here's our grocery list"), messages about writing (e.g., "Look at this! Shawn's sister published a story in the newspaper") and the children's writing;
- posters showing people engaged in writing;
- clipboards for children who want to write someplace other than at the table;
- mailboxes (one for each child, the teacher, the principal or center director, and other appropriate persons, as determined by the children) to encourage note and letter writing;

- alphabet strips on the writing table so that the children have a model readily available when they begin to attempt to link their knowledge of letter sounds with their knowledge of letter formations.

Mailboxes can be made in various ways. For example, they might be made from the large tin food cans available from the cafeteria. Kindergarten teacher Debbie Czapiga, a clever seamstress, made mailboxes for each child by sewing pockets of discarded jeans onto a colorful, stiff piece of fabric. She then attached the strip of fabric to the bottom of the chalkboard and labeled each pocket with a child's name.

Most teachers introduce the materials to the children gradually, that is, they do not place all these materials in the writing center on the first day of school, which young children would find overwhelming. They make the writing center new and exciting over the year by regularly adding new materials and tools. Pam Oken-Wright suggests that when new materials are added to the writing center, it is important not to substitute the new materials for the old materials; young children like the familiar along with the new.

ARRANGE THE MATERIALS.   With so many different materials in the writing center, keeping the supplies orderly and replenishing them can be time-consuming. Some teachers label the places where the various tools and paper belong in the writing center; this helps all the children know where to return used materials, and it helps a child "clerk" know how to straighten the center at cleanup time. Further, labeling the places where the items belong permits a quick inventory of missing and needed items. Figure 7.1 provides an illustration of a well-equipped, well-arranged writing center.

COMPUTERS AND WORD PROCESSING.   A growing number of early childhood classrooms have computers in the writing center. Teachers in these classrooms are indeed fortunate! Early childhood computer expert Dan Shade highly recommends the following relatively new software packages for their user-friendly qualities; that is, young children can easily use them to write: *Orly's Draw-a-Story* (Dan's personal favorite), *Claris for Kids,* and *The Writing Center* (the new and improved version). Some older favorites include *Kid Works 2* (Davidson), *Storybook Weaver* (MECC), *Wiggins in Storybook Land,* and *The Incredible Writing Machine* (The Learning Company).

Marilyn Cochran-Smith, Jessica Kahn, and Cynthia Paris (1986) point out that all writers, regardless of age, require time at the computer when their attention is focused on learning word-processing skills. For example, Bev Winston, a kindergarten teacher, introduced her young students to word processing during the school's orientation days, those days that precede the first full day of school. Then she watched her children as they played with word processing during their free-play time and provided instruction as each child needed it. Word processing is a tool to preserve children's important first writings. It is important for teachers to keep this in mind. Young children need time to experiment with this tool just as children need time to experiment with pencils, pens, markers, and so forth.

The Writing Workshop

By the time children reach kindergarten, many teachers add a writing workshop, with some direct teaching of writing, to the daily schedule at least once a week.

The writing workshop was first described by Donald Graves (1983) in his book *Writing: Teachers and Children at Work.* All members of the writing workshop meet to intensively study the art and craft of writing. The workshop typically has the following components:

- *Mini-lesson*—A five-minute lesson to teach children about the writing process ("I want to make a change in my writing. I'm going to *revise.* Here's how I'll do it."); a procedural aspect of the writing program ("We help our friends while they write. We say things like, 'Tell me more about your dog. What color is he?' "); a quality of good writing ("I can tell more about my dog by adding his color, black. So I'll write 'I hv a blk dg.' "); a mechan-

Figure 7.1   *A well-equipped writing center*

ical feature of writing ("Always make *I* a capital, a big letter."); or about why people write ("We need to make a list.").

■ *Writing*—A 10 to 15 minute period during which children write and meet with peers and the teacher.

■ *Group share*—A ten-minute period during which one or two children read their writing pieces to the group and receive positive feedback and content-related questions.

While the writing workshop was originally designed for use in the elementary grades, it can be easily adapted for use with younger children. Here are examples of how one kindergarten teacher has used variations of the workshop approach to help her students develop as writers.

MINI-LESSONS.   Mini-lessons are short lessons that focus on an aspect of writing. Kindergarten teacher Bernadette Watson uses mini-lessons to teach her students how to match letter sounds with the correct letter symbols. In one lesson, she helped the children sound out the spellings of the words in the sentence "I went to New York." She stretched the words out (e.g. w-e-n-t) and focused the children's attention on sound of each letter ("What letter makes the /w/ sound?) or letter cluster ("How about /ent/?). Because she knew that her students will not fully understand the relationship between sounds and symbols as a result of one lesson, Ms. Watson weaves the content of this lesson into many lessons and reinforces this understanding when she talks with her young writers about their writing.

Trade Secrets 7.1

Teaching About Sound–Symbol Relationships: An Invented-Spelling Mini-Lesson

Bernadette Watson

Teacher: I didn't tell you this before. I went on a trip to New York this weekend. The New York Marathon (the running race) was on this weekend, so there was a lot of traffic! It took us a long time to get to New York. That's what I'm going to write about today. I'm going to start by drawing a picture. I'll just draw a road. That will help me remember what I'm going to write about. [Teacher draws a road]. I'm going to write "I went to New York City." Will you help me write the words? "I" Oh, that's an easy one. [Writes "I"] W-e-n-t [stretches word]. "w"-"w"-"w."

Child: "Y."

Teacher: It does sound like a "Y." We'll use "Y" for that sound. E-N-T.

Children: "N!" "N!"

[Teacher writes "N."] Teacher:

W-E-N-T-T-T Children:

"T!" [Teacher writes "T."]

Teacher: to

Child: I know how to spell to—"t" "o."

Teacher: How do you know that?

Child: I don't know. I just do. [Teacher writes *to.*]

Teacher: [Reads, I went "to."] New. "N"-"N"-"N."

Child: It's like my name. "N"

... and so on.

WRITING TIME. The mini-lesson is followed by a time for the children to write. Ms. Watson teaches in a public school and has to make do with an occasional parent as a teacher assistant. She presents a writing lesson on Monday. Five children begin their free-play time in the writing center, writing with Ms. Watson's support and reading their text to Ms. Watson before they leave the writing center. The other children proceed to centers of their choice. Tomorrow another five children will begin their free-play time in the writing center. Each child begins free-play in the writing center once each week. Certainly the children can choose to write on more than their writing day, but all children must write at least one day each week. Requiring the children to begin their play time in the writing center one day each week allows Ms. Watson to support and observe each child's writing development at least once each week.

While the children write, Ms. Watson and other adults who might be in the classroom, meet with the young writers about their writing. The opportunity to talk while writing is a critically important component of writing workshop. The talk is about the content and the mechanics (usually the letter–sound relationships) of the piece. Through conferences, teachers can provide one-on-one instruction, providing the child with just the right help needed at that minute.

GROUP SHARE TIME. The workshop is culminated by group share time. During the group share session, two or three children sit, one at a time, in the author's chair and share their pieces with the other writers in the class. (See Trade Secret 7.2 for a description of how one teacher uses the "author's chair" strategy.) Typically, the other children are gathered at the sharing writer's feet, listening attentively while the writer reads the piece, preparing to make comments or ask questions. The following describes one group share in Ms. Bernadette Watson's kindergarten classroom.

Demetri: "I like your story."

Ms. Watson: "Remember, Demetri, when we talked about how we tell the writer what we really liked about his or her story? Can you tell Aaron what you liked about his story?"

Demetri: "I really liked the part where you thought you would get a dog, because I want a dog, too."

Aaron: "Thanks."

Trade Secret 7.2

The Author's Chair

Ms. Garcia has taken a regular classroom chair and taped the label "Author's Chair" on its backrest. The chair is placed in front of the carpeted area where her kindergartners sit during circle time. She uses this chair on a daily basis to read good literature to her class. Ms. Garcia also uses the Author's Chair to read stories that her students have written, treating them in the same manner as the adult-authored books. Her students use the chair too, taking turns reading their own writing from the Author's Chair.

Regardless of who is doing the reading (Ms. Garcia or her students) or what type of book is being read (adult-authored or child-authored), the children in the audience respond in the same way. First, they *receive* the story, making positive comments about their favorite part, what they liked best about the story (e.g., "It was funny!"), or their views of what the story was about. Then

the students may ask questions, requesting additional information or inquiring about specific events in the story. If the book was written by a professional author, Ms. Garcia and the children speculate on how the author might answer these questions.

The Author's Chair strategy, developed by Donald Graves and Jane Hansen (1983), provides a powerful incentive for young children to write. They know that selected pieces of their writing will be published by being read from the Author's Chair. Another advantage of this strategy is that the chair serves as a link between child and adult authors. When children sit in the chair and read their published books, their books are treated just like those of professional writers. They are received and questioned in the same manner. This adds status to their writing, helps children perceive themselves as being real authors, motivates young children to write, and helps them to develop a sense of authorship.

The classroom rule is that the writer calls on three children for a question or a comment. The first response is a comment. The other two must be questions. Ms. Watson uses this time to help her children begin to understand the difference between a comment (statement or sentence) and a question. Learning the difference takes lots of practice.

Aaron calls on another child, Luisa, for a question.

Luisa: "Did you draw your picture and write, or write and draw your picture?"

Aaron: "I drew the pictures and then wrote."
[Aaron calls on Bill.]

Bill: "I know how to spell *to.* Do you?"

Aaron is unsure how to respond to Bill's question. He writes a string of letters with no match to letter sounds. According to Elizabeth Sulzby's categories of emergent writing, Aaron's writing is representative of the nonphonetic letter strings (see Chapter 4, page 73 for a description).

Ms. Watson understands his confusion and comes to his rescue. She asks, "Bill, can you write *to* on the chart paper for us? [Bill eagerly displays what he knows.] Listen to Aaron's sentence. *I want to get a dog.* Count the number of words in Aaron's sentence." Ms. Watson says the sentence and raises a finger for each word. I want to get a dog. [Children respond correctly.] What Bill is saying is that Aaron's third word, I want *to,* is always written *t-o.* Should we add that to our word wall? Then you can look at the word wall when you need to write the word *to* in your sentences. [She takes a 3 × 5-inch card, writes *to* on the card, and ceremoniously adds it to the classroom word wall.] Thanks so much, Aaron and Bill. We learned about Aaron's hope for a birthday present and how to write the word *to* today. Who else would like to share?"

Through group shares, young children learn that writing is meant to be shared with others. Writers write to communicate their thoughts and ideas with their readers. Young children also learn about the how of sharing with others (reading in a loud voice so others can hear, holding their writing so others can see) and about the difference between a question and a comment. Teachers use children's texts and questions and comments as a context to teach about writing.

Journals and Interactive Forms of Writing

Teachers want to provide young children with opportunities to write for many different purposes and to use different forms (or modes) of writing. Ms. Murphy modeled writing a letter (a form or mode) to stay in contact with people (a purpose) in the writing center. Ms. Edwards demonstrated writing a list (a form or mode) to help her remember (a purpose) in a writing workshop group lesson. In this section, we describe three kinds of writing that are particularly beneficial for beginning writers: journals, dialogue writing, and pen pals.

JOURNALS.   Journals focus on personal expression and learning. Children write to themselves about what is happening in their lives in and out of school, the stories they are reading, and what they are learning in different subject areas. The writer is his or her own audience. The text might be pictures and writing, or just pictures, or just print.

In Trade Secret 7.3, Phoebe Ingraham describes several kinds of journal writing that her kindergartners use for many different purposes: creative journals, literature response journals, alphabet journals, theme journals, and learning logs.

Like Phoebe Ingraham, many teachers ask their children to keep learning logs while engaging in the study of different topics. Learning logs are little books in which children record their thinking and their discoveries. Children in Nancy Edwards' classroom keep a science learning log when they study the pond, a project that extends over several months. Each week the children record at least one new learning about the pond. Figure 7.2 shows examples of pages from several children's journals. Notice the range of ways these young children respond to the writing task—some draw, some draw and write letter strings, others draw and struggle with sound–symbol relationships.

DIALOGUE WRITING.   By the time children are four or five years old, most have become quite proficient at oral dialogue. Teachers can capitalize on this strength by engaging children in written conversations (Watson, 1983). In written conversations, the teacher and child use shared writing paper or dialogue journals to take turns writing to each other and reading each other's comments. This strategy makes children's writing more spontaneous and natural by helping them see the link between written and oral language. In addition, the teacher serves as an authentic audience of children's writing, providing motivation for engaging in the writing process.

The teacher initiates these written conversations by writing brief messages to each student, who in turn reads what the teacher has written and writes a response back to the teacher. The teacher then reads these responses and writes additional comments, and this continues in a chain-like fashion.

Teachers usually begin by making declarative statements about personal experiences rather than by asking children questions. Questions have a tendency to result in brief, stilted replies from children (similar to their oral responses to verbal interrogation by a teacher). For example,

Teacher: Did you do anything nice over the weekend?
Child: No.

On the other hand, when teachers write personal statements to the children, they respond more spontaneously. Nigel Hall and Rose Duffy (1987, p. 527) give the following example:

Teacher: I am upset today.
Child: What is the matr with you?
Teacher: My dog is sick. I took her to the vet, and he gave her some medicine.
Child: I hop she get betr sun did the medsn wok?

Obviously, it is helpful if children are able to use legible forms of invented spelling to write their messages. However, this strategy can be used even with children who are at the scribble or well-learned unit (random streams of letters) stage of early literacy. With these children, a brief teacher–child conference is needed so that children can read their personal script messages to the teacher.

PEN PALS.   Once children get used to engaging in written conversations with their teachers, they will naturally want to engage in written exchanges with their peers. Miriam Martinez

Trade Secret 7.3

Journal Experiences for Young Children

Phoebe Bell Ingraham

Young children love to imitate adult behaviors, especially reading and writing. Before ever entering school, young children can be caught "reading" stories to baby dolls or teddy bears, writing grocery lists, or taking phone messages in typical sloppy adult "cursive." Too often, once they begin school this experimentation with everyday functions and forms of literacy vanishes. Concerned parents, politically conscious school administrators, and stressed-out teachers in upper grade levels encourage kindergarten teachers to get the children reading and writing as soon as possible. The expectation to write using real words and read only what is on the page chases away all enthusiasm for risk taking. So, how do we merge these two philosophies, encouraging children to experiment with literacy while teaching them specific literacy skills at the same time?

The answer is journals! I use a variety of journals with my kindergartners. This gives me opportunities to scaffold their literacy skills, nudging them to use what they know and experiment with what is not secure. I can give mini-lessons to model literacy skills I see they are ready to begin using, and they can have a blank page of paper to try it out on their own.

Creative Journals

Open-ended creative journals can be purchased ready-made or put together with blank paper. Covers can simply be colored paper, with the children writing their names and the month, or drawing pictures of themselves. At the beginning of the year, I begin journaling with my kindergartners with a story. Sometimes I tell a story about my life, and then I draw a picture about it, making certain to include important details, such as the stripes on my favorite shirt or the color of my daughter's bicycle and the tassels that hang from the handle grips. On other days, I choose books about five-year-olds going to school, being part of a family, having friends, enjoying holidays; we then have a discussion about one of their experiences that relates to the story. Then each writer goes off to develop his or her ideas into pictures and words so that they can be kept forever on the pages of the journal. Even the first few days, when these "translations" don't quite fit the image in their minds, my young students learn that their thoughts can be communicated and saved.

Later in the year, I move on to mini-lessons to help them include writing with their pictures. We might notice how the words and illustrations go together in a favorite book, or how there are always spaces around words in text. As the year goes on, I may give a lesson on invented spelling, what we call the "sounding game" in my classroom. (I like to differentiate between writing the sounds

we hear in words and actual spelling. This allows me to avoid a negative response to the question "But is this spelled right?") On another day, we might brainstorm a list of sight words we can read and write independently to use in our journals. The children write the words on chart paper, and we hang them in our writing center to use throughout the week.

As the year progresses, my students move from scribbled designs and pictures to including a few words and then a sentence. Their pictures begin to show a sense of story, while their writing begins to demonstrate their increasing literacy skills. Sharing their entries with the class, their vocabulary and oral language skills show signs of growth. It is slow progress, but secure and stable.

Literature Response Journals

My classes always love books. I don't give them much of an opportunity to think that books are anything but wonderful! We have a variety of ways to write about our favorite books. During an author study, we might make a collection of journal entries to share our favorites of the stories the author has written. These make a nice collection in a loose-leaf notebook to have in our library throughout the year.

Another favorite group journal activity is a take-home literature suitcase. A favorite book is sent home with a journal. If the book has a stuffed animal, such as the bunny in *Goodnight Moon* or *Curious George,* it might also be placed in the suitcase or backpack. Simple instructions are secured to the inside lid of the suitcase with clear contact paper, telling the family to enjoy the book and then complete a page of the journal telling what they liked about the story or possibly what they did while their character was visiting.

Literacy Journals, Theme Journals, and Learning Logs

These journals are linked specifically to our learning in other areas. I have found that, while kindergartners know many things, they often do not understand what they know or how to use their knowledge. They are not mature enough in the learning process to have a metacognitive framework for using their knowledge independently on seemingly unrelated tasks. Writing in journals to record observations, questions, and insights helps children make important links between what they already know and what they are learning. Writing about what you want to know is a wonderful way to learn, even for adults!

For example, I created an alphabet journal one year with my class when I noticed that all their literacy learning was not showing up in their independent writing. They could write words in our group lessons. They could write a simple sentence independently in the writing center. But when I opened their journals, there was little or no writing. They weren't linking their literacy knowledge with

(continued on next page)

Trade Secret 7.3 *(continued)*

their ability to communicate their message in their journals. Now, these journals, published by Zaner-Bloser, Inc. (Ingraham, 1997), are a weekly event. Every Friday, we write in our ABC journals, linking what we are learning about letters and sounds to the concept of drawing and writing about our thoughts in a creative way.

Other curriculum journals that promote writing to learn include math journals, thematic journals, and learning logs. These are designed to allow young children to draw and write about their learning in a particular subject area. At the kindergarten level, we occasionally write and draw about what we are learning in math or science, or as part of our school-wide themes. These are put together into a book that can be placed in the appropriate center and reread often.

Figure 7.2 *Learning log entries (This is a cattail.)*

and Bill Teale (1987) describe how a "postal system/pen pal" program was successfully implemented in several Texas early childhood classrooms. Children in the morning half-day classes wrote weekly letters to pen pals in the afternoon classes; children in full-day programs were assigned pen pals in other full-day program classrooms. Children were purposely paired with partners who used different writing strategies. For example, a scribble writer was matched with an invented speller. Letters were exchanged once a week and placed in mailboxes located in the writing center. A teacher or aide was at the center to assist in cases where children received letters they could not read. Teachers reported that student response was overwhelmingly positive. Here, real audiences and real purposes for writing are provided.

Publishing Children's Writing

"Helping children make and publish their own books taps into [their] love of creating and owning written words" (Power, 1998, pp. 31–32). Brenda Power suggests several reasons why teachers should help young children publish their writing in books. Making their own books helps children learn:

- to hold the book right side up and to turn the pages correctly;
- that books have covers, titles, and authors;
- letter and sounds through their writing of the book and how to decode words by reading their own words;
- about the importance of an author and an illustrator to a book.

To publish with young children is to take their written texts and do something special with them. To publish is to make the writing public, to present it for others to read. There are many different ways to publish young children's writing. For example:

- Ask each child to bring a clear, plastic 8½ × 11-inch frame to school. (Of course, frames must be purchased for those children whose parents can not provide them.) Have the children publish their work by mounting their selected pieces, one at a time, in their frames. Hang the frames on the back wall of the classroom on a Wall of Fame.
- String a clothesline across the classroom. Using clothespins, clip the children's writings to the clothesline.
- Punch a hole in the upper left corner of several pages. All pages may be construction paper pages. If not, include a piece of colored construction paper or poster board on the top and bottom of the pile of pages for the book's cover. Thread string, yarn, or a silver ring through the hole to hold the book together.
- Ask each child to bring a light-colored T-shirt to school. (Again, teachers will need to provide T-shirts for children whose parents can not provide them.) Invite the children to use laundry marking pens and markers to write and illustrate their stories on their T-shirts.
- Purchase a low-cost photo album with large, stick-on plastic sleeves. (These can be found at discount stores and occasionally at flea markets or rummage and garage sales.) Place one page of each child's writing in one of the plastic sleeves. The same photo album can be used over and over as one piece of writing can be substituted for another piece of writing. Occasionally, all children might write on the same topic, and a class book might be created on this topic (e.g., a field trip to the apple orchard). Preserve these special books for the children's reading and rereading.
- While engaging in a special experience, take photographs of the children. Glue the picture to a piece of colored construction paper. Ask each child to select a photo. Ask the child to write about the chosen picture on a piece of white paper. Cut the white paper into an interesting shape, and mount it on the construction paper below the photo. Laminate each page and put the pages together with spiral binding. (Teachers might wish to type and mount the conventionally spelled version of the child's writing on the paper along with the child's personal script. Be sure to include both versions of the writing. If a child's script is not included, the child writer often does not recognize the writing and cannot read the print.)
- Cover a large bulletin board with bright paper or fabric. In large cut-out letters, label the bulletin board something like "Young Authors" or "Room 101 Authors." Divide the bulletin board evenly into rectangular-shaped sections, one section for each child in the class, using yarn or magic marker. Label each section with a child's name. Encourage the children to mount one of their pieces of writing in their special section each week. A staple or pushpin might be used to mount the writing.

These are but a few of the many ways that children's writing might be published. We repeat: Publishing with young children means making their writing public—available for others to read. It is important to note that it is developmentally inappropriate to require young children to revise or recopy their writing, though sometimes they are willing to add to their text. Most young children do not have the attention span or interest to make revisions or to recopy the text.

If the child's writing is a personal script—that is, if it is a form of emergent writing that needs the child's reading for meaning to be constructed—the teacher might elect to include a conventionally spelled version of the message with the child's personal script version. As noted above, it is important to include the child's personal script version on the page with the conventionally spelled version to avoid taking ownership from the child.

Handwriting

So far, we have focused on providing young children with opportunities to write. What about handwriting? Drilling young children on how to form the letters of the alphabet correctly also is a developmentally inappropriate practice. Forming letters correctly requires a good bit of manual dexterity, something most young children are developing. Teachers should provide young children with numerous opportunities to engage in activities that help develop their dexterity, like puzzles, sewing cards, table games, cutting, and drawing. Models of appropriately formed letters should be available for the children's reference. This means that teachers should correctly form the uppercase and lowercase letters when writing for and with the children, and an alphabet chart of uppercase and lowercase letters should be available at eye-level for the children's use in the writing center. When children have achieved some control, the teacher might work one-on-one with the children. Since the letters in a child's name are the most important, the teacher might choose to begin instruction by helping the child correctly form these letters. Do not expect perfection, and be sure to keep the instruction playful.

Reading/Decoding Instruction

How to teach children to read has been the subject of a series of controversies stretching back more than a century (Mathews, 1966). Initially, there was disagreement over whether alphabet names or letter sounds should be taught first. The argument then shifted to whether children should learn whole words or if they should be taught phonics (Chall, 1967). These debates have been accompanied by dramatic shifts in instructional methods, giving the unfortunate appearance of pendulum swings (Holdaway, 1979).

During the past decade, a furious debate has raged between proponents of skill-centered and meaning-centered methods of instruction. Proponents of skill-centered instruction favor systematic instruction that teaches all children a series of subskills that lead to proficient reading. Supporters of meaning-centered instruction (sometimes referred to as "whole language") believe that children learn to read by doing large amounts of reading and by having opportunities to discuss and respond to what has been read. Skill instruction is provided, but on an as-needed basis.

What is remarkable about this debate over beginning reading instruction is the polarization of the two positions, with each side believing that it is right and that the other side is totally wrong. Recently, there has been a call for balanced reading instruction that incorporates elements of both approaches (IRA, 1999), a position we strongly support.

Fortunately, the debate over how to teach reading is not nearly as volatile at the early childhood level. As explained in Chapter 4, the early literacy perspective has successfully replaced the readiness view as the dominant theory of early literacy development. According to the early literacy development view, the best way to help preschoolers and kindergartners learn to read is to provide them with the types of experiences described in Chapters 5 and 6.

However, when it comes to decoding instruction—helping young children learn the alphabetic principle and use this knowledge to recognize unfamiliar printed words—some controversy exists. While there is general agreement that most children need to be taught decoding skills, there are divergent views about when and how these skills should be taught. Morrow and Tracey (1997, p. 645) explain:

> Advocates of whole language suggest that phonics should be taught in the context of reading and writing activities and not be isolated. Materials such as worksheets and flashcards are considered inappropriate. Instead the teaching of skills emerges naturally from activities in which the class is engaged. . . . Others, however, contest that teaching phonics only through naturally occurring activities in context is not systematic enough and leaves a lot to chance. These writers argue that children need some systematic sound–symbol instruction to learn to read.

We prefer teachers to use an activity-based, in-context approach to skills instruction with young children. The sections that follow describe a number of strategies for teaching the major decoding skills: phonological and phonemic awareness, alphabet letter recognition, word recognition, and phonics. Readers will find examples of activity-based, in-context strategies for introducing and teaching these skills to young children.

Phonological and Phonemic Awareness

While current research is not clear on the role of knowing alphabet letter names in children's success as readers, the research is clear on the importance of phonological and phonemic awareness in children's literacy development (Stahl, Duffy-Hester, & Stahl, 1998). Phonological awareness is not the same as phonemic awareness. Phonological awareness is a broader term, referring to awareness of the sound structure of speech. Phonemic awareness is a subset of phonological awareness that involves awareness that spoken words are composed of individual sounds or phonemes (Yopp & Yopp, 2000). Both are important for all young children to possess if they are to become successful readers.

Marilyn Adams (1990) suggests that if children are to succeed at reading, especially if the reading program they meet in the primary grades relies heavily on phonics, phonemic awareness is the most crucial component of an early literacy program. Yet, again, the data challenge the use of highly structured training programs with young children (IRA/NAEYC, 1998). Therefore, early childhood teachers must look for ways to embed less-formal activities within their classroom settings that will help their young children attend to the sounds in the language. This is a new challenge for early childhood teachers. In the past, the teaching of letter–sound associations (phonics) has dominated early childhood programs; for the most part, children have been denied phonological and phonemic awareness experiences. Now we know that before phonics instruction can be fully useful to young children, they need phonological and phonemic awareness experiences. Even after children begin to read, they need continued instruction in phonological awareness, phonemic awareness, and phonics.

Growth in phonological awareness begins in infancy, so even the teacher of the youngest child is a phonological awareness instructor. Initially, babies hear language "as one big piece of 'BLAH BLAH BLAH'." However, as discussed in Chapter 2, babies quickly learn to hear the unique phonemes that comprise their native language. These early speech lessons occur naturally as most adults use parentese to communicate with infants (parentese is an exaggerated, slowed, and highly articulated form of speech that allows infants to see and hear their native language). Phonological awareness begins when young children are able to hear the boundaries of words (for example, *Seethekitty* becomes *See the kitty*). As sounds become words that are frequently used in context to label specific objects, the acquisition of word meaning begins.

The ability to hear distinct words and make meaningful associations usually emerges between 9 and 18 months (Cowley, 1997), and children quickly become specialists in their native tongue. However as children begin to hear and consistently produce the discreet sounds that comprise their language, the ability to hear and accurately produce the phonemes of other languages rapidly diminishes. Robert Sylwester (1995) calls this process "neural selectivity." The networks for phonemes that aren't in the local language may atrophy over time due to lack of use. This creates a challenge for children who do not speak the language of instruction when they enter school, as they often experience difficulty with hearing the phonemes and word boundaries of a second language. Therefore, oral language in the early childhood classroom is central and is a prerequisite to children's phonological and phonemic awareness development.

Marilyn Jager Adams (1990) suggests that before young children can become aware of phonemes—the individual sounds that make up spoken words—they first must become aware of larger units of oral language. Thus, children must first realize that spoken language is composed of words, syllables, and sounds. As mentioned earlier, this broader understanding is referred to as phonological awareness.

So, what can a child who is phonologically aware do? According to Catherine Snow, Susan Burns, and Peg Griffin (1998, p. 52), a child who is phonologically aware can enjoy and produce rhymes, count the number of syllables in a word, and notice when words begin or end with the same sound.

What kinds of preschool activities help children develop an appreciation of the sounds of spoken words? Marilyn Adams and several colleagues recommend a sequence of instructional activities that starts by building the most basic concepts of phonological awareness and then moves toward awareness of smaller and smaller units of sound (Adams, Foorman, Lundberg, & Beeler, 1998):

- *Listening games*—Plan activities that sharpen the children's ability to attend to sounds. For example, place objects that make noise into a bag. Invite a child to remove an object and demonstrate its sound (e.g., ring a bell). Ask the rest of the children to close their eyes and try to guess the identity of the object making the sound (Ericson & Juliebö, 1998).
- *Rhyming activities*—Plan activities that focus the children's attention on the sounds inside words. For example, invite the children to recite or sing well-known nursery rhymes such as "Jack and Jill," "Humpty Dumpty," or "Hickory Dickory Dock." Once children are familiar with the rhymes, repeat a rhyme leaving out the rhyming word. Ask the children to guess the missing rhyming words ("Humpty Dumpty sat on a wall. Humpty Dumpty had a big _____.") (Ericson & Juliebö, 1998).
- *Words and sentences*—Plan activities that develop children's awareness that language is made up of strings of words. For example, recite a familiar nursery rhyme and invite the children to join in. Explain that rhymes are made up of individual words. Recite the rhyme again, clapping as each word is spoken. Then construct the rhyme by inviting each child to say one word of the rhyme in sequence (The Wright Group, 1998). Activities in which children track print, such as the shared reading strategy described in Chapter 5, are also effective ways to help children discover the concept of words.
- *Awareness of syllables*—Plan activities that develop the ability to analyze words into separate syllables and to combine syllables into words. For example, clap and count the syllables in the children's first and last names. Start with several names with one syllable, then with multiple syllables. Say the names slowly, and clap for each syllable. Then ask the children to say the names and clap along. After each name has been "clapped," ask children how many syllables they heard.

Note that these phonological awareness activities are sequenced to provide progressively closer analysis of the units of sounds. Young children will need many of these kinds of activities. Teachers will need to be alert when their children are ready for a new challenge.

Phonological awareness exercises build a base for phonemic awareness activities in which children manipulate phonemes, the individual sounds that make up syllables and words. Phonemic awareness is a more advanced form of phonological awareness. Knowledge that speech can be broken down into phonemes is very important for learning to read. Here are some activities that can be used to develop awareness of phonemes:

- *Sound matching*—Plan activities that ask children to decide which of several words begins with a specific sound (Yopp & Yopp, 2000). For example, show children pictures of familiar objects (cat, bird, monkey), and ask which begins with the /b/ sound.
- *Sound isolation*—Plan activities in which children are given words and asked to tell what sound occurs at the beginning, middle, or ending (Yopp, 1992). For example, ask "What's the sound that starts these words: *time, turtle, top*?" Or ask children to "Say the first little bit of *snap*" (Snow et al., 1998).
- *Blending*—Plan activities that invite children to combine individual sounds to form words. For example, play "What am I thinking of?" (Yopp, 1992). Tell the class that you are thinking of an animal. Then say the name of the animal in separate phonemes: "/c/-/a/-/t/." Ask the children to blend the sounds to come up with the name of the animal.
- *Segmentation*—This is the flip side of blending. Here, teachers ask children to break words up into individual sounds (Stahl et al., 1998). Lucy Calkins (1994) calls the ability to segment words "rubber-banding," stretching words out to hear the individual phonemes. For example, provide each child with counters and Elkonin boxes (a diagram of three blank squares representing the beginning, middle, and ending sounds in a word). Ask the chil-

dren to place counters in the boxes to represent each sound in a word. For the word *cat,* a marker would be placed in the left-hand square for /c/, another in the center square for /a/, and a third in the right-hand square for /t/. The concrete props make this difficult task easier for children.

■ *Phonemic manipulation*—Ask the children to mentally add, delete, substitute, or reverse phonemes in words. For example, ask them to say a word and then say it again without the initial sound (farm > arm), to substitute initial sounds in lyrics of familiar songs (Fe-Fi-Fiddly-i-o > De-Di-Diddly-i-o) (Yopp, 1992), or to build words by substituting onsets and rimes (c-ake, b-ake, sh-ake, m-ake).

Other ways to increase phonemic awareness include reading children's books that play with sounds of language (see Opitz, 1998, for a list); reading alphabet books (Murray, Stahl, & Ivey, 1996); inviting children to use computer software like *Reader Rabbit's Ready for Letters, Kid Pix, A to Zp, Bailey's Book House,* and *The Playroom* (Snow, et al., 1998); and encouraging children to use invented spelling (Stahl, et al., 1998).

Some words of caution: Such activities can become developmentally inappropriate if the teacher does not keep them playful, weaving them intentionally and regularly into the day's activities in ways that do not dominate the early childhood program. Also, some of these activities will be inappropriate for some children. Children who are ready for such experiences will have had many experiences with books.

Alphabet Letter Recognition

What do children seem to be learning when they begin to name and write alphabet letters? By the time young children say the alphabet letter names, they have begun to make discoveries about the alphabet. Children who have had experiences with print come to understand that the squiggles on the paper are special; they can be named. Toddler Jed, for example, called all letters in his alphabet books or in environmental print signs either *B* or *D* (Lass, 1982). At this very young age, he had already learned that letters were a special form of graphics with names. Three-year-old Frank associated letters with things that were meaningful to him. He argued with his mother to buy him the *Firetruck* (not just the car) because "It's like me!" He pointed to the *F.* (Incidentally, his argument was successful.) Giti pointed to the *z* on her blocks and said, "Look, like in the zoo!" (Baghban, 1984, p. 30). These four young children have learned to associate letters with things important to them.

Should early childhood teachers expect all children to say and write all letters of the alphabet by the time the children are five? Certainly not! By the age of three, some children can name as many as ten alphabet letters (Heibert, 1981). Even children who read and write before entering kindergarten might not know the names of all the letters of the alphabet (Lass, 1982). As with other literacy learning areas, there is wide variation in what each child in a group of children will know and be able to do. Classroom strategies selected to teach young children alphabet letter names must be sensitive to these individual differences.

Knowing that some young children who are accomplished readers cannot name all the letters of the alphabet is a significant discovery. It is clear that learning to say the alphabet names need not be the first literacy skill children learn. Maybe it makes more sense to help children learn some whole words first, words that are important to them (e.g., their names, stores). Then, the letters within the words, like Cara's *C,* might hold more meaning.

Two methods are widely used to teach children the alphabet: the alphabet song and letter-of-the-week activities. Both methods have been criticized.

The alphabet song is the way children are most often introduced to letters at home (Adams, 1990). While there are some advantages to learning the names of letters in this fashion (e.g., the names give children a peg on which to attach perceptual information about letters), the song can also lead to misconceptions (e.g., that *lmnop* is one letter). In addition, Schickedanz (1998) argues that learning to recite the alphabet from memory is a trivial accomplishment that contributes little to children's learning to read. Yet, the recent report by the National Research Council (Burns, Griffin, & Snow, 1998) suggests singing the alphabet song as one of many activities early childhood teachers should use to support children's literacy learning.

The letter-of-week strategy involves introducing children to a different letter each week. During that week, children engage in a variety of activities related to the target letter. For example, during *A* week, children might establish an ant farm, eat apples, read a book about antelope, and the like. This strategy has been criticized for focusing on letters in isolation from meaningful reading and writing, for being too slow (it takes 26 weeks to introduce all the letters), and for not capitalizing on children's interests and prior knowledge (Schickedanz, 1998; Wagstaff, 1997–1998).

Rather than introducing letters in a fixed, arbitrary sequence, Lea McGee and Don Richgels (1989) believe that it is preferable to teach letters that match children's current interests and activities. In order to deliver this type of individualized alphabet instruction, teachers need to observe closely to learn about the types of contexts in which children notice letters (e.g., environmental print, computer keyboards, books, friends' T-shirts). These contexts provide wonderful opportunities for informal talk and instruction about the alphabet.

It is these other kinds of alphabet learning activities that are more typical of quality early childhood activities. They include:

- *Environmental print*—Bring environmental print items to class (empty cereal boxes, cookie bags, etc.) and encourage children to read the print's message and discuss prominent letters (e.g., the letter *C* on a box of corn flakes).
- *Reading and writing children's names*—As discussed in Chapter 6, printed versions of children's names can be used for a variety of functional purposes, including attendance charts, helper charts, sign-up lists, and so on. Names of classmates have inherent high interest. Take advantage of every opportunity to read these names and to call attention to letters in the names ("Look, Jenny's and Jerry's names both start with the same letter. What letter is it?").
- *Writing*—Whenever children engage in writing, on their own or with a teacher (e.g., shared writing), their attention can be drawn to the letters of the alphabet. Remember that even if children are using scribbles or another personalized form of script, they are attempting to represent the letters of alphabet and thus are learning about letters.
- *Alphabet books*—There are many types of alphabet books available. For young children who are just learning the alphabet, books with simple letter–object associations (e.g., illustrations that show a letter and objects that begin with the sound associated with the letter) are most appropriate (Raines & Isbell, 1994). Alphabet books offer an enjoyable way to introduce children to letters and the sounds they represent. Research has shown that repeated reading of ABC books can promote young children's letter recognition (Greenewald & Kulig, 1995). (See Chapter 5 for more information on alphabet books.)

It is also beneficial for children to make their own alphabet books. These child-made ABC books typically have a letter at the top of each page. Children then draw pictures and/or cut and paste illustrations of objects that begin with the sound of each letter. They can also write any words they know that contain the target letter. An adult can label the pictures.

- *Alphabet games*—Schickedanz (1998) recommends two alphabet games in particular:
  - alphabet-matching puzzles, in which the children must match loose letter tiles with letters printed on a background board;
  - an alphabet clue game, in which the teacher draws part of a letter and then asks children to guess which letter he or she is thinking of. After children make their guesses, the teacher adds another piece to the letter and has the children guess again.
- *Special alphabet activities*—Young children enjoy finger painting letters; painting letters on the easel or on the sidewalk on a hot day with a brush dipped in water; rolling and folding clay or playdough to make letters; and making and eating alphabet soup, puzzles, or pretzels. All of these activities provide meaningful, playful contexts within which young children can learn alphabet names.
- *Traditional manipulatives*—There are many traditional early childhood manipulatives that can be used to support children's alphabet letter name learning. These manipulatives include alphabet puzzles, magnetic uppercase and lowercase letters, felt letters, letter stencils, and chalk and chalkboards.

Incidentally, Adams (1990) recommends that teachers help children identify uppercase letters first, followed by lowercase letters. She thinks uppercase letters are more familiar to children and are easier for children to visually discriminate between than their lowercase counterparts.

Word Recognition

According to the old readiness view of reading, children needed to learn to recognize the letters of the alphabet before they were ready to learn to recognize and read whole words. Research on early literacy has shown this to be incorrect (see Chapter 4). We now know that many children learn to recognize personally significant words, such as their names and environmental print (*Pepsi*), before they learn to recognize the more abstract letters that make up these words. We recommend that teachers work on the two skills in a simultaneous and connected fashion: provide experiences that draw children's attention to highly meaningful words and, at the same time, point out key letters in those words.

We have already described several basic strategies that parents and teachers can use to help young children learn to recognize whole words:

- *Storybook reading*—When adults read favorite books to children over and over again, repeated exposure to a small number of words can lead to the beginning of word recognition.
- *Environmental print*—Words connected with environmental print (e.g., cereal boxes, soft drink cans, road signs, billboards, and restaurant menus) are often among the first words that children recognize. As explained in Chapter 4, this type of print is easy to learn to recognize because the context gives clues to the print's meaning. Adults can assist this process by drawing children's attention to environmental print and by using the environmental print and functional print strategies described at the beginning of Chapter 6.

In the following sections, we discuss two other strategies that are ideally suited for building young children's recognition of words: key words and word walls.

KEY WORDS.   The key word strategy, developed by Sylvia Ashton-Warner (1963), is an excellent way to build young children's ability to recognize words. It is a very simple and elegant strategy: children choose words that are personally meaningful and that they would like to learn to read. Real-life experiences, favorite children's books, writing workshop, and language experience stories are primary sources for these key words. Children learn to recognize these words quickly because of their high meaning and personal significance.

Here is how the key word strategy works: The teacher asks each child in the class to pick a favorite word that he or she would like to learn to read. This word is written on a large card while the child watches. (This is sometimes done in circle time so that the whole class learns about each child's key word.) The children then write their keys words plus any other words that they remember. Finally, they engage in various games and practice activities with their key words.

The following are some of the key word games and practice activities recommended by Jeanette Veatch and her associates (Veatch, Sawicki, Elliot, Flake, & Blakey, 1979, pp. 30–32):

- *Retrieving words from the floor*—The children's words (with young children this will be the words of a partner or a small group) are placed face down on the floor. On the signal, each child is to find one of her or his own words, hold it up, and read it aloud.
- *Claiming the cards*—The teacher selects many words from the class, holds them up, and the child who "owns" each word claims it.
- *Classifying words*—The teacher selects categories that encompass all of the words selected by the children. The categories are introduced, and labels are placed on the floor for each category. The children must then decide in which category their words belong. For example, the children who have animal words would stand next to the sheet of paper that says *animals*.
- *Making alphabet books*—Children record their words in the correct section of an alphabet book that is divided by initial letters. This is a good example of how children can learn about words and letters simultaneously.

- *Illustrating*—The child can draw a picture about the key word, dictate the word to a teacher to write on a card, and then copy the word into a picture dictionary word book.
- *Finding words*—Children might find their key words in books, magazines, and newspapers.

Veatch and her colleagues recommend that children collect key words and keep them in a box or on a ring file known as a "word bank." Another possibility is to have children keep their key words in a word book, as is illustrated in Trade Secret 7.4. In this variation, the teacher writes a word on a card for the child, then the child copies the word into his or her word book. Notice how the teacher, Bernadette Watson, prompts Amanda to use letter–sound relationships when she writes Amanda's key word, *elephant*, on the card.

Periodically, the teacher can have children review their words in their word banks or word books. Besides providing opportunities for children to practice recognizing key words, word banks and word books serve other valuable functions. They provide children with a concrete record of their reading vocabulary growth. It is very motivating for children to see their collections of words grow larger and larger. In addition, the words can be used to help children learn about letters and the sounds they are associated with. For example, if children are learning the sound associated with *b*, the teacher can have children find all the words in their collections that begin with that letter.

WORD WALLS.   A word wall is a word bank for an entire classroom. Category labels are posted at the top of one or more bulletin boards, and then words are selected by the teacher and/or children and placed on the board under the appropriate label. Wagstaff (1998) suggests a strategy that is appropriate for kindergartners: the ABC word wall. The category labels are the letters of the alphabet. Each week, the class focuses on a different poem or nursery rhyme. After the rhyme or poem is read for the first time, several words are selected that begin with different letters. For example, if the rhyme was "Jack and Jill," *Jack, hill,* and *pail* might be selected as the focus words. The following sequence is used to familiarize children with these words and their initial sounds:

- The teacher emphasizes the beginning sound of each word, helping children hear and say the sounds.
- The words are written on colored pieces of construction paper and added to the word wall under the appropriate letter labels.

Trade Secret 7.4

My Word Book

Bernadette Watson

As the children entered the classroom, Ms. Watson greeted them, gave them a 3 x 5-inch card, and asked them, "What is your word for today?" Children answered. Amanda said, "Elephant." Ms. Watson positioned her hand to write *elephant* on the card. Before she wrote the word, she asked Amanda how she decided on this word as her word for the day. Amanda had seen a program on television about elephants the night before and had decided, right then and there, that *elephant* would be her word today.

"So," asked Ms. Watson, "what letter do you think *elephant* begins with?"

"I don't know," responded Amanda.

"It's an *e*," said Ms. Watson. "What letter is next?" She stretched the sound, "l-l-l-l-l."

Amanda responded, "L!"

"You're right," exclaimed Ms. Watson, "and then it's another *e*, and a *p-h-a-n*. And what do you think the last letter is? T-t-t-t-t."

Amanda said, "T!"

"Absolutely," said Ms. Watson.

Amanda took her card with *elephant* written on it with her and set off to locate her word book. Having found it, she sat at a table to copy her word into her book. First, she drew a picture of an elephant. Above it, she copied the word *elephant*. At the beginning of the year, that is all she would have done. Now, she also wrote a sentence under the picture: "isnt.v" (I saw on TV).

When she was done, Amanda took her book to the library center. Here, she might read her words to herself or to a friend. The pictures she had drawn greatly help her remember her word for the day.

- The children engage in word play—putting thumbs up if words begin with the same sound as *Jack, hill,* or *pail,* and thumbs down if they start with a different sound; finding other words that start with the *j, h,* or *p* sounds; substituting words that rhyme with words in the nursery rhyme: "Back and Jill went up the pill to fetch a tail of water."
- The rhyme is reread, placing the words back into a meaningful context.

During the rest of the week, the rhyme can be revisited with shared reading, and the children can engage in different types of word play with the words on the word wall to build phonemic awareness and knowledge of letter–sound relationships.

Trade Secrets 7.5 describes another variation of the ABC word wall that might be used at the kindergarten level.

Phonics

Phonics involves using the alphabetic principle (letters have a relationship with the sounds of oral language) to decode printed words. Young children differ greatly in their need for instruction in this important decoding skill. Stahl (1992, p. 620) explains: "Some will learn to decode on their own, without any instruction. Others will need some degree of instruction, ranging from pointing out of common spelling patterns to intense and systematic instruction." Thus, as in all other aspects of literacy instruction, it is important for phonics teaching to match the needs of individual students.

The children who learn phonics more or less on their own simply need to be provided with the types of meaningful reading and writing activities described in Chapters 5 and 6—shared reading and writing, literacy-enriched play, and functional literacy activities. As these children engage in these purposeful literacy activities, they gradually discover the relationship between letters and sounds.

Those who need a moderate amount of assistance profit from what Morrow and Tracey (1997) term "contextual instruction." This type of instruction occurs in conjunction with the same types of activities described in the preceding paragraph—shared reading and writing, literacy-enriched play, and functional literacy activities. The only difference is that while children are engaging in these activities, the teacher draws children's attention to letter–sound relationships that are present.

Morrow and Tracey (1997, p. 647) give an example of how one teacher, Mrs. M., drew her students' attention to the letter *m* and its sound during an activity that involved both shared writing and functional writing:

Because her class had finished putting on a show for their grandparents, Mrs. M. thought it would be a good idea if they wrote a thank-you note to the music teacher who assisted them with the performance. The note was composed by the students with the teacher's help. She wrote the note on the board and sounded out each word to help the students with spelling. After they finished writing, Mrs. M. read the entire note and had the students read the note aloud:

> *Mrs. M.:* How should we start this letter?
>
> *Student:* Dear Mr. Miller.
>
> *Mrs. M.:* Very good [as she writes] "Dear Mr. Miller" has three words. *Dear* is the first word, *Mr.* is the second word, and *Miller* is the third word. I just realized that my name and Mr. Miller's name both begin with the same letter, *M.* Let's say these words together, "Mr. Miller, Mrs. Martinez."

This type of spontaneous teaching can occur in connection with all the literacy learning activities described in Chapters 4 and 5. Of course, such teaching requires a teacher who is on the lookout for teachable moments involving letter–sound relationships. Because most, if not all, preschool and kindergarten classes contain some children who need moderate assistance, we recommend that teachers make an effort to take advantage of these types of teaching opportunities when they arise.

Trade Secret 7.5

Word Walls

At the beginning of the kindergarten year, Mrs. Burl begins each school day by asking her class to share any print items they brought from home. These items are usually packages or wrappers of products the children's family use at home. She asks each child who brought an item to read the name of the item to the rest of the class. After the children have read their environmental print, Mrs. Burl selects one of the products, Aim toothpaste, and asks the children where they think the Aim toothpaste container should go on their ABC word wall? The children think for just a moment when Anissa suggests cutting the wrapper into two parts—one part for *Aim* to go under the letter *Aa* on the word wall and the second for *toothpaste* to go under the letter *Tt*. Mrs. Burl asks the class for a thumbs-up (for yes) or thumbs-down (for no) vote. The children give her a unanimous thumbs up. Mrs. Burl quickly cuts the package, circles the appropriate words, and asks the child who brought the wrapper

to pin each word under the correct letter on the word wall.

The word wall concept allows teachers to stimulate children's awareness of words and knowledge of letters and sounds (Hedrick & Pearish, 1999; Morrow, Tracey, Gee-Woo, & Pressley, 1999; Wagstaff, 1998). Teachers may use a range of word wall activities to reinforce and support young children's growing phonemic abilities and reading skills. Mrs. Burl begins the kindergarten year with an ABC word wall that focuses on the initial letter sounds. Later, when the children's awareness of the sound–symbol relationship grows, she will add blends and consonant digraphs to the ABC word wall (see Figure 7.3).

Mrs. Burl found the word wall concept to be useful for teaching a variety of mini-lessons and stimulating the children's interest in words and reading. She also found that parents are interested in the word walls because they provide an ongoing visual record of the many lessons Mrs. Burl uses to teach phonemic awareness to her students.

Figure 7.3 *ABC word wall*

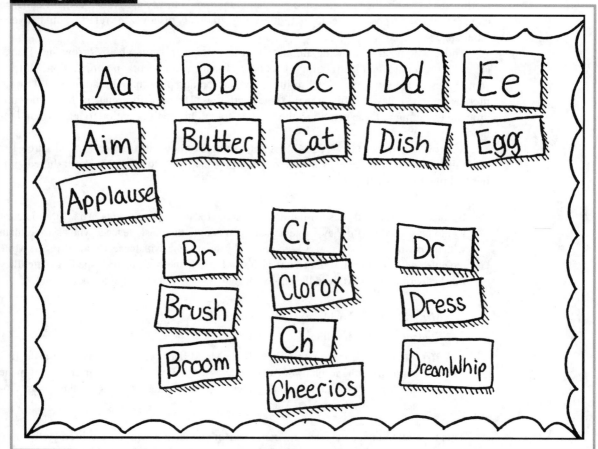

Another way to help children acquire knowledge about phonics is through writing (IRA/NAEYC, 1998; Stahl, 1992). Once children have reached the invented spelling stage in their writing development, they begin to use their knowledge of letter names and letter–sound relationships to spell words. During this stage, children spell words the way that they sound rather than how they are conventionally spelled. For example a child may spell the word *leave* with the letters *lev* because this is how the word sounds. When children use invented spelling, their attention is naturally focused on letter–sound relationships.

Research indicates that temporary use of invented spelling can promote children's reading development (IRA/NAEYC, 1998). For example, a study by Clarke (1988) found that young children who were encouraged to write with invented spelling scored higher on decoding and reading comprehension tests than children who were encouraged to use conventional spelling.

Finally, teachers can provide preplanned phonics activities to children who have developed an awareness of the sounds that make up spoken words and who can recognize some of the letters of the alphabet. This can be done by adapting the phonemic awareness, letter recognition, and word recognition activities discussed earlier in this chapter so that they focus on letter–sound relationships. We recommend that letter–sound relationships be selected that fit in with ongoing class activities or that fit the needs of specific children, rather than using an arbitrary sequence (consonants first, short vowels second, long vowels third, etc.).

Several of the phonemic awareness activities described earlier in this chapter can easily be modified to teach phonics by having children identify which letters represents the various sounds and then writing words so that children can see the letter–sound relationships:

- *Letter–sound matching*—Show pictures of familiar objects (cat, bird, and monkey) and ask children which begins with the /m/ sound. Then ask which letter *monkey* starts with. Write the word on chalkboard. Ask children for other words that start with the /m/ sound, and write these words on the board.
- *Letter–sound isolation*—Pronounce words and asks children what sounds are heard at the beginning, middle, or end. For example, ask the children, "What sound is in the middle of *man, cat,* and *Sam*?" Once the sound is identified, ask the children what letter represents the sound. The words can then be written on the chalkboard, along with other short-*a* words.

In a similar fashion, letter recognition activities can be modified to teach phonics by shifting the focus from letters to their sounds.

- *Environmental print*—Discuss letter–sound relationships that occur in environmental print. For example, if children have brought in cereal boxes from home, the teacher could ask questions such as "What letters make the /ch/ sound in Cheerios?" Children could then be asked to identify other words that start with the /ch/ sound, and these words could be written on the chalkboard.
- *Reading and writing children's names*—When referring to children's names in attendance charts, helper charts, and other places, call children's attention to letter–sound correspondences in their names. For example, the teacher might say, "Jenny's and Jerry's names start with the same sound. What letter does both their names start with?"
- *Games*—Create games that enable children to reinforce their growing knowledge of letter–sound relationships in an enjoyable manner. A popular type of phonics game requires children to match letters with pictures that begin with letter sounds. For example, the letter *b* might be matched with a picture of a bird. If you use this type of phonics matching game, be sure to tell the children the word that each picture represents in order to avoid confusion with other words that the picture could represent. In the example of the *b/bird* item, a child might justifiably believe that the picture of bird represented the word *robin* or *sparrow* rather than *bird.*

Word banks and word walls, discussed in the section on word recognition, can also be invaluable aids in helping children learn phonics. The words in these collections are familiar to children and often have strong personal significance and meaning. These high-meaning words can serve as pegs on which children can attach letter–sound relationships. Teachers should routinely take advantage of these words by linking them with phonics activities and lessons. For example, if a teacher were trying to help children learn the *ch* sound–symbol correspondence, children could be asked to find all the letters in their word banks or on the word wall that contain this letter combination.

Some children will need more direct instruction on letter–sound relationships, but not during the preschool years. Preschool and kindergarten children who need extensive help learning phonics really need more experience with phonemic awareness, letter recognition, and informal types of phonic instruction described in this chapter. These activities will build a foundation that will help these children benefit from more systematic approaches to learning phonics later.

Summary

Whereas Chapters 5 and 6 describe activities that can implicitly teach children how to write and read, this chapter deals with explicit literacy instruction. It describes a variety of developmentally appropriate strategies that teachers can use to directly teach children how to write and read. Each skill has been found to be important to children's success as readers and writers. What have you learned?

- *Why is a writing center an important area in the preschool classroom? How might an adult teach in the writing center?*

  A writing center is that area of the classroom in which the teacher has stocked materials (different kinds of papers, various writing tools, alphabet strips, computers) that invite children to write. The teacher is an important other in the writing center. As a co-writer, the teacher writes alongside the children and models the writing process, informally teaching children about the forms (letters, thank-you notes) and features (spelling, letter formation) of print. As a skilled writer, the teacher can teach children as he or she writes by casually talking about letter–sound relationships, how to begin a letter, or what might be said in a letter.

- *How does a teacher teach during a writing workshop?*

  Each writing workshop begins with a mini-lesson. The goal of these lessons is to teach children about some aspect of writing (e.g., how to make revisions; how to add describing words; how to spell words). The mini-lesson is followed by writing time. During writing time, the teacher talks with individual children about their writing. Here, the teacher might help a child stretch words to hear sounds, add details to the child's drawing, or talk with the child about the topic of the piece. Through conferences, the teacher provides one-on-one instruction. After the writing time, two or three children will share their work with their peers and the teacher. Now, the teacher and the other children can ask questions about the writing.

- *Why is it important to publish children's writing?*

  Publishing helps young children understand that they write so others can read their thoughts. Making young children's writing efforts public is important. The publishing process need not be complicated.

- *What does it mean to offer young children a balanced approach to reading instruction?*

  Balanced reading instruction combines elements of meaning-centered and skill-centered reading instruction. Children do large amounts of reading and have opportunities to discuss and respond to what has been read. In addition, they receive direct instruction on basic reading skills. This instruction is linked to the texts they are reading.

- *What is the difference between phonological awareness, phonemic awareness, and phonics? In what sequence do young children typically acquire these skills? What does this sequence suggest about classroom instructional strategies?*

  Phonological awareness (realization that spoken language is composed of words, syllables, and sounds) is broader than phonemic awareness (realization that words are composed of phonemes). Both are important for all young children to possess if they are to become successful readers. Whereas phonological and phonemic awareness just involve sound, phonics involves learning the relationship between letters and the sounds they represent. The instructional sequence now recommended by research is to begin by helping children build the basic concepts of phonological awareness, then to move toward helping children develop awareness that words are composed of phonemes, and finally to help children develop awareness of letter–sound associations. Therefore, the instructional sequence is from broad concepts to smaller and smaller units of sound.

■ *How might early childhood teachers introduce young children to the letters of the alphabet?*
   Some readers probably learned the names of the letters of the alphabet by singing the alphabet song. Today, the value of this activity gets mixed reviews. Some readers probably learned the names of the letters of the alphabet by studying a different letter each week. This approach receives strong criticism today. Early childhood teachers should teach their young learners the names of the letters that match their children's current interests and activities through informal talk and embedded in playful activities. Teachers should remember that most children will not know the names of all the letters of the alphabet before they recognize and read whole words. Skillful teachers can link drawing children's attention to highly meaningful words and key letters simultaneously.

■ *How can early childhood teachers reassure the public that they* are *teaching phonics?*
   Some children seem to learn phonics on their own; teachers need to provide them with numerous meaningful reading and writing activities that will allow them to discover how our language works. Other children need some phonics instruction; teachers need to offer them the same kind of meaningful reading and writing activities and also need to draw children's attention to letter–sound relationships present in these activities—not once, but often. Teachers need to be alert to teachable moments for drawing children's attention to letter–sound relationships in many reading and writing activities. Remember, phonics instruction is appropriate only when children exhibit phonological and phonemic awareness.

Linking Knowledge to Practice

1. Visit a classroom set up for three-year-olds and a classroom set up for five-year-olds in an early childhood center. Draw a diagram of each classroom's writing center, and make a list of the writing materials the teacher has provided. Describe the differences between the writing center set up for three-year-olds with that set up for five-year-olds. Observe the classrooms' teachers as they interact with the children in the writing center. Describe what they talk about with the children.

2. Create descriptions of several developmentally appropriate phonological awareness activities, from the most basic concepts to the more advanced, that might be used with young children. Make copies of your activities for others in your class.

3. Create descriptions of several developmentally appropriate phonemic awareness activities for use with young children. Make copies of your activities for others in your class.

4. Create a description of several developmentally appropriate alphabet recognition activities for use with young children. Make copies of your activities for others in your class.

Ongoing Assessment and Adapting Instruction to Meet the Needs of Diverse Students

8

Mrs. Saenz is observing four-year-old Martine and Monique playing together in the post office center. The children are pretending to be post office people and are busy sorting letters into a mail sorter (a plastic office sorter that is divided into 24 slots, each labeled with an alphabet letter sticker). As she watches the children put the letters in the slots, Mrs. Saenz notices that Martine is accomplishing this task by recognizing the first letter of each name, then matching it to the appropriately labeled slot. She also notices that Monique, who is learning English, is simply putting the letters into the slots without paying any attention to the names on the envelopes. After a few moments, Martine stops Monique.

Martine: No, Monique. Look at the name. See the big letter? That letter tells you to put it in this mailbox.

Monique: What it say?

Martine: It says B. I think it is for Bobby. See? [He puts the letter in the B mailbox.]

Monique: Gimme. [She reaches for another letter.] What it say?

Martine: It says R.

Monique: [Thinking for a moment, she starts to sing the alphabet song. She puts her hand on each letter as she sings them.]

Martine: That helps find 'em fast, uh?

Mrs. Saenz carefully observes this interaction and makes brief anecdotal notes describing what Monique and Martine know and can do. This information will also help her to adjust instruction to better meet both children's learning needs.

In the preceding three chapters we have presented strategies for implicit and explicit instruction in early literacy. While these instructional activities form the core of an effective language arts program, they cannot stand alone. Two other elements are needed to ensure that the instructional strategies meet the needs of every child in the class: assessment and adaptations for linguistic diversity and special needs.

We begin this chapter by describing the many ways teachers can gather information about children. Next, we explain how these data can be organized into portfolios and shared with others. In two special features, the authors present strategies for adapting instruction to meet the needs of second-language learners and children with special needs.

- how your teachers assessed your literacy progress. Did you take spelling tests? Did you read stories and answer comprehension questions? Did you ever evaluate your own progress?
- how information about your literacy progress was shared with your parents. Did your parents read your report card? Did your parents attend conferences? Were you involved in sharing information about your progress with your peers or parents?
- how children with special learning needs were accommodated in your classes. Were there children who spoke other languages in your classes? Did your teacher adapt instruction for children with different learning needs?

Focus Questions

- What is important for teachers to know about children's literacy development?
- What types of assessment methods are used to collect information about children's progress?
- How do teachers use the information they collect?
- How do ongoing assessment techniques help early childhood teachers meet the needs of diverse learners?

Assessment: Determining What Children Know and Can Do

Instruction and assessment are intertwined in excellent literacy instruction. In the opening vignette, Mrs. Saenz observed two children with differing levels of alphabet recognition. Mrs. Saenz's careful observations are supported by developmental guidelines created by early childhood experts. She knows that though Martine and Monique differ in their ability to recognize alphabet letters, both are making remarkable progress. She also knows that as a second-language learner, Monique has made tremendous strides. Further, Mrs. Saenz's observations

---

BOX 8.1

Definition of Terms

individual education plan (IEP): a written document developed by a multidisciplinary team that includes the student's parents, the student's regular and special education teachers, and other school administrative and support personnel. It describes the student's current level of functioning, his or her goals and objectives, the types of support the student needs, and the dates for the initiation and duration of that support.

individual family service plan (IFSP): a written document developed by a multidisciplinary team that focuses on the child's needs and goals. The focus of this type of plan may also include direct support for the family of a child with disabilities. In addition, the IFSP may specify the type of support parents may offer to their child to help the child successfully transition to school.

on-demand assessment: a type of assessment that occurs during special time set aside for testing. In most cases, teaching and learning come to a complete stop while the teacher conducts the assessment.

ongoing assessment: a form of assessment that relies on the regular collection of children's work to illustrate children's knowledge and learning. The children's products are created as they engage in daily classroom activities. Thus, children are learning while they are being assessed.

showcase portfolio: exhibits samples of student work that illustrate the student's efforts, progress, and achievements. The showcase portfolio is shared with others, usually the child's parents.

working portfolio: where the student and teacher place work that is reflective of the student's achievement. Both the student and the teacher may place work in the working portfolio.

provide her with a better understanding of the different strategies (alphabet song and one-to-one letter matching) Monique is using to learn the name of each of these symbols. The lessons Mrs. Sanez will teach tomorrow are guided by the observations she made of what and how the children learned today. As Lorrie Shepard, Sharon Kagan, and Emily Wurtz (1998, p. 52) note:

> When children are assessed as part of the teaching–learning process, then assessment information tells caregivers and teachers what each child can do and what he or she is ready to learn next. Finding out, on an ongoing basis, what a child knows and can do helps parents and teachers decide how to pose new challenges and provide help with what the child has not yet mastered. Teachers also use their assessment of children's learning to reflect on their own teaching practices so that they can adjust and modify curricula, instructional activities, and classroom routines that are ineffective.

What Is Important for Teachers to Know about Children's Literacy Development?

Sheila Valencia (1990) and Grant Wiggins (1993) agree on a primary principle of assessment: Teachers must begin assessment by determining what they value. "Only after goals have been established and clarified can attention turn to the appropriate tasks and contexts for gathering information" (Valencia, Hiebert, & Afflerback, 1994, p. 10). Teachers must answer the question: What is important for us to know about our children's development as readers, writers, speakers, and listeners?

The ideas in this book help readers answer this question. In addition, readers have two excellent new resources to guide their answer (IRA/NAEYC, 1998; Snow, Burns, & Griffin, 1998). Both include lists of literacy accomplishments that should be evidenced by young children of various ages. Teams of early childhood literacy experts created both lists following their reviews of what is known from research on young children's literacy development.

One of these reports was prepared by the Committee on the Preventing of Reading Difficulties in Young Children, appointed by the National Research Council. In their report, *Preventing Reading Difficulties in Young Children*, the committee provides teachers (and parents, administrators, curriculum consultants, textbook publishers, and legislators) with a list of "accomplishments that the successful learner is likely to exhibit during the preschool years" (Snow, Burns, & Griffin, 1998, p. 60).

In addition, in the summer of 1998, two major organizations—-the International Reading Association (IRA) and the National Association for the Education of Young Children (NAEYC)—issued a joint position statement on developmentally appropriate reading and writing practices for young children. "The primary purpose of this position statement is to provide guidance to teachers of young children in schools and early childhood programs (including child care centers, preschools, and family child care homes) serving children from birth through age eight" (IRA/NAEYC, 1998, p. 30). Like the report of the Committee on Preventing Reading Difficulties in Young Children, the joint position statement provides a list of what children of various ages and grade levels likely can do.

The authors of both reports acknowledge that their lists are not exhaustive and that children will function at a variety of levels along the reading–writing continuum. "Reading and writing acquisition is conceptualized better as a developmental continuum than as an all-or-nothing phenomenon" (IRA/NAEYC, 1998, p. 34). Further, since children differ maturationally and experientially, the accomplishments listed for each age group or phase are merely suggestive of the behaviors teachers might expect. A child will likely exhibit behaviors that span a variety of phases appropriate to various age groups. The authors of this book strongly encourage readers to obtain copies of these important new early childhood literacy resources.[1]

---

[1]For a complete copy of the position statement, *Learning to Read and Write: Developmentally Appropriate Practices for Young Children,* readers are encouraged to write to the International Reading Association, 800 Barksdale Road, Newark, Delaware 19714, or to the National Association for the Education of Young Children, 1509 16th St. NW, Washington, DC 20036. For a copy of *Preventing Reading Difficulties in Young Children,* write to the National Academy Press, 2101 Constitution Avenue, NW, Lockbox 285, Washington, DC 20053. You can also download this book off the Internet at the National Academy Press Web site (http://www.nap.edu/readingroom/books/prdyc/).

Figure 8.1	The Environmental Print Assessment kit consists of ten items that were identified as universal in American culture, being recognized by 60 to 80 percent of the children in the Phoenix pilot study. The pilot group consisted of children ages three to five from diverse ethnic, linguistic, and socioeconomic backgrounds.

The Environmental Print Assessment kit

- Level 1 consists of actual EP objects (M&M bag, stop sign, Oreo cookie wrapper, Band-Aid box, Pokemon plate, Burger King sack, Pepsi can, McDonald's fries container, Tele-tubbies plate, and a Blockbuster video container.
- Level 2 consists of ten cards with the color logo of each of the items.
- Level 3 consist of ten cards with black-and-white logo without the color or background clues.
- Level 4 consists of ten cards with each of the words printed in manuscript.

The activity is presented as a game, with prompt questions such as "Can you tell me what this is?" Or "Where is the container from?" Children are given

- 2 points if they recognize the correct word (Pepsi, McDonald's, Blockbuster),
- 1 point for meaningful answers such as correctly identifying the categories (soda for Pepsi, burger for McDonald's, movie or video for Blockbuster), and
- 0 points for no response or a wrong answer.

We begin this section by exploring the most appropriate ways teachers might gather information about their children's literacy development. We follow this description with specific guidelines for conducting ongoing assessment, the approach that best fits the constructivist orientation of this book. In this section, we describe the tools for the ongoing gathering of information about students' language and literacy learning, how to store information, and issues involved in interpreting and sharing the information gathered. Readers should know that it is generally believed to be more difficult to determine what young children know and can do than what older children know and can do. Both the nature of early learning and young children's developing language skills provide teachers and caregivers with assessment challenges.

The First Step—Gathering Information

Once teachers have decided what is important for them to know about their children's literacy development, they must then decide how to gather this information. There are two general options: on-demand tasks and ongoing assessment. We begin this section with brief descriptions of these two methods.

ON-DEMAND ASSESSMENT. On-demand assessments (Figure 8.1) occur at specific times. For example, on Tuesday all kindergarten children in the school district may be asked to take a pencil-and-paper test. They might be asked to listen to several short stories composed of two or three sentences. Then the children would be asked to put an X on the picture that best matches each story. They may be asked to circle the letters said aloud by the teacher. They might be asked to listen to sounds said aloud by the teacher (e.g., *b*) and to circle the letter that makes that sound.

Most readers likely would label these kinds of on-demand assessments as *tests*. Early childhood teachers often express concerns with the administration of these kinds of assessments to young children. Susan Andersen (1998), an early childhood consultant and former teacher, details several of these concerns. She objects to the "artificial situation" (p. 25)—children separated, each child working alone—in which children must be placed for such tests. There can be no responding to each other's questions, no cooperating with each other. Such tests place unnecessary stress and unrealistic expectations on young children (and their teachers) when children's performance is used as the measure to compare teachers against teachers, schools against schools, districts against districts, or states against states or to make decisions about the school's eligibility for federal programs for the coming school year.

Anderson (1998, p. 26) explains that "In theory we give young children standardized tests so we can use the results to improve teaching methods. But most teachers will admit the tests do more to disrupt learning than to benefit teaching."

No wonder many professional groups, including National Association for the Education of Young Children (NAEYC) and the other major early childhood education professional organization, the Association for Childhood Education International (ACEI), have called for a moratorium on the testing of children before the age of eight. Recently, the guidelines prepared by the Goal 1 Early Childhood Assessments Resource Group (an advisory group to the National Education Goals Panel, which is composed of governors, members of Congress, and administration officials) lend support to this moratorium on early testing (Shepard, Kagan, & Wurtz, 1998). These guidelines suggest that before age eight, standardized achievement measures are not sufficiently accurate to be used for high-stakes decisions about individual children and schools. Therefore, high-stakes assessments intended for accountability purposes should be delayed until the end of third grade (or preferably fourth grade).

The recent IRA/NAEYC joint position statement, *Learning to Read and Write: Developmentally Appropriate Practices for Young Children* (1998, p. 43) further reinforces this position:

> Group-administered, multiple choice, standardized achievement tests in reading and writing skills should not be used before third grade and preferably even before fourth grade. The younger the child, the more difficult it is to obtain valid and reliable indices of his or her development and learning using one-time test administration.

The primary purpose of standardized tests is accountability: How are the children in this classroom, school, school district, state, or nation doing, compared to the children in other classrooms, schools, school districts, states, and nations? The focus is on group performance rather than on the performance of individual students. Consequently, information on the performance of the group of children who participated in the assessment typically is reported to the parents, teacher, school, school district, state department of education, and often the broader community (e.g., parents, the newspaper, other public media) as a percentile, something like "Your child's score shows that your child scored better than 10 percent of the pupils in the state and that 90 percent of the children in the state scored better than your child did." Classroom, school, school district, and state data are aggregated so that comparisons can be made across classrooms in the school, schools in the school districts, school districts in the state, and states in the nation. We disagree with this excessive use of assessment for accountability purposes. We believe the main focus of assessment in the early years should be on promoting children's learning and development.

There are other kinds of on-demand tests administered in some early childhood programs. In these programs, teachers arrange to meet individually with each child three or four times a year to administer an on-demand assessment as one means of gathering specific information about each child's literacy development. Many use modified versions of Clay's (1972) *Concepts of Print* test. These teachers typically ask children to demonstrate their book awareness by doing several typical book behaviors. That is, teachers might ask the child to show them the front of the book or how to turn the books pages, or to point to the title. These teachers might ask children to demonstrate their understandings of print by showing them where they should begin reading, where to go after reading a line of text, and what is read, the print or the pictures. They might ask the children to point to a letter, a word, a period, and a question mark. They might ask them to listen to a story and read along, pointing while they read, when they can. They might ask them to retell the story.

ONGOING ASSESSMENT. Ongoing assessment relies on the regular collection of artifacts to illustrate children's knowledge and learning. The artifacts (the children's products) are produced by the children while they engage in their daily classroom activities, such as those described in every chapter in this book. The products of these activities, then, serve the dual purposes of instruction and assessment. Because the children's artifacts are stored in portfolios, ongoing assessment often is called portfolio assessment. Ongoing assessment differs from on-demand assessment in several ways:

- Children work on their products for varying amounts of time, and the procedures or directions often vary across the classroom or across classes in the building.

- What each child and the teacher select as evidence of literacy learning may be different, not only across the children in the school but also across the children in a teacher's class.
- The classroom teacher analyzes each child's performance on the tasks and makes judgments about each child's learning.
- The classroom teacher's judgments are used immediately to define the child's next learning goal. The assessment, then, has an immediate effect on instruction for each child.
- The assessment of the work produced over time in many different contexts permits the teacher and the child to gather more than a quick snapshot of what the child knows and is able to do at a given moment.

Ongoing assessment, then, permits both the teacher and the student to examine the child's knowledge and learning. Young learner Phyllis shares what this means as she uses her journal to describe her growth as a reader and writer:

I comed to this school a little bit nervous, you know. Nothin'. [She shakes her head for added emphasis.] I couldn't read or write nothin'. Look at this. [She turns to the first few pages of her writing journal.] Not a word! Not a word! [She taps the page and adds an aside.] And the drawin's not too good. Now, look at this. [She turns to the end of the journal.] One, two, three, four. Four pages! And I can read 'em. Listen. [She reads.] Words! [Nodding her head.] Yup! Now I can read and write a lotta words!

Phyllis' journal is one of several tools her teacher uses to gather information about Phyllis' literacy learning. Like Phyllis, her teacher can compare the writing at the beginning and at the end of the journal to learn about Phyllis' literacy development over time. Each tool used permits teachers to gather information about their children's literacy learning while the children perform the kinds of activities described in this book. Readers were introduced to several of these tools in previous chapters.

- *Anecdotal notes*—These are teacher notes describing a child's behavior. In addition to the child's name, the date, and the classroom area, the specific event or product should be described exactly as it was seen and heard. The following is an example of Karen Valentine's anecdotal notes:

Martia
M./ in the library center "reading" a page in a big book. As she reads 9/25, she points to the words. She runs out of words before she is done reading (each syllable = pointed to word). She tries again, and again, and again, and again. She leaves, shaking her head.

Teachers use many different kinds of paper (e.g., computer address labels, note pads, paper in a loose-leaf binder, index cards, Post-it® Notes) to make anecdotal records of children's behavior. Figure 8.2 shows an inexpensive flip chart a teacher developed to aid her anecdotal note record-keeping. The teacher used a clipboard and 3 × 5-inch index cards. She wrote each child's name on the bottom of a card; arranged the cards in alphabetical order; and then starting at the bottom of the clipboard, taped the child's card whose name began with the last letter of the alphabet onto the clipboard so that the bottom of the card was even with the bottom right-hand corner of the clipboard. Then she placed the card of the child whose name began with the next-to-last letter of the alphabet on the clipboard slightly above the first card. She mounted it so that the name of the other child was still visible. She continued this process with the remaining cards. When she finished, she had constructed an inexpensive flip chart.

Teachers use anecdotal notes to describe the strategies children use to decode words, the processes children use while they write, the functions of writing children use while they play, and characteristics of children's talk during a presentation to the class. "Taken regularly anecdotal notes become not only a vehicle for planning instruction and documenting progress, but also a story about an individual" (Rhodes & Nathenson-Mejia, 1992, p. 503). Note that anecdotal notes describe exactly what occurred and what was said verbatim, with no judgment or interpretation applied. Kindergarten teacher Lynn Cohen (1999) reminds teachers to "get the basic story and most significant details, keeping the information as factual as possible" (p. 27).

Figure 8.2

One record-keeping system—an inexpensive flip chart

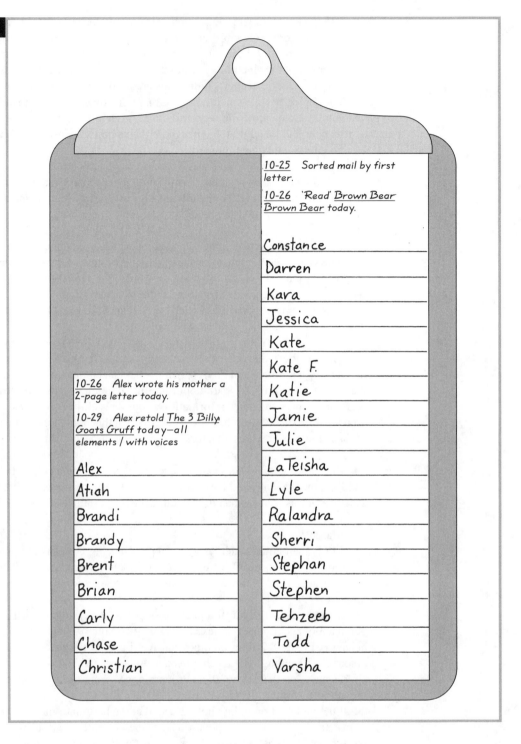

Vignettes or teacher reflections—Vignettes are recordings of recollections of significant events made after the fact, when the teacher is free of distractions. Because vignettes are like anecdotal notes except that they are prepared some time after a behavior has occurred and are based on a teacher's memory of the event, vignettes are used for purposes such as those identified for anecdotal notes. These after-the-fact descriptions or vignettes can be more detailed than anecdotal notes and are particularly useful when recording literacy behavior that is significant or unique for a specific child.

For example, Ms. Valentine observed a student attempting to control his peers' behavior by writing a sign and posting it in an appropriate place. Because she was involved with a small group of children, she did not have time to record a description of the student's behavior immediately. However, as soon as the children left for the day, she recorded her recollection of the event:

> For days Jamali had been complaining about the "mess" left by the children getting drinks at the classroom water fountain after recess. "Look at that mess! Water all over the floor!" At his insistence, the class discussed solutions to the problem. While the problem wasn't solved, I thought there was less water on the floor. Evidently, Jamali did not. Today he used the "power of the pen" to attempt to solve the problem. He wrote a sign:
>
> BEWR!! WTR SHUS UP
> ONLE TRN A LITL
> (Beware! Water shoots up. Only turn a little.)
> He posted his sign over the water fountain. This was the first time I had observed him using writing in an attempt to control other children's behavior.

Vignettes, then, are recollections of significant events. As such, they look much like an anecdotal note, except they are written in the past tense. Also, because teachers can write vignettes when they are free of distractions, they can be more descriptive about the child's concern that drove the literacy-oriented behavior, and they can connect this event to what is known about the child's previous literacy-oriented behaviors.

■ *Checklists*—Checklists are observational aids that specify which behaviors to look for and provide a convenient system for keeping records. They can make observations more systematic and easier to conduct. For example, an adapted version of Elizabeth Sulzby, June Barnhart, and Joyce Hieshima's (1989) Forms of Writing checklist can help identify the forms of emergent writing that children use during play and in other classroom situations (see Figure 8.3).

The number of checklists available to describe children's literacy development seems almost endless! For example, teachers can use an adapted version of Lesley Morrow's (1988) checklist to identify the elements present in a child's retelling of a story (see Figure 8.4), or Elizabeth Sulzby, June Barnhart, and Joyce Hieshima's (1989) checklist to identify what children attend to when they attempt to read books and other forms of print (see Figure 8.5).

Checklists are useful because they provide information that teachers can see at a glance, showing what children can do. Teachers have learned that (1) children sometimes engage in a behavior today that does not reappear for several weeks, and (2) many different variables (e.g., a storybook being read, other children in the group) can affect the literacy behaviors children show. Hence, teachers are careful to record the date of each observation and to use the checklist many times over the year in an attempt to create an accurate picture of their children's literacy development.

Figure 8.3	
Emergent writing checklist	

Child's Name _____

Forms of Writing	Date(s) Observed	Situation
■ uses drawing (might be circular scribbles)	_____	_____
■ uses drawing and writing	_____	_____
■ uses linear scribble	_____	_____
■ uses letter-like shapes	_____	_____
■ uses random letters	_____	_____
■ uses invented spellings	_____	_____
■ uses conventional spellings	_____	_____

Figure 8.4	

Story retelling checkist

Child's name _____ Date _____

Title of Story _____

Place a ✓ next to each element the child includes in his or her retelling.

Setting
Begins the story with an introduction, like
"Once upon a time . . ."   _____

Identifies the characters _____ of
_____ (total number)   _____

Theme
Tells what the main character(s) wanted
or needed   _____

Episodes
Recalls _____ episodes of the
episodes in the story   _____

Ending
Recalls how the story's problem was
solved or the goal was attained   _____

Sequence
Retells the story in the correct order
▪ from beginning to middle   _____
▪ from middle to end   _____

From L. M. Morrow, *Literacy development in early years.* Copyright © 1988 by Allyn & Bacon. Adapted by permission.

▪ *Questioning or interviewing*—Teachers interview to obtain information they cannot uncover any other way. Sometimes it is difficult to determine the significance of a literacy behavior, particularly when early forms of emergent writing, such as scribbles or random letters, are being used. For example, several preschoolers were observed in an airport play center. They were cutting out dollar-sized pieces of paper and writing on each piece with scribbles.

> ***Teacher:*** I wonder what you guys are making. Is it money? Are you making a lot of money?
>
> ***Buddy:*** These aren't money. They're tickets for the airplane!

Note how this brief, informal interview cleared up the teacher's initial misconception about the make-believe identity of the pieces of paper.

Unfortunately, young children often find it difficult to answer adult questions. Often the information involves tacit knowledge; young children may not know that they know the answer to the question. The kinds of questions teachers ask are very important. Peter Johnston (1992) suggests that there are three kinds of questions teachers might ask:

1. descriptive questions (e.g., What happens during storybook reading time in our classroom? What do you usually do when you are reading a book?);
2. structural questions (e.g., Do you read when you write? Can you tell me about how and when?); and
3. contrast questions (e.g., Who are your two favorite authors? How are their stories the same? How are their stories different?").

Figure 8.5

Emergent reading checklist

Child's Name _____

(You might say, "Please read me what you wrote" or "Please read this storybook to me.")

Read print by:	Print being read is:	Date
■ attending to the picture(s) and labeling the different objects	_____	_____
■ attending to the picture(s) and making up a story using a telling voice	_____	_____
■ attending to the picture(s) and making up a story using a reading voice	_____	_____
■ attending to the print and making up a story using a telling voice	_____	_____
■ attending to the print and making up a story using a reading voice	_____	_____
■ attending to the print and reading some words correctly and making up some words	_____	_____
■ attending to the print and reading most of the words correctly but with some difficulty	_____	_____
■ attending to the print and reading the words correctly	_____	_____

Note: If the print being read is written in invented spellings, indicate "child text—inv." in the "Print being read" column.

To Johnston's list, we could add Graves' (1983) process questions (e.g., I see you erased something here. Can you tell me why you made this change, this revision?).

Johnston noted that teachers might want to consider adding a pretend audience for the question. For example, a teacher might say, "Suppose a new child was added to our classroom. What things would you tell him or her about reading to help him or her know what to do and how to be good at reading?"

■ **Surveys**—Many teachers use reading or writing surveys to gather information about children's attitudes and their home literacy environments. Teachers often design their own surveys to help them acquire the information they wish to know. For example, Marianne Kellner wanted to learn about her children's home literacy experiences, so she designed the survey in Figure 8.6.

■ *Video and audio recordings*—Teachers often use audiotaping to document children's reading progress. For example, teachers might record a child's reading of a favorite book to study the child's reading attempts or children's retellings of stories read to them to study their comprehension of stories.

Teachers use videotape to capture children's literacy behaviors in a variety of contexts. Some teachers focus the camera lens on an area of the classroom, such as the dramatic play area or the writing center, to gather information about children's literacy-related social interactions during their play and work. Viewing the tapes provides valuable information not only about the children's knowledge of context-appropriate oral language and their ability to engage in conversations with others but also about the children's knowledge of the functions of writing. (See Chapter 3, page 63, for more details on using the video camera to gather information on children's literacy development.)

Figure 8.6

*Example of parent
literacy survey*

Parent Literacy Survey

Child's Name: _____   Parent Signature: _____

Date: _____

Please circle the most apporpriate of the six responses under each item.

1. My child and I discuss family happenings, school, and current events.
   Every Day   Every Other Day   Twice a Week   Once a Week   Twice a Month   Never

2. I read to my child.
   Every Day   Every Other Day   Twice a Week   Once a Week   Twice a Month   Never

3. My child reads to me.
   Every Day   Every Other Day   Twice a Week   Once a Week   Twice a Month   Never

4. How often does your child see you reading at home?
   Every Day   Every Other Day   Twice a Week   Once a Week   Twice a Month   Never

5. How often does your child see you writing at home?
   Every Day   Every Other Day   Twice a Week   Once a Week   Twice a Month   Never

6. How often does your child visit the public library?
   Every Day   Every Other Day   Twice a Week   Once a Week   Twice a Month   Never

7. How many books does your child have?
   30+ Books   20–30 Books   10–20 Books   5–10 Books   A Few Books   None

8. About how many hours of TV does your child watch every day?
   4+ Hours   3 Hours   2 Hours   1 Hour   Less Than 1 Hour   None

9. My child reads for his or her own enjoyment.
   Every Day   Every Other Day   Twice a Week   Once a Week   Twice a Month   Never

10. I would describe my child as a capable and confident reader.

◄───►
Strongly Agree   Somewhat   Strongly Disagree

■ **Products or work samples**—Some products, such as samples of children's writing, can be gathered together in a folder. If the children's original works cannot be saved (e.g., a letter that is sent to its recipient), a photocopy can be made of the product. Other products, such as three-dimensional structures the children have created with labels written by them, might not be conveniently saved. In these cases, a photograph—still or video—can be made. Because memories are short, the teacher should record a brief description of the product or the activity that resulted in the product.

ADDRESSING STORAGE PROBLEMS. Mrs. Saenz has developed an assessment notebook that helps organize information about children's literacy learning. Her notebook consists of several sections. One section contains a checklist she has developed to document children's emergent writing. Another section contains a checklist she created to document emergent reading behaviors, including information about concepts of print and alphabet recognition. Mrs. Saenz's notebook also has a section for writing vignettes. To prompt her memory of an event, Mrs. Saenz uses a digital camera that allows her to take pictures of the children engaging in specific literacy behaviors. Later in the day, she downloads the disk, prints the photo, and writes her interpretation of the event on the bottom margin of the photo. In addition, the camera automatically dates the picture, making it easier for Mrs. Saenz to document this information quickly. Using these various tools will result in the accumulation of many items that will need to be stored someplace.

For teachers to maintain this kind of assessment system, they must be very well organized! Typically, teachers maintain a folder on each child. Many teachers find that folders with pockets and center clasps for three-hold punched paper serve as better storage containers than file folders. Interview forms, running-record sheets, and other similar papers can be three-hole-punched, thus permitting their easy insertion into each child's folder. When anecdotal notes and vignettes are written on computer mailing labels, the labels can be attached to the inside covers of each child's folder. When these notes are written on index cards, the cards can be stored in one of the folder's pockets. Also, a plastic resealing sandwich bag might be stapled inside each child's folder to hold an audiotape. The self-sealing feature of the bag means that the tape can be securely held inside the folder. The class's folders might be housed in a plastic container or in hanging files in a file cabinet.

Although the plastic container or the file cabinet might be housed in the teacher's work area in the classroom, these folders and the information in them belong not only to the teacher but also to the children. Hence, while teachers may not want the children to personally insert material into the folders, the children should be able to gain access to their folders at their discretion. Likewise, teachers should share their discoveries with each child regularly.

Creating a Portfolio

There are at least two kinds of portfolios. Gaye Gronlund (1998) calls the folders described above "working portfolios." She suggests that the working portfolio should provide "accurate documentation about how a child is growing and developing" (p. 5). The work samples, anecdotal notes, and so forth housed in working portfolios are not representative of the child's best work. Rather, the items housed in working portfolios evidence a child's typical, everyday performance. Teachers use these working portfolios to guide their instructional planning for each child. From the working portfolios, children and their teachers select specific pieces for inclusion in each child's showcase portfolio. Here pieces that exhibit the best work the child produced are housed. For example, Ms. Gronlund describes how one "preschool program had children sign in each day by their names (in whichever way they could) in the special Sign-in Book. The teacher then cut out the best samples for the child's showcase portfolio" (p. 5).

WHAT IS A PORTFOLIO?   That question has been answered by F. Leon Paulson, Pearl Paulson, and Carol Meyer (1991, p. 60), who define a portfolio as "a purposeful collection of [a sample of] student work that exhibits the student's efforts, progress, and achievements. . . . The collection must include student participation in selecting [the] contents, the criteria for selection, the criteria for judging merit, and evidence of student self-reflection."

The purpose of portfolios, as defined by Frank Serafini (2001, p. 388), is "to uncover the possibilities for students to understand each child as a whole, and to attempt to provide a window into a student's conceptual framework and ways of seeing the world." What a working or a showcase portfolio actually looks like varies from teacher to teacher and school to school. The majority of teachers in a Delaware portfolio project used expandable file folders for their children's portfolios. Manila folders were placed inside each expandable file folder. Each class's portfolios were placed inside a large plastic container with a lid. These teachers liked having a lid on their portfolio boxes because it helped to reduce the amount of classroom dust on the children's portfolios.

Other teachers have created different kinds of portfolios. For example, a Colorado teacher used gallon-sized Ziploc™ bags bound together with large metal rings. This teacher's students decorated poster-board covers, which the teacher laminated (Wilcox, 1993). Some teachers use hanging files, each carefully labeled with a child's name, and the bottom drawer of a file cabinet (so young children can easily see into the drawer) as their children's portfolio. Other teachers use pizza boxes decorated by the children. One teacher used a handmade fabric wall-hanging with a pocket for each child.

Deciding what to use is the practical starting point with portfolio assessment. As Gaye Gronlund (1998) notes, "Decisions in this area must be made, experiments tried, and a comfortable style selected." There is no one right storage scheme for children's portfolios. Teachers might use one kind of system for their children's working portfolios and another for their children's showcase portfolios.

A large plastic container stores the children's portfolios; the expandable file folders are pictured in the foreground.

HOW ARE ARTIFACTS SELECTED FOR INCLUSION? Maintaining a classroom portfolio system does not mean saving everything the child does and sending nothing home. Saving everything creates what Gaye Gronlund calls "a storage nightmare!" The pieces placed in a working portfolio are selected because they show children's everyday performance related to the literacy accomplishments the program has determined the children should know and be able to do. The pieces placed in the showcase portfolio are selected from the working portfolio because they show the child's best accomplishment relative to the literacy accomplishments.

Having a specific reason for selecting each artifact is critically important. What are the specific reasons? Please recall IRA/NAEYC's and the Committee on Preventing Reading Difficulties in Young Children's lists of literacy accomplishments. These same literacy accomplishments might drive the teacher's and children's decisions about what should be selected for inclusion in each of the children's portfolios. For example, to demonstrate that Tyrone, a three-year-old, could identify labels and signs in the environment, Kristol, his teacher, included two pieces of evidence in Tyrone's working portfolio. First, one day Kristol observed Tyrone building roads for cars with Monica in the block area. One particular intersection proved dangerous; their cars were forever crashing. Initially the crashing was great fun; later Tyrone noticed a scratch on his car. He gathered red paper, cut the paper into something resembling the stop sign shape, and wrote his version of *STOP* on each sign. He placed the signs at the intersection and told Monica, "This means stop. Don't come if I'm here!" Kristol wrote a quick anecdotal note of her observation and tucked the note into Tyrone's working portfolio. Later she chose to include the note in his showcase portfolio as one piece of evidence of this literacy accomplishment.

On another day, the children were lining up for outdoor play. As they waited for someone to get ready, Tyrone looked at the sign above the door and said, "I know what that says." Surprised, Kristol said, "Really? What does it say?" Tyrone responded, "It says *out.*" It didn't; it said *exit.* However, Tyrone was using the context to attempt to decode the print above the door. Kristol responded, "What a great guess, Tyrone! I think you thought something like 'We use this door to go outside; that sign must say *out.*' It says *exit,* which means out. It's a really great idea to use what's around a word to help you figure it out." Since the children were on their way to outdoor play, Kristol had no time to write an anecdotal note. When the children left for the day, she wrote a vignette of this event. She included this vignette in Tyrone's working portfolio and later in his showcase portfolio as an illustration of the same literacy accomplishment. The anecdotal note and the vignette are called artifacts.

When Kristol wrote the anecdotal note and vignette, she was careful to date each artifact. Many teachers have discovered that it is helpful to have a date stamp readily available in the classroom in the area where the portfolios are stored. Dating each item selected for inclusion in working portfolios permits the teacher and the child to arrange the items in chronological order to show changes or learning over time.

There is another even more important reason beyond the storage for being selective about the artifacts chosen for inclusion in the children's portfolios. Without specific literacy accomplishments driving the selection of artifacts, it is possible—as Gaye Gronlund (1998) and Mary Roe and Carol Vukelich (1998) discovered—that the portfolios will contain a lot of "stuff" that reflects children's engagement in literacy activities or the lessons the teacher taught rather than how each child was learning and progressing. As Ms. Gronlund notes, teachers want to be able to answer the question "What does this artifact tell me about this learner?" Gronlund (1998, p. 5) summarizes this important point:

> By collecting all of the children's work, I had actually created far more work for myself! If I had done some careful consideration of curricular goals and identified criteria by which I would evaluate how children were meeting those curricular goals, then I could have looked for work samples that demonstrated that process. I would not have collected everything—instead, I would have watched for work that matched my educational objectives and collected only those pieces.

WHO SELECTS THE PIECES FOR INCLUSION? With young children, the majority of the items chosen for inclusion in working and showcase portfolios are selected by teachers or are chosen jointly by the children and their teacher. Even the youngest children, however, should be permitted to select some pieces independently—particularly for their working portfolios. Teachers must remember that the portfolios belong to the children and that student ownership is critically important. Hence, when teachers assist their students in the selection of artifacts, they must do so in ways that maintain the students' ownership of their portfolios. As Frank Serafini (2001) points out, portfolios are something teachers do with children, not to children.

WHY WAS EACH ARTIFACT SELECTED FROM THE WORKING PORTFOLIO FOR INCLUSION IN THE SHOWCASE PORTFOLIO? To encourage the thoughtful selection of items for inclusion in the children's showcase portfolios, portfolio experts suggest that an entry slip should be attached to each artifact when it is moved from the children's working portfolio to their showcase portfolios. "Writing the entry slips is a way for students [and teachers] to reflect on their work, as well as to give the background for the work to others" (New Standards Project [NSP], 1994, p. 12). Entry slips require students to engage in a "dialogue with their inner, critical selves" (Wilcox, 1993, p. 20). The NSP teachers and Carol Wilcox agree: An entry slip helps readers of children's showcase portfolios know the importance of the work selected for inclusion. "Why do I want this artifact in my (or this child's) showcase portfolio? What does it show about me (or this child) as a reader, a writer, a learner, a literate individual?"

Just what does an entry slip look like? See Figure 8.7 for an example of the entry slip used by Kristol with the anecdotal note and the vignette described above.

HOW OFTEN SHOULD ARTIFACTS BE SELECTED FROM THE WORKING PORTFOLIO FOR INCLUSION IN THE SHOWCASE PORTFOLIO? Teachers differ in how often they select items for inclusion in the children's showcase portfolios. The NSP and Samuel Meisels and his colleagues (1997) recommend that the selection of items for inclusion in children's portfolios should occur at least three times a year. The NSP teachers have discovered that too much accumulated work overwhelms children and their teachers, making it difficult for them to be selective, so it seems wise to follow this rule: The younger the child, the more frequently the artifacts should be selected from the working portfolio for the showcase

Figure 8.7 *Portfolio entry slip*

Portfolio Entry Slip

Name _____Tyrone_____ Date __3|11__

Child/(Teacher) chose to include this piece because it shows: _____Tyrone using____ writing to control a peer's behavior.

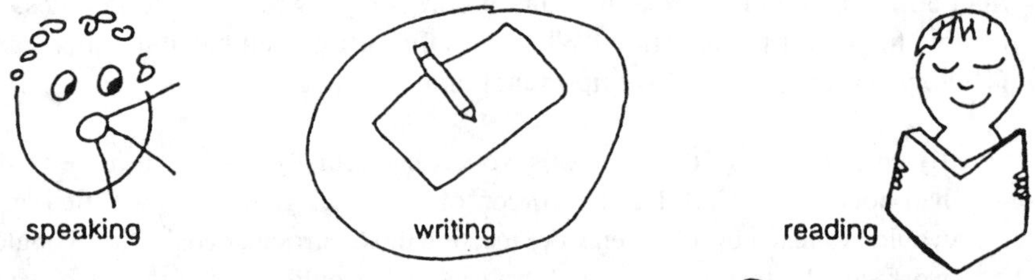

speaking   writing   reading

What does it show the child learned? __(1) a function of__ writing; we write to control others' behavior (2) exhibits knowledge learned from experiences in a play setting

portfolio. Perhaps once every four weeks would be a prudent guide. However, a key to the decision regarding frequency of selection will be the number of artifacts the children and their teachers have created and stored in their working portfolios. Having too few items also limits the children's and teacher's ability to select.

Another variable in determining when to select items will be the school's or center's identified times for reporting to parents through written reports and parent-teacher, parent-teacher-child, or parent-child conferences. The portfolios will serve as the information base for these reporting systems.

SHARING THE PORTFOLIOS WITH OTHERS. Carol Wilcox (1993, p. 33) reports teacher Karen Boettcher as saying, "The heart of portfolios is sharing." Following are some ways in which the information in portfolios can be shared with others.

■ *Sharing with peers*—One important audience for portfolios is the children's classmates. "Sharing portfolios is a powerful tool for building community within the classroom" (Wilcox, 1993, p. 33). Wilcox has elaborated this statement by noting that by sharing, children learn unique things about their classmates. They learn about the learning strategies their peers have used successfully. They learn what peers are struggling to learn, and they learn to offer assistance in their peers' struggles. They learn about peers' special talents. They learn about new ways of writing. They learn about how their peers read books. They set new goals for themselves.

How children share their portfolios, of course, will be determined by the age of the children. A common practice is for teachers to ask children to select one item from either of their portfolios to share with their peers. The children form a circle with the artifact of their choice in hand. The children describe why the artifact is important to them and what it tells about how they have changed as a reader, writer, or speaker. Sometimes the teacher asks children to select two artifacts that show how they have become better readers or writers. Such sharing calls for the teacher to show the children how and what to share. Such sharing also calls for the teacher to teach the children how to respond to each other. What questions might they ask? How might they tell their peer what they learned?

Ellen Booth Church (1999) proposes the following guidelines to ensure successful portfolio sharing:

1. Ask a different child to present once a week on a designated portfolio day.
2. Teach children how to interact with each other, by asking the presenter questions about the work. Expect that initially the children's questions will be stilted. Later, through modeling, children will learn important social, observational, and interviewing skills.
3. Teachers should show acceptance of the children's work.
4. Teachers should share their work.

■ *Sharing with parents*—The significant adults in each child's life are another important audience for portfolios. Of course, teachers will use the children's portfolios during parent-teacher conferences. Gaye Gronlund (1998) also recommends that the working portfolio be shared with parents during parent-teacher conferences. She believes parents might develop unrealistic expectations for their child if only the best examples of the child's literacy accomplishments are shared.

Sometimes children will join these conferences to provide their own perspective on their own development as readers, writers, and speakers. At other times, children will independently use their portfolios to explain their literacy development to their parents. Even Bernadette Watson's kindergartners ran their own portfolio conferences for their parents! (Ms. Watson and other teachers have discovered that it is important to have children practice how they plan to share their portfolios with their parents before they actually do so.) Lynn Cohen (1999) describes how some early childhood programs sponsor portfolio days, a special time when parents and family members come in to look at and enjoy the children's portfolios.

Teachers not only need to teach children how to respond to their peers, but also to inform parents about how to respond to their children's portfolios. Carol Wilcox (1993) has detailed the story of Michael, a young learner who had a devastating experience when sharing his portfolio with his parents. Their response focused on his poor spelling and handwriting performances, rather than on his accomplishments and his literacy development. He was not, after all, spelling words conventionally!

Some early childhood programs require teachers to report to parents at least four times a year, with two of these reports being oral and two being written. Certainly teachers can report to parents more often; this is a minimum. Written reports generally are called narrative reports. Teachers might wish to include a list of what the children can do. Stating what a child can do builds a positive picture of each child's development. Narrative reports should, after all, be progress reports. For this reason, the children's working portfolios serve as the data source for the report.

How does a portfolio assessment system *really* work in a classroom? Please read Dehbra Handley's brief description of her portfolio system in her preschool classroom (Trade Secrets 8.1).

Special Populations

The main purpose of this book has been to describe how to set up and implement an effective, developmentally appropriate language arts program for pre-K and kindergarten children. Chapter 3 presented strategies for promoting children's oral language development, and Chapters 5 through 8 have detailed best practice in teaching reading and writing to young children.

Recall that one of the underlying themes of this book is respecting the tremendous diversity of children who are enrolled in today's early childhood programs. It is not surprising, therefore, that the general strategies we have recommended for pre-K and kindergarten age children will sometimes need to be modified to meet the needs of specific children.

Trade Secret 8.1

Portfolio and Assessment: Paying Attention to What Kids Do

Dehbra Handley

How does the portfolio system work in a preschool setting? The portfolio system I use is a two-part system that includes the actual portfolio work and an assessment process. The process enables me to get a better look at how each of my students is doing. It helps me identify where little nudges might be needed. Through my children's work samples, I am able to see and share with my students' parents their child's literacy development.

My students' portfolios are created from large 36 x 24-inch pocket folders. The children decorate these, and then the folders are laminated. They are kept in a designated special place near our computers within the reach of each little learner. Everything and anything can (and often does) go into the portfolio.

In the beginning of the year, I explain to the students that their work is important. Therefore, they have the choice of displaying it in the classroom, taking it home, or saving it in their portfolio. They know that all work saved in their portfolio is still theirs, and any work displayed in the classroom can be saved or taken home. Choosing what to do with their work has several positive effects on the child: it fosters decision-making skills, develops ownership and control over the portfolio, and validates that

the child's work is important without having to have the teacher place any extrinsic value on it.

The other half of the portfolio system is the assessment and parent-reporting part. The assessment section is based largely on my observations that I describe in anecdotal notes or checklists. I spend part of each day making observations based on three areas: socioemotional development, cognitive development, and physical development. These observations then are distilled into a descriptive review of the student; a section reflects each of the three developmental areas noted.

The descriptive review and the portfolio are then shared with the parents during a home visit with the family. The student is always a part of the home visit; the child is the narrator for the work and is given the opportunity to select the pieces he or she would like to keep. In this way we are able to reduce the number of portfolio pieces and begin the collection process again. I explain and show the parents the developmental areas that each piece of work or photo demonstrates. Much of what I tell the parents is included in the descriptive review. The parents are given a copy of the review to keep for their own records.

After our second and final home visit, the student work is then incorporated into a big book. This book contains all of the special pieces the parent and child have decided together (during the home visit process) should be saved for this purpose. With the completion and presentation of the big books to the families, our portfolio process comes to an end.

As explained earlier in this chapter, ongoing assessment is a key requirement for providing this type of individualized instruction. Another important requirement is for teachers to be aware of the needs of special populations—groups of children who face common problems and challenges.

This section contains information on adapting instruction to meet the needs of two groups of children—bilingual second-language learners and children with various types of disabilities. Early childhood educators will undoubtedly encounter many members of both groups of children during their teaching careers. Tailoring instruction to meet the needs of linguistically and developmentally diverse children is one of the hallmarks of excellent teaching. The special features that follow give practical tips to assist teachers in this challenging task.

Bilingual and Second-Language Learners

Currently, more than one in seven students in U.S. schools speak English as a second language (Barone, 1998), and the proportion is much higher in some areas such as California and other parts of the Southwest. In addition, the percentage of second-language learners tends to be higher in the earliest grades, forecasting even greater linguistic diversity in future classrooms. For example, one survey of Head Start programs reported that 22 percent of the students spoke Spanish at home and that 4 percent came from families who spoke one of 139 other languages (Tabors, 1998)! It is vitally important for early childhood educators to be prepared to help these children learn to speak, read, and write English. These children also need to be helped to learn content knowledge in subjects such as math, science, and social studies. Whenever possible, second-language learners should also be helped to continue to master their native languages.

In Special Feature 8.1, Sarah Hudelson and Irene Serna describe how two master teachers, Ms. Espinosa and Ms. Moore, meet the needs of second-language learners in their kindergarten classroom. The reader will note that these two teachers use many of the same literacy strategies we recommended for young children in general: a print-rich classroom environment, frequent teacher read-alouds, language-experience dictation, and journal writing. The major adaptations Ms. Espinosa and Ms. Moore make to these strategies are (1) exposing children to books and other print in both the children's native language and English, and (2) allowing the children lots of opportunities to speak, listen, read, and write in their native language.

Special Feature 8.1

Promoting Emergent Literacy Development in Bilingual and Second-Language Learners

Sarah Hudelson and Irene Serna

In Chapters 5 through 8, you have learned about ways to organize pre-kindergarten and kindergarten classrooms, and about instructional strategies that promote the natural emergence of literacy. In this special feature, we provide an illustration of how the emergent literacy perspective proposed for native-English speakers applies to bilingual and second-language learners. We describe selected literacy practices of two excellent bilingual kindergarten teachers, Cecilia Espinosa and Karen Moore. We begin with a description of their kindergarten classroom environments and the daily schedule. Then some of their instructional strategies are highlighted and consideration is given to working with pre-kindergarten children. Finally, we offer some implications of their work for other teachers.

The Classroom Environment

In Ms. Espinosa's and Ms. Moore's classrooms, print in both English and Spanish is everywhere: alphabet trains, calendars, sign-in sheets for attendance, labels on objects around the room, labels for centers and activities, words to songs on chart paper, posters, and instructions. Because at the beginning of the school year most children do not read independently and do not distinguish English print from Spanish print, the teacher-prepared print is color-coded. Everything in English is written with a black marker; everything in Spanish is written in red.

In the book corner, books in Spanish are on one set of bookshelves and books in English are on another set of shelves. The children straighten and shelve the books according to language. Even if the children are not able to read the book titles, they quickly begin to recognize books by the covers and illustrations. For books available in both languages, (for example Maurice Sendak's *Where the Wild Things Are* and its Spanish translation, *Donde Viven Los Monstruos,* 1996), the Spanish language titles are coded with a red dot.

In both classrooms, multiple hanging charts contain the lyrics for songs, chants, finger plays, and poems in both languages. These are also color-coded (English in

black print and Spanish in red print). Teachers and children make use of these charts on a daily basis, reciting poems and chants, and using the lyrics as they sing their favorite songs. Sometimes Ms. Moore and Ms. Espinosa lead the class in making voice–print connections by pointing to the words on the chart; sometimes one of the children takes over this task. Instead of translations from English to Spanish, Ms. Espinosa and Ms. Moore often use poems or songs that reflect the same theme or topic but that have been created originally in one language or the other and thus are culturally authentic. For example, the children learn "Old MacDonald Had a Farm" in English and "Mi Chacra" (My Farm), a traditional Latin American song, in Spanish. Also placed prominently in the classrooms are charts and webs (also color-coded) that are evidence of children's content study. These charts list (1) what the children already know about a topic; (2) what the children want to learn; and (3) what they learned during their investigation (a technique that is sometimes referred to as KWL, for know, want to learn, and learned).

In these classrooms, both languages are used for instruction, and children are encouraged to develop literacy first in their native language. Thus, the fluent Spanish speakers are becoming writers and readers initially in Spanish, while the English speakers are writing and reading in English. In addition, all children are encouraged to participate in literacy events in their second language, whether that language is English or Spanish. Both languages are valued and promoted.

Daily Schedule

Ms. Espinosa and Ms. Moore teach two half-day kindergarten sessions approximately three hours in length. The daily schedule is flexible but generally includes the following:

- arrival of the children, including children checking in by putting an X next to their their names on a daily attendance sheet, and a few minutes of free time, during which the children look at books, observe some of the animals in the room, play with blocks, or chat with others;
- opening circle, which includes the children's contributions to the News of the Day/ Noticias written down by the teacher, calendar activities, and a song and/or poem read aloud by the teacher or by one of the children and then reread by everyone;

(continued on next page)

Special Feature 8.1 *(continued)*

- writing time, which involves drawing and writing in journals and creating personal narratives;
- daily read-aloud time in both English and Spanish;
- hands-on mathematics activities;
- content study of topics of interest to the children.

Instructional Strategies

In this section, specific features of the curriculum that contribute to the children's emergent literacy are discussed. We also consider variations on each instructional strategy that would be appropriate for pre-kindergarten bilingual and second-language learners.

Read-Aloud

Read-aloud experiences are an important daily activity, and they are conducted in both English and Spanish. The two teachers read different kinds of books to the children. Some books are selected for the quality of the story and the potential for discussion. Some books (for example, nonfiction informational books, alphabet books) relate to the content unit under study. Still others are chosen for their predictability.

Predictable stories are especially important in providing the kind of comprehensible input mentioned in Chapter 2 as crucial for language acquisition. These stories are also important because, as the teachers read the stories multiple times, the children begin to memorize parts of them and reread and retell the content themselves. In both the native and the second language, this kind of reading has been shown to contribute to young ESL learners in two ways: (1) they begin to view themselves as readers, and 2) they develop their vocabulary in English (Carger, 1993; Seawell, 1985).

Usually Ms. Espinosa and Ms. Moore read a story out loud to all the children. If the stories are in English, the bilingual children explain it to those just learning English (and vice versa if the stories are in Spanish). In this way, all children in the group can follow the story. In addition, the teachers suggest strategies the children can use, such as looking at the pictures carefully, to help them understand a story read in their nonnative language. The teachers also encourage the children to listen carefully to the stories. After reading a story, the group goes back through the story, using both languages to communicate their constructions of meaning and to get clarification. Multiple readings of the same story contribute to greater comfort with second-language stories. Children are more likely to pick up a book to peruse it independently or with a friend if the teacher has read it aloud.

With some of the predictable books, Ms. Moore engages the children in a variation of reader's theater (children reading orally from scripts based on stories). For example, when she chose the predictable story *Caps for Sale* by Slobodkina (1947), she read the book multiple times over several days and encouraged the children to read along with her. She then chose specific children to act out the parts of the peddler and the monkeys who

steal his caps. The class decided on actions these characters would perform to accompany the story action. Ms. Moore then read the story again, pausing throughout to help the children act out their parts and say their lines. Later, one of the ESL learners in the class took over the role of story narrator. Because she had listened to Ms. Moore's expressive reading, this child also read (from memory) the story with enthusiasm and expression. This kind of dramatization of selected stories is an excellent vehicle for children's second-language development.

Is read-aloud equally important for bilingual and second-language pre-kindergartners? Our answer is a definite yes. Many ESL youngsters first experience the wonder of books in classroom settings. Pre-kindergartners need multiple opportunities for read-aloud during the day. In our view, it is especially important for preschool teachers to select some books for read-aloud that are highly predictable, involve repetition, and invite children's active involvement in reading along and (when possible) acting along with the story. Bill Martin's *Brown Bear, Brown Bear, What Do You See?* is such a book. Familiar tales such as "The Three Little Pigs," "The Three Bears," "Little Red Ridinghood," and others may be familiar to some very young second-language learners because they have heard versions in their home settings. These are also excellent for read-alouds. We encourage inviting parents and other community members into pre-kindergarten classrooms to tell and/or read these stories in children's native language before they are read in the second language. We also recommend that children's early experiences with read-alouds be carried out in their native languages, even if it requires splitting a class into smaller groups.

Pre-kindergarten bilingual and second-language learners need to be exposed to many different kinds of books. Concept books, such as those of Tana Hoban that utilize high-quality photographs, should be available. Number books and alphabet books are also plentiful, and some, for example, Pat Mora's *One Two Three/Uno Dos Tres* (2000) and Tabor's *Albertina Anda Arriba*, (1993) are written bilingually. We also urge teachers to look for some books that reflect the actual life experiences and cultural experiences of young learners, so that children are able to see themselves in books. Finally, in terms of selecting books to use, there are many fine collections of folk songs, finger plays, and action songs that pre-kindergarten teachers may want to make a part of their daily activities—for example, Lulu Delacre's *Arroz con Leche*, (1989) Leslie Alexander's *Mother Goose on the Rio Grande,* (1997) and *Diez Deditos/Ten Little Fingers and Other Play Rhymes and Action Songs from Latin America* by José Luis Orozco. (1997)

If pre-kindergarten children have not had a lot of experiences with books, they need time to accustom themselves to attending to a book, listening to a reader's voice, looking at the illustrations, and following the story line. Such familiarization with books may be accomplished

(continued on next page)

more easily in small groups and in informal settings, rather than solely in large group read-aloud. Additionally, pre-kindergarten children need time simply to look at books on their own or with a peer or adult, so that they may interact with them and savor them on their own, using whatever language they choose. They may also want to carry books into classrooms centers such as the housekeeping center and "read" to their babies.

What do Ms. Espinosa's and Ms. Moore's read-aloud practices suggest to other educators working with young bilingual and second-language learners? Several things. Reading aloud needs to be considered a basic aspect of instruction, not a frill. It is important to read to children in their native language, as well as in English. If the teacher cannot read in the children's native language, a parent or community volunteer should be recruited to read. Another possibility is to use older elementary-school learners who read in the children's native language and create buddy readers (Samway, Whang, and Pippitt, 1995). If live reading is not possible, readers may tape-record stories for classroom use. Audiotapes that accompany some of the Spanish language Troll and Scholastic books might be used.

Reading aloud is a time to contribute to ESL children's language development. For children just beginning to learn English, teachers should choose books to read carefully, keeping in mind aspects of language predictability and the relationship of the pictures to the story line. Reading the same story multiple times provides an excellent context for second-language learning. Choral reading and readers theater may provide relatively low-risk opportunities to try out the new language. It is important to allow children to work through the construction of the meanings of stories in their native language, as well as in English (Battle, 1995; Fessler, 1998).

Language-Experience Dictation

On a regular basis, the children in Ms. Moore's and Ms. Espinosa's rooms engage in content study, choosing topics want to investigate. These studies begin with the children's brainstorming what they already know about the topic to be studied. The teacher records in writing what the children dictate, thus providing a written transcription of the spoken language. After the children have generated what they know, they share what they still want to learn. Again, the teacher writes what the children dictate, writing what is expressed in Spanish in red and what is expressed in English in black.

The questions raised by the children become the basis for the unit study itself. In small groups, with multiple print and nonprint resources, and with considerable assistance from teachers and other adults, the children investigate their topics and create representations of what they have learned to share with others. Often these representations are in the form of drawings, clay creations, or dioramas. Sometimes the teachers take dictation as the children prepare what they want to share with their classmates.

At the end of a unit of study, the children often come together to record what they have learned. Once again the teacher records the children's contributions. The teacher's use of language experience provides children with repeated demonstrations of the relationship between spoken and written language. Here, for example, is the chart generated by a small group of children who had studied llamas as part of a larger study of animals:

> Llamas
> Aprenden a caminar rapidito.
> When they are born, they are all wet.
> Comen zacate como las avestruces.
> Es un herbívoro.
> They are mammals.
> They drink milk from their moms.

And what of pre-kindergartners and language experience? We are not specifically advocating the kind of extensive topic study carried out in these bilingual kindergartens for younger children. In our view, language-experience dictation may be used with younger children, but we advocate using this strategy on a more limited and often on a one-to-one basis. In several bilingual Head Start classrooms, for example, we have seen teachers engage in brief conversations with children about something they have created through painting or clay work, and then write a sentence or two reflecting what the child has said: "This is a boat. Me and my dad go fishing." We also have seen Head Start teachers use language experience to follow up a field trip, eliciting comments from children and putting them in written form—"Vi un elefante en el zoo" (I saw an elephant at the zoo). Dictation may also occur if children have used art to reflect on a group experience. Thus, a walk to see various kinds of cactus resulted in children's cactus paintings and in writing about that experience: "Alex saw a big cactus." "Eva likes the flowers on the cactus." So we view dictation, used sensitively by teachers who take their views from children about their interest in such an activity, as an appropriate strategy for pre-kindergarten.

For many years bilingual and ESL educators have advocated using language experience as a way both of demonstrating the connections between spoken and written language and of providing children with some texts they will be able to read successfully because they have created them themselves (Heald-Taylor, 1986; Rigg, 1989). If possible, teachers should transcribe children's contributions in their native language as well as in English. If teachers do not write the children's native language, other adults or older children may take dictation. For second-language learners, it is especially important to accept the contributions as the children express them, rather than converting them to adult forms of conventional English.

Writing Experiences

Writing forms an important part of the curriculum in these kindergartens. The teachers demonstrate writing as they

(continued on next page)

Special Feature 8.1 *(continued)*

take dictation from children. In addition, the children engage in writing on a daily basis. Early in the year, most of the writing takes place in the children's journals. Later, some of the children branch into creating more extensive personal narratives, and writing becomes one of the ways children can represent what they are learning in content study. As in other aspects of the school day, the children are encouraged to write in their native language. Thus, the teachers encourage the Spanish speakers to write in Spanish, explaining that after they have learned to write in Spanish, they will be helped to write in English.

At the beginning of the year, before asking the children to write, Ms. Moore and Ms. Espinosa pair the learners and engage them in conversations between peers, asking them to share information about themselves with their partners. This extended talking provides a way of generating possibilities for writing, as the teachers explain to the children that they can write about the same kinds of topics they have been sharing orally.

As is common with young children, at the beginning of the school year many of the children's journal entries consist either entirely of drawings or include a great deal of drawing accompanied by strings of lines, circles, or other forms that do not correspond to specific sounds. Some of the children may copy words from print around the room. What is significant, however, is that many of the children, when asked what they have written, relate specific language to the pictures and graphic forms. They understand that they can represent their ideas on paper. There is intentionality in their work (Harste, Woodward, & Burke, 1984), even though they use nonconventional symbol systems to represent their meanings (Dyson, 1993).

As the school year progresses, while some children continue to rely on pictures and letter forms, more and more kindergartners begin to use invented spelling in their writing, reflecting a growing awareness of grapheme–phoneme correspondences in their native language. As this occurs, Ms. Espinosa and Ms. Moore create small alphabet charts (*abecedarios*) the children use at their desks to help them with their writing.

On a regular basis, during the second-half of the school year, children work together to sound out words that one child is writing and then to find the letters that represent those sounds. A few children earn the reputation of being good spellers, and they are frequently in demand by some of the others. There is a phenomenon in Spanish invented spelling that is quite different from what has been reported about invented spelling in English. Beginning inventions in Spanish often consist of vowel strings rather than the more common occurrence in English of strings of consonants. Thus, a child just beginning to use sound–letter correspondences in Spanish might write the word *zapato* as *aao*.

The teachers' roles during writing time vary. At times they will move among the children, inviting them to share what they have created. This provides an opportunity for the children to connect their pictures and letter strings and for the teachers to understand better the children's creations. Sometimes, especially for the purpose of noting the children's changes as writers, the teachers might jot on Post-it® Notes a child's interpretations of her or his work and later affix the note to the child's text. As some of the children use increasing amounts of invented spelling, Ms. Espinosa and Ms. Moore sit with individuals, helping them sound out the words they want to write. Such careful repronunciation by the teacher often enables the child writer to produce more of the letters than if the child worked without assistance.

Sometimes the teachers engage in what might be called shared writing (Serna & Hudelson, 1993) with selected children. The child creates part of a text, and the teacher writes another part from the child's dictation, thus sharing the transcription. This is especially helpful for some children who are daunted by the task of getting all their ideas down. Ms. Moore and Ms. Espinosa, are especially sensitive to individual differences in children, and they observe and facilitate the learners' writing based on each child's unique needs.

The teachers also serve as editors of the children's stories that go into published form. Final versions of some of their personal narratives are typed using conventional spelling, after which the authors create illustrations to accompany the print on each page. Typing their stories in 18- to 24-point fonts helps young authors make one-to-one correspondences of spoken words with those in written form. Children enjoy sharing the final versions of their stories with their classmates.

And what of writing experiences for second-language preschoolers? We would suggest a less structured approach to writing, one that is connected directly to the multiple functions of writing that nonnative English-speaking children become aware of in normal family living and that they may enact in centers and play time in the classroom. In the Head Start center connected to the school at which Ms. Espinosa and Ms. Moore teach, for example, there is a housekeeping center. As children take on adult roles, they use the paper and pencils provided in the center to create lists of items they need to buy at the store, or lists of items they will send their children to buy. In an organized area that sometimes serves as a restaurant, menus have been written by the restaurant owners, and servers write down the orders of the customers. When this area becomes a store stocked with food items contributed by the children, customers arrive with their lists and ask the storekeepers for what they want. In the block area, as children construct roads and buildings, an adult writes such environmental signs for the builders as STOP, BANK, and SCHOOL. A writing center is stocked with all kinds of paper, crayons, pencils, and markers. In this center, some children write letters to grandparents in distant places as they have seen their parents do. Other

(continued on next page)

children choose to experiment with written forms, writing their own names and the names of friends, copying words from around the room or from a favorite book. These preschoolers are engaged in constructing their understandings of the multiple purposes for which people use the written word. We believe that they need ample opportunity to do this before moving into more formal activities such as journal or story writing. We also believe that children need to be able to write in the language or languages they choose.

A classroom environment that encourages children to express themselves in their native language is an optimal one for second-language learners. Teachers who are literate in the native language of their ESL children can demonstrate native-language writing for the children and can encourage the children to write in their native language. Teachers who are not able to do this themselves need to recruit adults or older children to perform these functions. Teachers who are unable to use the children's native language should be positive about the children's attempts to write in English. ESL children may be reluctant to write in English, especially if they do not yet speak the language fluently. It is a daunting task to be asked to create a text in a second language. Teachers should respond to the intentionality of children's work, valuing the multiplicity of ways that ESL children may express their meanings.

Clearly, there are important parallels between the emergent literacy practices proposed in this book for native speakers of English and those advocated for children learning English as a second language. The following list suggests additional instructional adaptations possible to help second-language learners:

- Carefully select stories for reading aloud, giving particular attention to comprehensibility (especially the relationship of text to pictures) and predictability.
- Consider reading stories multiple times, and provide opportunities for children to join in with the reading through such practices as choral reading.
- Utilize language-experience narrations as a way of both providing second-language learners with texts that they will understand and encouraging them to use English to share an experience.
- Be sensitive to learners' second-language abilities, and recognize that the way they express themselves reflects their second-language competence at the time. Do not correct their efforts.
- Encourage writing in a second language for a variety of purposes, and acknowledge whatever children produce as they work to express their intentions.
- Allow the use of the native language and utilize bilingual individuals to interpret, as needed.

Children with Special Needs

Recent legislation has mandated that children with disabilities be placed in the least restrictive environment. The goal is inclusion, allowing each child with special needs to have the maximum amount of integration into general education classrooms that is possible. The resulting mainstreaming of children with special needs into regular classrooms has radically changed the role of classroom teachers at all grade levels. Teachers are now expected to work as part of a multidisciplinary team (along with special education teachers, psychologists, and other specialists) to develop an individualized education program (IEP) for each child with identified special needs.

While this movement toward full inclusion has generated new challenges and responsibilities for teachers, it has also created wonderful new opportunities for children with disabilities. Koppenhaver, Spadorcia, and Erickson (1998, p. 95) explain:

The importance of inclusive instruction for children with disabilities is that they receive instruction from the school personnel who have the greatest knowledge of literacy theory and practice, the most training, and the greatest print-specific resources. They are surrounded by models of varied print use, purposeful reading and writing, frequent peer interaction and support, and the expectation that children can, should, and will learn to read and write.

These types of positive literacy experiences are especially important for children with disabilities. Marvin and Mirenda (1993) investigated the home literacy experiences of children enrolled in Head Start and special education programs. They found that the parents of children with special needs placed a much higher priority on oral communication than on learning to read and write. Parents of preschoolers with disabilities reported less adult-initiated literacy activity in the home, less exposure to nursery rhymes, and fewer trips to the library.

In Special Feature 8.2, Karen Burstein and Tanis Bryan describe how teachers can make accommodations to promote language and literacy learning for children with a variety of special needs. These adaptations, when combined with the activities described in this book, should enable teachers to get all students off to a good start in learning language and literacy.

In Special Feature 8.3, we share the case study of Terrel, a child who receives special education services. We include a copy of the IEP that was developed with his teachers and parents.

Special Feature 8.2

On Your Mark, Get Set, Go: Strategies for Supporting Children with Special Needs in General Education Classrooms

Karen Burstein and Tanis Bryan

Previous chapters in this book have described how to set up and implement a balanced language and literacy program for young children. In this special feature, two early childhood special needs experts describe strategies for supporting children with special needs in such programs.

On Your Mark

Teachers in preschools, kindergartens, and the primary grades are increasingly likely to have children with special needs in their classrooms. Typically, the majority of these children have speech and/or language impairments, developmental delays, and learning disabilities. A smaller number of these children have mental and or emotional disturbances, sensory disabilities (hearing or visual impairments), and physical and health impairments. The latter reflects increases in the number of children surviving serious chronic conditions (e.g., spina bifida, cystic fibrosis) and attending school as well as increases in the number of children with less life-threatening but nonetheless serious health (e.g., asthma) and cognitive (e.g., autism) problems.

Public policy and law, including the 1997 Individuals with Disabilities Education Act (IDEA), along with humane and ethical considerations dictate that children with disabilities receive optimal educational programs, given our knowledge bases and resources. Further, *IDEA* stipulates that children with special needs be provided their education in classes with their age-same peers to the greatest extent possible.

One of the primary goals of early education is to prepare all young children for general education classrooms. Making this a reality for children with special needs requires that teachers make accommodations and adaptations that take into account the individual child's special needs. Teachers' willingness to *include* children with disabilities and their skillfulness in making adaptations are critical determinants of effective instruction. This special feature outlines strategies and suggestions for teachers who have young children with special needs in their classrooms. Our purpose is to provide suggestions for making adaptations so that teachers feel comfortable,

confident, and successful including these children in their classrooms.

Get Set

Cognitive, physical, sensory, developmental, physical, emotional—there are so many variations in development! It is not reasonable to expect general education teachers or special education teachers to be experts on every childhood malady. The primary lesson to remember is that children are far more alike than they are different from one another. Whatever their differences, children desire and need the company of other children. They are more likely to develop adaptive behaviors in the presence of peers. Children with special needs can succeed academically and socially in mainstreamed settings (Stainback, & Stainback, 1992; Thousand & Villa, 1990).

Setting the stage for an inclusive classroom takes somewhat more planning. Effective planning includes input and support from the school administration, other teachers, parents of children with special needs, and possibly the school nurse. Early and frequent collaboration with your special education colleagues is particularly helpful. There are significant differences between general and special education teachers' perspectives on curriculum and methods of instruction. Sometimes they differ in expectations for children.

Collaboration works when teachers constructively build on these different points of view. Collaboration produces multiple strategies that can be tested for effectiveness (as in the proverbial "two heads are better than one"). For collaboration to work, teachers have to respect different points of view, have good listening skills, and be willing to try something new. It also requires systematic observation and evaluation of strategies that are tested. Teachers have to ask, "How well did the strategy/adaptation work? What effect did it have on the children in the class?" Here are some strategies for collaboration:

- Attend the student's multidisciplinary team meeting.
- Keep a copy of the individual family service plan (IFSP) or individualized education plan (IEP) and consult it periodically to ensure that short- and long-term goals are being achieved.
- Arrange to have some shared planning time each week with others who work with children with special needs.
- Brainstorm modifications/adaptations to regular instructional activities.

(continued on next page)

Special Feature 8.2 *(continued)*

- Identify who will collect work samples of specific tasks.
- Assess the student's language, reading, and writing strengths, and give brief probes each week to check on progress and maintenance.
- Share copies of student work with your collaborators and add these artifacts to the child's portfolio.
- Collaborate with families. Parents are children's first and best teachers. Additionally, they possess personal knowledge of their children that far surpasses any assessment data we may collect.

Go

As previously mentioned, the majority of children with special needs have difficulties in language, reading, and written expression. Research indicates that these problems stem from deficits in short-term memory, lack of self-awareness and self-monitoring strategies, lack of mediational strategies, and inability to transfer and generalize learned material to new or novel situations. Hence, many children with special needs may have difficulty in classroom setting that utilize a high degree of implicit teaching of literacy. These children typically can benefit from explicit instruction. Here are some general teaching strategies that teachers can use to support children with special needs:

- Establish a daily routine on which the child with special needs can depend.
- Allocate more time for tasks to be completed by children with special needs.
- Structure transitions between activities, and provide supervision and guidance for quick changes in activities.
- Adapt the physical arrangement of the room to provide a quiet space free of visual and auditory distractions.
- Plan time for one-on-one instruction at some point in the day.
- Use task analysis to break learning tasks into components.
- Recognize the different learning styles of all students, and prepare materials in different ways—for example, as manipulatives, audio recordings, visual displays, and the like.
- Try cross-ability or reciprocal peer tutoring for practice of learned material.
- Begin teaching organization skills such as the use of a simple daily planner.
- Teach positive social behaviors to all children.
- Consistently implement behavior change programs.
- Recognize and help children with special needs deal with their feelings.
- Encourage all children to respect and include children with special needs in their academic and play activities.

- Establish a routine means of communication with parents.
- Locate strategies that help parents that select materials that are developmentally and educationally appropriate for their children.

Speech Development

When children come to school, they are expected to be able to communicate. Language is the ability to communicate using symbols; it includes comprehension of both oral and written expression. Speech is one component of oral expression. Many young children come to school with delays in speech and language (comprehension and expression). Speech problems such as misarticulations and dysfluencies are frequently seen in young children with and without special needs. Less obvious are problems understanding others' speech. Fortunately, the majority of children with language problems are able to successfully participate in all aspects of general education with a few modifications to the environment or curriculum.

Frequently, children with language problems receive special education services provided by a speech and language pathologist. However, the classroom teacher also has important roles to fulfill: (1) monitoring children's comprehension of instructions and classroom activities, and (2) providing opportunities for oral language practice and interaction with peers and adults.

The following are strategies that classroom teachers can use to help promote speech development in children with oral language delays:

- Collaborate with the speech and language pathologist in selecting activities, materials, and games that promote language development.
- Model appropriate grammar, rhythm, tone, and syntax.
- Keep directions simple, brief, and to the point.
- For students who have difficulty expressing themselves, do not rely solely on open-ended questions. Use yes or no questions that are easier to answer.
- When students with speech problems speak, give them your full attention and ensure that other students do the same.
- Errors should not be criticized. Pay attention to the content of the child's message. Do not call attention to misarticulations, especially dysfluencies, as the problem may become more serious if attention is called to it (Lewis & Doorlag, 1999).
- Children who stutter may have improved speech quality if alternate styles of communication are used, such as whispering, singing in a higher or lower pitch, or choral reading.
- Give children with special needs multiple opportunities across the day to converse with you.
- Encourage parents to routinely engage in conversations using children's new words, experiences, and relationships.

(continued on next page)

Special strategies are also needed to help language-delayed children learn the meanings of new words (receptive vocabulary) and be able to use these new words in their speech (expressive vocabulary):

- Teach vocabulary in all subjects: math, science, social studies, health, and so on.
- Assess the child's prior knowledge before introducing a new topic.
- Have the student develop a word book of new words for practice. Pair these words with pictures.
- Encourage children to ask about words they do not understand. Pair these new words with concepts already known.
- Have the students paraphrase new words they are acquiring.
- Use physical demonstrations of words, such as verbs and prepositions, that are difficult to explain. Show children the meanings of these words.
- Have the students physically demonstrate the meanings of words.
- Use manipulatives that children can handle to teach new words.
- Give multiple examples of word meanings.
- Teach students to use picture dictionaries to locate unfamiliar words.
- Keep parents informed of these special strategies and urge them to continue their use outside of school.

For children with more severe special needs, secure the services of a specialist in augmentative communication. These individuals have specific skills in communication boards, electronic communication devices, and computer voice synthesis. For more information about this special area, contact the Assistive Technology On-Line Web site at www.asel.udel.edu?at-online, sponsored by the DuPont Hospital for Children and the University of Delaware.

Reading Assessment and Instruction

For many young children with or at-risk for special needs, reading is a very difficult task. Many of these children benefit greatly from explicit instruction in the basic tools of reading (Chall, 1983, 1989; Slavin, 1989; Stahl & Miller, 1989) using a direct instruction model. Assessments of children's phonemic awareness (Torgesen, 1994) provide valuable information about the student's skills and deficits in basic manipulation of phonemes. Additionally, it is essential for teachers to match reading materials to the skills of students with special needs.

Once a student's instructional reading level has been identified and appropriate reading materials have been obtained, teachers can use the following strategies to help promote the reading development of the child with special needs:

- Use books without words to provide early readers with an overview of the sequence of story content.

- Teach students to use the context clues available in the text such as the title and pictures.
- Use cross-age tutors, pairing older children such as second-graders with kindergarteners, for drill and practice of sight words and newly learned words.
- Increase fluency by having students repeat readings often.
- Have students use a straightedge under a line of text to eliminate visual distractions and keep place and pace.
- Have students use their finger to point and keep place and pace.
- Tape text read by the teacher or other children. Have the student follow along and read aloud while listening to correct pronunciation, expression, phrasing, and punctuation.
- Echo read with the students. Sit behind and to the side of the child out of his or her line of sight. Read the text with the child softly into his or her ear, providing a model of pacing, pronunciation, and corrective feedback.

Writing Instruction

Most young children with special needs do not have physical impairments. However, many may experience delays in both fine and gross motor development. These delays may affect a child's ability to effectively grasp a pencil or shape letters and numbers. Large or ball-shaped crayons are often effective writing tools for children who have not developed a pencil grip. Many commercial built-up pencils or pencil grips are also available. When using these grips, be sure to instruct the child in the proper finger and hand placement on the pencil. For very young children with special needs, tracing letters in sand is a good place to start. Practicing letter structure in finger-paints or liquid soap is also effective. Paper used by young children can be brightly colored in order to produce a contrast between the writing and the background. Initially, plain paper without lines is preferable to that with lines, as printing is similar to drawing. Using successive approximation of the appropriate size and shape of letters can be accomplished with wide-lined paper with different colored lines. These lines serve as cues for the child to stop or go. Young children with more severe special needs may require the support and services of occupational therapists. These therapists can provide you with expertise and specialized equipment to promote fine motor development.

Written expression by young children with special needs may present several problems for the teacher and the child, as writing is both a process and a product that requires physical and cognitive skills. The written product should be assessed using observable and measurable goals that correspond with the strengths and weaknesses of the child. Teachers need patience and repeated observations of children's written work in order to effectively evaluate and plan for writing in-

(continued on next page)

Special Feature 8.2 *(continued)*

struction. The following are strategies for promoting written expression by young children with special needs:

- Allocate time for writing each day.
- Have children create simple stories from tangible objects that they can touch and manipulate, rather than asking for a memory or a concept. For example, give a ball to the child and ask the child to tell you about this ball. Have an adult serve as a scribe for the child and take dictation, writing down the story as it is composed. When the child is able, ask the child to copy the dictated copy and draw a picture of the ball.
- Compliment children on the content of their stories. Ask for more information about the topic and help them expand their stories.

- Develop a template for writing—for example, putting name and date on a specific area of the paper.
- Celebrate the child's successes!
- Exhibit examples of all children's work.

Including young children with special needs in the general education setting can be a rewarding experience for the children and their teachers. Assisting children to meet their potential is a teacher's responsibility. These strategies have proven to be effective for teachers supporting children with special needs in special and general education classrooms. However, the most effective tool for teachers is shared planning and collaboration. We urge teachers in all settings to share their skills, experience, and techniques with one another and celebrate the diversity of learners in the schools of this new century.

Special Feature 8.3

Helping Terrel

Terrel was born with a lateral cleft palate.* He had his first corrective lip surgery when he was 3 months old. He was able to have corrective surgery for the palate when he was 18 months old. A further complication of cleft palate is frequent ear infections because the eustachian tube, which connects the ear to the nose, does not open properly, allowing fluid to build up in the middle ear. Terrel is a bright child with a large receptive vocabulary, but his ability to express himself orally is greatly limited. He misarticulates most words and often becomes frustrated and then begins to stutter.

Terrel is entering a preschool associated with a university that has a speech clinic. Terrel is fortunate. His progress has been assessed by a speech pathologist, and today Terrel's parents are meeting with the preschool teacher, the speech pathologist, and the preschool administrator to develop a Individual Family Service Plan (IFSP). The IFSP like the IEP, is a written document developed by a multidisciplinary team that focuses on the child's needs and goals. The focus of this type of plan may also include direct support for the family of a child with physical challenges as well as learning disabilities. The IFSP usually specifies the type of support parents may offer to their child to help the child successfully transition to school.

*A cleft palate is a division or separation of parts of the lip and/or roof of the mouth that is formed during the early months of development of the unborn child. Children born with cleft palates are carefully assessed by a crainiofacial team in order to detect potentially serious abnormalities that can be associated with clefting. The objective of cleft palate surgery is to close the palate to restore normal functions of eating and drinking and to enhance the development of normal speech. Cleft lip and/or palate affects one of every 700 babies. Cleft lip and cleft palate are genetic birth defects that are usually associated with what is called multifactorial inheritance. This means that in the vast majority of cases, multiple genes contributed from both parents, as well as a number of environmental factors that doctors do not yet fully understand, cause the condition.

(continued on next page)

Special Feature 8.3 *(continued)*

Figure 8.8

Terrel's Individual Family Service Plan (IFSP)

Date of IFSP Meeting: *8-14-00*	Anticipated Duration of IFSP: *9-14-00 to 12-14-00*	IFSP Type: ☒ Initial ☐ Annual ☐ Interim

Student: *Terrel Jackson* School: *Apple Elementary* Grade: *Preschool* Placement: *Regular Class/SpEd Consultant/Co-teacher* Birthdate: *September 1, 1997* Address:	District Representative: *Dr. Ryan, Principal* Regular Education Teacher: *Mrs. Hansen, Preschool* Special Education Teacher: Parent(s): *Wendy & Bob Jackson* Evaluator: Student: *Terrel Jackson* Other(s): *Ms. Marquez—Speech Therapist*

Present Educational Level	Tri-Annual Goal	Instructional & Social Skills Objectives	Evaluation
Language: Strengths 1. Surgery successful 2. Excellent receptive vocabulary 3. Highly motivated 4. Strong family support **Weaknesses** 1. Articulation 2. Disfluency 3. One or two word utterances **Social Skills** 1. Shy, hesitant to interact with same-age peers 2. Refuses to speak in front of a group 3. Becomes frustrated with trying to communicate with others	Terrel will improve his articulation and begin to use multi-word sentences. Terrel will develop confidence in his social skills.	1. Terrel will work with speech therapist to practice articulating targeted sounds and high-frequency words. 2. Teacher and speech therapists will identify target words that use target sounds. 3. Terrel will answer close-ended questions during social-circle and storybook time. 4. Terrel's social goal will be to verbally interact with at least one classmate during center time. 5. Terrel's parent's will sing songs with Terrel to help his fluency. 6. Terrel's parents will play age-appropriate games like Candy Land to help Terrel build turn-taking skills and reinforce articulation and fluency.	Articulation of target words is assessed on a weekly basis. Teacher anecdotal notes will document social goals. Parents will have a quarterly conference with teacher and speech therapist to reassess Terrel's progress and establish new goals.

Summary

Chapters 5 through 7 presented the instructional strategies that create the framework for an effective early childhood language arts curriculum. However, these strategies by themselves are not sufficient to construct a program that ensures optimal language and literacy learning for all children. This chapter presents the other two key ingredients: ongoing assessment and adapting instruction to meet the needs of second-language learners and children with special needs.

- *What is important for teachers to know about children's literacy development?*

  Teachers need a through knowledge of language and literacy guidelines for young children. This information may be obtained from several sources, including state and local district guidelines for kindergarten children. In addition to information provided throughout this text, the authors also recommend reports prepared by the Committee on the Preventing of Reading Difficulties in Young Children and a joint report published by the International Reading Association and the National Association for the Education of Young Children (IRA/ NAEYC).

- *What types of assessment methods are used to collect information about children's progress?*

  Changes in what we know about literacy learning have necessitated major changes in our ways of measuring young children's literacy accomplishments and progress. Instead of sporadic tests and quizzes that yield isolated samples of student literacy behavior, teachers now rely on ongoing assessment procedures that are connected with the daily literacy activities that take place in the classroom. This ongoing assessment makes heavy use of systematic observation and the collection of samples of children's work. The classroom library, writing center, and dramatic play areas are ideal settings for this type of assessment, and anecdotal notes, vignettes, and checklists provide effective ways to record data.

- *How do teachers use the information they collect?*

  Teachers (and children) collect information and store it in working portfolios. The products and information contained in a working portfolio are analyzed by the teacher (and the student) to assess the student's progress over time. These types of authentic assessment provide just the type of information that teachers need to know to provide effective literacy learning experiences for children.

  Teachers also use the information they collect in portfolios to share with parents. Parents need to know how their children are progressing, and most parents need to have concrete examples with explicit information provided by the teacher to see how their child's early literacy efforts will develop into conventional reading and writing. Most early childhood educators recommend showing parents examples from the working portfolio and the showcase portfolio.

- *How do ongoing assessment techniques help early childhood teachers meet the needs of diverse learners?*

  In order to make literacy learning experiences accessible to all children in the classroom, teachers also need to make accommodations for the tremendous diversity that is present in today's classrooms. Special features by Sarah Hudelson and Irene Serna and by Karen Burstein and Tanis Bryan explain how instructional activities can be modified to meet the needs of children who are learning English as a second language and those who have language disabilities and other special needs.

Linking Knowledge to Practice

1. One way teachers determine what they want and need to know about children's literacy development is by reviewing national, state, and local standards. Contact a local school district to obtain a copy of the local standards for language arts at the kindergarten level.

Given what you have learned about children's early literacy development in this textbook, do these standards appear to be reasonable goals for language arts instruction at the kindergarten level?

2. Interview a pre-K or kindergarten teacher about the information-gathering tools that he or she typically uses to collect information about children's literacy development. How does the teacher organize this information to share with parents?

Organizing the Curriculum and Classroom Environment

The four-year-olds in Mrs. Flores' preschool class had been talking about their experiences at the grocery store. Mrs. Flores decided to use a KWL chart to find out what the children already knew about grocery stores ("They have lots of food." "I like the cereal place.") and what they wanted to learn ("Where does the food come from?"). The class decided to study grocery stores to find the answers to their questions. During the weeks that followed, the class took several field trips to nearby grocery stores, invited store employees to visit their classroom, read books about grocery stores, and engaged in dramatic play in a grocery store play center stocked with store-related literacy (signs, empty product containers, note pads for grocery lists) and mathematics (scales, calculator) props. While engaging in their investigations and play, the children learned quite a lot about grocery stores (social studies concepts), and they also developed important literacy and mathematic skills.

For many years, early childhood teachers have connected, or integrated, the curriculum. This approach to curriculum planning and implementation has had a variety of labels. Some teachers use the term interdisciplinary curriculum (Jacobs, 1989), while others speak about immersing their children in the study of a theme (Manning, Manning, & Long, 1994). More recently, many early childhood teachers suggest they are using the project approach (Katz & Chard,1993).

Whatever the label, these teachers are heeding the advice of the National Council of Teachers of English (NCTE, 1993):

> Rather than working on subjects in isolation from one another, studying reading apart from writing, and apart from math, science, social studies, and other curricular areas, children learn best when they are engaged in inquiries that involve using language to learn, and that naturally incorporate content from a variety of subject areas.

When the language arts are woven into the very fabric of all subject matter areas, it is a classic win-win situation. Subject matter content and the language arts are both learned more effectively. As teacher Tarry Lindquist (1995, p. 1) points out:

> It is through the language arts that my students most often reveal their knowledge and apply their skills. Reading, writing, listening, and speaking are integral to all learning. Without language arts, the construction of meaning in specific topics is impossible.

An integrated approach to curriculum has three basic requirements: (1) a classroom environment rich with materials to support children's investigations, (2) a daily schedule that permits interweaving the various subject matter areas and focusing on a topic for sustained periods of time, and (3) teachers who view their role as a facilitator of learning rather than as a transmitter of knowledge. According to Goodlad and Oakes (1988, p. 19), these teachers "function more like orchestra conductors than like lecturers; getting things started and keeping them moving along, providing information and pointing to resources, coordinating a diverse but harmonious buzz of activity."

In this chapter we describe how many teachers are connecting the language arts, helping children use literacy to learn, planning integrated curriculum designed to meet their children's interests and needs, designing classroom environments that support their children's investigations, and arranging for the time that is needed for their children's study and play.

Before reading this chapter, think about . . .

- The types of projects and units that you participated in when you were in school. What topics do you remember studying? Were these topics selected by the teacher, by the students, or both? What sorts of activities were included in the projects or units? How did you share the findings or products?

Focus Questions

- What are the major differences between the subject-by-subject, correlated, and integrated approaches to early childhood curricula?
- How can teachers plan and implement an integrated curriculum unit or project?
- How can teachers arrange the classroom's physical environment and daily schedule to support the integrated curriculum?

Approaches to Curriculum Design

Before examining just how teachers are connecting the language arts and implementing an integrated curriculum, we briefly consider the range of curriculum choices available to teachers.

Subject-By-Subject

Some teachers use a subject-based approach in which each subject (language arts, mathematics, science, social studies, art, music, and physical education) has a separate time block during the day. These teachers make no deliberate effort to show the relationship between or among the subjects. When reading is over, the children put their reading books away and take out their spelling books. In these classrooms, the textbook determines the curriculum. These teachers

---

BOX 3.1

Definition of Terms

correlated curriculum: activities in different subjects are selected that are related to to a given theme or topic.

integrated curriculum: activities in different subject areas are selected in order to help children find answers to questions about a topic that is of interest to them.

KWL chart: a strategy for facilitating comprehension. Prior to studying a topic, the teacher makes a chart listing what children already know about the topic and what they want to learn about the topic. After the topic has been studied, the teacher makes a list of new things that the students learned about the topic.

learning log: a notebook in which children record their thinking about the topic being studied in a project or unit.

subject-by-subject curriculum: a curriculum in which each subject area has a separate time block during the day. For example, math is scheduled from 9:00 to 9:30, and the language arts are taught from 9:30 to 10:30.

webbing: a visual organizer that shows how various facets of a topic are related to each other. Teacher use webs to help children to generate ideas linked to a topic and to organize the investigation of the topic.

seem to believe that children are vessels into which knowledge can be poured. Fortunately, this compartmentalized option is seldom used in preschool and kindergarten classrooms. The authors of this book believe it should not be used at all.

Correlated

Many early childhood teachers use a correlated approach to curriculum planning (also commonly referred to as the multidisciplinary approach). These teachers choose a topic for study, such as the circus, bears, monsters, or pigs. Sometimes the topic is selected because its study is required by the state or district social studies or science curriculum. For example, the district may require that all children in kindergarten study sinking and floating. Other times, the topic is selected because teachers know it is of interest to their children.

Typically, these teachers begin their planning by examining their district's suggested learning goals or objectives in each subject area for their grade level. Then, they design activities or learning experiences that correlate with the selected topic and that permit their students to achieve these learning goals. Often, activities exhibit the planner's creativity, and usually these activities are fun for the children. Typically, these teachers plan lots of activities, and they gather all the children's books they can find on the topic.

One group of early childhood teachers chose rabbits as a topic of study for their four- and five-year-olds in April. These teachers made a deliberate decision to bring together the various discipline areas. Together, they planned a range of activities that would be placed in the various centers (e.g., the mathematics center, the writing center) in their classrooms. Figure 9.1 provides an illustration of the activities offered to the children on one day.

Figure 9.1

One day of a multidisciplinary rabbit study

One Day of a Multidisciplinary Rabbit Study

RABBIT UNIT

Writing Center
The teacher had traced a large bunny pattern on 8½" x 11" paper. On each page the following verse had been written:

I baked a carrot pie.
It was very sweet.
I baked a carrot _____ for
my friends to _____ .

The children were to cut out the bunny pattern and to fill in the blanks.

Reading Center
In addition to lots of books on rabbits and bunnies, the teachers had made a game. On the left side of the file folder, the teachers had placed 12 rabbit patterns. Each rabbit pattern had a bow tie with an alphabet sequence

(e.g., f g / i j).

In addition, the teachers had cut 12 circles out of tag board. On each circle was a letter

(e.g., h).

The children were to put the correct circle onto the correct bow tie.

Math Center
The teachers had traced five bunny patterns. Each bunny held a circle, square, triangle, or rectangle. The teachers had cut five triangles, five circles, five squares, and five rectangles the same size as the shapes held by the bunnies. The children matched the shapes to the correct bunny.

Dramatic Play Center
The teachers had created Mr. McGregor's garden. The children dressed as bunnies or the farmer and acted out *Peter Rabbit.*

Science Center
The teachers had drawn the outline of a bunny shape on each of twelve 4" x 6" index cards. On two shapes, they had glued sandpaper; on two shapes, they had glued a cotton ball; on two shapes, they had glued corduroy; and so on. The children took turns matching the bunnies by the textures of their tails.

There are several shortcomings with this approach to designing curriculum. First, what did the children learn about the rabbits during this day? What major concepts or understandings about this animal were addressed? Often when teachers seek to have each of the subject matter areas represented in a theme, the topic serves as the conduit to teach or reinforce skills. Learning about the topic is subjugated to a minor position.

A second problem relates to the activities themselves. Was matching the shapes in the math center or matching the textures in the science center right for all children in the three classrooms? In all likelihood, some children could already sort and even label the shapes. Was this activity an appropriate use of their valuable school time?

Were these activities worth the tremendous investment of the teachers' time? A comparison of the teachers' construction time with the children's doing time would reveal that the teachers spent far more time constructing the activities than the children spent doing them.

Finally, is the activity in the writing center a writing activity? To provide activities in each of the centers sometimes results in a deviation from the principles of quality instruction we have described in this book. Clearly, the links or connections across the various curricular areas are artificial.

Integrated

The topic of dinosaurs was chosen by a group of teachers in Colorado and was developed into an integrated unit. Judith Gilbert (1989) described these teachers' unit. First, the teachers decided on the concepts they wanted to address and queried their young students about the questions they wanted answered during their study of dinosaurs. For example, one concept centered on one of the children's question about the size of dinosaurs: How big were dinosaurs? The teachers designed an activity to help their young children understand dinosaurs' size and to answer their question. One of the teachers drew a full-sized outline of a dinosaur on the school's parking lot. The number of children who could fit inside a dinosaur was estimated and calculated. Many children could fit inside the dinosaur outline! Then the teachers had the children lie flat, with one child's feet touching the top of another child's head, on the parking-lot outline, extending from the bottom of the dinosaur drawing's feet to the tip of the dinosaur's nose. In this way, the children were able to determine that a dinosaur was about ten children tall. Did that mean a dinosaur could see over the school building? To help the children answer this question, ten children's silhouettes were traced vertically on a roll of butcher paper. The school's custodian kindly climbed to the roof of the building and hung the butcher paper from the top of the school building. The children discovered that the paper was longer than the school building was high! This helped the children understand that dinosaurs could see over their school building. Numerous other activities were implemented to help the children answer their questions and understand the major concepts about dinosaurs.

In the preceding example, concepts about dinosaurs and children's questions drove the teachers' creation of the educational activities. Subject-matter areas appropriate to the activities or projects were woven naturally into the children's investigations. The seams among the subject-matter areas were erased. Notice that school time was structured around the children's needs. Thus, the schedule had to be flexible. The teachers had to be alert to the knowledge and skills the children were acquiring through the activities. In addition, the teachers had to consider new ways to legitimately weave subject areas and skill development into the activities.

This integrated curriculum approach (also called the interdisciplinary approach) "trusts the teacher to be a good problem solver and wise decider" (Lindquist, 1995, p. 2). This kind of instruction, which is an integral element of the constructivist philosophy, requires a teacher who

- Shows innate curiosity, sharing children's interests and enthusiasm about the world
- Supports children's intellectual curiosity by organizing the environment and the schedule in ways that encourage children to pursue their ideas
- Willingly collaborates with children in the designing of the curriculum. (Klein, 1991)

How do teachers make the right decisions and design quality curricula? What might their classroom schedules look like? How do they design their classroom environments? These questions are the focus of this chapter.

Erasing The Seams: Designing Integrated Curricula

Phase 1: Selecting a Topic

Teachers begin by selecting what Heidi Hayes Jacobs (1989, p. 54) calls "an organizing center." She and several other writers identify different criteria that should be used in the selection of the topic of study. For example, Jacobs (1989) warns teachers that they must discover topics that are not too broad and not too narrow and that lend themselves to children's study. Other writers (e.g., Manning, Manning, & Long, 1994) nudge teachers toward broad topics, such as endangered species, homelessness, and human rights. Lillian Katz and Sylvia Chard (1993) use relevance to young children's daily lives to drive their identification of topics appropriate for children's study. They suggest topics like the children's homes, families, and food; the local community's people and businesses; important local events and current affairs; nearby landmarks, rivers, hills, or woods; and natural phenomena like the weather, water, wind and air, plants, and animals. Note how topics such as these, regardless of their breadth, help children "make sense of their own personal experience and of life around them" (Katz & Chard, p. 68).

It is clear that if children are to invest themselves in the study, the topics selected must be important to them. Blending these experts' suggestions, the writers of this book advise early childhood teachers to consider broad topics relevant to the lives of their children and their community.

EXACTLY WHICH TOPICS?   In the ideal school, topic selection would be negotiated between the teacher and the children, with the teacher attempting to be responsive to as many children's interests as possible. Topics would emerge from collective planning with the children. However, state departments of education, school districts, and schools often mandate some topics. So, in practice, the topics selected by early childhood teachers who work within a school system likely will be a blend of those chosen by the children and those mandated. Of course, within some topics chosen by the children may be elements of mandated topics. Teachers need to be alert to the overlaying possibilities.

HOW MIGHT THE CHILDREN'S CHOICES BE IDENTIFIED?   Many teachers begin by holding a brainstorming session where the children identify topics they want to study. As one of the members of the community of learners, these teachers feel free to contribute topics of interest to them or to the state or district. With young children, they often need to begin the session by suggesting some possibilities. In this way, the children come to understand the request. As the group discusses each of the topics listed, some topics might be combined. Then, the class might narrow the options by identifying what they would like to learn about first. Nancy Edwards' children might have been influenced by the sound of the fire alarm from the nearby fire station, which blared as they tried to talk about what they'd like to learn about during the year. Firemen and fires was a popular topic among her children. Photography was the topic that interested the four-year-olds at the school described by Judy Helm (1999). Helm described how a professional photographer used the four-year-olds' school as the setting for some pictures he needed. Their teacher listened to the children and used the children's piqued interest in photography as the focus for an in-depth exploration.

Phase 2: Determining What the Children Already Know and What They Want to Learn about the Topic

Once the topic or theme has been selected, it is important for the teacher to know what the children already know and what misconceptions the children possess about the topic before activity planning begins. Often teachers begin by constructing a KWL chart with their children—a chart with three columns, the first two of which show the answers to the questions: What do you already know? What do you want to learn? After the study of the topic is completed, the third column of the chart shows the answer to, What did you learn? (Ogle, 1986). The teacher serves as the recorder of the children's collective knowledge.

At this stage of information-gathering, it is important to accept and record all comments made and questions generated by the children. Not only is knowing what children know important for their teachers, but knowing children's misconceptions also provides their teachers with insights into needed learning experiences. As Sandra Wilensky (1995, p. 43) suggests, teachers "have an obligation . . . [to] dissolve stereotypes and generalizations such as 'All Africans live in huts.' and 'All Eskimos live in igloos.' "

Certainly, during the group discussion, because teachers are members of the classroom learning community, the teacher might raise questions to extend the children's thinking about what they might learn. For example, as the children consider the topic of dinosaurs, a popular topic with many groups of children, if no child raises the question about how big they really were, the teacher might suggest that this is something she or he would like to learn. "Do we know how big dinosaurs really were? I've seen them on television, but I've always wondered: If a dinosaur stood beside me, how much taller than me would it be? I've also wondered: Could a dinosaur fit in this room? I don't think so, but how tall and long were they? I'm interested in answers to these questions." With that, the teacher's question (How big were dinosaurs?) could be added to the What do you want to learn? column on the KWL chart.

Observant teachers often see links between the topics the children want to study and what their districts or states say the children must study. When such links are possible, they alert their children to the questions the district or state wants them to be able to answer. All teachers are not free to do anything they choose!

Carol Avery (1993) described another reason teachers need to understand what their children know about a topic before they plan activities. In a 45-minute discussion, her young students demonstrated their knowledge of all of the concepts about urban, suburban, and rural communities outlined in the Lancaster County, Pennsylvania, district curriculum guide. Her students had lived in the area for all their young lives and had attended to their environment. Life had provided her children with this knowledge. Had Carol not begun with a What do you already know? discussion, she would have wasted time presenting information and offering her children activities on concepts they already understood.

What subtopics are represented by the children's questions? By looking over all the questions, it is possible to develop a list of subtopics. For example, following a group discussion on the environment, a teacher identified the following subtopics embedded within the children's questions: recycling/disposing, pollution, litter, and garbage.

After the list of subtopics has been generated, the teacher can construct a web. "A web is a kind of visual brainstorm that helps to generate ideas and link them to a theme or central focus" (Huck, Hepler, Hickman, & Kilfer 1997, p. 652). It is also "a mapping of the key ideas and concepts that a topic comprises and some of the major subthemes related to it" (Katz & Chard, 1993, p. 88). By preparing a web, teachers can see whether the topic has sufficient depth and breadth to warrant the children's investigation. Figure 9.2 is a sample web on homes written by Karyn Wellhousen (1996).

Phase 3: Determining Ways to Answer Children's Questions: The Activities or Projects

The concepts to be addressed, the questions generated, and the children's misconceptions drive the decisions about which activities these children will do during their study of the topic of interest. Since major concepts relative to each topic are embedded in children's and teachers' questions, teachers know their children will come away from their study with important understandings. In addition, teachers know that the various subject matter areas are embedded in the questions. In contrast to when the multidisciplinary approach is used in curriculum planning, integrated curriculum teachers are not concerned that every subject matter area or every classroom learning center is blended into the study of each topic. Teachers using the integrated approach do not set out at the beginning of their planning with the intention of ensuring that all subject matter areas are covered. They know that most, if not all, subject areas will be embedded in each topic's study using this approach. If activities are planned thoughtfully, the activities will draw

Figure 9.2   *Web on Homes*

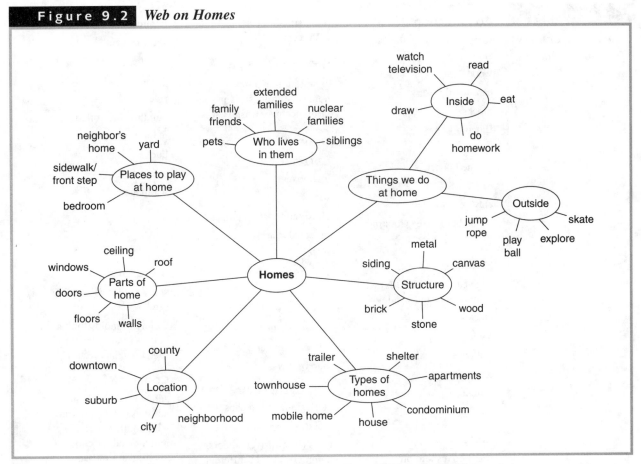

Reprinted with permission from the National Association for the Education of Young Children. Karen Willhousen
(1996). Social studies: Why not study homes? *Young Children,* p. 75.

heavily on a variety of disciplines for facts, skills, concepts, and understanding. In fact, it will be
nearly impossible not to weave the language arts into nearly all of the activities. The children will
be doing lots of listening, reading, writing, enacting, speaking, and observing.

Judy Helm (1999) describes how a group of four-year-olds approached their study of photography. The children interviewed and worked with experts. That is, their teacher made
arrangements for them to interact with adults who knew a lot about photography. Helm reminds
teachers to talk with the experts before their visit to the classroom about the children's developmental level and to encourage the experts to consider leaving something with the children,
perhaps something like "a small light table so that the children can view slides they've taken
together" (p. 28). The class also went on various field trips. Helm reminds teachers to make
the following preparations before each field trip:

- Make a pre-trip visit to explain that the children will have specific tasks they are hoping
  to do while they are at the site.
- Prepare the children by reviewing what they want to learn from their visit to the site.
- Decide how the children will make a record of their trip.
- Make a list of the questions they want to have answered.

Children might bring clipboards, paper, and pencils with them to make sketches of what they
see, or they might bring cameras.

Finally, children can explore the topic using various resources in classroom learning centers. The teacher's task is to collect and organize materials related to the topic and then observe
and listen to the children's interactions with these materials. These observations provide insight
into what children are learning about the topic of study. Figure 9.3 is a list of resources children might use in the various classroom learning centers when studying homes.

Figure 9.3 *Learning centers for unit on homes*	**Construction** scraps from house-building sites wood scraps cardboard boxes blocks Lincoln Logs Legos notched popsicle sticks rocks clay adobe bricks (see Cooking for recipe) **Home** large cardboard box(es) with cutout doors and windows blocks paint wallpaper samples carpet scraps shingles tile **Crafts** small boxes and other materials to be covered, painted, decorated for creating a neighborhood, apartment complex, trailer park **Art** pictures of various architectural structures drawing pencils and large paper triangles and T-squares	other supplies used by architects **Science** exploration of animal homes—bird nests, ant farm, beehive, wasp nest **Dramatic Play Themes** *Post Office* mailboxes stickers old shoulder-strap purses canceled stamps seals stickers envelopes paper postage scale rubber stamp and ink pad map of city *Hardware Store* clerk smocks and caps wood tools (screwdrivers, pliers, hammers, etc., of different sizes) on peg board cash register play money price tags *Construction Site* work gloves hard hats boots goggles tool belt	hammer screwdrivers clamps wrench ruler paintbrushes/rollers paint trays buckets sandpaper wallpaper nails pipe lunchpails **Sand Table** spray bottles for wetting sand variety of molds for building houses (margarine tubs, food containers, etc.) **Cooking** adobe bricks—(1) mix dirt, a little sand, some straw with a little water; (2) pour into a metal ice cube tray; (3) bake at low heat **Blocks** large supply and variety of blocks and other building materials sticky-notes, index cards, and tape for labeling windows and doors cut from construction paper or transparencies dollhouse with family microfigures	

Reprinted with permission from the National Association for the Education of Young children. Karen Willhousen (1996). Social studies: Why not study homes? *Young Children*, p. 75.

SHARING LEARNING WITH OTHERS. As teachers plan for and consider various ways for children to express their learning, they want to be cognizant that knowledge can be expressed in many different ways. The question is, What is the best way for children to share their learning with others? Several different kinds of products will be possibilities. Typically, the children will choose the product that seems most appropriate for them. Judy Helm suggests that sharing is a wonderful means of concluding the project. She suggests that children might make a large display, make a book about what they learned, produce a videotape that "tells the story of their project," or hold an open house for their families (1999, p. 31).

INTEGRATING LITERATURE INTO THE STUDY. As young children engage in investigation activities, they will be "reading" many different materials (books, encyclopedias, pamphlets), or more likely having information read to them. The teacher's role is to gather trade books (fiction and nonfiction) that are correlated with the topic under study. For example, when Nancy Edwards' kindergartner's studied the pond, Nancy's library corner was filled with books about water and the animals who live in it.

Readers should become familiar with the American Library Association bimonthly magazine *Book Links: Connecting Books, Libraries and Classrooms.* This magazine lists books, suggests activities, and recommends literature useful across the curriculum. Each month it contains annotated bibliographies of books connected to a theme, possible discussion questions, author interviews, activities, and lists of related books.

Another must-have for teachers of young children is *Once Upon a Time: An Encyclopedia for Successfully Using Literature with Young Children* (Hurst, 1991). Not only does this book contain background information on numerous children's authors and illustrators, but also it provides their mailing addresses—if the authors answer letters—and information on whether they will visit schools.

Finally, teachers of young children will find Mary Jett-Simpson's (1989) book *Adventuring with Books: A Booklist for Pre-K–Grade 6* helpful. It contains nearly 2000 recommended children's titles grouped by subjects.

LEARNING LOGS.   Many teachers request their children to keep learning logs while they engage in the learning activities or projects. Learning logs are notebooks in which children record their thinking and their discoveries. Unlike diaries, they are meant to be shared with others and to be reflected upon. In their logs, children

- systematically record the data they obtain through observations, reading, talking, and interviewing (e.g., the number of pets each classmate has, their classmates' favorite colors or sports);
- make predictions and speculations;
- describe experiences;
- record descriptions of activities;
- identify problems; and
- write summaries.

Of course, preschool and kindergarten children will use personalized, emergent forms of writing to record these types of information.

Carol Avery (1993) summarizes: Learning logs "are vehicles that can be used for speculating, predicting, recording, documenting, webbing, charting, listing, sketching, brainstorming, questioning, imagining, hypothesizing, synthesizing, analyzing, and reflecting" (p. 444). They are, says Nancie Atwell (1990, p. xviii), "tools [for children] to generate their own knowledge."

While students write in their learning logs, their teachers can have informal conferences with them. As her children wrote in their learning logs, Carol Avery (1993, p. 444) moved among them, asking "How do you know this?" "Why is this important?" "What do you think?" She reports that the children began posing similar questions to each other. Can young children really keep learning logs? Nancy Edwards' young learners certainly can and do (see Figure 7.2 in Chapter 7).

Phase 4: Assessment and Evaluation

Recall what you read in Chapter 1: Assessment and evaluation are intricately woven into the learning process; teachers gather data about their children's study of topics (assessment), and they make judgments about what their children have learned and need to learn (evaluation) while their children are engaged in learning.

While children work, teachers gather evidence to document their children's learning, skill development, and dispositions toward learning. Using these data, teachers and the children themselves make judgments about the children's learning. Note that, unlike in past years, it is not just the teacher making judgments about the children's learning. Child self-evaluation is a critical component of the new assessment and evaluation procedures.

Two teachers, Lisa Burley Maras and Bill Brummett (1995, p. 100), summarize their new view of assessment:

> We no longer viewed assessment and evaluation as something that comes at the end of a learning experience. For us, they occurred at all stages of the study—from our first wonderings and formulations of questions, through our active engagement, to our final products, and beyond to new topics. Assessment constantly functioned to support learners by enabling them to move beyond their current understandings.

Evidence, then, of the children's learning is demonstrated by the products created during the children's investigations, constructions, dramatic play, writing, and speaking while they study topics. Not only is the teacher gathering information about what the children are learning about the topic of study, but the teacher is also gathering information about each child's reading, writing, speaking, and listening learning. Every activity is an opportunity to gather data about the children.

Phase 5: Involving Parents

While "Involving Parents" is listed as the fifth phase of designing and implementing an integrated unit, parents can and should be involved throughout the study of a topic. If teachers want parents to be involved in what is going on in the classroom, then parents must be brought into each topic's study.

Lilian Katz and Sylvia Chard (1993) suggest that teachers can help parents become involved in their children's study by:

1. Helping children share information about their study with their parents while the study is progressing. For example, newsletters, written by or with the children, detailing the classroom activities can provide information for conversations. Similarly, occasionally photocopying a page form the children's learning logs provides a record of what the children learned on a particular day. Some teachers bring parents together regularly as a group to speak to them about their curricular intentions. Knowing that some parents will be unable to attend such a meeting, a follow-up summary can be sent to those parents who were unable to attend. Perhaps a parent with secretarial skills would be willing to prepare minutes of the meeting. Many parents want to be involved and need teachers assistance in the how of their involvement.

2. Encouraging parents to ask questions of their children about their study and to become involved in their children's study. Some children are excellent at responding to the age-old parent question, "What did you learn in school today?" Many children, however, answer "Nothing." Effective teachers look for ways to help parents structure their questions so that they generate a genuine parent–child conversation about children's learning. These teachers might include illustrations of possible kinds of questions (sometimes constructed with the children) at the end of a classroom newsletter. Other teachers hold a meeting for helping parents ask the kinds of questions that generate more than a "yes," "no," or "nothing" answer.

3. Involving parents "in providing information, pictures, books, and objects for the whole class in its pursuit of knowledge on the topic" (Katz & Chard, 1993, p. 106). Are there parents who hold jobs who are willing to speak to the children about their occupations? Could the children interview their parents to discover what they do?

These kinds of involvement activities help parents feel they are taking an active part in their children's education. Parents are important partners in their children's education. For additional suggestions on ways to involve parents in their children's education, see Chapter 10.

Implementing the Plan

Are you ready to initiate the study of a topic using the project approach with a group of young children? After learning about this approach, Donna Manz was. In Trade Secrets 9.1, she describes her use of the project approach with her young children during their study of the topic "House."

Trade Secrets 9.1

This Is the House That Kindergarten Built

Donna Manz

I am a kindergarten teacher who started teaching 20 years ago in a very traditional, worksheet-oriented environment. For the last 10 years, I have been moving toward a more child-sensitive, project-oriented classroom. I teach approximately 20 children of mixed ability and varied socioeconomic backgrounds, affluent to homeless. I am very pleased with the enthusiasm and far-reaching educational benefits that I see from all my students. They have learned to be planners, organizers, researchers, and problem solvers. They have learned lifelong skills that I never saw developing during fill-in-the-blank time.

This is about a project that I have used in my classroom. Maybe it will work as a starter for other teachers wanting to move toward a project approach.

How do you teach a group of five- and six-year-old children who come from the full spectrum of socioeconomic levels (affluent to homeless), who have a wide range of learning abilities (exceptionally gifted to severely disabled) and a diversity of life experiences? You develop projects around science and social studies themes that integrate specific skills through real-life activities.

One of the classroom projects my children worked on this year was constructing a "people shelter." We did research through observation and the literature about the different kinds of homes that people use for shelter. The children took walks around the school neighborhood and brought in pictures of their own homes so that they could observe the many styles and details of different types of shelters. Follow-up discussions made the children aware of the variety of homes, the need for homes, and the economics of building and buying or renting a home.

Through brainstorming and planning, children divided up into construction crews of painters, brick masons, carpenters, decorators, and landscapers. They had to work together in these groups, planning, organizing, and cooperating while turning a large washing-machine cardboard box into a beautiful house.

At the start of each class period, the "workers" punched their time clock and put on their hard hats. At the end of the work period, children again punched the time clock and used money stamps to record how much money they had earned. Throughout the project, children were using rulers to measure the sizes of windows and doors, sizing up the lengths of wallpaper needed, measuring for and sewing curtains, constructing a fence out of cardboard tubes, cutting cardboard bricks to build a fireplace, applying patterning skills to put shingles on the roof, and constantly reading and writing.

During the three-week project, children also made daily observations and recorded data through their drawing and writing about each stage of construction. When the house was finished, the children turned in their time cards and were paid for their work with play money. Kindergartners then had to pay a portion of their earnings to the Realtor (the teacher) as a fee to move into the house. They used the rest of the money to buy treats from the teacher's snack store.

Upon completion of the project, the entire school and parents were invited for a home tour while kindergarten children acted as tour guides. This project took three weeks to complete but had a lasting effect through the year. Children often used the house for playtime or as a quiet-time area. At the end of the year, we auctioned the house for real money at an all-school event.

When I asked the children at the end of the year to draw and write about their favorite kindergarten activity, many of them wrote about "The House That Kindergarten Built."

Manz, D. (1996). This is the house that kindergarten built. *Young Children,* 70–71.

Designing the Classroom's Physical Environment to Support the Integrated Curriculum

The classroom is the stage on which the drama will be played. The props it contains and how it is set up are critically important to the successful implementation of an integrated curriculum. Both the materials provided and the physical arrangement of these materials in the available space affects children's behaviors (Gump, 1989; Morrow & Weinstein, 1982, 1986). The classroom floor plan used by one teacher of young children, Sandra Lawing, is shown in Figure 9.4 as an illustration of several points teachers need to consider in arranging their classrooms.

Carve the Large Classroom Space into Small Areas

Notice how Sandra Lawing's classroom is divided into small, well-defined activity areas. Small, clearly defined areas encourage more interaction and sustained activity than do large areas. In addition, smaller areas accommodate fewer children, which leads to a quieter

Figure 9.4

Sandra Lawing's classroom floor plan

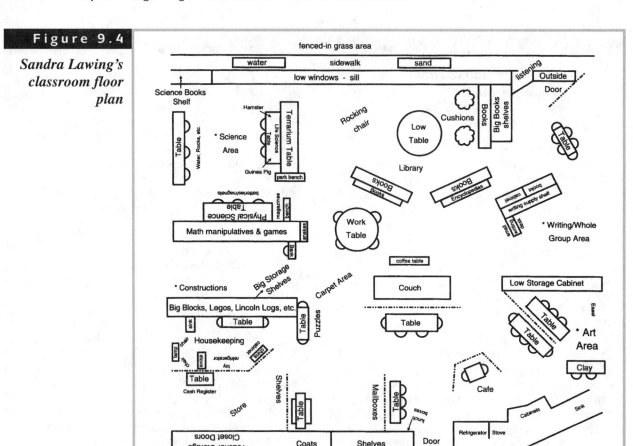

Reprinted from "Building Generative Curriculum" by Lester L. Laminick and Sandra Lawing, *Primary Voices K–6,* August 1994. Copyright 1994 by the National Council of Teachers of English.

classroom and fewer behavior problems. Each area (or center, as it is often called) needs to be clearly evident to its users. Areas can be clearly defined by using available classroom movable furniture (such as book shelves, cupboards, tables, boxes), screens, and large plants (real, if possible, but if not, artificial will do).

Typically, these centers are designed around each content area. Hence, classrooms have a science center, a mathematics center, a library center, a writing center, a dramatic play center, and so forth. To assist children's understanding of the purposes of the areas, each area should be clearly labeled with a sign mounted near the children's eye level. With young children, an appropriate picture or symbol should accompany the written label.

Gather Appropriate Resources to Support the Children's Learning

Typically, the materials needed to support children's engagement in activities are housed in the various centers. For example, we include a list of the materials found in Sandra Lawing's classroom's centers in Figure 9.5 and an extensive equipment and materials checklist prepared by Kimberly Kneas (1998) for rooms being set up for children of various ages. In addition, suggestions for materials for the writing center can be found in Chapter 7 and for the reading/library area in Chapter 5.

Each item should have a designated storage place. This designation helps children to find the materials with ease and to replace the materials for the next child's use. This means that each center needs shelves, tables, or boxes for the materials, with the designated spot for each material clearly labeled.

Within each center, the method of exhibiting the materials should be considered. For example, blocks of like sizes, like shapes, or like materials should be grouped together in the block

Figure 9.5 *Resource Materials to Support Children's Learning*

Use the four checklists that follow to guide your evaluation of your program and each learning center. Classroom teachers should complete the age-specific lists. A supervisor or administrator should take responsibility for the program-wide list. Use different-colored highlighters to note your "like-to-have" and "wish list" items so you can find them quickly later.

Infant/Toddler Room

For older infants who are crawling and younger toddlers who are pulling up, cruising, and walking:

❏ sturdy furniture that children can hold on to

❏ interesting things to move toward and around

❏ colorful things of different textures to grasp and examine (should be easy to disinfect)

For older toddlers and 2-year-olds:

❏ duplicate to avoid quarrels over sharing

❏ simple dramatic-play and dress-up props

Sleeping Area

❏ sturdy cribs

❏ cots for toddlers

❏ crib and cot sheets

❏ pictures of family on cribs

❏ crib mirrors

❏ busy boxes

❏ mobiles

❏ cassette recorder or CD player

❏ cassettes or CDS

❏ soft stuffed toys (if regulations permit)

Diapering Area

❏ rattles and squeak toys (should be easy to disinfect)

❏ mirrors

❏ mobiles

❏ pictures covered with clear contact paper

❏ diaper pail with lid

❏ disposable gloves

❏ bleach solution

❏ paper towels

❏ tissue paper

❏ newsprint

❏ yarn and string

❏ feathers

❏ craft sticks

❏ storage bins for each child's personal items

❏ hand soap and lotion

Eating Area

❏ infant seats

❏ small high chairs

❏ sturdy straight or rocking chairs

❏ small table with 9" chairs

❏ crock pot

❏ refrigerator

❏ small disposable plates and spoons

Activity Areas *(where soft, colorful toys and manipulatives can be explored)*

❏ simple lightweight, open-ended, easily washable toys containers

❏ balls

❏ spinning top

❏ nesting cups

❏ action/reaction toys

❏ shape-sorting box or cube

❏ stacking toys

❏ simple puzzles with knob handles

❏ pretend toys

❏ dolls

❏ telephone

❏ paper and large crayons

❏ individual pans for water and sand play

❏ dramatic-play props

Movement Area

❏ tiered, padded structures to crawl up, down, inside, and over

❏ push and pull toys

❏ pounding bench

❏ sand and water bins with toys

❏ small stacking blocks made of plastic or cardboard

Block/Woodworking Area

❏ block shelf

❏ intermediate unit blocks

❏ accessories such as wooden or plastic people, animals, cars, trucks, boats

❏ activity mat

(All these items can be taken outside for play as well.)

Reading Area *(where babies can look at books or be read to)*

❏ rocking chair

❏ beanbags

❏ carpet pieces

❏ cassettes

❏ cassette recorder

❏ cardboard or cloth books

❏ flannelboard and large, colorful pieces

Cuddle Area *(a place for babies to explore things and to be comforted)*

❏ cuddly, soft toys

❏ teethers and rings

❏ rocking chair

❏ beanbags

❏ foam-padded cushions and shapes

❏ eye-level aquarium

Preschool Classroom

Art Center

❏ tempera and finger paints

❏ crayons and markers

❏ story-and-stack utility center

❏ 30" × 48" table

❏ double easel

❏ vinyl smocks

❏ adjustable chalkboard easel and chalk

❏ non-spill plastic paint pots

❏ easel and paintbrushes

❏ child-sized safety scissors

❏ rolling pin

❏ clay and hammers

❏ glue and paste

(continued on next page)

| Figure 9.5 | *Continued* |

❒ collage materials
❒ props such as trees and benches
❒ cellophane to make rivers and lakes
❒ block mobile
❒ block patterns
❒ architectural block set
❒ tunnel and arch set
❒ block-play props
❒ super building blocks
❒ hollow blocks
❒ work vehicles
❒ railway and traffic sign set
❒ bucket of vehicles
❒ wedgie community workers
❒ wedgie family
❒ pegboard hook set
❒ workbench with vise and safety goggles
❒ tool set
❒ wood glue and wood scraps

Science Center

❒ tray cubby
❒ 24" × 48" table scale or balance
❒ 6" prism
❒ color paddles
❒ easy-view magnifier
❒ giant magnet
❒ plastic magnet wands
❒ bird-study package
❒ aquarium system
❒ weather props
❒ plants
❒ naturally found items
❒ science books

Sensory Center

❒ sand and water table with cover and water exploration activity top
❒ props for experiments
❒ water kit
❒ water pump
❒ boat set
❒ geometric-shape sand molds
❒ water play set
❒ double sand and water wheel

❒ sand builder set
❒ plastic scoops and funnels
❒ sand sieve and containers
❒ vinyl smocks

Computer Center

❒ computer table
❒ computer with monitor and printer
❒ simple software with concept games for matching, sorting, sequencing, counting, color and number recognition, drawing, and logical-thinking processes

Private Spaces

❒ furniture, carpet squares, small rugs, or a table and chair to define the space

Language/Listening Center

❒ double-sided library shelf
❒ book stand
❒ photo cards
❒ memory games
❒ sequencing shapes and pattern cards
❒ flannelboard with easel stand
❒ felt primary shapes
❒ flannelboard story kits
❒ chalkboards
❒ chart paper
❒ pencils, rulers, and tape
❒ tactile letters
❒ alphabet stepping stones (uppercase)
❒ letter and number stamp set
❒ lotto games
❒ Big Books
❒ self-concept books
❒ primary rhythm set
❒ cassette recorder/CD player
❒ cassettes and CDS (classical, popular, jazz, children's, soundtracks)
❒ books with cassettes

Manipulative/Math Center

❒ modular organizer/double unit with trays
❒ 30" × 48" table
❒ jumbo building blocks

❒ large Duplo basic set
❒ magnetic activity center
❒ learning-to-dress boards
❒ lacing shoe
❒ 1" beads
❒ strings and pattern cards
❒ jumbo lacing buttons
❒ lacing sets
❒ puzzle rack
❒ animal puzzles with knobs
❒ early concept puzzles
❒ nonstereotyped occupations, community, family, and children of the world puzzles
❒ colors and shapes bingo
❒ pencils, rulers, and tape
❒ books (enough to rotate often)
❒ cassette player/recorder with headphones

Outdoor-Play Area

❒ climbing and balancing equipment
❒ balls
❒ beanbags and targets
❒ ring-toss game
❒ bucket and paintbrushes for water painting

Kindergarten Classroom

❒ tactile letters
❒ primary shape sorter
❒ sequential sorting box
❒ colored geo forms
❒ counting pegs with base
❒ assorted counters
❒ sorting kit and tray
❒ attribute blocks
❒ pattern stacker
❒ interlocking cubes with storage tray
❒ parquetry blocks and pattern cards
❒ large pegs and pegboards
❒ child-sized counting frame
❒ unifix cubes and patterns

Dramatic-Play Center

❒ dolls, doll clothes, and furniture
❒ dress-up clothes and props

(continued on next page)

Figure 9.5 *Continued*

- ❏ child-sized furniture
- ❏ puppets and puppet stand
- ❏ circular table and chairs set
- ❏ four-unit kitchen set
- ❏ kitchen utensils, pots, and pans
- ❏ food sets
- ❏ fruits and vegetables with basket
- ❏ two-position plexi-mirro
- ❏ housecleaning set and stand
- ❏ wooden push-button phone
- ❏ reversible role vests
- ❏ career hats (plastic only)

Cooking Center
- ❏ plastic measuring cups and spoons
- ❏ plastic or aluminum mixing spoons
- ❏ rubber spatula
- ❏ muffin tins
- ❏ cookie sheets (large and small)
- ❏ rebus recipe cards
- ❏ hot-air popcorn popper

Creative-Arts Area
- ❏ 30" × 48" table
- ❏ double-sided easel
- ❏ vinyl smocks
- ❏ adjustable chalkboard easel and chalk
- ❏ non-spill plastic paint pots
- ❏ easel brushes
- ❏ child-sized scissors
- ❏ rolling pin
- ❏ clay hammers
- ❏ construction paper
- ❏ tissue paper
- ❏ glue and paste
- ❏ collage materials
- ❏ markers and crayons
- ❏ tempera and finger paints
- ❏ watercolors
- ❏ brushes and newsprint
- ❏ yarn and string

Block/Construction Area
- ❏ intermediate unit block set
- ❏ block patterns
- ❏ jumbo building blocks

- ❏ architectural blocks
- ❏ tunnel and arch blocks
- ❏ block-play props
- ❏ large hollow blocks
- ❏ work vehicles
- ❏ railway and traffic signs
- ❏ small vehicles
- ❏ community workers
- ❏ family and world people
- ❏ workbench with vise
- ❏ safety goggles
- ❏ tool set
- ❏ pegboard with hooks
- ❏ picture books about buildings and structures

Natural Sciences Area
- ❏ 24" × 48" table
- ❏ scale and weights
- ❏ 6" prism
- ❏ color paddles
- ❏ easy-view magnifier
- ❏ giant magnet
- ❏ magnetic wants
- ❏ bird-study package
- ❏ aquarium system
- ❏ microscope
- ❏ compass
- ❏ timers
- ❏ leaves, pinecones, shells, and other natural items
- ❏ science books

Sensory Center
- ❏ sensory table with cover
- ❏ water kit
- ❏ water pump
- ❏ boat set
- ❏ geometric-shape sand molds
- ❏ water play set
- ❏ sand and water wheel
- ❏ sand builder set
- ❏ plastic scoop and funnels

Language Arts Center
- ❏ books and stand
- ❏ writing materials

- ❏ double-sided library shelf
- ❏ chart stand
- ❏ sentence strips and holder
- ❏ photo cards
- ❏ memory game
- ❏ sequencing shapes and pattern cards
- ❏ flannelboard with easel stand
- ❏ felt primary shapes
- ❏ flannelboard story kits
- ❏ child-sized chalkboards
- ❏ tactile letters
- ❏ uppercase and lower case letters
- ❏ number stamp set
- ❏ lotto games
- ❏ classic books
- ❏ self-concept books
- ❏ books with cassettes
- ❏ rhythm set
- ❏ listening center
- ❏ cassette recorder
- ❏ cassettes
- ❏ lined paper
- ❏ pencils and sharpener
- ❏ erasers
- ❏ dictionary

Math/Manipulative Area
- ❏ modular organizer/double unit with trays
- ❏ 30" × 48" table
- ❏ educational area rugs
- ❏ magnetic activity center
- ❏ interstar links
- ❏ gear-building set
- ❏ flexiblocks
- ❏ lacing shoe
- ❏ puzzle rack
- ❏ nonstereotyped occupations, community, family, and children of the world puzzles
- ❏ colors and shapes bingo
- ❏ sequential sorting box
- ❏ colored geo forms
- ❏ sorting kit and tray
- ❏ attribute blocks

(continued on next page)

| **Figure 9.5** *Continued* |

❏ pattern stackers

❏ interlocking cubes with storage tray

❏ parquetry blocks and pattern cards

❏ counting frame (student size)

❏ time-sequence puzzle set

❏ Cuisenaire rods

❏ Cuisenaire patterns or base-10 block set

❏ clock

❏ play money

Cooking Area

❏ hot-air popcorn popper

❏ electric skillet

❏ measuring cups and spoons

❏ mixing bowls and spoons

❏ cookie sheets

❏ muffin tins

❏ rebus recipe book or cards

❏ cookbooks

Dramatic-Play Area

❏ dolls and doll clothes

❏ dress-up clothes and props

❏ child-sized furniture

❏ puppets and stand

❏ circular table and chairs set

❏ four-unit kitchen set

❏ tableware

❏ kitchen utensils

❏ pots and pans

❏ food sets

❏ fruits and vegetables with basket

❏ two-position plexi-mirror

❏ housecleaning set and stand

❏ wooden push-button phone

❏ reversible role vests

❏ career hats (plastic only)

Private Space

Individual learning center where one child can:

❏ draw

❏ write

❏ read

❏ listen

❏ dictate or create a sculpture

(Plan for and rotate at least one new idea per week.)

Computer Center

❏ computer table

❏ computer with monitor and printer

❏ software that integrates with curriculum and supports concepts introduced in classroom, such as counting, letter recognition, multiple-attribute matching, drawing, and map reading

Outdoor-Play Area

❏ balls (including kickball, soccer ball, football, softball, and basketball)

❏ Nerf Frisbees

❏ jumpropes

❏ gloves and bats

❏ activity tubs

From Scholastic's *Early Childhood Today,* May/June 1998. Copyright © 1998 by Scholastic Inc. Reprinted by permission of Scholastic Inc.

center (sometimes called the construction site). The labels might read: long, rectangular, wooden blocks; or small square wooden blocks; or red Lego blocks. Pictures of each kind of block by the words will support the youngest children's reading. Similarly, paper in the writing center can be grouped by color, kind, and size. Labels might include those for publishing paper, rough-draft paper, stationery, and cards.

Functional signs (e.g., "Make construction plans here!") can also be used to guide children's behavior in each center. Experiences with such signs encourage even the youngest children to attend to the functional purposes of print and to begin to make use of signs to achieve their purposes. We present an example of a kindergartner named Adam's use of a functional sign, "Dot toht" (Don't touch) in Figure 9.6. (No one touched his paper while he was away from the writing center.)

In addition, many teachers prepare an inventory of the items available in each center in enlarged print. Remember that with young children, the use of print with pictures on the inventory list is important. Posting the inventory in a location visible from various spots in the classroom assists the children in independently gathering the resources they need to support their work. Because the children will be engaged in interdisciplinary projects, they may need materials from several different centers.

In addition to the regularly used resources, centers often will contain special displays and materials related to the topic under study. Like the regularly used center resources, these also need to be grouped into meaningful collections, labeled, and displayed attractively.

Place Similar or Related Centers Near Each Other

Sandra Lawing placed the library center and the writing center close to each other. These two centers belong together because they both encourage children's development and use of liter-

Figure 9.6

Adam's sign

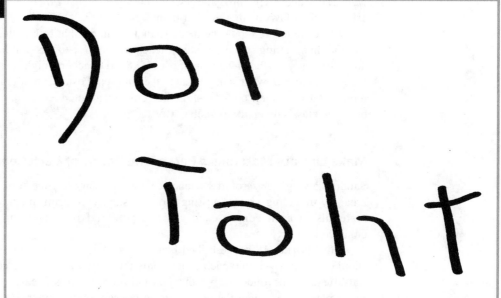

acy. In fact, some educators combine these centers together into a literacy center because their focus is children's literacy development. The two centers occupy a major portion of the classroom space: the library center with its posters, many books of many different genres displayed in different kinds of ways (e.g., as in a public or school library with spines visible, with the covers visible), puppets, literature on tapes, flannel boards with story characters, magazines, stuffed animals wanting to hear stories read to them, a rocking chair, pillows, and more; and the writing center with its many writing tools, different kinds of paper, cards, resources to assist with the writing process, and more.

Many educators divide the centers into potentially noisy centers and potentially more quiet centers. Based on their predictions, they place the potentially noisy centers near each other (e.g., the block center is placed near the dramatic play center, and both centers are near the art center) and the potentially quiet centers are near each other (e.g., the literacy center is placed near the science and mathematics centers, as they are in Ms. Lawing's classroom).

Involve the Children in Designing the Classroom

After years of teaching in the same classroom, kindergarten teacher Dee Dougherty was required to move to a new classroom. In August, as she surveyed the boxes and boxes of materials and reflected on what she had learned in a summer design technology workshop she had attended, she decided to try meeting the children on the first day of school in a different manner than previously. The classroom would be undecorated, and they would design it together. They talked about what they needed and considered where the various centers might be located. They drew blueprints, drawings done on beige construction paper in blue pen or blue crayon. They considered safety rules, traffic patterns, electrical outlet placement, and much more. Eventually, they voted upon the best design. With the help of the custodian, materials were moved to the designated areas, materials were arranged, and their placements were labeled. (A note to new teachers: Make friends immediately with the custodian!)

Some teachers find that this level of involvement by their children in the classroom's construction makes them feel uncomfortable. However, these teachers look for other ways for their children to feel ownership of the classroom. Instead of decorating the walls with displays of commercial items, these teachers look for ways to celebrate their children's products. They mount exhibitions of their children's work. They look for ways to provide opportunities for the children to share messages with each other. Recall the mailboxes recommended as equipment in the writing center in the Chapter 7. How about a suggestion box for sharing ideas, recommendations, and complaints? How about a message board where children exchange personal notes? How about a picture gallery where children can hang their favorite photographs of themselves or their favorite drawings or paintings?

A special effort should be made to include items that reflect the children's cultures. Recall that in selecting topics for study, teachers look for topics that have meaning to the children. Similarly, as the environment is considered, teachers might ponder what to include that is representative of what is important to the children. Posters, photographs, objects, and so forth representative of their cultures should be embedded into each center. The intention is to celebrate the class's diversity in visible ways.

Make Literacy Materials a Part of the Fabric of Each Center

Sandra Lawing's classroom's science center has many science books in it. So does her block area. By including books, writing tools, posters with print, magazines, and other relevant materials in each center, each center's potential for developing children's literacy is enhanced.

Jim Christie (1995) described how, in his early teaching days, he believed that literacy should not be woven into each center; only the library and writing centers had literacy materials. He recalled wondering whether he would confuse his students by putting books in the dramatic play center when the center was a housekeeping center. He now knows that putting literacy materials in the various centers supports children's literacy development and is an important way for teachers to enhance children's literacy learning. By enriching all centers, children read, write, speak, listen, and observe to learn.

Create an Aesthetically Pleasing, Inviting Environment

Attention to detail and careful organization of each center will be rewarded by children's increased attention to the activities and materials offered in each center and by children's increased care in maintaining the center and using the materials.

Cleotis Stevens' classroom immediately communicates a positive message to the observer. The color scheme of blues and grays projects a feeling of calmness. Extra table and floor lights in various areas lessen the harshness of the overhead fluorescent lighting. On occasion, Ms. Stevens can turn off the overhead lights, turn on the large table lamp in the library center, and create a new atmosphere for sharing a story with her children. Large soft pillows and beanbag chairs make the library center an inviting atmosphere for reading books, listening to tapes of stories, using the flannel board and story characters, and so forth. The rugs in most centers in the classroom (not the art center) absorb the sound of many little feet traveling about the room to collect needed resources. Ms. Stevens' classroom is in an older building; the classroom floors are tiled, not carpeted. When a friend of a friend replaced her family-room carpeting, Ms. Stevens was able to secure the used carpet. Teachers need to be scroungers!

Lots of natural objects from the world outside the classroom are available for the children's manipulation. For example, different kinds of seashells are available in the math center for the children's sorting, counting, and examination. Ms. Stevens borrowed an idea from another teacher, Roxanne Nelson: When the children went to a pond that had been overrun with *phagmites* (a weed that grows in ponds), they returned to the classroom with a pile of these destructive weeds. (This is one of the few items environmentalists eagerly support having removed from a pond area.) Together, the children wove an area divider from the weeds. Ms. Stevens looks for ways to bring natural items from the children's outside world into the classroom.

Creating this kind of environment required thought, work, and scrounging on Ms. Stevens' part. Ms. Stevens is expert at knowing which yard sales in which neighborhoods to shop. She's even learned that if she arrives the night before and pleads her case as a teacher in need of resources for her classroom, often the owner will permit her early access to the goods at a reduced rate. The outcome for her classroom is worth the work, evoking a sense of pride in Cleotis and enhancing her children's learning.

Organizing The Classroom's Daily Schedule: Creating A Rhythm To The Day

Recall that children need chunks of time to investigate topics alone, with small groups of other children, and with the whole group. On the one hand, there needs to be flexibility in the schedule to permit students to focus on flowers or insects for a block of time when their needs and interests dictate. On the other hand, there needs to be some predictability to life in the classroom. In this section, we consider how to create a schedule that supports children's engagement in meaningful learning.

Sample classroom schedules are provided in Figure 9.7. In each of these schedules, the teachers followed several common principles. They have

- balanced quiet times with noisier times, and sitting and listening time movement time;
- provided large chunks of time for individual and small-group investigations and shorter amounts of time for whole-group activities;
- recognized their children's need for time to work together as a whole group, to work with peers in small groups, and to work independently;
- shown that they value having children choose and make decisions about how to structure their personal time.

Through the use of these principles, these teachers demonstrate their recognition of children's need for diversity and variety in their daily activities. They also recognize children's need for predictability and a not-so-hidden structure to each day—a rhythm.

How firmly should teachers hold to a time schedule? Carol Wien and Susan Kirby-Smith (1998) suggest that teachers consider having an order of events, but allowing the children to dictate the timing of the changes in activities. They contend that the " 'Schedule,' determined by the 'clock,' often interrupts productive play and intrudes upon young children's natural, creative activities. This creates unnecessary transitions and stress" (p. 9).

Kirby-Smith worked with two teachers of toddlers (age 18 to 30 months) to test the idea of letting children's interests dictate the length of activities. After an initial period when the teachers experienced frustration and a period when the children were very happy, the teachers came to see that allowing the children's rhythm to control the timing allowed the children to focus. The teachers discovered that children preferred (1) being greeted on arrival and helped to make an activity choice; (2) having a long free-play period with snack and toileting naturally occurring without interrupting the whole group's play; (3) having a short circle time with music and action after the long free-play period; and (4) ending the morning with outdoor playtime. Now the toddlers "co-own" the curriculum.

What Happens During Whole-Group Times?

Some teachers call whole-group sessions group time or circle time. Of course, it is during these times that the children and their teacher come together, typically in a carpeted area of the classroom. During the first group time of the day, teachers usually take attendance; make announcements; with kindergarten and older children, recite the pledge of allegiance to the flag; check the date on the calendar; report on the news of the day; and discuss plans for the day. Other whole-group sessions are used to introduce and to discuss the integrated unit being studied, for the teacher to read literature aloud, for teacher presentation of a lesson on a writing or reading strategy, for singing songs, for the choral reading of poems, and for bringing closure to the day.

These group sessions typically last 10 to 30 minutes, depending on the children's developmental needs and the teacher's intentions. Many of these whole-group times have been discussed in detail in other chapters. As Susan Neuman and Kathy Roskos (1993, p. 147) suggest, teachers' intent during whole-group sessions often is "to actively engage [all the children] in thinking and talking, reading and writing about ideas related to [the] topic of interest."

Figure 9.7	
Daily schedules	

A Toddler Schedule

9:00	Arrival
9:00–10:15	Activity Time
10:15–10:25	Clean-Up
10:25–10:40	Snack
10:40–10:50	Book Time (individual lap reading)
10:50–11:20	Outdoor Play
11:30	Dismissal

A Preschool Class Schedule—A.M.

9:00–10:30	Activity Time (snack is brought into the room at 10:05 A.M. to be one of the activities the child can choose)
10:30–10:35	Clean-Up (each child will be given a specific job)
10:35–10:50	Gathering Time
10:50–11:20	Outdoor Play
11:20–11:45	Lunch
11:45–11:55	Clean-Up and Toothbrushing
11:55	Closing and Dismissal

A Preschool Schedule—P.M.

1:10–1:40	Outdoor Play Time
1:40–1:55	Group Time
1:55–3:10	Free-Play Time
3:10–3:20	Independent Reading Time
3:20–3:30	Snack
3:30–3:45	Story Time
3:45–4:00	Outdoor Play

A Kindergarten Schedule

9:00–9:20	Circle Time
9:20–10:20	Activity or Free-Play Time
10:20–10:30	Clean-Up
10:30–10:45	Snack and Quiet Reading
10:45 -11:10	Group Time
11:10–11:30	Outdoor Play
11:30–11:45	Literature Time
11:45	Dismissal

What Happens During Small-Group Activity Time?

Typically, the children's curiosity will be aroused or their focus will be directed during the whole-group meetings. During the small-group activity times (a bit of a misnomer, since the children will also be engaged in independent activities during these times), the children can act on their interests. During these times, the children might move freely about the classroom, selecting the area or center of interest to them. They might write in the writing center, read books in the cozy corner library, build structures in the block or construction center, or investigate and record their observations in the science center. It is important for teachers to provide children with time to engage in activities of their choice and to plan the use of their time.

It is also important for teachers to actively engage in learning with their children during these free-choice times. This is not the time for teachers to work at completing administrative tasks. It is the time to read a book with a child or two, take a child's dictation, happen upon a child at just that moment when she or he needs instruction, or play with the children in dramatic play area.

During these free-choice times, the children might work with a small group of peers to answer questions of shared interest. In other instances, groups might form spontaneously; those five children who are interested in playing in the dramatic play area come together for play and stay until they are tired of playing in the center.

Integrated Units Alive In A Classroom

How do the parts of the day come together in the interdisciplinary study of a topic of interest to the children? How is it that children engage in purposeful activities that support the development of their abilities to speak, listen, read, and write? The following special feature provides an example of a developmentally appropriate integrated unit.

Special Feature 9.1 presents a unit on babies that Charlotte Woodward uses with her three-year-olds at the College of Education Preschool at Arizona State University. As Charlotte explains, the topic is of high interest to this age group because many three-year-olds have baby brothers and sisters. Notice how, even at this young age, children can use reading and writing as part of their investigation of babies and can even engage in some simple experimentation to learn more about babies' toy preferences.

Special Feature 9.1

The Baby Project

Charlotte Woodward

Integrated projects play an important role at the College of Education preschool at Arizona State University. These projects, or explorations, enable children to delve deeply into an area of special interest and to develop language and literacy skills at the same time. The interest and curiosity of the young preschool students initiate these projects. Although projects vary widely from year to year, one project that makes the exploration list frequently is the baby project. We think this is a popular subject for several reasons. The preschool's three-year-olds frequently have a baby brother or sister at home. And, of course, three-year-olds were babies themselves not long ago. They soon become the school's experts on the subject.

A baby project is usually initiated when a young student's mother gives birth to a baby. We begin the project with a special event, such as a visit of a mother and her baby. (It is sometimes not a good idea to have the baby belong to one of the three-year-olds, as sibling rivalry or sibling overprotectiveness can make it hard for the big brother or sister.) The mother brings along a baby bath, towels, powder, and so on, and gives the baby a bath. The children watch and talk about what they are seeing.

Following the initial event, the children who wish can bathe doll babies at the water tables. We provide them with all the necessary supplies: towels, diapers, powder (cornstarch), baby soap, and the like.

As the project progresses, we have one or two more visits from mother and baby. If the mother has a scale, we might see how much the baby has grown and how it has changed. Things such as being able to turn over and sit up without being held are discussed. Another time the mother might come before snack time and feed the baby a bottle, baby food, cereal, or a teething cracker (depending on the age of the child.) During snack time, the young students are offered a taste of the baby food or teething cracker.

For a culminating visit, the class conducts its own experiment with the baby. Prior to the visit, the children look through selected toys from a baby catalog and decide on several toys that the baby might like to play with. Three toys are then purchased. When the mother and baby arrive, these toys are put on the baby's blanket, and the children watch closely to see which toy the baby goes to first. Last year it was a soft red ball with a bell inside. Later, when the children discussed why this toy was chosen they decided it was the red color and the noise the bell made.

Once the project is underway, books about babies are displayed in the class library and featured in the daily story reading time. Here are some of the popular titles,

Special Feature 9.1 *(continued)*

many of which have a multicultural perspective, since as the COE Preschool has a multicultural enrollment:

- *Bend's Baby* by Michael Foreman (1987))
- *Tell Me a Story, Mommy* by Angel Johnson (1989)
- *The Berenstain Bear's New Baby* by Stan and Jan Berenstain (1974)
- *Eat Up Gamma* by Sarah Hayes (1988)
- *In the Middle of the Night* by Kathy Henderson and Jennifer Eachus (1992)
- *Geraldine's Baby Brother* by Holly Keller (1994)
- *On Mother's Lap* by Ann Scott (1972)
- *Mama, Do You Love Me* by Barbara Joose (1991)
- *Peter's Chair* by Ezra Jack Keats (1967)

We also stock our dramatic playroom with an extra supply of baby dolls and baby accessories. Taking care of baby develops into a very popular activity, as make-believe parents bathe, feed, and play with their "babies." This dramatic play provides an ideal context for children to work through and assimilate the knowledge about babies that they are gaining from other parts of the curriculum. This play also offers a wonderful opportunity for teachers to assess children's learning.

The project might end with construction of baby albums. Children bring to class several of their own baby pictures. Children mount them inside a blank book. A teacher assists by printing the child's name and "Baby Book" on the cover. The children can then dictate to the teacher words to go with the photos. Children are encouraged to draw in the books, perhaps a self-portrait. The books are taken home to share the results of the project with their parents.

Summary

Children learn best when they are engaged in inquiries that involve using their language to learn. For this to happen, the various content areas need to be naturally integrated. Through immersion in the study of a broad topic that is relevant to the lives of the students and their community, children read, write, speak, listen, and observe. How does this approach to integrated curriculum match with your memories of projects and units when you were in school?

To summarize the key points about facilitating oral language learning, we return to the guiding questions at the beginning of this chapter:

- *What are the major differences between the subject-by-subject, correlated, and integrated approaches to early childhood curricula?*

A subject-by-subject curriculum has a separate time block for each subject area. In this type of compartmentalized curriculum, each subject is taught in isolation. In a correlated curriculum, activities in different subjects are selected that are related to a given theme or topic. The goal is to master subject-area content and skills, not to learn about the topic. There is some degree of subject-area integration in this approach, but the links or connections across the various curricular areas tend to be artificial. In an integrated curriculum, activities in different subject areas are selected in order to help children find answers to questions about a topic that is of interest to them. In this approach, subject-matter areas appropriate to the topic are woven naturally into the children's investigations, and there is true curricular integration.

- *How can teachers plan and implement an integrated curriculum unit or project?*

The teacher begins by helping children select a topic for study and by determining what the children already know and want to learn about the topic. Next, the teacher helps the children plan learning activities or projects. As children work on their investigations, the teacher engages in ongoing assessment and evaluation of children's learning. The teacher also involves parents in all phases of the unit.

- *How can teachers arrange the classroom's physical environment and daily schedule to support the integrated curriculum?*

Teachers can create a classroom environment that supports an integrated curriculum by (1) carving classroom space into small, well-defined areas; (2) gathering appropriate resources to support the children's learning; (3) placing similar or related centers near each other, (4) involving children in designing the classroom; (5) making literacy materials part of the fabric of each center; and (6) creating an aesthetically pleasing environment.

The daily schedule should also support the integrated curriculum. A wonderful environment without blocks of time to use it is worthless. There need to be large chunks of time for individual and small-group investigations and shorter amounts of time for whole-group activities. Quiet times during which children sit and listen should be balanced with active times. The schedule should also feature flexibility, so that children have the freedom to pursue their interests, and predictability, so that there is a rhythm to the day.

Linking Knowledge to Practice

1. Kathy Roskos (1995) worked with a group of teachers to design a set of criteria and a scale that can be used to assess the quality of integrated units. An adaptation of these teachers' and Kathy's ideas is presented in Table 9.1. Visit a preschool or kindergarten classroom and use this scale to evaluate an ongoing unit or project.
2. While visiting the classroom, observe the physical environment. How does the classroom match up with the six criteria for a supportive physical environment presented in this chapter?
3. What is the daily schedule in this classroom? Does this schedule support or hinder integrated curriculum?

Table 9.1		Yes	Somewhat	No
Evaluating the Quality of Interdisciplinary Units	The topic is . . .			
	■ child-centered	├────────────────────┤		
	■ broad in scope	├────────────────────┤		
	■ relevant to these children	├────────────────────┤		
	■ relevant to real-life in these children's community	├────────────────────┤		
	During the study of the topic . . .			
	■ the teacher begins by discovering what these children know (their prior knowledge) and what they want to learn	├────────────────────┤		
	■ children are given choices about which aspect of the topic they wish to investigate	├────────────────────┤		
	■ reading, writing, speaking, and listening are naturally woven into the activities	├────────────────────┤		
	■ activities are planned to help develop concepts and to answer the children's questions	├────────────────────┤		
	■ children share what they have learned with others	├────────────────────┤		
	■ the teacher provides information (e.g., how to take notes, how to write an informative report, how to make an oral presentation) the children need to successfully complete their projects and activities	├────────────────────┤		
	■ quality literature is woven into the study	├────────────────────┤		

(continued on next page)

Table 9.1	Assessing students' learning . . .	
Continued	■ is ongoing, while the children complete the activities	├──────────────────────┤
	■ includes student self-evaluation	├──────────────────────┤
	Teaching this unit, the teacher . . .	
	■ involves the students' parents	├──────────────────────┤
	■ functions like an orchestra conductor, getting things started and moving them along, providing information and resources, and coordinating the buzz of activities	├──────────────────────┤
	■ conferences with the students	├──────────────────────┤

chapter 10

Helping Families Facilitate Language and Literacy Development

Nestling close on Grandma's big, soft, feather bed, Grandma reads Billie her favorite book, The Little Engine That Could. *Grandma barely finishes the last word in the book when Billie asks her to read it again. As Grandma rereads, Billie echoes the refrain, "I think I can, I think I can, I think I can!" After the story, Grandma always says, "If you think you can, you can do anything." To this day, whenever Billie is challenged to learn new concepts or deal with difficult situations, she remembers Grandma saying, "Just think you can, just think you can!"*

If you share memories like Billie's, you are indeed fortunate. Research demonstrates that a family's role in a child's language and literacy development is directly related to the child's communicative competence (Hart & Risley, 1995), positive attitudes toward reading and writing, and literacy achievement (e.g., Christian, Morrison, & Bryant, 1998; Epstein, 1986; Sulzby, Teale, & Kamberelis, 1989).

When parents and teachers share information the child benefits

Before reading this chapter, think about . . .

- Your early literacy experiences. Do you remember precious moments snuggling with a special person and sharing a book? Do you remember talking with an adult who provided you with many experiences and the words to describe these experiences? Do you remember an adult helping you read words in your environment?
- Your memories of a parent's report of a parent–teacher conference about your classroom behavior and learning. Do you remember if your parents always heard positive reports about your learning? Do you remember what happened if the teacher made suggestions for home learning activities?
- News flashes, newsletters, and other written communication you carried home from school. Do you remember these being posted in your home, perhaps on the refrigerator door? Do you remember them helping you answer the question: What did you do in school today?

Focus Questions

- What is known about the relationship between what parents do and children's language and literacy development?
- In what ways might early childhood teachers communicate personally with parents?
- How might teachers run a parent–teacher conference?
- In what ways might teachers communicate with parents in writing?
- What resources might an early childhood teacher provide to parents and parents provide to teachers to support young children's early literacy learning?

BOX 10.1	**developmental spelling:** another name for invented spelling, where children use two or three letters to phonetically represent a word (e.g., *happy* might be spelled as *hape*).
Definitions of Terms	

What Roles Do Families Play?

Collin (1992, p. 2) refers to the parents' nurturing role in their child's literacy development as "planting the seeds of literacy." Almost all parents want to plant these seeds, but many are unsure of the best way to begin. Similarly, most parents and other primary caregivers vastly underestimate the importance of their role in helping children become competent language users. In this chapter, we discuss strategies teachers can use to inform parents of all cultures and other primary caregivers about the critical role they play in their child's language and literacy development, and how parents and teachers can work together to enhance language and reading and writing opportunities in the home. Special Feature 10.4 Parental Involvement in Bilingual/ Second Language Settings provides a multicultural perspective on this issue.

Language Development

In Chapters 2 and 3, we discussed how families provide the rich social context necessary for children's language development. The thousands of hours of parent–child interactions from the moment of birth through the preschool years provide the foundation for language. As children acquire language, they are able to share with others what they feel, think, believe, and want. While most children begin to use their expressive vocabulary in the second year of life, research has long documented that children differ in their ability to learn and use new words (Smith & Dickinson, 1994). In an effort to understand what accounts for these differences, researchers Betty Hart and Todd Risley (1995) documented parent and child interactions during the first three years of children's lives. The research team observed 42 families from different socioeconomic and ethnic backgrounds one hour each month for two-and-a-half years. Their data revealed vast differences in the amount of language spoken to children. Children from welfare homes heard an average of 616 words an hour; children from working-class families heard 1251 words an hour; while children from professional homes heard 2153 words per hour! If one thinks of words as dollars, the children from these different socioeconomic homes would have significantly disparate bank accounts. Further, this long-term study revealed that early language differences had a lasting effect on childrens' subsequent language accomplishments both at age three and at age nine. In other words, talk between adults and children early in life makes a significant difference.

Reading and Writing Acquisition

Parents also play a critical role in helping children learn about print. Many children learn about literacy very early. This task is accomplished quite naturally as children sit on the laps of parents, other family members, or caregivers sharing a storybook. Surrounded by love, these children easily learn about the functions of print and the joys of reading. Being read to at home facilitates the onset of reading, reading fluency, and reading enjoyment. Unfortunately, a growing number of studies have documented a lack of parent–child reading opportunities, especially in low-income homes (Christian, Morrison, & Bryant, 1998; Griffin & Morrison, 1997). Lesley Morrow (1988) surveyed parents of children in three preschools serving poor families (incomes of less than $10,000, 40 percent minority, 75 percent single-parent headed). Ninety percent of these parents indicated that they read to their children only once a month or less! This lack of parental involvement may have a significant effect on the children's learning throughout their schooling. For example, Billie Enz's (1992) study of 400 high school sophomores revealed that 70 percent of the remedial readers could not recall being read to by their parents as children, while 96 percent of the students in advanced placement courses reported that their parents had read to them regularly. In essence, it appears that a child's future literacy and subsequent success in school depend on parents' ability and willingness to provide the child with thousands of planned and spontaneous encounters with print (Enz & Searfoss, 1995).

Parental involvement also has an important effect on children's writing development. In the following example, notice how four-year-old Timeka's early attempts at writing are subtly supported by her mother:

> Sitting at a table with crayon in hand, Timeka is engrossed in making squiggly lines across a large paper. Timeka's mother, sitting across from her, is busy writing checks. After Timeka finishes her writing, she folds her paper and asks her mother for an envelope so she can "pay the bank, too." As mother smiles and gives Timeka the envelope, she remarks, "Good, our bank needs your money."

This brief example illustrates how Timeka is taking her first steps to becoming literate. While most children need formal instruction to learn to read and write conventionally, children who have parents who guide and support their beginning literacy efforts learn to read and write more quickly. As Timeka observes her parents and other adults writing, she discovers that these marks have purpose and meaning. Timeka then imitates, to the best of her ability, this process. Since the adults in Timeka's life also regard her efforts as meaningful, Timeka is encouraged to refine both her understanding of the functions of print and her writing skills. In that regard, Timeka's scribbles are to writing as her babbling was to talking. Because her parents approve and support her attempts instead of criticizing or correcting them, Timeka practices both talking and writing. This dual effort also simultaneously develops her understanding that words and thoughts can be expressed both orally and in print (Fields, Spangler, & Lee, 1991; Sulzby, Teale, & Kamberelis, 1989). Unfortunately, too few parents know how to help their young children become writers or how to support their children's attempts at written communication (Bus, Belsky, van IJzendoorn, & Crnic, 1997).

Dilemmas Facing Modern Families

The "family in America—Black, White, Hispanic, and Asian—is actually in the throes of basic upheaval" (Carlson, 1990, p. xv). As evidence, Carlson cites the three factors most likely to affect school performance: the employment of both parents in more than 70 percent of nuclear families, the high divorce rate, and the increase in single-parent families. Recent research studies report that 40 percent of today's school children will have lived with a single parent by the time they reach the age of 18 (Flaxman & Inger, 1991). The financial and psychological stresses many single-parent families face may not allow parents either the time or emotional energy to sustain conversation or read to their children on a regular basis.

Another significant factor is the cycle of poverty and undereducation. Research consistently reveals that a child whose parent has poor literacy skills is at great risk of repeating the illiteracy cycle (Christian, Morrison, & Bryant, 1998; Lonigan & Whitehurst, 1998). Likewise, Betty Hart and Todd Risley's (1995) study clearly demonstrates that welfare parents often transmit their limited vocabulary and lower oral communicative competence to their children.

Two factors span socioeconomic and cultural differences. First, as educators we must help parents understand the crucial role they play in helping their children become successful communicators, readers, and writers (Epstein, 1995). Secondly, we must build parents' knowledge of how to support their child's language and literacy development. How else will parents be able to fulfill their role as their child's first and most important teacher?

Helping Parents and Primary Caregivers Become Effective First Teachers

Helping parents become successful language and literacy models is one of early childhood teachers' most important tasks. To fulfill this responsibility, teachers must interact with parents constantly! However, this role may be more challenging than many teachers initially anticipate. In this chapter, we describe two categories of communication efforts—personal interactions and classroom instructional publications.

Personal Interactions

Personal interactions are opportunities for parents, other family members, and early childhood teachers or caregivers to share information about a child's individual needs in two-way conversations. Personal interactions also offer unique opportunities for modeling communication and literacy strategies. These personal interactions include home visits, parent workshops, parent–teacher conferences, and telephone calls.

Today's teachers need to be aware that English may not be their children's parents' dominant language; therefore, a teacher may need to have a translator help with communication during personal interactions. Regardless of how teachers choose to communicate, observation shows that whatever the content, medium, or language, any message is enhanced if it is delivered warmly, respectfully, and with genuine concern.

HOME VISITS.   Perhaps the best way to reach parents prior to children's formal entry into preschool or kindergarten is through home visits.

"We are going to be heroes today," Dana Donor said as she sat down on the couch in the living room of the Youtie family. She was met by four-year-old Tate and three-year-old Darrin. They watched as Dana opened the children's storybook, *One Duck Stuck.*

"Are you ready to help?" Dana asked as she sat between Tate and Darrin. For the next 15 minutes, Dana and Marie, the children's mother, take turns reading to the children and encouraging them to interact with the pictures in the book. "How many frogs are trying to help this silly duck? Let's count them," Marie suggests, and Tate and Darrin use their fingers to count the fearless frogs. Dana asks, "What animal do you think will try to help next? How many animals do you think will be on the next page? How would you have helped the duck?" After they had read the story, two very happy children asked to have it read again!

After the second reading, Dana passes out crayons and paper and asks the children to draw their favorite animal. "I'm gonna write my name," says Tate. "See T-A-T-E." Tate has recently begun using conventional print to write her name. Darrin announces loudly, "Me too!" Darrin uses scribble writing for his name. As the children work on their pictures, Dana and Marie step back to engage in a brief conversation about the children's stage of development in the writing process. After the children complete their pictures, they tape them to the refrigerator.

Dana Donor is a teacher-demonstrator in a well-documented parent–child home program that has a long track record of helping at-risk families. Her job is to help bring stories to life for children as young as two. The demonstrator also helps parents learn how to make reading fun. During the twice-a-week visits, Marie is able to observe Dana model story reading strategies, encourage language interactions, and support beginning writing opportunities. Marie and Dana also discuss age appropriate language and literacy behavior (see Table 10.1). After several weeks of participating in the program, Marie is more confident and has begun to try some of these techniques using the storybooks Dana leaves in the home for between-visits use. Marie is pleased that she is learning how to keep her children actively engaged during storytime.

Table 10.1 *Age-Appropriate Support Activities*

| Months | | Language | Print Recognition | |
		Speaking/Listening	Receptive/Reading	Expressive/Writing
0–6	CD	Babbling, extensive sound play.		
	PS	Talk to baby. Sing to baby. Make direct eye contact with baby when speaking. Use parentese.		
6–12	CD	Echolia, vocables, first words.	Is able to listen to short stories. Wants to handle books.	
	PS	Label objects. Scaffold child's language efforts.	Provide cloth and cardboard book. Read to your child.	
12–24	CD	Begins to use words and gestures. Responds to simple requests.	Begins to recognize environmental print/logos.	Begins to use writing implements to make marks.
	PS	Listen and actively respond. Read stories. Engage in frequent conversations.	Confirm print recognition, "Yes, that is Coke." Read to your child.	Offer chalk/chalkboard, paper, and crayons.
24–36	CD	Uses simple sentences, adds new words rapidly, and experiments with inflection.	Attends to pictures—describes pictures, then begins to form oral studies reflecting pictures.	Knows print has meaning and serves practical uses. Uses scribble marking.
	PS	Engage child in complex conversations frequently. Listen to child.	Read, read, read to your child. Ask child to label characters and objects.	Provide access to many types of writing implements/paper.
36–48	CD	Proficient language user. Engages in dramatic play. Likes to learn songs.	Attends to pictures. Repeats familiar story phrases.	Print recognition—may write letter-like units, and nonphonetic letter-like string.
	PS	Serve as co-player in dramas. Teach new songs. Ask child questions to encourage two-way dialogue.	Reread familiar stories. Ask open-ended questions. Begin home library.	Model writing process. Demonstrate your interest in your child's writing efforts.
48–60	CD	Uses language to obtain and share information.	May begin to recognize individual words.	Conventional writing emerges as letter–sound relationship develops.
	PS	Offer logical explanations. Listen and respond thoughtfully and thoroughly.	Shared reading. Frequent visits to library and expand home library. Demonstrate your enjoyment of reading.	Being writing notes to child. Read your child's writing.

CD: Child's development
PS: Parental support

Since the 1970s, these types of home-visit programs have increased in number, especially as states and communities refocus attention and resources on young children. The programs can have long-term benefits, by offering maternal and child health care, parenting education, school readiness skills, guidance on how to create a literate home environment, and a direct link to other social services (Jacobson, 1998; Ryan, 1999).

PARENT WORKSHOPS. Another strategy for involving and directly informing parents of preschool and kindergarten students about how to support their children's language and literacy learning is through parent workshops. The purpose of the workshops is to share explicit information about the children's development and the class curriculum, and to provide practical suggestions that parents may use at home to support their child's learning (Brown, 1994).

To begin, the teacher should design a needs assessment survey to determine parents' special interests and needs. In Figure 10.1, we provide an example of a survey that covers possible workshop topics, meeting times, and child care needs.

After the survey has been returned and the results tallied, the early childhood teacher should publish and advertise the schedule of workshops. We recommend selecting the top two or three

Figure 10.1

Needs assessment survey

Dear Parents,

Did you know you are your child's first and most important teacher? One of my responsibilities as a teacher is to work with all my teaching colleagues for the benefit of the special student we share—your child. I would like to conduct several workshops this year, and I need to know what topics you are most interested in learning about. Please complete the survey and have your child return it by _____. Place an X by topics you would like to attend.

____Storytelling techniques   ____Linking Play and Literacy

____Writers Workshop   ____Kitchen Math and Science

____Rainy Day Fun   ____Learning Motivation

____Other_____

_____

What is the most convenient day? What time is the most convenient for you to attend a workshop?

____Monday   ____Tuesday   ____9:00 A.M.   ____4:00 P.M.   ____7:00 P.M.____

____Wednesday   ____Thursday

____Friday   ____Saturday

Would you use a child care service if one was provided?

____Yes – list number of children needing care ____.

____No.

topics and identifying the time(s) and day(s) listed as convenient for most of the parents. Generally the most convenient meeting place is the classroom or the school's or center's multipurpose room. Scout troops, parent volunteers, or older students may provide child care. Teachers should be sure to have parents confirm their participation in the workshop (see Figure 10.2). This will allow the teacher to prepare sufficient materials and secure appropriate child care arrangements. Send reminders the day before the workshop. Don't be surprised if only a few parents attend initially. Parent workshops may be a new concept, and it might take a little time for parents to become comfortable with this approach to parent–teacher interactions.

Teachers must prepare for a parent workshop. They need adequate supplies. They may need to organize the room. They need to set up refreshments. (Parent Teacher Organizations or center budgets can often reimburse teachers for refreshments.) Teachers need to prepare name tags, double-check child care arrangements, develop an evaluation form for the workshop, and create a detailed lesson plan!

There are several points for teachers to remember when running a parent workshop. First, the workshop should begin promptly. Second, start with a get-acquainted activity to put people at ease and begin the workshop on a relaxed, positive note. Third, remember that parents

---

Figure 10.2

Workshop confirmation form

Dear Parents:

The topics that most most of you wanted to learn more about were Writing Workshop, Kitchen Math and Science, and Rainy Day Fun!

The times that were convenient to most of you were:

Wednesdays at 7:00 P.M. and Saturdays at 9:00 A.M.

I have used this information to create a schedule of workshops for the fall semester. Please fill out the personal information and put an X by the workshops you plan to attend. All workshops will be in my classroom. Refreshments will be served. Dress comfortably as we might be getting messy. Children will be cared for in the cafeteria by the Girl Scouts and their leaders.

_____

Name_____ Phone_____

Number of children needing child care_____.

_____Writers Workshop - Wednesday, October 2, 7:00–8:30 P.M.

_____Kitchen Math and Science - Saturday, November 4, 9:00–10:30 A.M.

_____Rainy Day Fun - Wednesday, November 9, 7:00–8:30 P.M.

should not be lectured to; instead, they should experience hands-on, highly engaging activities. After the parents have engaged in the activity, provide brief, specific information about the theory underlying the process. Most importantly, remember to smile. When the teacher has a good time, the parents will also! Finally, have parents complete the workshop evaluation form; this will help to continually refine the quality of the workshops (see Figure 10.3).

PHONE CALLS.   Another powerful tool for communicating with parents is the telephone. Unfortunately, phone calls have traditionally been reserved for bad news. However, successful teachers have found that brief, positive, frequent telephone conversations help establish a strong partnership with parents (Fredericks & Rasinski, 1990). When parents receive a phone call about something exciting at school, they immediately sense the teacher's enthusiasm for teaching their child and are more likely to become involved in classroom activities. Thus, whenever possible, the phone should be used as an instrument of good news. Whenever a call is made and for whatever reason, it is important to have the parents' correct surname; there are many stepfamilies in today's schools. All calls to parents should be documented. A phone log can be effective method to manage and maintain a record of phone conversations (see Figure 10.4).

Figure 10.3

Workshop evaluation

Workshop Name_____ Date_____

List two activities you enjoyed or learned the most about.

1.

2.

List any information that was not useful to you.

The workshop was (mark all that apply)

____clear   ____confusing   ____enjoyable   ____boring

____too short   ____too long   ____informative

Any other comments?

Thanks for attending!

Figure 10.4

Phone call log

> **Child:** Robert Romero   **Parent's name:** Mrs. Rodriguez
> **Phone #:** 555-7272
>
> **Date:** *Feb. 2*   **Regarding:** *Robert has been absent for 3 days*
> **Action:**
> *Robert has chicken pox, he will be out at least 4 more days.
> Older brother will pick up get well card from class and bring home
> storybooks for entertainment.*
> **Date:** *March 3*   **Regarding:** *Academic Progress*
>
> **Action:**
> *Robert having great success with reading, especially paired-reading.
> Is hesitant to write during writer's workshop. Teacher will send
> home writing briefcase and have parents write stories with him.*
> **Date:** *April 12*   **Regarding:** *Writing progress*
>
> **Action:**
> *Robert showing more confidence and comfort with his writing. He
> shared a story he wrote with parents to the class today.*
>
> **Date:**   **Regarding:**
> **Action:**
>
> **Date:**   **Regarding:**
> **Action:**
>
> **Date:**   **Regarding:**
> **Action:**
>
> **Date:**   **Regarding:**
> **Action:**

This log should contain a separate page or section for each child in the class, making it easy to trace the contacts with specific parents (Enz & Cook, 1993).

PARENT–TEACHER CONFERENCES.   Children are complex, social individuals who must function appropriately in two very different cultures—school and home. Parents need to understand how a child uses his or her social skills to become a productive member of the school community. Likewise, experienced teachers appreciate the child's home life and recognize its significant influence on a child's behavior and ability to learn. Partnerships reach their full potential when parents and teachers share information about the child from their unique perspectives, value the child's individual needs and strengths, and work together for the benefit of the child.

The best opportunity teachers have for engaging parents in this type of discussion is during parent–teacher conferences. Conferences should feature a two-way exchange of information. There are generally two types of parent–teacher conferences—pre-established conferences that review the child's classroom progress, and spontaneous conferences that deal with a range of specific concerns that occur throughout the year.

Progress Review Conference.   The progress review conference is an opportunity for parents and teachers to share information about children's social interactions, emotional maturity, and cognitive development. One way to help a parent and teacher prepare to share information during the conference is a preconference questionnaire. The teacher sends the questionnaire home to the parent to complete and return prior to the conference. In Figure 10.5, we present the notes made by Manuel's mother as she prepared for her conference with Ms. Jones, her son's kindergarten teacher. The information Mrs. Rodriquez provides also tells Ms.

Figure 10.5

Preconference questionnaire

Dear Parent,

 To help us make the most of our time, I am sending this questionnaire to help facilitate our progress review conference. Please read and complete the questions. If you have any other concerns, simply write them down on the questionnaire and we will discuss any of your inquiries during our time together. I look forward to getting to know both you and your child better.

1. How is your child's overall health?
 Good, but Manuel gets colds alot.

2. Are there specific health concerns that the teacher should know about? (include allergies)
 Colds and sometimes ear infections.

3. How many hours of sleep does your child typically get?
 About 9

4. Does your child take any medication on a regular basis? If so, what type?
 He takes penicillin when he has ear infections.

5. What are the names and ages of other children who live in your home?
 Maria, 9; Rosalina, 7; Carlos, 3.

6. How would you describe your child's attitude toward school?
 He likes school.

7. What school activity does your child enjoy most?
 P.E. and art

8. What school activity does your child enjoy least?
 Math

9. What are your child's favorite TV shows?
 Power Rangers, Ninja Turtles

 How many hours of TV will your child generally watch each night?
 Three

10. What is the title of your child's favorite storybook?
 Where the Wild Things Are.

11. How often do you read to your child?
 His sisters read to him most nights.

12. What other activities does your child enjoy?
 Playing soccer.

Other concerns:
 I can't read his writing. His sisters' was good in Kindergarten.

Jones what concerns she has; therefore, Ms. Jones has a better idea about how to focus the conference. Remember, it may be necessary to have this letter and questionnaire translated into the language spoken in the home.

During the progress review conference, the teacher, of course, will share information about the child's academic progress. In Chapter 8, we discussed how to develop and maintain assessment portfolios and document observational data for each child. The portfolio allows the teacher an opportunity to document the child's development over time. In addition to academic progress, most parents want to know about their children's social interactions and classroom behavior. The observational data that the teacher has recorded helps provide a more complete picture of the child in the classroom context.

When working with parents of young children, teachers are encouraged to use a structured format during the progress review conference. The structure keeps the conference focused and increases the chance of both teachers' and parents' concerns being adequately discussed. Billie Enz and Susie Cook (1993) recommend that progress review conferences be structured as follows:

■ *Positive statement and review conference format*—The teacher's first sentence helps establish a foundation for a proactive conference. Positive statements are sincere and usually personal—for example, "Your child is so eager to learn." Next, the teacher should briefly review the three steps of the conference: (1) parent input, (2) teacher input, and (3) closure. Reviewing the conference process relieves stress and actually helps keep the conference moving in a positive direction.

■ *Ask for parental input*—"First, I am going to ask you to share with me what you have observed about your child this year that makes you feel good about his learning and then what concerns you have about his progress." It is important for parents to focus on their child's academic and social strengths when they meet with you. It is also important for you to know the parents' view of their child's major academic and social concerns.

■ *Offer teacher input*—"Then I will share some of your child's work with you and my observations about his progress. We'll discuss ideas that will continue to encourage his learning."

■ *Closure*—"So, let's review the home and school (or center) activities that we think will best help your child continue to progress."

The success of the parent–teacher relationship depends on the teacher's ability to highlight the child's academic and social strengths and progress. When areas of concern are discussed, it is important to provide examples of the child's work or review the observational data to illustrate the point. Often, the issues the parents reveal are directly related to the concerns the teacher has. Whenever possible, connect these concerns, as this reinforces the feeling that the teacher and the parents have the same goals for helping the child learn. It is essential to solicit the parents' views and suggestions for helping the child and also to provide concrete examples about how they might help the child learn.

To make sure both teacher and parents reach a common understanding, briefly review the main ideas and suggestions for improvement that were discussed during the conference. Allow parents to orally discuss their views of the main ideas of the conference. Check the parents' perceptions. Finally, briefly record the parents' oral summary on the conference form. Figure 10.6 is a progress review conference form from Manuel's conference.

Specific Problem Conference.

Occasionally, concerns will emerge that require the teacher to work with the family immediately. The following case study illustrates how teacher and parents worked together to help identify and resolve a specific problem in the home that was creating tension in the child's school life.

Four-year-old Sibby started preschool as a happy, confident child. She loved storytime and had memorized several stories that she had heard her family read to her over and over again. Sibby had learned to print her name and was excited about writing her own letters and stories (scribble writing and some letter-like streams). Sibby was interested in environmental print and often brought empty product boxes and wrappers to preschool because she was proud that she recognized words and specific letters. She loved playing in the dramatic play center and frequently demonstrated her understanding of the many practical functions of print. After winter break, Sibby's behavior changed abruptly. She said she didn't know how to read when she went to the library center, and she refused to write during journal time. Her teacher, Mrs. Role, quickly called Sibby's parents.

Mr. and Mrs. Jacobs came to preschool the following day. Mrs. Role described the dramatic change in Sibby's behavior and asked the Jacobs' if they had any ideas about what may have caused the change. The Jacobs had also noticed a change in Sibby's confidence. After discussing her behavior, they mentioned that Sibby's grandmother, a retired high school English teacher, visited their home over winter break. They were surprised that Sibby's grandmother had been critical of their display of Sibby's stories on the refrigerator. Grandmother stated "That youngster needs to know the correct way to write!" She felt that "Praising Sibby's scribbles kept her from wanting to learn the right way to form letters," but they were sure Sibby had not overheard any of these comments. However, they remembered that Grandmother baby-sat Sibby one afternoon just before her visit was over. Mrs. Jacobs promised she would talk to Grandmother about the baby-sitting episode.

The following week, Mrs. Jacobs reported that Grandmother had decided "It was time someone taught Sibby how to print her letters properly." During the afternoon Grandmother and Sibby were together, Sibby had spent most of the time practicing making letters correctly. In addition, Grandmother required Sibby to say the letter sounds as she repeatedly wrote each letter. Grandmother told Sibby that she "would not be able to read and write until she knew all her letters and their sounds."

Figure 10.6

Progress-review conference form

Student's name: *Manuel Romero*　　　　Parent's name: *Mary Romero*

Conference date: *Nov. 1*　　　Time: *4:30 p.m.*

Positive Statement: *Manuel is so eager to learn*

Review Conference steps:

Our conference today will consist of three parts. First, I will ask you to review your child's progress, sharing with me both academic/social strengths and areas of concern. Next, I'll review Manuel's work with you and discuss his academic/social strengths and areas in which we will want to help him grow. Finally, we will discuss the main points we discussed today, and review the strategies we decided would help Manuel continue to make progress.

1. Ask for Parent Input: What have you observed about Manuel this year that makes you feel good about his learning? (Take notes as parent is sharing)

Manuel likes school, drawing, friends, stories.

What are your main concerns?

His writing looks like scribbles. He's not reading yet but he likes stories read to him.

2. Teacher Input: I would like to share some observations about Manuel's work and review both areas of strengths and skills that need to be refined. *Manuel interest in reading is wonderful. He is eager to write in class journal. Though his printing is still developing, he is beginning to use "invented" spelling. Look at this example in his portfolio.*

> MT MpN PR RG2
>
> Mighty Morphin Power Rangers

Notice how he is separating the words. Ask him to read his work for you if you are having difficulty decoding or deciphering it. His printing skills will improve naturally with time and encouragement. He is really progressing well. Sometimes young girls develop finger muscles sooner. We need to support his efforts. Manuel enjoys sharing his writing in class with his friends and his art work is full of detail. Manuel has many friends and gets along easily with others.

3. Closure: Let's review those things we talked about that will facilitate continued success. (Teacher needs to write down this information as the parent talks)

a. *Manuel's printing is "okay" for him.*

b. *Manuel is writing. I am surprised to see that he really is writing. I just need to have him read for me. Then it's easier for me to figure out what his*

c. *letters say.*

The Jacobs and Mrs. Role attributed Sibby's reluctance to read and write to her Grandmother's inappropriate instructional efforts. Sibby was going to need a great deal of encouragement and support from her parents and her teacher to regain her confidence.

Classroom Instructional Publications

Classroom instructional publications are designed to describe the children's learning activities or directly inform parents about specific literacy concepts. They may include informal news flashes, weekly notes, and a more formal monthly newsletter that features regular columns, such as Dear Teacher, Family Focus, and Center Highlights. With the growing number of homes with computers and Internet access, some teachers may be able to publish their classroom instructional publications on a classroom Web site or listserve. Of course, teachers must check with their children's parents to learn which homes have access to these services. Sadly, those teachers who work with young children from low socioeconomic families likely will find few families with Internet access. The digital divide is widening, rather than narrowing, in the United States. Communities are struggling to learn how to increase Internet access to families of modest financial means.

INFORMAL WEEKLY NOTES. Because consistent communication helps create a sense of community, the authors strongly recommend weekly, or at minimum, bimonthly notes. Frequent communications allow teachers the opportunity to

- provide a bond between school and home experiences,
- extend parents' understanding of developmentally appropriate curriculum,
- involve parents in assessing the child's growth and development,
- encourage parents to reinforce and enrich children's learning, and
- strengthen the working partnership between parents and teacher.

Weekly notes are typically one page in length and generally include (1) information about upcoming events; (2) items about children's achievements; (3) explanations about the curriculum that help parents understand how children learn to read and write; (4) practical and developmentally appropriate suggestions for working with children; and (5) recognition of parents who have helped support classroom learning—for example, parents who accompanied the class on a field trip (Gelfer, 1991).

It is important for informal weekly notes to be reader-friendly and brief and to suggest successful activities for parents and children to do together (see Special Feature 10.1 for home literacy ideas). These suggestions typically are well received if they are stated in a positive, proactive manner—for example, "Reading to your child just ten minutes a day helps your child become a better reader," not, "Your child will not learn to read unless you read to her or him."

Figure 10.7 is a sample of an informal weekly note. Observe how Ms. Jones reviews the previous week's activities, taking the opportunity to thank parents who have provided supplies or support. Next, she describes the focus of this week's curriculum and provides suggestions that will help parents reinforce this information at home. Notice how Ms. Jones uses friendly, everyday language to introduce and explain new concepts, and suggests realistic, content-appropriate literacy activities that encourage parents to become involved in classroom learning.

NEWS FLASHES. There are times when events occur that require immediate publication or an upcoming activity warrants attention, such as reminding parents that their children will attend school only a half day because of parent–teacher conferences or alerting parents that their children will be on the TV news tonight. Teachers may use news flashes to inform parents about TV programming that is relevant to curriculum the class is currently studying. News flashes might also be used to tell a parent about a noteworthy event in the child's life that day (e.g., Zack said, "Mama" lots today!). In Figure 10.8, we illustrate how Ms. Jones informs parents about an upcoming activity sponsored by the local library.

Special Feature 10.1

Home Literacy Ideas

Mitsuka Fukuda

Dear Parents:

There are many easy and inexpensive literacy ideas a parent can use to help make reading and writing a wonderful experience for their children. The following list offers a few examples of how to make a literacy-rich environment in your home.

Create a cozy reading corner—Throw an old sheet over a card table or large cardboard box, add a couple of pillows and a few books, and you have a personal library corner.

Make a writing kit—Use a double-sided plastic tote. Include all sorts of writing implements, pencils and markers, paper of all sizes, shapes, and colors, tape, and glue. For variety, add old envelopes and stickers that children may use to write letters.

Create a home library—Shop at garage sales and used-book stores or purchase inexpensive books from children's book clubs (like Scholastic or Troll). Organize books on a bookshelf or in a book box and label the shelf or box with the child's name—for example, "Mabel's Books." The pride of ownership can inspire most young readers.

Make environmental print books—Use toy catalogs, advertisements, and coupons to create "My Favorite Toy Book" or "My Favorite Foods Book." Children read through the catalogs and ads to identify the items they wish to include in their book. The construction of the book may require adult help (if the child is under the age of four or five) but the finished product is usually read over and over again.

Subscribe to children's magazines—Children enjoy receiving mail, and children's magazines are designed to delight the young reader. Some children's magazines include *Ladybug, Cricket, Zoo Book,* and *Scienceland.*

Be a reader—Parents who read are likely to have children who read. Show them that there are many opportunities to read—for example, recipes, television listings, magazines, newspapers, novels, and storybooks.

Be a writer—Allow your children to watch you compose a grocery list or write a letter to Grandmother. Demonstrate how you use print to accomplish many goals.

Read, read, read to your child—Parents who read to their children usually have children who become readers. Literacy is a lifelong gift. Be sure to share it with your child.

MONTHLY NEWSLETTERS.　Like weekly notes, monthly newsletters create a sense of community. The goal of monthly newsletters should be to provide parents with specific information about children's literacy development. In addition, monthly newsletters offer parents an opportunity to preview the curriculum and classroom projects for the upcoming month. As most parents have extremely busy schedules, monthly newsletters help them plan ahead and thus increase the likelihood that they will be able to participate in school activities. Monthly newsletters are generally two or three pages in length and typically use a two- or three-column format. Regular features, such as Dear Teacher, Family Focus, Curriculum Overview, Center Highlights, and Monthly Calendar inform parents in a direct but fun and interesting manner. In Figure 10.9, we provide a sample kindergarten newsletter written for the month of October. Notice the regularly featured columns.

Dear Teacher Letters.　As the sample newsletter demonstrates, parents frequently have questions about reading to their children. An effective way to address these inquires is through Dear Abby type letters. The teacher frames the questions based on common concerns she hears from the parents. The following are examples of typical parent questions, answered by advice based on Jim Trelease's (1989) work.

> **Dear Teacher:**
> My three-year-old often becomes restless when I read stories to him. What can I do to keep his interest? *Signed, Wiggle-Worm's Mom*
>
> **Dear Wiggle-Worm's Mom:**
> While most children enjoy having stories read to them, most young children also have a short attention span. Hence, younger children need to be actively involved in the reading. Asking your son to predict what he thinks will happen next or asking him to point to a character or discuss some aspect of the illustration is an excellent way to keep his attention.

Figure 10.7

Informal weekly note

Dear Parents:

Last week our field trip to the hospital was exciting and we learned even more about how doctors and nurses serve our community. Have your child read you the story they wrote and illustrated about what we learned on our hospital journey. One of the most exciting stops in the hospital was the baby nursery. All of the children were interested in their own first stay at the hospital. Perhaps you will be able to share your memories about that event. A great big thank you to Mrs. Delgato and Cecille Ortiz for helping to chaperon. They also helped our students write their stories.

This week we will discuss fire safety at home and school. Our first lesson is called "Stop, Drop, and Roll," which teaches us what to do if our clothes catch on fire. Next, we will discuss the proper use and storage of matches and lighters. We will also map a safe exit from our room in case of fire and review appropriate behavior during an emergency (no talking, listen to teacher's directions, leave all possessions, walk the planned escape route). We will actually have a schoolwide fire drill to practice these skills. Because you and your child's safety is so important, I am asking that you work with your child to draw and label a map of your house and design the best fire escape route. Drawing the map and labeling the rooms of your house teach your child vocabulary words and reinforce the fire safety concepts I am teaching in school. On Friday we will go to our local Fire Station. Attached to this note is a permission slip. Since this is a walking field trip, I will need at least four parent volunteers. I hope you can join us. To help all of us learn more about fire safety, the Fire Marshall will provide the children and their families with a booklet called "Learn Not To Burn." The book is available in Spanish also. If you would like additional copies, let me know. Please review this informative and entertaining booklet with your child.

To learn even more about fire safety and fire fighters, you might wish to read the following books to your child. These books are available in the classroom, school, and local public library.

EL Fuego, by Maria Ruis and Josep McParramon, Harron's.
Pumpers, Boilers, Hooks and Ladders: A Book of Fire Engines,
by Leonard Everett Fisher, Dail Press.
Fire Fighters, by Ray Brockel, Children's Press.
Curious George at the Fire Station, by Margret and H.A. Rey, Houghton Mifflin.
Puedo Ser Bombero, by Rebecca Hankin, Children's Press.
The Whole Works: Careers in a Fire Department, by Margaret Reuter, Children's Press.

If you have any personal experiences in the area of fire safety, please let me know and you can be an Expert Speaker for our classroom.

Sincerely, Mrs. Jones

Figure 10.8

News flash

Ms. Jones' class will be studying the writings of Mercer Mayer! Some of his books include

Little Monster's Neighborhood
Little Monster At School
Little Monster At Home
Little Monster's Alphabet Book
Little Monster's Bedtime Book
Just For You
Just Me and My Dad
Just Grandma and Me
Just Me In the Tub
Just Go To Bed
I Just Forgot
Just Me and My Friend
Just Me and My Mom
Just Shopping With Mom
The New Baby

All of these books are published by Western Publishing Company, Inc. Racine, Wisconsin. Look for these and other Mercer Mayer books in your public library!

Figure 10.9

Monthly newsletter

Ms. Jones' October Newsletter

Kindergarten Curriculum

 It's October and the Kindergartners in Ms. Jones' class are learning about our 5 senses— Halloween style! During this month we will learn about sight: how our eyes work, and eye health and safety. We will also have our vision tested. We will study the super sense of smell: How the nose and olfactory nerves work, and how smell and memory are related. We will learn how the ear hears and discover how hearing aids work. We will test our tongues to determine how the sense of taste works to detect sweet, salty, sour, and bitter. Finally, we will learn about the largest organ on our bodies—our skin! The sense of touch can teach us many things about our world.

Dear Teacher: Questions about Reading.

Dear Teacher,
Hola! Both my husband and I speak and read Spanish. Though our son speaks both languages, would it confuse him if we read him story books in Spanish?
Signed, Bilingual/Biliterate

Dear Bi-double L,
How wonderful it is that your son is already speaking two languages! It is perfectly fine to read books written in Spanish to him in Spanish—just as you would read books written in English to him in English. While he is learning to read in both languages, he will also begin to write in English and Spanish.

Parent Partnership: Your Child Learns to Write.

DR TUTH FRE ILS MI TUTH
PLS HEL ME FD et

Can you read this? This is a note to the tooth fairy. It was written by a child who lost her first baby tooth. Let's decode this note together.

DR TUTH FRE ILS MI TUTH

Dear Tooth Fairy, I lost my tooth.

PLS HEL ME FD et

Please help me find it.

As adults, we have been conditioned to read only conventional spelling. On first glance, this note may resemble only a string of letters. On closer inspection, we detect that its writer is trying to convey an important message. When young children begin to use print, their parents and teachers should encourage all attempts. Treating a child's scribbles or letter streams as important and meaningful encourages the child to continue her efforts. As she experiments with reading and writing, her understanding of the rules of our language increases. Eventually, developmental or invented spelling matures into more conventional spelling. To read more about this process you might want to read *Spell. . . is a four letter word* by J. Richard Gentry, (1987) from Heinemann Publishing Company in Portsmouth, New Hampshire.

(cont.)

Dear Teacher:

I have three children, and our evenings are hectic to say the least! I also work, so the time I have is limited. When is the best time and for how long should I read to my kids? *Signed, Watching the Clock*

Dear Watching:

Excellent question! Many parents have multiple responsibilities, and time is always an issue. The best time is whenever you can consistently schedule about 15 to 20 minutes alone. For most parents, that time appears to be just before bed. However, some parents report that they find time right after the evening meal. Whenever you feel rested and can give your children 15 to 20 minutes of undivided time is the best time to read to them.

Dear Teacher:

My four-year-old son wants to hear the same story over, and over, and over. Is this normal? Shouldn't I read a new book each night? *Signed, Repeating Myself*

Dear Repeating:

As adults we tend to like variety, but most young children between the ages of two and seven have a favorite story, and this storybook may be as comforting to them as their best-

Figure 10.9

Continued

Preparing for Parent/Student/Teacher Conferences

Conferences are wonderful opportunities for parents, student, and teacher to sit beside one another to share the students' work and review their progress. In our class each student will share the contents of his/her portfolio with both parents and teacher.

In the first half of the 20-minute conference, students will display and discuss their writing and perhaps read some of their stories. They will explain why certain products were included in the portfolio and why they believe these particular pieces best demonstrate their learning efforts. The students will also show the parents and teacher some of the work they completed at the beginning of the school year and compare it to how they are performing today. During this part of the conference, it is important for parents to listen to the student's self-evaluation. Parents are encouraged to ask open-ended questions, such as:

• What did you learn the most about?
• What did you work the hardest to learn?
• What do you want to learn more about?

These questions encourage students to analyze their own learning and also help them set new learning goals for themselves. Parents should not criticize the child's work or focus on any negative aspect of any material that is presented from the portfolio. Negative comments will only inhibit learning and dampen excitement about school. During the last ten minutes of the conference, the student will be excused so that parents and teacher have an opportunity to talk about any concerns the parents may have. Be sure to complete the Preconference Questionnaire and return it prior to the conference so that the teacher may be better prepared to discuss your concerns.

October Calendar

3rd	– Visit with the eye doctor: vision testing
7th	– Visit the audiologist: hearing tests
15th	– My Favorite Smells Day: bring in your favorite smell
18th	– Taste-testing day
19th	– School pictures day – dress bright
23rd	– Touch and tell day
28th–29th	– Parent/Student/Teacher Conference
31st	– Halloween/5 senses party

Remember: Weekly notes will provide details for each event.

Story Books for October

Georgie's Halloween, by Robert Bright (Doubleday)
The Teeny-Tiny Woman, by Paul Galdone (Clarion)
The Berenstain Bears: Trick or Treat, by Stan and Jan Berenstain (Random House)
Clifford's Halloween, by Norman Bridwill (Scholastic)
ABC Halloween Witch, by Ida Dedage (Garrard)
Who Goes Out on Halloween, by Sue Alexander (Bank Street)
It's Halloween, by Jack Prelutsky (Greeenwillow)

loved stuffed toy. So the question becomes how to have both variety and comfort. At this age, favorite books tend to be short, so one suggestion is to read two or three books at storytime. Try reading the new books first and the favorite book last. When your child begins to read along with you, this is the perfect time to have him read this favorite book to you or to another child in your household. Frequently a child's favorite book becomes the first one he will read independently.

Dear Teacher:

When I read my five-year-old daughter a book at storytime, I worry about her comprehension skills. Should I ask questions? *Signed, Just the Facts*

Dear Facts:

I'm so glad you asked that question. The stories you read will frequently inspire your child to share many of her thoughts, hopes, and fears. These discussions are obviously more important than reciting any particular detail. In fact, quizzing children about story details will only make storytime an unpleasant activity for both of you. Instead, ask open-ended, opinion questions, such as "Which was your favorite part?" or "Why do you think Max stared at the Wild Things?" Storytime will also motivate your children to ask you questions! Take your time, share your views, and allow your child to hear your thought process. This activity will do more to teach them about story interpretation than 1000 fact questions! P.S. Did you know that Sendak's relatives served as the model for the Wild Things?

Family Focus. Because many parents have a number of questions about how their child will learn to write, it becomes essential for teachers to proactively communicate information about the normal developmental process of writing. To help parents learn about emergent writing, teachers may wish to use a more formal, direct instruction approach, such as a Your Child Learns to Write column in the monthly newsletter, like the example in Figure 10.9. We recommend that before any children's writing is sent home, the teacher educate parents about the developmental writing stages. The following is an example of the most common questions parents ask about their child's writing development. The answers provide a sample of the tone and depth of information the column should contain.

When does my child really start to write? We live in a culture where print is used to communicate. Therefore, children begin to read and write informally long before they enter school. By the time children are able to pick up a pencil or crayon and draw or scribble, they are demonstrating their knowledge that these marks mean something, and the first step toward written communication has begun.

When my child draws or scribbles, does that mean that I should begin to teach him or her how to hold the pencil and form letters correctly? When your child first began to sing songs, did you start teaching him to play the piano? No, of course not! But you did enjoy the songs he or she sang, and you sang along. This is exactly the approach parents should take when their child first begins to draw or scribble write. Say, "Tell me about what you wrote about." Listen to the answer and compliment the effort.

How can I encourage my child's writing? When children watch adults write a grocery list or a letter or pay bills, they are often motivated to imitate this writing. Usually, all children need are the writing materials—paper, markers, crayons, pencils—and they will take the ideas from there. Occasionally, you could suggest that they might wish to write a letter to Grandmother or leave a note for the tooth fairy. Another perfect opportunity to encourage writing is during their dramatic play. When children play house, they can write grocery lists or leave phone messages—all you need to do is provide the writing materials and praise. A particularly exciting activity is to have your child choose a favorite stuffed animal. The stuffed animal takes a field trip to Grandmother's house or to preschool with the child. That night, parents and child may write about and illustrate a story about "The Adventures of _____ at _____." Children will write frequently if they feel their attempts to communicate are accepted and valued as meaningful.

Isn't handwriting practice important for learning to read and write? Learning the correct written form of a letter is called handwriting. It is an opportunity for children to gain control of the small muscles in their fingers and hands. However, handwriting drills do not teach children how to read and write. A child who exhibits excellent penmanship will not necessarily learn to read or communicate in written form any faster than the child whose writing still resembles scribbles. Critical comments about a child's handwriting efforts can stifle the joy of communicating. When a new scribe begins to learn the "how" of writing, it is far better to praise the efforts. This will encourage the child to write more.

How do I read my child's written work? Start by asking your child to tell you what was written. The information provided will give you context. These clues should enable you to figure out what the scribble, shapes, or letters represent. Children tend to progress through predictable developmental stages on the way to conventional spelling. This progression may proceed from scribbles, to letter strings, to single letters representing whole words or thoughts, to invented spelling, to conventional spelling. Invented spelling is using two or three letters to phonetically represent a word—this is sometimes called developmental spelling.

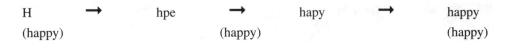

| H | → | hpe | → | hapy | → | happy |
| (happy) | | | | (happy) | | (happy) |

Should I correct my child's invented/developmental spelling? Have you ever changed what you wanted to write simply because you were unsure of the spelling of a word? Research reveals that children write less and use only a limited vocabulary of known words if their spelling is criticized. However, young children of six or seven who are encouraged to use their invented spelling will often write extensive stories with complex vocabularies. Parents may help children sound out phonetic words or spell more difficult words if the child asks for assistance.

CENTER HIGHLIGHTS. Another feature that can be included in weekly notes or monthly newsletters is Center Highlights. In this segment, the types of learning opportunities children experience when they work together in learning centers are described. This is particularly important as many parents are unsure how learning centers, especially dramatic play centers, contribute to a child's literacy development. In Figure 10.10, we provide an example of a Center Highlights feature.

Thus far, this chapter has provided a number of communication strategies and highlighted the importance of ongoing communications to parents. One-shot publicity campaigns (e.g., read to and write with your child) do not provide parents with sufficient information or the long-term motivation they need to become involved in a meaningful literacy program. Instead, consistent, frequent, positive information that includes highly practical suggestions will help parents support their child's education. Beyond communicating, however, teachers may also need to provide other types of support to help parents fulfill their role as their child's first teachers. In the remainder of this chapter, we discuss the teacher's role as educational resource and community connection.

Teachers and Schools as Professional Resources

"In some schools there are still educators who say, 'If the family would just do its job, we could do our job.' And there are still families who say, 'I raised this child; now it is your turn to educate her' " (Epstein, 1995, p. 702). Most often, children who need the most help come from families that need the most support. Schools and centers that wish to make a significant difference in the lives of these children must find ways to offer support and forge successful school–family partnerships (Gardner, 1993–1994). Fortunately, most early childhood educators find that educating a child requires at least two teachers—the one at school or the center and the one at home. Following are concrete suggestions that teachers may use to help parents fulfill their role as first teacher.

Sharing Instructional Materials and Offering Guidance

Preschool teachers frequently recommend that parents read to their young children (Becker & Epstein, 1982). Unfortunately, many parents face great financial hardships and cannot provide a large number of quality reading materials in their homes. Further, parents may not know how to encourage and engage their children's interest in reading (Richgels & Wold, 1998). To help parents to fulfill their role as partners in literacy programs, it is vital for teachers to work with these families to offer easy access to both books and writing materials (Brock & Dodd, 1994) and guidance in how to use them (McGee & Richgels, 1996).

CLASSROOM LENDING LIBRARY. Susan Neuman's 1999 study examined the effect of flooding more than 330 child care centers with storybooks. The results of her study confirm that children who have access to high-quality storybooks and teachers who are trained to support children's storybook interactions score significantly higher on several early reading achievement measures than children who have not experienced high-quality storybooks and trained teachers. In other words, it is critically important for young children to have easy access to

Figure 10.10 *Center highlights*

Thematic Play—Grocery Store

Story Retelling

Thematic Play—Cafe

Dramatic Play Centers provide children with an opportunity to reveal thoughts and attitudes through conversations; use knowledge of print to enhance play; learn to share, plan, organize, and take turns; and demonstrate understanding of the many functions of print.

high-quality storybooks. Further, it is essential that parents and child care providers know how to support a child's early interactions with print. Though most public schools possess libraries, children generally are restricted to borrowing only one or two books a week. Some child care centers use public libraries with similar restrictions. While this may be appropriate for older children who can read chapter books, this quantity is insufficient for young children who are learning how to read. Young children should have the opportunity to have at least one new book an evening. One way to ensure early literacy development at home and foster the home–school connection is through a classroom lending library. A classroom lending library allows children to check out a new book each day, thus ensuring that all parents have an opportunity to read to their child frequently.

The acquisition of quality books for daily checkout is the first step in establishing a classroom lending library. Since the children will exchange their book each day, all a teacher needs to begin a library is one book per child. For tips on acquiring inexpensive children's books, see Trade Secrets 5.1 in Chapter 5.

Managing the classroom lending library requires that all books contain a library pocket and identification card. The teacher needs to create a classroom library checkout chart. When a child borrows a book, she simply removes the book's identification card and replaces it in her or his name pocket on the classroom checkout chart. The teacher can easily see what book each child has checked out at a glance.

The rules that accompany the classroom lending library are simple. A child may borrow one book each day. When the book is returned, the child may check out another. Teaching the children to manage the checkout routine is easy. When the children enter the classroom in the morning, they return their books to the library by removing the book's identification card from their name pocket. They place the identification card back in the book's library pocket, and they place the book back on the shelf. The children may select new books anytime throughout the day. See Trade Secret 5.2 for a description of Lynn Cohen's classroom lending library.

WRITING BRIEFCASE. Another popular option that may be included as part of the classroom lending library is the writing briefcase. The briefcase can be an inexpensive plastic carrying case or a canvas portfolio. Inside the briefcase, the teacher may provide writing paper, colored construction paper, markers, pens and pencils, glue, tape—anything that might stimulate a child to write a story, make a greeting card, design a book cover, or create whatever they can imagine. Depending on the size of the class, teachers may have seven or eight writing briefcases—enough so that four or five children may check out the materials each day, and two or three extras so that the teacher has time to replenish the briefcase supplies frequently and conveniently. The briefcases are numbered, and each has a library pocket and identification card. The checkout procedures follow the same routine as for library books.

The writing briefcase may also contain explicit suggestions that encourage parents to use writing to communicate with their children. In Special Feature 10.2, we describe how one father used notes to spark his child's interest in learning to read and write.

BOOK BAGS. Yet another way to encourage family participation and successfully engage and guide parents' literacy interactions with their children is through book bags (Barbour, 1998–1999). Like writing briefcases, book bags may be checked out of the classroom lending library for a week at a time. Book bags contain a collection of high-quality books and offer informal, interactive activities for extending children's language and literacy acquisition. When designing the bags, teachers need to consider their children's developmental stages, interests and experiences, and literacy levels. The book bags (nylon gym bags) typically contain three

Special Feature 10.2

Love, Letters, and Literacy Learning

Mikeal Killeen

My plan was simple. I would write a short love note to my five-year-old daughter and leave it by her bed after she had fallen asleep. When she awoke she would see the note and come running to find me. My first message was "*Come hug me. Love, Daddy.*" To my dismay there was no enthusiastic visitor the next morning. At the breakfast table, my daughter informed me that "It was fun to get a note, but it was too hard to read." I learned a valuable lesson that morning, for in my excitement I used

cursive! My daughter emphatically made me promise to "Print the letters neatly, Daddy, cause I can't read that scribble stuff."

True to my promise, the next few notes were neatly printed and contained several symbols to help my daughter decode my messages. Soon our communication developed into a treasure hunt; one note would give clues about where to find the next note and, occasionally, a treat. As you might guess, my modeling was quickly imitated, and it was not long before notes began to appear under my pillow or on the mirror. As you can imagine, the paper, tape, and pencil consumption in our house went way up, but those things are just the tools of the trade of communicating your ideas to the world.

or four books and activities inspired by a specific theme (see Figure 10.11 for sample book bag themes). In addition, each bag contains two response journals (one for the child and one for the parent). Some bags contain tape recorders and the tapes that accompany the books. The tapes and tape recorders are particularly important for parents who may not be able to read English. Each bag also contains an inventory that helps parents and children keep track of and return materials assigned to each bag. (For more information see Lynn Cohen Trade Secret 5.2.)

Teachers typically initiate the program by sending home a letter describing the program. In addition to the introductory letter, each family also receives a contract. The terms of the contract are simple: Parents promise to spend time regularly reading to their children; children promise to spend time with the books and activities and treat each bag with care; and teachers promise to instill a love of reading in children and to manage the program. All three participants sign the contract.

The book bag project has been highly successful in many teachers' classrooms. The book bags supply parents the appropriate materials and explicit guidance, which in turn

- empower and motivate them to become teachers of their own children,
- encourage them to provide supportive home learning environments, and
- expand their knowledge of how to interact with their children.

VIDEOTAPE. As more schools have access to video cameras, another option to consider is creating a videotape lending section for the classroom library. Videotape has the potential to become an exceptional tool for teaching parents about storybook reading skills. The teacher may wish to videotape himself or herself reading an exciting storybook. While reading a book to the children, the teacher has the opportunity to demonstrate oral fluency, enthusiasm, and the use of different voices to make the story characters come alive. In addition, the teacher can illustrate how open-ended, predictive questioning strategies can facilitate children's ac-

---

Figure 10.11	
Sample book bag themes	**Counting Theme** Hillanbrand, W. (1997). *Counting Crocodiles.* Orlando: FL: Harcourt Brace. Kirk, D. (1994). *Miss Spider's Tea Party.* New York: Scholastic Editions Inc. Barbieri-McGrath, B. (1998). *Hershey's Counting Board Book.* Wellesley, MA: Corporate Board Book. **Alphabet Theme** Wilbur, R. (1997). *The Disappearing Alphabet.* New York: Scholastic. Alexander, M. (1994). *A You're Adorable.* New York: Scholastic. Martin, B., & Archambault, J. (1989). *Chicka, Chicka, Boom Boom.* New York: Simon & Schuster Children's Publishing. **Rhyming Books** Goldston, B. (1998). *The Beastly Feast.* New York: Scholastic. Slate, J. (1996). *Miss Bindergarten Gets Ready for Kindergarten.* New York: Scholastic. Wood, A. (1992). *Silly Sally.* Orlando: FL: Harcourt Brace. **Getting Dressed** Degen, B. (1996). *Jesse Bear, What Will You Wear?* New York: Simon & Schuster Children's Publishing. London, J. (1997). *Froggy Gets Dressed.* New York: Viking Children's Press. Regan, D. (1998). *What Will I Do if I Can't Tie My Shoe?* New York: Scholastic.

tive involvement during storytime. Likewise, using retelling prompts, the teacher can demonstrate how children discuss story events with each other and share their unique and meaningful perspectives. These informal instructive videos may significantly help parents improve and expand their own story-reading skills. Children may check out both the videotape and the storybook. The video and accompanying storybook may be stored in a large self-sealing plastic bag. The same checkout procedures as for the library books or writing briefcases may be used.

The job of communicating with parents and providing instructional resources and guidance is comprehensive. In Trade Secrets 10.1, teacher Maureen Jobe shares the different strategies she uses in her classroom.

Schools as Community Resource

Because literacy is a critical component for success in all aspects of community life, schools are beginning to extend opportunities for all community members to become involved in producing literate citizens. In extending our view of literacy beyond the classroom, we also expand our views of the traditional roles of schools. In the past decade, an increasing number of schools have chosen to provide for the social, medical, and educational needs of the families in their community. In Special Feature 10.3, readers will find a discussion of the major components of family resource schools.

Trade Secrets 10.1

Sharing Information and Resources

Maureen Jobe

It is critical for teachers to encourage parents to get involved in the reading process with their children. I believe teachers should encourage parents to read with their children as much as possible. In my preschool classroom, I try many strategies to encourage parents to read to their children. I begin the year by sending home a classroom newsletter. In the newsletter I write about the benefits, based on current research, of reading to children. I offer parents ideas on how to make reading enjoyable and also give ideas about where to get high-quality literature. Over the years, I have found it very difficult to get parents to read my classroom newsletters. In order to encourage parents to read the information I am sending home, I add comments from the children in the classroom. For example, I asked the children, "What do you enjoy most about your parents reading to you?" The comments I received back from the children were published in the classroom newsletter. This was a great motivator, and more parents began reading the information.

I also have the red bookbag program in my classroom. I designed this program after I read Lynn E. Cohen's article about the book backpack program. Since the children in my classroom really enjoy reading Clifford books, I put together a red bag that consisted of many Clifford books, a Clifford puppet, and a journal for the children to draw and/or write about their experience with

the bag. When children bring back the bookbag, they have an opportunity to tell the class about their entries in the journal. The thinking behind this program is that parents will read to their children and the children will interact with the Clifford puppet in retelling their favorite stories. The journal is to encourage emergent writing skills. The children in my class have had a good time with the red bag this year.

Another program is the parent library. The objective of this program is to encourage parents to model reading to their children. In the parent library I have many books focusing on parental issues. I have books about child development, discipline, and sibling interactions. I have also included books about my classroom teaching philosophy. I send parents a letter at the beginning of the year introducing them to the parent library and the benefits for their children in modeling reading at home. The program is managed based on a sign-in and -out method. This approach has been beneficial for me in many ways. First, parents are provided with many resources to help support them with their parenting issues. Also, parents learn more about the classroom philosophy of teaching, which reduces conflicts later.

Finally, I always communicate with parents on a personal level. I do this through phone calls and conferences. I always talk about positive points in their child's literacy development and give them practical suggestions about things they can do at home with their child. I find that communicating on a personal note with parents really strengthens the parent–teacher relationship and the child benefits.

Family Resource Schools

The way schools care about children is reflected in the way schools care about the children's families. If educators view children simply as students, they are likely to see the family as separate from the school. That is, the family is expected to do its job and leave the education of children to the schools. If educators view students as children, they are likely to see both the family and the community as partners with the school in children's education and development. (Epstein, 1995, p. 701)

The major goal of family resource schools (also called learning community schools) is to strengthen the social and economic foundations of the neighborhood community. This goal is accomplished by providing extensive support to families, both before and after school. Family resource schools offer a broad range of service, including

Student achievement and activity programs, such as
- community study hall with volunteer tutors,
- family read-alongs and family math classes,
- physical activity classes (gymnastics, dance, etc.),
- fine arts classes (arts and crafts, chorus, guitar, etc),
- community garden.

Adult education and skill building, such as
- adult basic education,
- general equivalency diploma,
- English as a second language,
- Spanish as a second language,
- conflict management seminars,
- employment workshops.

Parent education courses, such as
- parenting education programs,
- positive discipline workshops,
- sex education workshops,
- gang prevention workshops.

Family support services, such as
- on-site case management,
- alcohol and drug prevention programs,
- before- and after-school child care,
- baby-sitting co-ops,
- food and clothing banks,
- primary health care,
- mental health services.

Teacher as Community Contact

Teachers also need to think beyond the classroom and consider the many ways reading, writing, talking, and listening enhance all facets of a person's life in the home, school, church, and workplace. Teachers then must consider how they can provide opportunities for students to learn about community literacy activities.

VIP PROGRAM. The VIP, or very important person, program is an effective strategy for involving community members in classroom activities. Community members of all types—secretaries, politicians, lawyers, construction workers, computer programmers, maids, chefs, fire fighters, flight attendants, store clerks, doctors, farmers, and professors—are invited to visit the classroom. When they arrive, they may read their favorite childhood story or perhaps an appropriate story that provides information about their career. After the VIP reads the story, she or he may wish to tell how reading and writing are used in the job. Children are sometimes surprised to hear how all types of jobs require literacy.

Another version of VIP is "Very Important Parents." As the name implies, this program features the children's parents. Parents may read their favorite childhood story to the class, share a favorite oral story, engage in a cooking activity using a favorite recipe, or perform another interesting activity.

BUSINESS ADOPTION PROGRAMS. In this type of community involvement program, the school or classroom is adopted by a business in the community. Businesses often provide some financial support for the purchase of books or writing briefcases. In addition, employees of the businesses may be encouraged to be VIPs or help arrange a field trip to see business literacy in action (Rasinski & Fredericks, 1991). Children viewing the work of adults may be inspired to imitate and practice many of the reading and writing activities they see performed. Teachers may capitalize on this interest by creating dramatic play centers where the adopted business is a play theme, including all the literacy props and activities the children observed.

COMMUNITY TUTORS. Perhaps the most inclusive and dynamic method for involving adult community members in your classroom is as volunteer reading tutors. Retirees in particular enjoy the role of classroom grandparents. Classroom tutors regularly volunteer each week to cuddle with and read to a child. This consistent involvement is pleasurable for the volunteer and benefits the young children. The value of spending individual time with another caring adult is beyond calculation.

BUDDY READING PROGRAMS. To make a significant improvement in family literacy practices, it is essential that educators begin to develop the skills of tomorrow's parents. Older students may benefit greatly by participating in a parent apprenticeship program called Buddy Reading. Unfortunately, many older children do not have strong reading skills themselves. One major strength of the Buddy Reading program is that it has the potential to simultaneously improve older students' skills while supporting young students as they learn to read.

Primary, middle, or high school teachers may arrange to have their students work with preschool children during the school day, during lunch or recess, or in an after-school program. Whatever the time arrangement, the older reading buddies need to

- learn appropriate read-aloud behaviors, such as using an expressive voice, sharing and discussing pictures and print, and facilitating comprehension;
- identify characteristics of appropriate trade books, such as predictable books with repetitive, cumulative, rhythm and rhyme, and/or chronological patterns; and
- determine the younger reading buddy's interests and how to select appropriate books of interest to the child.

Sharing your literacy program within the school and throughout the local community is a win-win proposition. Older children learn how and why it is important to read to young children, while community members learn to appreciate the work of children and teachers in the schools. The following is a list of agencies that teachers may contact for more information and specific brochures about family involvement in the literacy process:

- Association for Childhood Education International
    The Olney Professional Building
    17904 Georgia Avenue, Suite 215
    Olney, MD 20832
- National Association for the Education of Young Children
    15009 16th Street, NW
    Washington, DC 20036-1426
- American Library Association
    50 E. Huron Street
    Chicago, IL 60611
- International Reading Association
    800 Barksdale Road
    Newark, DE 19714
- Reading Is Fundamental
    P.O. Box 23444
    Washington, DC 20026

Special Feature 10.4

Parental Involvement in Bilingual and Second-Language Settings

Sarah Hudelson and Irene Serna

This chapter discusses the importance of involving parents in their children's education. In the home setting, parents are their children's first teachers. There is no reason for this role to cease when children begin their formal schooling. In this special feature, the perspective already developed in this chapter is extended by exploring several issues that are particularly important to keep in mind when planning for the involvement of parents who are native speakers of a language other than English.

The Problem of Stereotyping

Even in the 1990s, when educators worked to be more sensitive to diversity (Brandt, 1992), comments about parents, especially parents of color, parents who do not speak English, and parents who are not middle class were heard.

- "Those parents are poor and uneducated; they don't have any idea of how to help their children."
- "The parents at my school don't value education; they don't even come to parent-teacher conferences."
- "Some parents can't even speak English and read and write themselves. How are they supposed to help their kids?"
- "These poor babies come from homes with no books; no wonder they are so behind. They have no understanding of literacy before they come to school."

Comments such as these reflect stereotyping and negative attitudes toward some parents. Some non-English-speaking parents have not been fortunate enough to complete even elementary school; some have had limited opportunities to develop literacy. Some are uncomfortable in the school setting because they do not speak English; some have difficulty attending school functions because they are holding down two or three poorly paying jobs in order to support their families. The presence of these challenging obstacles does not mean that parents are unable and unwilling to participate in their children's education. In fact, non-English-speaking parents are especially concerned about education because they view education as the key to a better life for their children.

Recent studies (Allexsaht-Snider, 1991; Delgado-Gaitan & Trueba, 1991; Schieffelin & Cochran-Smith, 1984; Vasquez, 1991) (e.g., of home literacy practices in working-class, non-English-speaking, immigrant families) have found that these families do engage in a variety of literacy practices. However, these practices tend to be focused on literacy for daily life, survival, and communication with relatives in their native countries, rather than on more middle-class purposes for reading (for example, literacy for pleasure or to pass leisure time). Reading for pleasure or leisure is difficult when a parent is working multiple jobs.

Therefore, educators must avoid making assumptions about non-English-speaking parents. Instead teachers are encouraged to (1) acknowledge and understand parental and family realities; (2) work to establish relationships with parents that will allow them to feel valued for who they are; and (3) help parents recognize the important contributions they make to their children's continued education.

Understanding Different Cultural Norms Regarding Schooling

For individuals raised in mainstream, middle-class settings, parental involvement in education may be considered a given. Parents assume that they are welcome at school and that they ought to have a say in their children's educational experiences. However, such assumptions are not necessarily the case in all communities, and they are particularly unlikely in culturally and linguistically diverse settings.

In the Miami community of Little Haiti, for example, Creole-speaking parents from Haiti historically had been excluded from the French-language schools their children attended. Parents viewed the schools as places where they sent their children to do as the schools instructed, with no input from parents. The schools, in turn, emphasized learning via memorization rather than through active construction of knowledge (Hudelson, 1990).

Similarly, in many communities populated by Mexican and other Latin American immigrants, parents believe that when they send their children to school, they turn over the responsibility for the child's education to that institution. Traditionally, there has been a separation of functions. The parents' role is to instruct their children to behave and to listen carefully to their teachers. The parents' job is also to discipline children who misbehave in school. The teachers' function is to teach (Delgado-Gaitan & Trueba, 1991). Additionally, Mexican and Mexican-American parents have not been schooled in the constructivist perspective advocated by so many educators today. These parents may hold views of literacy learning that may be much more traditional than those of the teacher. Also like most parents, they may be reticent to participate in pedagogies that they have not experienced (Enz & Searfoss, 1995; 1996).

Authoritarian views of schooling and the separation of parents from schools and teachers, then, have been experiences that parents from many cultural backgrounds may have shared. Given such socialization, it is understandable that parents may initially be uncomfortable seeing themselves in formal teaching roles and working in more interactional ways. They may also believe that they should come to school only for disciplinary

(continued on next page)

reasons. It is important, therefore, to appreciate that parents may have been socialized to view schools and teacher-parent roles in ways that significantly differ from the views that the teacher expects. Teachers need to learn from community members what parents' views about schools and about experiences with schools have been so that they may more effectively invite parents to work with them.

Encouraging Native Language Use

One of Irene Serna's most vivid memories of her own elementary schooling is having a teacher tell her parents that they should not use Spanish with her in their home. If her parents continued to speak Spanish to her, they were told, Irene would be retarded in her academic development. The way to help Irene was to use English. More than 30 years later, this advice continues to be given to parents who are not proficient users of English. Simply stated, this advice is wrong.

In Special Feature 2.3 accompanying Chapter 2, you read about immigrant parents' problems in communicating effectively with their young children who no longer acknowledged their native languages. How were these adults who spoke little or no English to raise their children to be decent human beings if they could not use the language they spoke fluently (Fillmore, 1991)? In addition, think about what language means to humans, what humans use language for. People use both spoken and written language for a broad spectrum of purposes: to provide information, to persuade others to a point of view, to argue, to tell jokes, to share stories, to scold, to ask questions, to share opinions, to make interpersonal connections, to express emotions, and so on. Language is a powerful force in our lives.

In order to understand language's potential, children need to be exposed to a wide range of language uses (Heath, 1986). Such exposure is much more likely to happen when adults interact in a language they control (i.e., their native language), rather than in a language they are still struggling to learn. Unless second-language learners have achieved high levels of proficiency in the second language, they will not use this newer tongue for the full range of uses in which they will use the native language. To deny children access to this full range of language functions is to impoverish children's language and to put them at risk for lower achievement in school. David Dolson (1985) has demonstrated that children who come from monolingual homes where a language other than English is spoken perform better in school than children from homes where parents try to use their second language, English, with their children.

Therefore, parents who are more proficient in their native language than in English must be encouraged to use the native language with their children, thus providing the young learners with demonstrations of a broad range of possibilities of language use. Learners then take these understandings into the second-language setting.

Expanding Our Views of the Roots of Literacy

As this book has demonstrated, one place where children learn about reading and writing is the home, where the children see their parents engage in reading and writing and where they themselves engage in a variety of literacy events. One such event is storybook reading. Because storybook reading has been found to be a predictor of later success in reading (Wells, 1986), suggestions to parents for assisting their children to become literate generally include reading out loud.

For many non-English-speaking parents, economic circumstances and limited availability of materials in their native languages often mean that storybook reading is limited. However, in many cultures, a tradition of oral storytelling exists. Research has demonstrated that the elements of story, as well as the strategies or ways of thinking about or responding to text that schools expect (for example, sequencing, evaluating, elaborating, clarifying) are developed during these storytelling events (Guerra, 1991; Pease-Alvarez, 1991; Vasquez, 1991).

Juan's family is an example. Juan came from a home in which oral storytelling was a family ritual that took place as Juan's mother prepared the family dinner. Juan's mother would tell a story, and then the children were expected to tell stories. This home literacy practice provided Juan with a sophisticated understanding of story development. His stories demonstrated a complexity and creativity that many of his classmates (who did not engage in such storytelling) did not have. For example, during kindergarten, Juan created "Los Osos Malos" (The Bad Bears). In Juan's story, some bad bears chased him, even turning themselves into ghosts in an effort to capture him. However, through a series of moves and countermoves, Juan finally escaped. Juan's story was by far the most complex of any produced by the kindergarten children, and this, at least in part, can be attributed to his background in hearing and then telling stories.

Non-English-speaking parents who come from cultures with strong oral traditions should be encouraged to tell stories at home. Parents could be invited to tell stories at school. By broadening our base of understanding of what contributes to children's school literacy success, another avenue is provided for meaningful participation by non-English-speaking parents.

Family Literacy Demonstrations

The present chapter makes a series of excellent suggestions for providing workshops for parents on aspects of curriculum. The workshop format allows parents to participate in and try out some classroom instructional strategies that promote literacy. Educators involved with parents in bilingual and second-language settings also have worked in this hands-on way, but they have found particular success in organizing the workshops somewhat differently. They have involved parents and young children together in carrying out the kinds of activities and strategies that are a part of the children's ongoing literacy

(continued on next page)

Special Feature 10.4 *(continued)*

development; thus, the focus is on family and intergenerational literacy (Weinstein-Shr & Quintero, 1995).

In an elementary school in central Phoenix, Arizona, primary-grade bilingual teachers have invited parents and children to participate in literature study groups with high-quality picture books. The teacher begins by reading the story aloud, followed by opportunities for adults and children to share their responses to the book. Often, parents and children then choose other books to take home. While this activity is usually carried out in Spanish, a variation of it could involve parents and children in listening, one time or several times, to a carefully selected predictable book in English. Parents who are ESL learners have reported that they themselves learn more English when they listen to predictable stories.

In a family literacy project involving Spanish-speaking mothers and their four-year-old preschoolers, experienced early childhood educators engaged parents and children in hands-on activities, followed by language-experience-type dictation. These parent- and child-generated stories became comprehensible reading material for the workshop participants. Teachers also urged the mothers to encourage their young children's experimentations with written language, even though the writing was not conventional (Macías-Huerta & Quintero, 1990).

In a project in Atlanta, Georgia, ESL parents with some ability in English came together with their children so that the parents could share stories of their lives in their various homelands. Teachers involved in the program helped put these stories into written English narratives, which then became a source of reading material for children and their parents. This project also utilized computers, motivating adults and children to learn to use the computer so that they could produce final versions of their stories (Nurss & Hough, 1992).

Consider bringing parents and children together in workshop sessions that will both facilitate better understanding of your philosophy and pedagogy and contribute to children's and adult literacy.

Use Parental Knowledge

There is substantial evidence indicating that working-class immigrant families engage in a variety of home literacy practices. However, because these events often do not match the schools' views of literacy, family literacy practices may go unacknowledged or may even be viewed as standing in the way of children's academic development. For several years, educator Luis Moll and some of his colleagues have been working with teachers both to investigate literacy practices in U.S. and Mexican households and to develop innovations in literacy teaching in the schools based on these practices, related to what Moll calls, "funds of knowledge" (Moll, Amanti, Neff, & González, 1992). Moll has used the term *funds of knowledge* to describe bodies of skills and knowledge that accumulate in all communities and households. He and his colleagues contend that family and local community knowledge and skills can be tapped strategically by teachers and used to promote academic achievement (González, 1995).

Early childhood education teacher Marla Hensley (1995) wrote about how she applied the concept of funds of knowledge to her kindergarten classroom. Hensley chose the family of one of her students for a series of extended home visits in which, with the assistance of a questionnaire, she learned about this family in depth. As she got to know the child's father, she discovered that he was an expert gardener, and she recruited him to help her class prepare and plant both a vegetable and a flower garden. As she continued to visit in the home, Hensley found that the father had excellent communication skills and that he was a skilled musician, playing both keyboard and guitar and composing original songs. This parent agreed to write some children's songs and to help create a musical based on the folktale "The Little Red Hen." Then Hensley and this parent worked together to help the children learn the songs and later to rehearse and perform the musical.

Learning in detail about the talents and abilities of one parent gave this teacher an appreciation for parental funds of knowledge in general. This teacher developed a sensitivity to the possibilities of making use of parental experts across her school curriculum.

It may not be feasible for you to spend extensive amounts of time visiting families and conducting in-depth interviews with parents. Nonetheless, it is still possible to learn something about the kinds of knowledge and skills possessed by the parents of your learners. Parent-teacher conferences might be one venue for asking parents about their talents and interests. You may want to send a letter home asking parents to jot down hobbies, areas of expertise, and so on that they would be willing to share with the children. Listen to your children as they talk about the activities they engage in at home. Bring parental expertise into the classroom. Make parents' real-life knowledge an integral part of your curriculum, thus providing children with the opportunity to use spoken and written language to accomplish real-world learning.

Summary

Families play a critical role in nurturing young children's literacy learning. Early childhood teachers must be prepared to reach out to parents to form two-way partnerships aimed at building parents' awareness of the important role they play in their children's literacy learning and providing them with strategies for nurturing their children's early reading, writing, and speaking development. Here, we return to the questions posed at the beginning of the chapter and briefly summarize the information presented.

■ *What is known about the relationship between what parents do and children's language and literacy development?*

Research demonstrates that when parents converse a great deal with their young children, the children's vocabulary and language fluency increase. Likewise, if parents consistently engage their children in storytime and storytelling, there is a greater likelihood that their children will enjoy reading and become interested in and knowledgeable about the reading process. Parents who support young children's early reading and writing attempts encourage their children to begin to read and write. In short, what parents do makes a great deal of difference in their children's literacy learning and success. The data suggest that many parents need their children's teachers' assistance in understanding the crucial role they play in helping their children become successful readers, writers, and speakers and that all parents need teachers to share strategies for nurturing their young children's early literacy learning.

■ *In what ways might early childhood teachers communicate personally with parents?*

Communication is the key to successful parent–teacher partnerships. True two-way communication must take place between parents and teachers. Teachers can communicate personally with parents through regular phone calls and conferences. Phone calls should be used to communicate good news, not just troubling news. Regularly scheduled progress review conferences offer opportunities for parents and teachers to share information about factors influencing children's reading and writing development. Specific problems conferences are needed when difficulties arise between regularly scheduled conferences. Sharing information about the child's literacy development might occur during a home visit, another forum for personal communication. Home visits also can be used to share information with parents on how to support their children's literacy learning. While teachers can share information one on one with parents during home visits, groups of parents can learn and interact together during parent workshops.

■ *How might teachers run a parent–teacher conference?*

Structuring the parent–teacher conference keeps the conference focused and increases the chance of both the teacher's and the parents' concerns being addressed. The teacher might begin with a positive statement and review the conference format, then ask for the parents' input, then offer input, and finally summarize points agreed on in the conference.

■ *In what ways might teachers communicate with parents in writing?*

Teachers can send home a variety of written publications including informal weekly notes, news flashes, and monthly newsletters. News flashes might be about classroom-related events, or they might be about something special the child has done that day. Some teachers might be able to use electronic mail to communicate with parents.

■ *What resources might an early childhood teacher provide to parents and parents provide to teachers to support young children's early literacy learning?*

Teachers of young children are an important resource for parents. Through the use of classroom lending libraries, book bags, and writing briefcases, teachers can provide parents with the materials needed for home literacy activities. In addition, teacher-made videos can be sent home to show parents what they might do during an activity, like storybook reading, to help their child get the most from the activity.

Parents can be an important resource for teachers also. Teachers can recruit parents and other community adults to assist them in their efforts to offer young children the best literacy education possible. Parents and members of the community might come to the classroom to read favorite stories to the class; local businesses might adopt the school or center and offer material and people resources; senior citizens might serve as classroom volunteers, offering a lap and cuddle for one-to-one sharing of a story; and older students might be reading buddies. Bringing parental and community expertise into the classroom does much to help build powerful partnership links between home and classroom and between classroom and community.

These links are critical for all children. They offer young children the opportunity to use spoken and written language to accomplish real-world learning.

Linking Knowledge to Practice

1. With a group of colleagues, plan a workshop for parents on some aspect of young children's language and literacy learning. Write a letter to invite parents to the workshop. List the supplies you will need. List the refreshments. Develop an evaluation form. Create a detailed lesson plan. Offer your workshop to a group of parents.
2. Based on a classroom experience, write a one-page weekly note for parents.
3. Work with a group of colleagues to write a monthly newsletter for your class (the one for which you are reading this book).
4. Write a Dear Teacher question and answer for inclusion in a preschool classroom's newsletter. Make a photocopy for everyone in your college class.
5. Visit a school or public library. Question a librarian about their check-out policy for young children. If this library allows young children to check out only one book per week, write a letter to convince the librarian that this is inappropriate for young children.
6. With a colleague, develop a bookbag around a theme for use by parents of young children.

appendix

Quality Literature
for Young Children

Alphabet Books

Anno, M. (1975). *Anno's alphabet: Adventure in imagination.* New York: Thomas Y. Crowell.

Baker, A. (1995). *Black and white rabbit's ABC.* New York: Kingfisher.

Cohen, I. (1998). *ABC discovery!* New York: Dial Books.

Fujikawa, G. (1974). *A to Z picture book.* New York: Grosset & Dunlap.

Gag, W. (1933). *The ABC bunny.* New York: Coward, McCann & Geoghegan.

Johnson, S. (1995). *Alphabet city.* New York: Penguin Group.

King, D. (1997). *Alphabet book.* New York: DK Publishing.

Krauss, R. (1972). *Good night little ABC.* New York: Scholastic.

Larrick, N. (1965). *First ABC.* New York: Platt & Munk.

Lester, A. (1998). *Alice and Aldo.* Boston: Houghton Mifflin Company.

McDonnell, F. (1997). *Flora McDonnell's ABC.* Cambridge, MA: Candlewick Press.

Pallotta, J. (1998). *The boat alphabet book.* Watertown, MA: Charlesbridge.

Pallotta, J., and Masiello, R. (1991). *The yucky reptile alphabet book.* Watertown, MA: Charlesbridge.

Pallotta, J., and Stewart, E. (1991). *The bird alphabet book.* Watertown, MA: Charlesbridge.

Penny, I. (1998). *Ian Penny's ABC.* New York: Harry N. Abrams.

Schnur, S., and Evans, L. (1997). *Autumn. An alphabet acrostic.* New York: Clarion.

Schnur, S., and Evans, L. (1998). *Spring. An alphabet acrostic.* New York: Clarion.

Seuss, Dr. (1963). *Dr. Seuss' ABC.* New York: Random House.

Shelby, A., and Trivas, I. (1994). *Potluck.* New York: Orchard.

Tobias, T., and Malone, P. (1998). *A world of words. An ABC of quotations.* New York: Lothrop, Lee & Shepard.

Wegmann, W. (1994). *ABC.* New York: Hyperion.

Whitford, P., and Winter, J. (1991). *Eight hands round. A patchwork alphabet.* New York: Harper Collins.

Wildsmith, B. (1963). *Brian Wildsmith's ABC.* New York: Franklin Watts.

Counting Books

Alda, A. (1998). *Arlene Alda's 1 2 3 what do you see?* Berkeley, CA: Tricycle Press.

Anholt, C., & Anholt, L. (1996). *One, two, three, count with me.* New York: Puffin.

Anno, M. (1977). *Anno's counting book.* New York: Thomas Y. Crowell.

Beaton, C. (1999). *One moose, twenty mice.* New York: Barefoot Books.

Carle, E. (1968). *1, 2, 3 to the zoo.* New York: William Collins.

Fujikawa, G. (1977). *Can you count?* New York: Grosset & Dunlap.

Geddes, A. (1996). *Down in the garden counting book.* San Rafael, CA: Cedco.

Giganti, P. (1992). *Each orange had 8 slices. A counting book.* New York: Mulberry.

Hoban, T. (1972). *Count and see.* New York: Macmillan.

Holloway, Z. (1999). *Water babies counting 1, 2, 3.* New York: Scholastic.

Jahn-Clough, L. (1998). *1, 2, 3 yippie.* New York: Houghton Mifflin.

Johnson, S. T. (1998). *City by numbers.* New York: Viking.

Keats, E. J. (1972). *Over in the meadow.* New York: Four Winds Press.

King, D. (1998). *Counting book.* New York: DK Publishing.

Lesser, C. (1999). *Spots: Counting creatures from sky to sea.* Orlando, FL: Harcourt Brace & Company.

Livermore, E. (1973). *One to ten, count again.* Boston: Houghton Mifflin.

Mack, S. (1974). *10 bears in my bed.* New York: Pantheon.

Merriam, E. (1999). *Ten rosy roses.* New York: HarperCollins.

Moore, L. (1956). *My first counting book.* New York: Simon & Schuster.

Morozumi, A. (1999). *One gorilla.* Hong Kong: Sunburst (Farrar, Strauss, & Giroux).

Oxenbury, H. (1968). *Numbers of things.* New York: Franklin Watts.

Potter, B. (1999). *Peter Rabbit's counting book.* New York: Frederick Warne.

Reidy, H. (1999). *How many can you see?* New York: Zero to Ten Ltd.

Saul, C. P. (1998). *Barn cat.* Boston: Little, Brown and Company.

Sierra, J. (1997). *Counting crocodiles.* San Diego, CA: Gulliver Books.

Vischer, P. (1997). *How many veggies?* Nashville, TN: Tommy Nelson.

Wildsmith, B. (1965). *Brian Wildsmith's 1, 2, 3.* New York: Franklin Watts.

Concept Books

Anderson, S. (1988). *Colors.* Bridgeport, CT: Penguin.

Baker, A. (1994). *Brown rabbit's shape book.* New York: Kingfisher.

Beck, J. (1991). *Shoes.* Bothell, WA: The Wright Group.

Berenstain, S., & Berenstain, J. (1968). *Inside, outside, upside down.* New York: Random House.

Bogdaniwicz, B. (1997). *Quiet bear, noisy bear.* Brookfield, CT: Millbrook.

Boone, E. (1986). *It's spring.* Peterkin, NY: Random House.

Brady, P. (1996). *Freight trains.* Mankato, MI: Bridgestone Books.

Byron, B. (1981). *Wheels.* New York: Thomas Y. Crowell.

Cartwright, S. (1973). *Water is wet.* New York: Coward, McCann & Geoghegan.

Cowley, J. (1987). *I'm bigger than you!* Bothell, WA: The Wright Group.

Crews, N. (1995). *One hot summer day.* New York: Greenwillow Books.

Cutting, B., and Cutting, J. (1988). *Wheels.* Bothell, WA: The Wright Group.

Fleming, D. (1992). *Lunch.* New York: Henry Holt and Company.

Garelick, M. (1998). *Who likes it hot?* Greenvale, NY: Mondo.

Hands, H. (1985). *First-look nature books.* New York: Grosset & Dunlap.

Hill, E. (1985). *Spot at play.* New York: Putnam.

Hoban, T. (1972). *Push, pull, empty, full.* New York: Macmillan.

Hoban, T. (1976). *Big ones, little ones.* New York: Greenwillow.

Hoban, T. (1997). *Is it larger? Is it smaller?* New York: Mulberry.

Howard, A. (1996). *When I was five.* San Diego, CA: Harcourt, Brace & Company.

Kessler, E., & Kessler, L. (1966). *Are you square?* New York: Doubleday.

Lobban, J. (1991). *Paddington's opposites.* New York: Viking.

Lousada, S. (1995). *Playskool: My nose, my toes.* New York: Dutton.

Murphy, C. (1992). *My first book of shapes.* New York: Scholastic.

Oxenbury, H. (1986). *I can.* New York: Random House.

Pienkowski, J. (1975). *Shapes.* New York: Harvey House.

Provensen, A., & Provensen, M. (1967). *What is color?* New York: Golden Press.

Robbins, K. (1983). *Tools.* New York: Four Winds Press.

Rotner, S., and Olivo, R. (1995). *Close, closer, closest.* New York: Atheneum.

Round, G. (1976). *Top and bottom.* New York: Grosset & Dunlap.

Seuss, Dr. (1996). *My many colored days.* New York: Alfred A. Knopf.

Steffof, R. (1997). *Snake.* Tarrytown, NY: Marshall Cavendish.

Tefft, C. P., Mitchell, C. C., and Porter, G. R. (1997). *Football.* Bothell, WA: The Wright Group.

Williams, R. (1993). *Tracks.* Bothell, WA: The Wright Group.

Williams, R. (1998). *The nine days of camping.* Bothell, WA: The Wright Group.

Williams, R. (1998). *Whose shoes?* Bothell, WA: The Wright Group.

Young, C. (1993). *The zoo.* Bothell, WA: The Wright Group.

Informational Books

Aardema, V. (1983). *Bringing the rain to Kapiti.* New York: Pied Piper.

Ajmera, M., and Versola, A. R. (1997). *Children from Australia to Zimbabwe.* Watertown, MA: Charlesbridge.

Asch, F. (1985). *Bear shadow.* Englewood Cliffs, NJ: Prentice Hall.

Barton, B. (1979). *Wheels.* New York: Crowell.

Bessar, M. (1967). *The cat book.* New York: Holiday House.

Bonners, S. (1978). *Panda.* New York: Delacorte.

Bridwell, N. (1999). *Big book of things to know.* New York: Scholastic.

Carrick, D. (1985). *Milk.* New York: Greenwillow.

Cole, J. (1983). *Cars and how they go.* New York: Thomas Y. Crowell.

Cole, J. (1987). *The magic school bus inside the earth.* New York: Scholastic.

Gackenbach, D. (1984). *Poppy the panda.* New York: Clarion.

Ganeri, A. (1994). *I wonder why the wind blows and other questions about our planet.* New York: Kingfisher.

Gentner, N. L. (1993). *Bear facts.* Bothell, WA: The Wright Group.

Gershator, D., and Gershator, P. (1998). *Bread is for eating.* New York: Henry Holt.

Gibbons, G. (1984). *Tunnels.* New York: Holiday House.

Graham, I. (1998). *The best book of spaceships.* New York: Kingfisher.

Hutchins, R. (1960). *The amazing seeds.* New York: Dodd, Mead & Co.

Jones, G. (1995). *My first book of how things are made.* New York: Scholastic.

Kettlekamp, L. (1959). *Kites.* New York: William Morrow & Co.

Krauss, R. (1945). *The carrot seed.* New York: Harper & Row.

Lane, M. (1981). *The squirrel.* New York: Dial.

LeSieg, T. (1961). *Ten apples up on top.* New York: Beginner Books.

Lowrey, J. (1971). *Six silver spoons.* New York: Harper & Row.

Maestro, B., & DelVecchio, E. (1983). *Big city port.* New York: E. P. Dutton.

May, J. (1971). *Why people are different colors.* New York: Holiday House.

Miles, M. (1969). *Apricot ABC.* Boston: Little, Brown & Co. Inc.

Monjo, F. N. (1969). *The drinking gourd.* New York: Harper & Row.

Morris, N. (1996). *Deserts.* New York: Crabtree.

Nathan, C., and McCourt, L. (1999). *The long and short of it.* Moraga, CA: Bridgewater Press.

Norris, L., & Smith, H. (1979). *An oak tree and a journey begins.* New York: Crown Publishers.

O'Brian, W. (1968). *Ear book.* New York: Random House.

Parker, S. (1989). *Seashore.* New York: Alfred A. Knopf.

Rayston, A. (1992). *Trains.* New York: Little Simon.

Rockwell, A. (1972). *Machines.* New York: Macmillan.

Scary, R. (1989). *All about cars.* New York: Golden Book.

Selsam, M. (1966). *When an animal grows.* New York: Harper & Row.

Selsam, M. (1973). *How kittens grow.* New York: Four Winds Press.

Skaar, G. (1966). *All about dogs.* New York: Young Scott Books.

Spier, P. (1980). *People.* New York: Doubleday & Co.

Swallow, S. (1973). *Cars, trucks and trains.* New York: Grosset & Dunlap.

Taylor, B. (1995). *I wonder why zippers have teeth and other questions about inventions.* New York: Kingfisher.

Trussel-Cullen, A. (1996). *This is the seed.* Glenview, IL: Good Year Books.

While, R. (1972). *All kinds of trains.* New York: Grosset & Dunlap.

White, F. (1969). *Your friend the tree.* New York: Alfred A. Knopf.

Wildsmith, B. (1971). *The owl and the woodpecker.* Oxford, England: Oxford University Press.

Young, R. (1990). *A trip to Mars.* New York: Orchard Books.

Multicultural Books—Folk Tales

Belafonte, H., and Burgess, L. (1999). *Island in the sun.* New York: Dial.

Bunting, E. (1999). *I have an olive tree.* New York: Harper Collins.

Chang, M., and Chang, R. (1999). *Da Wei's treasure.* New York: Margaret McElderry Books.

Echewa, T. O. (1999). *The magic tree.* New York: Morrow Junior Books.

Ehlert, L. (1997). *Cuckoo.* San Diego, CA: Harcourt, Brace & Company.

Gill, J. (1999). *Basket weaver and catches many mice.* New York: Alfred A. Knopf.

Grifalconi, A. (1986). *The village of round and square houses.* Boston: Little, Brown and Company.

Ho, M. (1996). *Hush.* New York: Orchard.

Lewin, T. (1999). *Nilo and the tortoise.* New York: Scholastic.

Look, L. (1999). *Love as strong as ginger.* New York: Simon & Schuster.

Madrigal, A. H. (1999). *Erandi's braids.* New York: Putnam.

McCain, B. R. (1998). *Grandmother's dreamcatcher.* Morton Grove, IL: Albert Whitman & Company.

Mitchell, B., and Doney, T. W. (1996). *Red bird.* New York: Lothrop, Lee & Shepard.

Musgrove, M. (1976). *Ashanti to Zulu: African traditions.* New York: Dial.

Oppenheim, S. L. (1999). *Yanni Rubbish.* Honesdale, PA: Boyds Mills Press.

Raczek, L. T. (1999). *Rainy's powwow.* Flagstaff, AZ: Rising Moon.

Ringgold, F. (1999). *The invisible princess.* New York: Crown.

Santiago, C. (1998). *Home to medicine mountain.* San Francisco: Children's Book Press.

Say, A. (1999). *Tea with milk.* Boston: Houghton Mifflin Company.

Shange, N. (1997). *White wash.* New York: Walker and Company.

Tarpley, N. A. (1998). *I love my hair!* Boston: Little, Brown and Company.

Wyeth, S. D. (1998). *Something beautiful.* New York: Bantam Doubleday Dell.

Young, E. (1997). *Mouse match: A Chinese folktale.* San Diego, CA: Silver Whistle/Harcourt, Brace & Company.

Picture Storybooks

Ahlberg, J., and Ahlberg, A. (1986). *Each peach pear plum.* New York: Puffin Books.

Anno, M. (1978). *Anno's journey.* New York: Philomel Books.

Appleby, E. (1984). *The three billy-goats gruff: A Norwegian folktale.* New York: Scholastic.

Aruego, J. (1988). *Look what I can do.* New York: Aladdin.

Aruego, J., & Dewey, A. (1992). *Raffi: Five little ducks.* New York: Crown Publishers.

Barret, J. (1970). *Animals should definitely now wear clothing.* New York: Antheneum.

Barton, B. (1995). *Buzz buzz buzz.* New York: Aladdin.

Berenstain, S., & Berenstain, J. (1966). *The bear's picnic.* New York: Random House.

Berger, B. (1997). *A lot of otters.* New York: Philomel.

Brown, M. (1972). *The runaway bunny.* New York: Harper & Row.

Brown, M. W. (1957). *Goodnight moon.* New York: Harper & Row.

Browne, A. (1997). *Willy the dreamer.* Cambridge, MA: Candlewick Press.

Carle, E. (1969). *The very hungry caterpillar.* New York: Philomel.

Carle, E. (1971). *The grouchy ladybug.* New York: Crowell.

Carle, E. (1971). *Do you want to be my friend?* New York: Crowell.

Cohen, M. (1967). *Will I have a friend?* New York: Collier Books.

Daniel, A. (1990). *The eensy weensy spider.* New York: The Wright Group.

DePaola, T. (1975). *Strega Nona: An old tale.* Englewood Cliffs, NJ: Prentice Hall.

Flack, M. (1932). *Ask Mr. Bear.* New York: Macmillan.

Fleming, D. (1991). *In the tall, tall grass.* New York: Holt, Rinehart & Winston.

Fleming, D. (1997). *A time to sleep.* New York: Henry Holt.

Gag, W. (1938). *Millions of cats.* New York: Coward-McCann.

Galdone, P. (1975). *The little red hen.* New York: Scholastic.

Glazer, T., and Barber, R. (1995). *On top of spaghetti.* Glenview, IL: Good Year Books.

Hoban, R. (1969). *Best friends for Frances.* New York: Harper & Row.

Hoban, T. (1971). *Look again.* New York: Macmillan.

Kasza, K. (1995). *Grandpa Toad's secrets.* New York: G. P. Putnam Sons.

Keats, E. J. (1962). *The snowy day.* New York: Viking.

Keats, E. J. (1967). *Peter's chair.* New York: Harper & Row.

Kellogg, S. (1971). *Can I keep him?* New York: Dial Press.

Kennedy, J., and Hague, M. (1997). *The teddy bears' picnic.* New York: Henry Holt.

Kraus, R. (1971). *Leo the late bloomer.* New York: Windmill Books.

Langstaff, J. (1974). *Oh, a-hunting we will go.* Boston: Houghton Mifflin Company.

Lionni, L. (1966). *Frederick.* New York: Pantheon.

Lionni, L. (1973). *Swimmy.* New York: Random House.

Mayer, M. (1987). *There's an alligator under my bed.* New York: Dial.

McCloskey, R. (1941). *Make way for ducklings.* New York: Viking.

McCloskey, R. (1948). *Blueberries for Sal.* New York: Penguin.

McCloskey, R. (1952). *One morning in Maine.* New York: Viking Press.

McCloskey, R. (1957). *Time of wonder.* New York: Viking Press.

McGeorge, C. W., and Whyte, M. (1999). *Boomer's big surprise.* San Francisco: Chronicle Books.

Melser, J., Cowley, J., and Bailey, M. (1998). *The big toe*. Bothell, WA: The Wright Group.

Oran, H., and Varley, S. (1998). *Princess Chamomile gets her way*. New York: Dutton.

Otey, M. (1990). *Daddy has a pair of striped shorts*. New York: Farrar, Strauss & Giroux.

Pfister, M. (1997). *Mils and the magical stones*. New York: North-South Books.

Piper, W. (1954). *The little engine that could*. New York: Platt & Munk.

Reiser, L. (1994). *The surprise family*. New York: Greenwillow Books.

Rey, H. A. (1952). *Curious George rides a bike*. Boston: Houghton Mifflin.

Riley, L. (1997). *Mouse mess*. New York: Blue Sky Press/Scholastic.

Scheer, J. (1964). *Rain makes applesauce*. New York: Holiday House.

Sendak, M. (1963). *Where the wild things are*. New York: Harper & Row.

Seuss, Dr. (1940). *Horton hatches the egg*. New York: Random House.

Seuss, Dr. (1957). *The cat in the hat*. New York: Random House.

Shannon, D. (1999). *David goes to school*. New York: The Blue Sky Press.

Shaw, C. (1947). *It looked like spilt milk*. New York: Harper.

Slobodkina, E. (1947). *Caps for sale*. Reading, MA: Addison-Wesley.

Steig, W. (1969). *Sylvester and the magic pebble*. New York: Simon & Schuster.

Steig, W. (1998). *Pete's a pizza*. New York: Harper Collins.

Stevens, J. (1987). *The three billy goats gruff*. Orlando, FL: Harcourt, Brace, & Company.

Tafuri, N. (1991). *Have you seen my duckling?* New York: Mulberry.

Udry, J. (1961). *Let's be enemies*. New York: Harper & Row.

Viorst, J. (1972). *Alexander and the terrible, horrible, no-good, very bad day*. New York: Atheneum.

Waber, B. (1972). *Ira sleeps over*. Boston: Houghton Mifflin Company.

Wells, R. (1973). *Noisy Nora*. New York: Dial.

Young, E. (1989). *Lon Po Po: A red riding hood story from China*. New York: Philomel Books.

Zelinsky, P. O. (1990). *The wheels on the bus*. New York: Dutton Children's Books.

Predictable Books

Anderson, S. (1988). *Colors*. Bridgeport, CT: Penguin.

Arno, E. (1970). *The gingerbread man*. New York: Scholastic.

Aruego, J., & Dewey, A. (1989). *Five little ducks*. New York: Crown Publishers.

Aylesworth, J. (1995). *Old black fly*. New York: Henry Holt.

Baker, A. (1994). *Brown rabbit's shape book*. New York: Kingfisher.

Bonnie, R. (1961). *I know an old lady*. New York: Scholastic.

Brown, M. (1957). *The three billy goats gruff*. New York: Harcourt Brace Jovanovich.

Carle, E. (1969). *The very hungry caterpillar*. Cleveland, OH: Collins-World.

Carle, E. (1987). *Have you seen my cat?* New York: Aladdin.

Cameron, P. (1961). *"I can't," said the ant*. New York: Coward-McCann.

Chistelow, E. (1989). *Five little monkeys jumping on the bed*. New York: Houghton Mifflin Company.

Cowley, J. (1996). *Where are you going, Aja Rose?* Bothell, WA: The Wright Group.

Cowley, J. (1998). *The red rose*. Bothell, WA: The Wright Group.

Cowley, J. (1998). *Oh, jump in a sack*. Bothell, WA: The Wright Group.

Daniel, A., and Daniel, L. (1990). *Down by the bay*. Bothell, WA: The Wright Group.

Daniel, A., and Daniel, L. (1990). *She'll be comin' round the mountain*. Bothell, WA: The Wright Group.

Daniel, A., and Daniel, L. (1992). *The ants go marching.* Bothell, WA: The Wright Group.

Daniel, A., and Daniel, L. (1992). *Old MacDonald had a farm.* Bothell, WA: The Wright Group.

Daniel, A., and Daniel, L. (1993). *Goober peas.* Bothell, WA: The Wright Group.

Daniel, A., and Daniel, L. (1993). *This old man.* Bothell, WA: The Wright Group.

Daniel, A., and Daniel, L. (1993). *I've been working on the railroad.* Bothell, WA: The Wright Group.

Daniel, A., and Daniel, L. (1995). *Over the meadow.* Bothell, WA: The Wright Group.

DePaola, T. (1978). *Pancakes for breakfast.* New York: Harcourt Brace Jovanovich.

Eastman, P. D. (1960). *Are you my mother?* New York: Random House.

Emberly, B. (1967). *Drummer Hoff.* Englewood Cliffs, NJ: Prentice Hall.

Feely, J. (1999). *Making lunch.* Littleton, MA: Sundance.

Galdone, P. (1970). *The three little pigs.* New York: Seabury Press.

Galdone, P. (1972). *The three bears.* New York: Scholastic.

Galdone, P. (1975). *Henny penny.* New York: Houghton Mifflin.

Galdone, P. (1975). *The gingerbread boy.* New York: Houghton Mifflin.

Galdone, P. (1975). *The little red hen.* New York: Scholastic.

Guilfoile, E. (1962). *The house that Jack built.* New York: Holt, Rinehart & Winston.

Ho, M. (1996). *Hush.* New York: Orchard.

Hoberman, M. A. (1978). *A house is a house for me.* New York: Viking.

Hutchins, P. (1972). *Goodnight, owl!* New York: Macmillan.

Johnson, C. (1959). *Harold and the purple crayon.* New York: Harper & Row.

Keats, E. J. (1972). *Over in the meadow.* New York: Four Winds.

Kent, J. (1971). *The fat cat.* New York: Scholastic.

Kraus, R. (1970). *Whose mouse are you?* New York: Macmillan.

Lanczak-Williams, R. (1994). *Who will help?* Cypress, CA: Creative Teaching Press.

Lewison, W. C. (1992). *Buzz said the bee.* New York: Scholastic.

Lobel, A. (1979). *A treeful of pigs.* New York: Greenwillow.

Mahy, M. (1986). *When the king rides by.* Greenvale, NY: Mondo Publishing.

Martin, B. (1967). *Brown bear, brown bear, what do you see?* New York: Holt, Rinehart and Winston.

Mayer, M. (1975). *What do you do with a kangaroo?* New York: Scholastic.

McCracken, R., and McCracken, M. (1989). *Teddy bear, teddy bear.* Winnipeg, Canada: Peguis Publishers.

Melser, J., & Cowley, J. (1980). *In a dark, dark wood.* Bothwell, WA: New Zealand: The Wright Group.

Piper, W. (1954). *The little engine that could.* New York: Platt & Munk.

Robart, R. (1986). *The cake that Mack ate.* Boston: Little, Brown and Company.

Sendak, M. (1962). *Chicken soup with rice.* New York: Harper & Row.

Seuss, Dr. (1940). *Horton hatches an egg.* New York: Random House.

Seuss, Dr. (1960). *Green eggs and ham.* New York: Random House.

Slobodkina, E. (1947). *Caps for sale.* Glenview, IL: Addison-Wesley Publishing Co.

Spier, P. (1971). *Gobble, growl, grunt.* Garden City, NJ: Doubleday & Co.

Stott, D. (1990). *Too much.* New York: Dutton.

Westcott, N. (1980). *I know an old lady who swallowed a fly.* Boston: Little, Brown & Co.

Literature for Hispanic Children: Preschool and Kindergarten Level

by Sara Hudelson

Bilingual

Ada, A. F. (1995). *Mediopollito/Half-chicken.* New York: Delacorte Doubleday.

Ada, A. F. (1997). *Gathering the sun: An alphabet in Spanish and English.* New York: Lothrop Lee.

Delacre, L. (1989). *Arroz con leche: Popular songs and Rhymes from Latin America.* New York: Scholastic.

Emberley, R. (1990). *Taking a walk: Caminando.* Boston, MA: Little Brown.

Mora, P. (1994). *Listen to the desert/Oye al desierto.* New York: Houghton Mifflin.

Reed, L. (1995). *Pedro, his perro and the alphabet sombrero.* New York: Hyperion.

Reiser, L. (1993). *Margaret and Margarita/Margarita y Margaret.* New York: Greenwillow.

Rodriguez, G. (1994). *Green corn tamales/Tamales de elote.* Tucson, AZ: Hispanic Book Distributors.

Roe, E. (1991). *Con mi hermano/With my brother.* New York: Bradbury Press.

Stevens, J. (1995). *Carlos and the cornfield/Carlos y la milpa de maiz.* Flagstaff, AZ: Northland Publishing.

Spanish Language

Carle, E. (1994). *La oruga muy hambrienta.* New York: Philomel Books.

Guarino, D. (1993). *Tu mama es una llama?* New York: Scholastic.

Hill, E. (1995). *Spot hace un pastel.* New York: G. P. Putnam & Sons.

Kraus, R. (1980). *De quien eres, ratoncito?* New York: Scholastic.

Tafuri, N. (1991). *Has visto a mi patito?* New York: Scholastic.

English Language

Brown, T. (1986). *Hello, amigos.* New York: Henry Holt.

Cooper, M., & Gordon, G. (1996). *Anthony Reynoso: Born to rope.* New York: Clarion.

Dooley, N. (1991). *Everybody cooks rice.* Minneapolis, MN: Carolhoda.

Dorros, A. (1991). *Abuela.* New York: Dutton.

Ets, M. H. (1963). *Gilberto and the wind.* New York: Viking.

Lowell, S. (1992). *The three little javelinas.* Flagstaff, AZ: Northland Publishing.

Palacios, A. (1993). *A Christmas surprise.* New Jersey: Bridgewater Books.

Soto, G. (1987). *Too many tamales.* New York: Puffin.

Wing, N. (1996). *Jalepeno bagels.* New York: Atheneum.

Caldecott Medal Books

Fish, H. D. (1938). *Animals of the bible.* New York: Harper Collins.

Handforth, T. (1939). *Mei Li.* New York: Doubleday.

Parin D'Aulaire, I., & Parin D'Aulaire, E. (1940). *Abraham Lincoln.* New York: Doubleday.

Lawson, R. (1941). *They were strong and good.* New York: Viking.

McCloskey, R. (1942). *Make way for ducklings.* New York: Viking.

Burton, V. L. (1943). *The little house.* Boston: Houghton Mifflin.

Thurger, J. (1944). *Many moons.* San Diego, CA: Harcourt, Brace & Co.

Field, R. (1945). *Prayer for a child.* Old Tappan, NJ: Macmillan.

Petersham, M. (1946). *The rooster crows.* Old Tappan, NJ: Macmillan.

MacDonald, G. (1947). *The little island.* New York: Doubleday.

Tresselt, A. (1948). *White snow, bright snow.* New York: Lothrop.

Hader, B., & Hader, E. (1949). *The big snow.* Old Tappan, NJ: Macmillan.

Politi, L. (1950). *Song of the swallows.* Old Tappan, NJ: Macmillan.

Milhous, K. (1951). *The egg tree.* Old Tappan, NJ: Simon & Schuster.

Will, N. (1952). *Finders keepers.* San Diego, CA: Harcourt, Brace & Co.

Ward, L. (1953). *The biggest bear.* Boston: Houghton Mifflin.

Bemelmans, L. (1954). *Madeline's rescue.* New York: Viking.

Perrault, C., & Brown, M. (1955). *Cinderella, or the little glass slipper.* New York: Scribner's.

Langstaff, J. (1956). *Frog went a-courtin'.* San Diego, CA: Harcourt, Brace & Co.

Udry, M. (1957). *A tree is nice.* New York: Harper Collins.

McCloskey, R. (1958). *Time of wonder.* New York: Viking.

Chaucer, G. (1959). *Chanticleer and the fox.* New York: Harper Collins.

Ets, M. H., & Labastida, A. (1960). *Nine days to Christmas.* New York: Viking.

Robbins, R. (1961). *Baboushka and the three kings.* Boston: Houghton Mifflin.

Brown, M. (1962). *Once a mouse. . . .* Old Tappan, NJ: Simon & Schuster.

Keats, E. J. (1963). *The snowy day.* New York: Viking.

Sendak, M. (1964). *Where the wild things are.* New York: Harper Collins.

de Regniers, B. S. (1965). *May I bring a friend?* Old Tappan, NJ: Simon & Schuster.

Leodhas, S. N. (1966). *Always room for one more.* San Diego, CA: Holt.

Ness, E. (1967). *Sam, bangs and moonshine.* San Diego, CA: Holt.

Emberley, B. (1968). *Drummer Hoff.* Upper Saddle River, NJ: Prentice Hall.

Ransome, A. (1969). *The fool of the world and the flying ship.* New York: Farrar.

Steig, W. (1970). *Sylvester and the magic pebble.* Old Tappan, NJ: Simon & Schuster.

Haley, G. E. (1971). *A story, a story.* New York: Antheneum.

Hogrogian, N. (1972). *One fine day.* Old Tappan, NJ: Macmillan.

Mosel, A. (1973). *The funny little woman.* New York: Dutton.

Zemach, M. (1974). *Duffy and the devil.* New York: Farrar.

McDermott, G. (1975). *Arrow to the sun.* New York: Viking.

Aardema, V. (1976). *Why mosquitoes buzz in people's ears.* New York: Dial.

Musgrove, M. (1977). *Ashanti to Zulu: African traditions.* New York: Dial.

Spier, P. (1978). *Noah's ark.* New York: Doubleday.

Goble, P. (1979). *The girl who loved wild horses.* Old Tappan, NJ: Simon & Schuster.

Hall, D. (1980). *Ox-cart man.* New York: Viking.

Lobel, A. (1981). *Fables.* New York: Harper Collins.

Van Allsburg, C. (1982). *Jumanji.* Boston: Houghton Mifflin.

Cendrars, B. (1983). *Shadow.* New York: Scribner's.

Bleriot, L. (1984). *The glorious flight: Across the channel.* New York: Viking.

Hodges, M. (1985). *St. George and the dragon.* New York: Little Brown & Company.

Van Allsburg, C. (1986). *The polar express.* Boston: Houghton Mifflin.

Yorinks, A. (1987). *Hey, Al!* New York: Farrar, Strauss & Giroux.

Yolen, J. (1988). *Owl moon.* New York: Putnam.

Ackerman, K. (1989). *Song and dance man.* New York: Knopf.

Po, L. P. (1990). *A red riding-hood story.* New York: Putnam.

Macaulay, D. (1991). *Black and white.* Boston: Houghton Mifflin.

Wiesner, D. (1992). *Tuesday.* Boston: Houghton Mifflin.

McCully, E. A. (1993). *Mirette on the high wire.* New York: Putnam.

Say, A. (1994). *Grandfather's journey.* Boston: Houghton Mifflin.

Bunting, E. (1995). *Smoky night.* San Diego, CA: Harcourt, Brace & Co.

Rathman, P. (1996). *Officer Buckle and Gloria.* New York: Putnam.

Wisniewski, D. (1997). *Golem.* Boston: Houghton Mifflin.

Zelinsky, P. O. (1998). *Rapunzel.* New York: Dutton.

Martin, J. B. (1999). *Snowflake Bentley.* Boston: Houghton Mifflin.

Taback, S. (2000). *Joseph had a little overcoat.* New York: Viking.

For updates, see http://www.mgprogeny.com/progeny/calmedal.html

Internet Resources for Children's Book Authors, Illustrators, and Storytellers

Web Sites

African-American Images
http://www.scils.rutgers.edu/special/kay/afro.html

The Annual Digital Storytelling Festival
www.dstory.com

Australian Storytelling Guild (NSW) Inc.
www.home.aone.net.au/stories/

Books for Children and More: An Editor's Site
http://www.users.interport.net/~hdu/

Children's Book Council
http://www.cbcbooks.org/index.html

Children's Literature Web Guide
http://www.ucalgary.ca/-dkbrown/index.html

Electronic Resources for Youth Services
http://www.ccn.cs.dal.ca/~aa331/childlit.html

Internet Public Library—Youth Division
http://ipl.sils.umich.edu/youth

Multicultural Publishing and Education Council
http://www.qulknet.com/mbt/mpec/mpec.html

The Storytelling Home Page
members.aol.com/storypage

The Storytelling Ring
www.tiac.net/users/papajoe/ring.htm

Vandergrift's Children's Literature Page
http://www.scils.rutgers.edu/special/kay/childlit.html

Storytelling Resources

Bailey, C. S., Lewis, C. M. (1965). *Favorites stories for the children's hour.* New York: Platt & Munk Publishers.

Baltuck, N. (1995). *Apples from heaven: Multicultural folk tales about stories and storytellers.* North Haven, CT: Shoe String Press.

Bryant, A. (1952). *Stories to tell boys and girls.* Grand Rapids, MI: Zonderman Publishing House.

Buck, P. S. (1940). *Stories for little children.* New York: The John Day Co.

Hart, M. (1987). *Fold-and-cut stories and fingerplays.* Cathage, IL: Fearon Teacher Aids

Oldfield, M. J. (1973). *Lots more tell and draw stories.* Minneapolis, MN: Creative Storytime Press.

Olsen, M. J. (1969). *More tell and draw stories.* Minneapolis, MN: Creative Storytime Press.

Pellowski, A. (1984). *The story vine: A source book of unusual and easy-to-tell stories from around the world.* New York: Macmillan.

Children's Literature Cited

Alexander, L. (1997). *Mother Goose on the Rio Grande.* Dallas: NTC Publishing Group.

Anderson, S. (1998). *Colors.* Bridgeport, CT: Penguin

Anno, M. (1975). *Anno's alphabet: Adventure in imagination.* New York, NY: Thomas Y. Crowell.

Arno, Ed. (1970). *The Gingerbread Man.* New York, NY: Scholastic.

Aylesworth, J. (1995). *Old black fly.* New York, NY: Henry Holt.

Azarian, M. (1981). *A farmer's alphabet.* Lincoln, MA: Godine.

Baker, A. (1994). *Brown rabbit's shape book.* New York, NY: Kingfisher.

Baker, A. (1994). *Black and white rabbit's ABC.* New York, NY: Kingfisher.

Berenstain, S., & Berenstain J. (1974). *Berenstain bear's new baby.* New York: Random House.

Brown, J. (1964). *Flat Stanley.* New York: HarperCollins Children's Books.

Caines, J. (1977). *Daddy.* New York: Harper & Row.

Carle, E. (1984). *The very busy spider.* New York: Philomel Books.

Carle, E. (1969). *The very hungry caterpillar.* New York: Philomel Books.

Carlson, A. (1990). *Family questions.* New Brunswick, NJ: Transaction.

Carter, N. (1991). *Where's my fuzzy blanket?* New York: Scholastic, Inc.

Cohen, I. (1998). *ABC discovery!* New York, NY: Dial Books.

Crew, D. (1980). *Truck.* New York, NY: Greenwillow.

Crews, D. (1991). *Bigmama's.* New York, NY: Greenwillow.

Cuyler, M. (2000). *ROADSIGNS: A harey race with a tortoise.* Delray Beach, FL: Winslow Press.

Delacre, L. (1989). *Arroz con leche: Popular songs from Latin American.* New York: Scholastic, Inc.

dePaola, T. (1974). *Charlie needs a new cloak.* New York: Prentice-Hall.

dePaola, T. (1978). *The popcorn book.* New York: Holiday House.

dePaola, T. (1977). *The quicksand book.* New York: Holiday House.

dePaola, T. (1985). *Tomie dePaola's Mother Goose.* New York: Putnam, G. S. Sons.

Dodds, S. (1993). *Grandpa Bud.* Cambridge, MA: Candlewick Press.

Dorros, A. (1991). *Abuela.* New York: Dutton.

Fleming, D. (1993). *In the small, small pond.* New York: Henry Holt.

Fleming, D. (1991). *In the tall, tall grass.* New York: Henry Holt.

Forman, M. (1987). *Ben's baby.* New York: Harper & Row.

Fujikawa, G. (1974). *A to Z picture book.* New York, NY Grosset & Dunlap.

Gag, W. (1933). *The ABC bunny.* New York: Coward-McCann, Inc.

Galdone, P. (1970). *The three little pigs.* New York: Clarion

Galdone, P. (1972). *The three bears.* New York: Clarion.

Galdone, P. (1973). *The three billy goats gruff.* New York: Clarion.

Garza, C. L. (1990). *Family pictures/Cuadros de familia.* New York: Children's Book Press.

Gibbons, G. (1982). *The tool book.* New York: Holiday House.

Graham, I. (1998). *The best book of spaceships.* New York, NY: Kingfisher.

Grime, N. (1995). *C is for City.*

Grimm, J. (1983). *Little Red Riding Hood.* New York: Holiday House.

Hayes, S. (1988). *Eat up Gemma.* New York: Lothrup, Lee, & Shepard.

Henderson, K., & Eachus, J. (1992). *In the middle of the night.* New York: Bantam Books.

Hoban, R. (1960). *Bedtime for Frances.* New York: Harper & Row.

Hoban, R. (1960). *Bread and jam for Frances.* New York: Harper & Row.

Hoban, T. (1970). *Shapes and things.* New York: Macmillan Co.

Hoban, T. (1972). *Count and see.* New York: Macmillan Co.

Hoban, T. (1974). *Circles, triangles, and squares.* New York: Macmillan Co.

Hoban, T. (1976). *Big ones, little ones.* New York: Greenwillow Books.

Hoban, T. (1978). *Is it red? Is it yellow? Is it blue?* New York: Greenwillow Books

Hoban, T. (1985). *What's that?* New York: Greenwillow Books.

Hoffman, M. (1991). *Amazing Grace.* New York: Dail Books for Young Readers

Holloway, Z. (1999). *Water babies counting 1, 2, 3.* New York, NY: Scholastic.

Johnson, A. (1989). *Tell me a story, Momma.* New York: Bantam Books.

Johnson, S. (1995). *Alphabet city.* New York, NY: Viking Penguin Publishers.

Joose, B. (1991). *Mama, do you love me?* New York: Chronicle Books.

Keats, E. J. (1964). *A letter to Amy.* New York: Harper & Row Publishers.

Keats, E. J. (1967). *Peter's chair.* New York: Harper & Row Publishers.

Keats, E. J. (1962). *The snowy day.* New York: Viking Press, Inc.

Keats, E. J. 1969). *Goggles.* New York: Macmillan.

Keats, E. J. (19). *Louie.* New York: Greenwillow Press.

Keats, E. J. (1964). *Whistle for Willie.* New York: Viking Press, Inc.

Keller, H. (1994). *Geraldine's baby brother.* New York: Greenwillow.

King, D. (1997). *Alphabet book.* New York, NY: DK Publishing.

Krauss, R. (1945). *The carrot seed.* New York, NY: Scholastic.

Kunhardt, D. (1940). *Pat the bunny.* New York: Golden Press.

Lanczak-Williams R. (1994). *Who will help?* Cypress, Ca: Creative Teaching Press.

Larrick, N. (1965). *First ABC.* New York, NY: Platt & Munk.

Lester, A. (1998). *Alice and Aldo.* Boston, MA: Houghton Mifflin Company.

Lionni, L. (1962). *Inch by inch.* New York: Mulberry.

Lobel, A. (1986). *The Random House book of Mother Goose.* New York: Random House.

Lowell, S. (1992). *The three little javelina.* Arizona: Northland Publishing.

Martin, B., Jr. (1967). *Brown bear, brown bear, what do you see?* New York: Holt.

Martin, B., Jr. (1991). *Polar bear, polar bear, what do you hear?* New York: Holt.

McCloskey, R. (1948). *Blueberries for Sal.* New York: Viking Press.

McDonnell, F. (1997). *Flora McDonnell's ABC.* Cambridge, MA: Candlewick Press.

Mora, P. (2000). *One, two, three/Uno dos tres.* New York: Houghton Mifflin.

Orozco, J. (1997). *Diez Deditos: Other play rhymes and action songs from Latin America.* New York: Dutton Children's Books.

Paley, V. (1984). *Boys and girls: Superheroes in the doll corner.* Chicago: University of Chicago Press.

Paley, V. (1990). *The boy who would be a helicopter.* Cambridge, MA: Harvard University Press.

Pallotta, J. (1998). *The boat alphabet book.* Watertown, MA: Charlesbridge.

Pallotta, J., and Masiello, R. (1991). *The yucky reptile alphabet book.* Watertown, MA: Charlesbridge.

Pallotta, J., and Stewart, E. (1991). *The bird alphabet book.* Watertown, MA: Charlesbridge.

Parish, P. (1963). *Amelia Bedelia.* New York: Harper & Row.

Penny, I. (1998). *Ian Penny's ABC.* New York, NY: Harry N. Abrams.

Ringgold, F. (1991). *Tar beach.* Boston, MA: Crown.

Rockwell, A., & Rockwell, H. (1979). *The supermarket.* New York: Macmillan Co.

Say, A. (1991). *Tree of cranes.* Boston, MA: Houghton Mifflin.

Scarry, R. (1964). *Best Mother Goose ever.* Racine, Wisconsin: Western Publishing Co., Inc.

Scheer, J. (1964). *Rain makes applesauce.* New York: Holiday House, Inc.

Schlein, M. (1974). *What's wrong with being a skunk?* New York: Four Winds Press.

Schon, I. (1994). *Tito, tito: Rimas, adivinanzas, y juegos infantiles.* Leon: Editorial Everest.

Schnur, S., and Evans, L. (1998). *Spring. An alphabet acrostic.* New York, NY: Clarion.

Schnur, S., and Evans, L. (1997). *Autumn. An alphabet acrostic.* New York, NY: Clarion.

Scott, A. (1972). *On Mother's lap.* New York: Clarion.

Selsam, M. (1966). *Benny's animals and how he put them in order.* New York: Harper & Row, Inc.

Selsam, M. (1973). *How kittens grow.* New York: Four Winds Press.

Selsam, M., & Hunt, J. (1974). *A first look at insects.* New York: Walker.

Sendak, M. (1962). *Chicken soup with rice.* New York: Harper & Row.

Sendak, M. (1996). *Donde viven los mostruos.* New York: HarperCollins.

Seuss, Dr. (1963). *Dr. Seuss' ABC.* New York, NY: Random House.

Shelby, A., and Trivas, I. (1994). *Potluck.* New York, NY: Orchard.

Shulevitz, U. (1974). *Dawn.* New York: Farrar, Straus, & Giroux.

Slobodkina, E. (1947). *Caps for sale.* New York: Addison.

Spier, P. (1972). *Fast-slow high-low.* New York: Doubleday & Co.

Tabor, N. (1993). *Albertina Anda Arriba.* Watertown, MA: Charlesbridge Publishing Company, Inc.

Tafolla, C. (1992). *Sonnets to human beings.* Santa Monica, CA: Lalo Press.

Takeshita, F. (1988). *The park bench.* New York: Kane/Miller

Tobias, T., and Malone, P. (1998). *A world of words. An ABC of quotations.* New York, NY: Lothrop, Lee & Shepard.

Tolstoy, A. (1968). *The great enormous turnip.* New York: Watts, Franklin, Inc.

Vance, E. G. (1974). *The everything book: A treasury of things for children to make and do.* New York, New York: Golden Press.

Ward, C. (1988). *Cookie's week.* New York, NY: Putman & Grossett.

Wagman, W. (1994). *ABC book.* New York, NY: Hyperion.

Wells, R. (1997). *Bunny cakes.* New York, NY: Dial Books for Young Readers.

Whitford, P., and Winter, J. (1991). *Eight hands round. A patchwork alphabet.* New York, NY: Harper Collins.

Wildsmith, B. (1963). *Brian Wildsmith's ABC.* New York, NY: Franklin Watts, Inc.

Young, E. (1989). *Lon Po Po: A red-riding hood story from China.* New York: Putnam

References

Adams, M. (1990). *Beginning to read: Thinking and learning about print.* Cambridge, MA: MIT Press.

Adams, M., Foorman, B., Lundberg, I., & Beeler, T. (1998). The elusive phoneme: Why phonemic awareness is so important and how to help children develop it. *American Educator, 21*(1&2), 18–29.

Afflerbach, P., Moni, K., Dwyer, S., & Kleindinst, C. (1994). Involving students in assessing their reading: The winter count. *The Reading Teacher, 48,* 80–84.

Andersen, S. (1998). The trouble with testing. *Young Children, 53,* 25–29.

Anderson, G., & Markle, A. (1985). Cheerios, McDonald's and Snickers: Bringing EP into the classroom. *Reading Education in Texas, 1,* 30–35.

Anderson, P. (1962). *Flannelboard stories for the primary grades.* Minneapolis: T. S. Denison & Co., Inc.

Anderson, R., Heibert, E., Scott, J., & Wilkinson, I. (1985). *Becoming a nation of readers: The report of the Commission on Reading.* Washington, DC: National Institute of Education.

Allen, R. (1976). *Language experiences in communication.* Boston: Houghton Mifflin.

Allen, V. (1991). Teaching bilingual and second language learners. In J. Flood, J. Jensen, D. Lapp, & R. Squires (Eds.), *Research in the teaching of the English language arts.* New York: Macmillan.

Allexsaht-Snider, M. (1991). Family literacy in a Spanish-speaking context: Joint construction of meaning. *The Quarterly Newsletter of the Laboratory of Comparative Human Cognition, 13,* 15–21.

Altwerger, B., Diehl-Faxon, J., & Dockstader-Anderson, K. (1985). Read-aloud events as meaning construction. *Language Arts, 62,* 476–484.

Archbald, D., & Newman, F. (1988). *Beyond standardized testing: Assessing authentic academic achievement in secondary schools.* Washington, DC: National Association of Secondary School Principals.

Ashton-Warner, S. (1963). *Teacher.* New York: Simon & Schuster.

Atwell, N. (1990). *Workshop 1: By and for Teachers,* Vol. 1. Portsmouth, NH: Heinemann.

Au, K. (1993). *Literacy instruction in multicultural settings.* Fort Worth, TX: Harcourt Brace Jovanovich.

Au, K., & Jordan, C. (1981). Teaching reading to Hawaiian children: Finding a culturally appropriate solution. In H. Tureba, B. Guthire, & K. Au (Eds.), *Culture and the bilingual classroom.* Rowley, MA: Newbury House.

Au, K., & Kawakami, J. (1991). Culture and ownership: Schooling of minority students. *Childhood Education, 67,* 280–284.

Avery, C. (1993). *And with a light touch: Learning about reading, writing, and teaching with first graders.* Portsmouth, NH: Heinemann.

Baghban, M. (1984). *Our daughter learns to read and write.* Newark, DE: International Reading Association.

Ballenger, C. (1997). *Teaching other people's children: Literacy and learning in a bilingual classroom.* New York: Teachers College Press.

Barbour, A. (1998–1999). Home literacy bags: Promote family involvement. *Childhood Education, 75*(2), 71–75.

Barone, D. (1998). How do we teach literacy to children who are learning English as a second language? In S. Neuman & K. Roskos (Eds.), *Children achieving: Best practices in early literacy* (pp. 56–76). Newark, DE: International Reading Association.

Barrentine, S. (1996). Engaging with reading through interactive read-alouds. *The Reading Teacher, 50,* 36–43.

Barrera, R., Ligouri, O., Salas, L. (1992). Ideas literature can grow on: Key insights for enriching and expanding children's literature about the Mexican-American experience. In B. Harris (Ed.), *Teaching multicultural literature in grades K–8.* Norwood, MA: Christopher-Gordon.

Bass, G., & Bass, D. (1998). Joel's language development: The parent's perspective. Field notes and commentary.

Bateson, G. (1979). *Mind and Nature.* London: Wildwood House.

Battle, J. (1995). Collaborative story talk in a bilingual kindergarten. In N. Roser & M. Martinez (Eds.), *Book talk and beyond: Children and teachers respond to literature.* Newark, DE: International Reading Association.

Beane, J. (1995). Curriculum integration and the disciplines of knowledge. *Phi Delta Kappan, 76,* 616–622.

Bear, D. & Barone, D., (1998). *Developing literacy: An integrated approach to assessment and instruction.* Boston: Houghton Mifflin Co.

Becher, R. (1985). Parent involvement and reading achievement: A review of research and implications for practice. *Childhood Education, 62,* 44–49.

Becker, H., & Epstein, J. (1982). Parent involvement: A study of teacher practices. *Elementary School Journal, 83,* 85–102.

Bhavnagri, N., & Gonzalez-Mena, J. (1997). The cultural context of infant caregiving. *Childhood Education, 74,* 2–8.

Bishop, R. (Ed.). (1994). *Kaleidoscope: A multicultural booklist for grades K–8.* Urbana, IL: National Council of Teachers of English.

Bissett, D. (1969). *The amount and effect of recreational reading in selected fifth grade classes.* Unpublished doctoral dissertation, Syracuse University.

Bissex, G. (1980). *GNYS AT WRK: A child learns to read and write.* Cambridge, MA: Harvard University Press.

Black, J., Puckett, M., & Bell, M. (1992). *The young child: Development from prebirth through age eight.* New York: Merrill.

Booth-Church, E. (1998). From greeting to goodbye. *Scholastic Early Childhood Today, 13*(1), 51–53.

Bosma, B. (1992). *Fairy tales, fables, legends and myths* (2nd ed), New York: Teachers College Press.

Bradshaw, J., & Rogers, L. (1993). *The evolution of lateral asymmetries, language, tool use, and intellect.* New York: Academic Press.

Brandt, R. (1992). Overview: A caring community. *Educational Leadership, 49,* 3.

Bravo-Villasante, C. (1980). *Historia y antologia de la literatura infantile iberoamericanan* (Vol. 1 and 2; 2nd ed.). Madrid: Edita Doncel.

Bredekamp, S. (1989). *Developmentally Approptriate Practice.* Washington, D.C.: National Association for the Education.

Bredekamp, S., & Copple, C. (1997). *Developmentally appropriate practice in early childhood programs* (rev. ed.). Washington, DC: NAEYC.

Brock, D., & Dodd, E. (1994). A family lending library: Promoting early literacy development. *Young Children, 49*(3), 16–21.

Bromley, K. (1988). *Language arts: Exploring connections.* Boston: Allyn & Bacon.

Brooks, J., & Brooks, M. (1993). *In search of understanding: The case for constructivist classrooms.* Alexandria, VA: Association for Supervision and Curriculum Development.

Brown, J. (1994). Parent workshops: Closing the gap between parents and teachers. *Focus on Early Childhood Newsletter, 7*(1).

Bruner, J. (1980). *Under five in Britain.* Ypsilanti, MI: High/Scope.

Bruner, J. (1983). Play, thought, and language. *Peabody Journal of Education, 60*(3), 60–69.

Bruner, J. (1986). *Actual minds, possible worlds.* Cambridge, MA: Harvard University Press.

Bus, A., Belsky, J., van IJzendoorn, M., & Crnic, K. (1997). *Attachment* and bookreading patterns: A study of mothers, fathers, and their toddlers. *Early Childhood Research Quarterly, 12*(1), 81–98.

Bus, A., van IJzendoorn, M., & Pellegrini, A. (1995). Joint book reading makes for success in learning to read: A meta-analysis on intergenerational transmission of literacy. *Review of Educational Research, 65,* 1–21.

Butler, A., & Turbill, J. (1984). *Towards a reading–writing classroom.* Portsmouth, NH: Heinemann.

Calkins, L. (1994). *The art of teaching writing.* Portsmouth, NH: Heinemann.

Cambourne, B. (1988). *The whole story: Natural learning and the acquisition of literacy in the classroom.* Auckland, New Zealand: Ashton Scholastic.

Canizares, S. (1997). Sharing stories. *Scholastic Early Childhood Today, 12,* 46–48.

Carey, S. (1979). The child as word learner. In M. Halle, J. Bresnan, & G. Miller (Eds.), *Linguistic theory and psychological reality.* Cambridge, MA: MIT Press.

Carger, C. (1993). Louie comes to life: Pretend reading with second language emergent readers. *Language Arts, 70,* 542–47.

Carlson, A. (1990). *Family questions.* New Brunswick, NJ: Transaction.

Carlson, K., & Cunningham, J. (1990). Effect of pencil diameter on the graphomotor skill of preschoolers. *Early Childhood Research Quarterly, 5,* 279–293.

Casper, L., Hawkins, M., O'Connell, M. (1991). *Who's Minding the Kids: Child Care Arrangements Fall 1991.* DIANE Publishing Company.

Cazden, C. (1976). Play with language and meta-linguistic awareness: One dimension of language experience. In J. Bruner, A. Jolly, & K. Sylva (Eds.), *Play: Its role in development and evolution.* New York: Basic Books.

Cazden, C. (1988). *Classroom discourse.* Portsmouth, NH: Heinemann.

Cazden, C. (1992). *Whole language plus: Essays on literacy in the United States and New Zealand.* New York: Teachers College Press.

Chall, J. (1967). *Learning to read: The great debate.* New York: McGraw-Hill.

Chall, J. (1989). *Learning to read: The great debate* 20 years later—A response to "Debunking the great phonics myth." *Phi Delta Kappan, 70,* 521–538.

Chomsky, C. (1969). *The acquisition of syntax in children from 5 to 10.* Cambridge, MA: MIT Press.

Chomsky, N. (1965). *Aspects of the theory of syntax.* Cambridge, MA: MIT Press.

Christian, K., Morrison, F., & Bryant, F. (1998). Predicting kindergarten academic skills: Interaction among child-care, maternal education, and family literacy environments. *Early Childhood Research Quarterly, 13,* 501–521.

Christie, J. (1991). *Play and early literacy development.* Albany, New York: State University of New York Press.

Christie, J. (1995). *Linking literacy and play.* Newark, DE: International Reading Association.

Christie, J., & Enz, B. (1992). The effects of literacy play interventions on preschoolers' play patterns and literacy development. *Early Education and Development, 3,* 205–220.

Christie, J., Johnsen, E. P., & Peckover, R. (1988). The effects of play period duration on children's play patterns. *Journal of Research in Childhood Education, 3,* 123–131.

Christie, J., & Stone, S. (1999). Collaborative literacy activity in print-enriched play centers: Exploring the "zone" in same-age and multi-age groupings. *Journal of Literacy Research, 31,* 109–131.

Chukovsky, K. (1976). The sense of nonsense verse. In J. Bruner, A. Jolly, & K. Sylva (Eds.), *Play: Its role in development and evolution.* New York: Basic Books.

Church, E. (1998). Meet the authors. *Scholastic Early Childhood Today, 12*(5), 38–39.

Church, E. (1999). Sharing portfolios. *Scholastic Early Childhood Today, 13,* 13.

Clark, E. (1983). Meanings and concepts. In J. Flavell & E. Markman (Eds.), *Handbook of child psychology: Vol. 3. Cognitive development* (4th ed.). New York: Wiley.

Clark, M. (1976). *Young fluent readers.* London: Heinemann.

Clarke, A., & Kurtz-Costes, B. (1997). Television viewing, educational quality of the home environment, and school readiness. *Journal of Educational Research, 90,* 279–285.

Clarke, L. (1988). Invented spelling versus traditional spelling in first graders' writing: Effects on learning to spell and read. *Research in the Teaching of English, 22,* 281–309.

Clay, M. (1966). *Emergent reading behavior.* Unpublished doctoral dissertation, University of Aukland.

Clay, M. (1972). *Reading: The patterning of complex behaviour.* London: Heinemann.

Clay, M. (1975). *What did I write?* Auckland, New Zealand: Heinemann.

Clay, M. (1979). *Concepts about Print.* NH: Heinemann.

Clay, M. (1985). *The early detection of reading difficulties* (3rd ed.). Portsmouth, NH: Heinemann.

Clay, M. (1989). Telling stories. *Reading Today, 6*(5), 24.

Clay, M. (1991). *Becoming literate.* Portsmouth, NH: Heinemann Books.

Cochran-Smith, M. (1984). *The making of a reader.* Norwood, NJ: Ablex.

Cochran-Smith, M., Kahn, J., & Paris, C. (1986, March). *Play with it; I'll help you with it; figure it out; here's what it can do for you.* Paper presented at the Literacy Research Center Speaker Series, Graduate School of Education, University of Pennsylvania.

Cohen, L. (1999). The power of portfolios. *Scholastic Early Childhood Today, 13,* 22–29.

Collin, B. (1992). *Read to me: Raising kids who love to read.* New York: Scholastic.

Collins, M. (1997). Sounds like fun. In B. Farber (Ed.), *The parents' and teachers' guide to helping young children learn* (pp. 213–218). Cutchoque, NY: Preschool Publications, Inc.

Collins, R. (1993). Head Start: Steps towards a two-generation program strategy. *Young Children, 48,* 25–33.

Coody, B. (1997). *Using literature with young children.* Chicago: Brown & Benchmark Publishing.

Corballis, M. C. (1991). *The lopsided ape: Evolution of the generative mind.* New York: Oxford University Press.

Cowley, F. (1997, Spring/Summer). The language explosion. *Newsweek: Your Child,* 16–18, 21–22.

Cunningham, A., & Stanovich, K. (1998). What reading does for the mind. *American Educator, 21*(1&2), 8–15.

Cunningham, P. (1995a). *Phonics they use: Words for reading and writing.* New York: Harper Collins.

Cunningham, P. (1995b). *Words they use: Words for reading and writing* (2nd ed.). New York: Harper Collins.

Dailey, K. (1991). Writing in kindergarten: Helping parents understand the process. *Childhood Education, 3,* 170–175.

Danst, C., Lowe, L., & Bartholomew, P. (1990). Contingent social responsiveness, family ecology, and infant communicative competence. *National Student Speech-Language-Hearing Association Journal, 17*(1), 39–49.

Delgado-Gaitan, C., & Trueba, H. (1991). *Crossing cultural borders: Education for immigrant families in America.* Philadelphia, PA: Falmer Press.

DeLoache, J., (1984). *What's this? Maternal questions in joint picture book reading with toddlers.* Paper presented at the Annual Meeting of the American Educational Research Association, New Orleans, LA.

DeStephano, J., Pepinsky, H., & Sanders, T. (1982). Discourse rules for literacy learning in a classroom. In L. Wilkinson (Ed.), *Communicating in the classroom.* New York: Academic Press.

Dewey, J. (1938). *Experiences and education.* New York: Collier Books.

Dickinson, D., & Tabors, P. (2000). *Beginning Literacy with Language: Young Children Learning at Home and School.* Baltimore: Paul H. Brookes.

Dillon, D., & Searle, D. (1981). The role of language in one first grade classroom. *Research in the Teaching of English, 15,* 311–328.

Dodge, D., & Colker, L. (1992). *The creative curriculum for early childhood education.* Washington, DC: Teaching Strategies.

Dolson, D. (1985). The effects of Spanish home language use on the scholastic performance of Hispanic pupils. *Journal of Multilingual Multicultural Development, 6,* 135–155.

Downing, J., & Oliver, P. (1973–1974). The child's concept of a word. *Reading Research Quarterly, 9,* 568–582.

Durkin, D. (1966). *Children who read early.* New York: Teachers College Press.

Durkin, D. (1987). *Teaching young children to read* (4th ed.). Boston: Allyn and Bacon.

Dyson, A. (1993). From prop to mediator: The changing role of written language in children's symbolic repertoires. In B. Spodek & O. Saracho (Eds.), *Language and literacy in early childhood.* New York: Teachers College Press.

Dyson, A., & Genishi, C. (1983). Children's language for learning. *Language Arts, 60,* 751–757.

Edelman, G. (1995, June). Cited in Swerdlow, J. Quiet miracles of the brain. *National Geographic, 187*(6), 2–41.

Edelsky, C. (1978). "Teaching" oral language. *Language Arts, 55,* 291–296.

Ehri, L. (1991). Development of the ability to read words. In P. D. Pearson (Ed.), *Handbook of Reading Research* (Vol. II, pp. 383–417). New York: Longman.

Ehri, L. (1997). Phonemic awareness and learning to read. *Literacy Development in Young Children, 4*(2) 2–3.

Eldredge, J. (1995). *Teaching decoding in holistic classrooms.* Englewood Cliffs, NJ: Prentice Hall.

Elkind, D. (1990). Academic pressures—Too much, too soon: The demise of play. In E. Klugman & S. Smilansky (Eds.), *Children's play and learning: Perspectives and policy implications.* New York: Teachers College Press.

Ellis, (1985). *Understanding second language acquisition.* New York: Oxford University Press.

Elster, C. (1998). Influences of text and pictures on shared and emergent readings. *Research in the Teaching of English, 32,* 43–63.

Enright, D. (1986). Use everything you have to teach English: Providing useful input to young second language learners. In P. Rigg & D. Enright (Eds.), *Children and ESL: Integrating perspectives.* Washington, DC: Teachers of English to Speakers of Other Languages.

Enright, D., & McCloskey, M. (1988). *Integrating English: Developing English language and literacy in the multilingual classroom.* Reading, MA: Addison-Wesley.

Enz, B. (1992). *Love, laps, and learning to read.* Paper presented at International Reading Association Southwest Regional Conference, Tucson, AZ.

Enz, B., & Christie, J. (1997). Teacher play interaction styles: Effects on play behavior and relationships with teacher training and experience. *International Journal of Early Childhood Education, 2,* 55–69.

Enz, B., & Cook, S. (1993). *Gateway to teaching: From pre-service to in-service.* Dubuque, IA: Kendall-Hunt.

Enz, B., & Searfoss, L. (1995). Let the circle be unbroken: Teens as literacy teachers and learners. In L. M. Morrow (Ed.), *Family literacy: Multiple perspectives.* Reston, VA: International Reading Association.

Enz, B., & Searfoss, L. (1996). Expanding our views of family literacy. *The Reading Teacher, 49,* 576-79.

Epstein, J. (1986). Parent's reactions to teacher practices of parent involvement. *Elementary School Journal, 86,* 277–294.

Epstein, J. (1995). School/family/community partnerships: Caring for the children we share. *Phi Delta Kappa, 76,* 701–712.

Ericson, L., & Juliebö, M. (1998). *The phonological awareness handbook for kindergarten and primary teachers.* Newark, DE: International Reading Association.

Ernst, G. (1994). "Talking circle": Conversation and negotiation in the ESL classroom. *TESOL Quarterly, 28,* 293–322.

Espinosa, C. & Fournier, J. (1995). Making meaning of our lives through literature: Past, present, and future. *Primary Voices, 3*(2), 15–21.

Faltis, C. (2000). *Joinfostering: Teaching and learning in multicultural classrooms.* (3rd ed.). Upper Saddle River, NJ: Prentice Hall.

Farr, M. (1994). En los dos idiomas: Literacy practices among Chicago Mexicans. In B. Moss (Ed.), *Literacy across communities* (pp. 9–48). Creskill, NJ: Hampton.

Farris, P. (1982). *A comparison of handwriting strategies for primary grade students.* Arlington, VA: ERIC Document Reproduction Service.

Fein, G., Ardila-Rey, A., & Groth, L. (2000). The narrative connection: Stories and literacy. In K. Roskos & J. Christie (Eds.), *Play and literacy in early childhood: Reseach from multiple perspectives.* Mahwah, NJ: Lawrence Erlbaum.

Feitelson, D., & Goldstein, Z. (1986). Patterns of book ownership and reading to young children in Israeli school-oriented and nonschool-oriented families. *The Reading Teacher, 39,* 924–930.

Fenson, L. (1984). Developmental trends for action and speech in pretend play. In I. Bretherton (Ed.), *Symbolic play: The development of social understanding.* Orlando, FL: Academic Press.

Ferreiro, E., & Teberosky, A. (1982). *Literacy before schooling.* Exeter, NH: Heinemann.

Fessler, R. (1998). Room for talk: Peer support for getting into English in an ESL kindergarten. *Early Childhood Research Quarterly, 13,* 379–410.

Field, T., Woodson, R., Greenberg, R., & Cohen, D. (1982). Discrimination and imitation of facial expressions by neonates. *Science, 218,* 179–181.

Fields, M., Spangler, K., & Lee, D. (1991). *Let's begin reading right: Developmentally appropriate beginning literacy.* New York: Merrill-Macmillan.

Fillmore, L. (1976). *The second time around: Cognitive and social strategies in second language acquisition.* Unpublished doctoral dissertation, Stanford University.

Fillmore, L. (1982). Instructional language as linguistic input: Second language learning in classrooms. In L. Wilkinson (Ed.), *Communicating in the classroom.* New York: Academic Press.

Fillmore, L. (1983). The language learner as an individual: Implications of research on individual differences for the ESL teacher. In J. Handscombe and M. Clarke (Eds.), *On TESOL '82: Pacific perspectives on language learning and teaching.* Washington, DC: Teachers of English to Speakers of Other Languages.

Fillmore, L. (1991). When learning a second language means losing the first. *Early Childhood Research Quarterly, 6*(3), 323–346.

Fisher, B. (1995). Things take off: Note taking in the first grade. In P. Cordeiro (Ed.), *Endless possibilities: Generating curriculum in social studies and literacy.* Portsmouth, NH: Heinemann.

Flanigan, B. (1988). Second language acquisition in the elementary schools: The negotiation of meaning by native-speaking and nonnative-speaking peers. *The Bilingual Review/La Revista Bilingue, 14*(3), 25–40.

Flaxman, E., & Inger, M. (1991). Parents and schooling in the 1990s. *ERIC Review, 1*(3), 2–5.

Fournier, J. Landsdowne, E., Pasteries, Z. Steen, P., & Hudelson, S. (1992). Learning with, about and from children: Life in a bilingual second grade. In C. Genishi (Ed.), *Ways of assessing children and curriculum Voices form the classroom.* New York: Teachers College Press.

Fox, M. (1993). *Radical reflections: Passionate opinions on teaching, learning, and living.* San Diego: Harcourt Brace.

Fox, S. (1983). Oral language development, past studies and current directions. *Language Arts, 60,* 234–243.

Fractor, J., Woodruff, M., Martinez, M., & Teale, W. (1993). Let's not miss opportunities to promote voluntary reading: Classroom libraries in the elementary school. *The Reading Teacher, 46,* 476–484.

Fredericks, A., & Rasinski, T. (1990). Involving the uninvolved: How to. *The Reading Teacher, 43,* 424–425.

Freeman, Y., and Freeman, D. (1994). Whole language learning and teaching for second language learners. In C. Weaver (Ed.), *Reading process and practice: From sociopsycholinguistics to whole language.* Portsmouth, NH: Heinemann.

Galda, L., Cullinan, B., & Strickland, D. (1993). *Language, literacy, and the child.* Fort Worth, TX: Harcourt Brace Jovanovich.

Gallas, K. (1992). When the children take the chair: A study of sharing in a primary classroom. *Language Arts, 69,* 172–182.

Gardner, S. (1993–1994). Training for the future: Family support and school-linked services. *Family Resource Coalition, 3*(4), 18–19.

Garvey, C. (1977). *Play.* Cambridge, MA: Harvard University Press.

Garvey, C. (1984). *Children's talk.* Cambridge, MA: Harvard University Press.

Geller, L. (1982). Linguistic consciousness-raising: Child's play. *Language Arts, 59,* 120–125.

Gelfer, J. (1991). Teacher–parent partnerships: Enhancing communications. *Childhood Education, 67,* 164–167.

Genishi, C. (1987). Acquiring oral language and communicative competence. In C. Seefeldt (Ed.), *The early childhood curriculum: A review of current research.* New York: Teachers College Press.

Genishi, C., & Dyson, A. (1984). *Language assessment in the early years.* Norwood, NJ: Ablex.

Gesell, A. (1928). *Infancy and human growth.* New York: Macmillan.

Gilbert, J. (1989). A two-week K–6 interdisciplinary unit. In H. Jacobs (Ed.), *Interdisciplinary curriculum: Design and implementation.* Arlington, VA: Association for Supervision and Curriculum Development.

Gleason, J. (1967). Do children imitate? In C. Cazden (Ed.), *Language in early childhood education.* Washington, DC: National Association for the Education of Young Children.

Golden, J. (1984). Children's concept of story in reading and writing. *The Reading Teacher, 37,* 578–584.

Golinkoff, R. (1983). The preverbal negotiation of failed messages: Insights into the transition period. In R. Golinkoff (Ed.), *The transition from prelinguistic to linguistic communication.* Hillsdale, NJ: Erlbaum.

González, N. (1995). The funds of knowledge for teaching project. *Practicing Anthropology, 17*(3), 3–7.

Gonzalez-Mena, J. (1997). *Multicultural issues in childcare* (2nd ed.). Mountain View, CA: Mayfield Publishing Company.

Goodlad, J., & Oakes, J. (1988). We must offer equal access to knowledge. *Educational Leadership, 45,* 16–22.

Goodman, Y. (1981). Test review: Concepts About Print test. *The Reading Teacher, 34,* 445–448.

Goodman, Y. (1986). Children coming to know literacy. In W. Teale & E. Sulzby (Eds.), *Emergent literacy: Writing and reading.* Norwood, NJ: Ablex.

Goodman, Y., & Goodman, K. (1994). To err is human: Learning about language processes by analyzing miscues. In R. Ruddell, M. Ruddell, & H. Singer (Eds.), *Theoretical models and processes of reading* (4th ed.). Newark, DE: International Reading Association.

Goodman, Y., Watson, D., & Burke, C. (1987). *Reading miscue inventory: Alternative procedures.* Katonah, NY: Richard C. Owen.

Goodz, N. (1994). Interactions between parents and children in bilingual families. In F. Genesee (Ed.), *Educating second language children: The whole child, the whole curriculum, the whole community.* New York: Cambridge University Press.

Graham, S. (1992). Issues in handwriting instruction. *Focus on Exceptional Children, 25,* 1–4.

Graves, D. (1983). *Writing: Teachers and children at work.* Portsmouth, NH: Heinemann.

Graves, D., & Hansen, J. (1983). The author's chair. *Language Arts, 60,* 176–183.

Greenfield, P. (1984). A theory of the teaching in the learning activities of everyday life. In B. Rogoff & J. Lave (Eds.),*Everyday cognition: Its development in social context* (pp. 117–138). Cambridge, MA: Harvard University Press.

Greenewald, M. J., & Kulig, R. (1995). Effects of repeated readings of alphabet books on kindergartners' letter recognition. In K. Hinchman, D. Leu, & Kinzer, C. (Eds.), *Perspectives on literacy research and practice: Forty-fourth yearbook of the National Reading Conference* (pp. 231–234). Chicago: National Reading Conference.

Griffin, E., & Morrison, F. (1997). The unique contribution of home literacy environment to differences in early literacy skills. *Early Child Development and Care*(127–128), 233–243.

Gronlund, G. (1998). Portfolios as an assessment tool: Is collecting of work enough? *Young Children, 53,* 4–10.

Guerra, J. (1991). The role of ethnography in the reconceptualization of literacy. *The Quarterly Newsletter of the Laboratory of Comparative Human Cognition, 13,* 3–8.

Guerra, J. (1998). *Close to home: Oral and literate practices in a transnational Mexican community.* New York: Teachers College Press.

Gump, P. (1989). Ecological psychology and issues of play. In M. Bloch & A. Pellegrini (Eds.), *The ecological context of children's play* (pp. 35–36). Norwood, NJ: Ablex.

Hakuta, K. (1986). *Mirror of language: The debate on bilingualism.* New York: Basic Books.

Hall, N. (1987). *The emergence of literacy.* Portsmouth, NH: Heinemann.

Hall, N. (1991). Play and the emergence of literacy. In J. Christie (Ed.), *Play and early literacy development.* Albany, NY: State University of New York Press.

Hall, N. (1999). Real literacy in a school setting: Five-year-olds take on the world. *The Reading Teacher, 52,* 8–17.

Hall, N., & Duffy, R. (1987). Every child has a story to tell. *Language Arts, 64,* 523–529.

Hall, N., & Robinson, A. (1995). *Exploring writing and play in the early years.* London: David Fulton.

Han, M., Chen, Y., Christie, J., & Enz, B. (2000). Environmental Kit Assessment. Created for New Directions Institute, First Teacher Project. Arizona State University, Tempe, AZ.

Hansen, C. (1998). *Getting the picture: Talk about story in a kindergarten classroom.* Unpublished doctoral dissertation, Arizona State University.

Hansen, J. (1994). Literacy profiles: Windows on potential. In S. Valencia, E. Hiebert, & P. Afflerbach (Eds.), *Authentic reading assessment.* Newark, DE: International Reading Association.

Harris, V. (Ed.). (1992). *Teaching multicultural literature in grades K–8.* Norwood, MA: Christopher-Gordon.

Harris, V. (1997). *Using multiethnic literature in the K–8 classroom.* Norwood, NJ: Christopher-Gordon.

Harste, J., Short, K., & Burke, C. (1988). *Creating classrooms for authors: The reading-writing connection.* Portsmouth, NH: Heinemann.

Harste, J., Woodward, V., & Burke, C. (1984). *Language stories and literacy lessons.* Portsmouth, NH: Heinemann.

Hart, B., & Risley, T. (1995). *Meaningful differences in the everyday experience of young American children.* Baltimore, MD: Paul H. Brookes Publishing Company.

Heald-Taylor, G. (1986). *Whole language strategies for ESL primary students.* Toronto: OISE Press.

Healy, J. (1997, August–September). Current brain research. *Scholastic Early Childhood Today,* 42–43.

Healy, J. M. (1994). *Your child's growing mind: A practical guide to brain development and learning from birth to adolescence.* New York, NY: Doubleday.

Heath, S. (1982). What no bedtime story means: Narrative skills at home and school. *Language in Society, 11,* 49–76.

Heath, S. (1983). *Ways with words.* Cambridge, England: Cambridge University Press.

Heath, S. (1986). Sociocultural contexts of language development. In Bilingual Education Office, California State Department of Education (Ed.), *Beyond language: Social and cultural factors in schooling language minority students.* Los Angeles: Evaluation, Dissemination and Assessment Center, California State University.

Hedrick, W., & Pearish, A. (1999, April). Good reading instruction is more important than who provides the instruction or where it takes place. *The Reading Teacher, 52,* 716–725.

Heibert, E. (1981). Developmental patterns and interrelationships of preschool children's print awareness. *Reading Research Quarterly, 16,* 236–260.

Helm, J. (1999). Projects! Exploring children's interests. *Scholastic Early Childhood Today, 14,* 24–31.

Hensley, M. (1995). From untapped potential to creative realization: Empowering parents. *Practicing Anthropology, 17*(3), 13–17.

Hicks, D. and Mahaffey's, S. *Flannelboard classic tales.* Chicago: American Library Association.

Hirschler, (1994). Preschool children's help to second language learners. *Journal of Educational Issues of Language Minority Students, 14,* 227–240.

Hoff-Ginsberg, E. (1991). Mother–child conversations in different social classes and communicative settings. *Child Development, 62,* 782–796.

Hoffman, J., Roser, N., & Battle, J. (1993). Reading aloud in classrooms: From modal toward a "model." *The Reading Teacher, 46,* 496–503.

Holdaway, D. (1979). *The foundations of literacy.* Sydney: Ashton Scholastic.

Howard, S., Shaughnessy, A., Sanger, D., & Hux, K. (1998). Let's talk! Facilitating language in early elementary classrooms. *Young Children, 53*(3), 34–39.

Huck, C., Hepler, S., Hickman, J., & Kiefer, B. (1997). *Children's literature in the elementary school.* New York: Holt, Rinehart, & Winston.

Hudelson, S. (1990). Bilingual/ESL learners talking in the English classroom. In S. Hynds & D. Rubin (Eds.), *Perspectives on talk and learning.* Urbana, IL: National Council of Teachers of English.

Hudelson, S., Fournier, J. Espinosa,C., & Bachman, R. (1994). Chasing windmills: Confronting the obstacles for literature based reading program. *Language Arts, 71,* 164–171.

Huey, E. (1908). *The psychology and pedagogy of reading.* New York: Macmillan.

Hurst, C. (1991). *Once upon a time: An encyclopedia for successfully using literature with young children.* Allen, TX: Developmental Learning Materials.

Huttenlocher, J. (1991). Early vocabulary growth: Relations to language input and gender. *Developmental Psychology, 27*(2), 236–248.

Ingraham, P. (1997). *My ABC journal: An emergent literacy journal.* Columbus, OH: Zaner-Bloser.

IRA. (1997). *The role of phonics in reading instruction.* Newark, DE: International Reading Association.

IRA. (1999). *Using multiple methods of beginning reading instruction.* Newark, DE: International Reading Association.

IRA/NAEYC. (1998). Learning to read and write: Developmentally appropriate practices for young children. *Young Children, 53*(4), 30–46.

IRA/NCTE. (1994). *Standards for the assessment of reading and writing.* Newark, DE, and Urbana, IL: International Reading Association and National Council of Teachers of English.

Jackman, H. (1997). *Early education curriculum: A child's connection to the world.* Albany, NY: Delmar Publishers.

Jacobs, H. (1989). *Interdisciplinary curriculum: Design and implementation.* Alexandria, VA: Association for Supervision and Curriculum Development.

Jacobson, L. (1998, February 11). House calls. *Education Week,* 27–29.

Jacobson, R., & Faltis, C. (Eds.). (1990). *Language distribution issues in bilingual schooling.* Clevedon, UK: Multilingual Matters.

Jalongo, M. (1995). Promoting active listening in the classroom. *Childhood Education, 72*(1), 13–18.

Jaramillo, N. (1994). Grandmothers' nursery rhymes/Las nana de abuelita. New York: Henry Holt, 1994.

Jett-Simpson, M. (1989). *Adventuring with books: A book list for pre-K–grade 6.* Urbana, IL: National Council for the Teachers of English.

Johnson, J., Christie, J., & Yawkey, T. (1999). *Play and early childhood development* (2nd ed.). Glenview, IL: Scott, Foresman.

Johnston, P. (1992). *Constructive Evaluation of Literate Activity.* New York: Longman.

Jones, E., & Reynolds, G. (1992). *The play's the thing: Teachers' roles in children's play.* New York: Teachers' College Press.

Kalb, C. & Namuth, T. (1997, Spring/Summer). When a child's silence isn't golden. *Newsweek: Your Child,* 23.

Karmiloff-Smith, A. (1979). Language development after five. In P. Fletcher & M. Garman (Eds.), *Language acquisition.* Cambridge, England: Cambridge University Press.

Katz, L., & Chard, S. (1993). *Engaging children's minds: The project approach.* Norwood, NJ: Ablex Publishing Corporation.

Klein, A. (1991). All about ants: Discovery learning in the primary grades. *Young Children, 46,* 23–27.

Kneas, K. (1998). What every classroom needs. *Scholastic Early Childhood Today, 12,* 33–37.

Koppenhaver, D., Spadorcia, S., & Erickson, K. (1998). How do we provide inclusive early literacy instruction for children with disabilities. In S. Neuman & K. Roskos (Eds.), *Children achieving: Best practices in early literacy* (pp. 77–97). Newark, DE: International Reading Association.

Kotulak, R. (1997). *Inside the brain: Revolutionary discoveries of how the mind works.* Kansas City, MO: Andrews McMeel Publishing.

Krashen, S. (1982). *Principles and practices in second language acquisition.* Oxford, England: Pergamon.

Krashen, S. (1987). Encouraging free reading. In M. Douglass (Ed.), *51st Claremont Reading Conference Yearbook.* Claremont, CA: Center for Developmental Studies.

Kuhl, P. (1993). *Life language.* Seattle, WA: University of Washington.

Kupetz, B., & Green, E. (1997). Sharing books with infants and toddlers: Facing the challenges. *Young Children, 52*(2), 22–27.

Ladson-Billings, G. (1994). *The dreamkeepers.* San Francisco: Jossey-Bass.

Lamme, L., & Ayris, B. (1983). Is the handwriting of beginning writers influenced by writing tools? *Journal of Research and Development in Education, 17,* 32–38.

Lamme, L., & Childers, N. (1983). The composing processes of three young children. *Research in the Teaching of English, 17,* 33–50.

Lapointe, A. (1986). The state of instruction in reading and writing in U.S. elementary schools. *Phi Delta Kappan, 68,* 135–138.

Lass, B. (1982). Portrait of my son as an early reader. *The Reading Teacher, 36,* 20–28.

Lemish, D. (1987). Viewers in diapers: The early development of television viewing. In T. Lindlof (Ed.), *Natural audiences: Qualitative research of media uses and effects* (pp. 33–57). Norwood, NJ: Ablex.

Lenneberg, E. (1967). *Biological foundations of language.* New York: Wiley.

Leseman, P., & de Jong, P. (1998). Home literacy: Opportunity, instruction, cooperation, and socio-emotional quality predicting early reading achievement. *Reading Research Quarterly, 33,* 294–318.

Lessow-Hurley, J. (1990). *Foundations of dual language instruction.* New York: Longman.

Levin, D., & Carlsson-Paige, N. (1994). Developmentally appropriate television: Putting children first. *Young Children, 49,* 38–44.

Lewis, R., & Doorlag, D. (1999). *Teaching special students in general education classrooms.* Columbus, OH: Prentice Hall.

Lindfors, J. (1987). *Children's language and learning* (2nd ed.). Englewood Cliffs, NJ: Prentice-Hall.

Lindquist, T. (1995). *Seeing the whole through social studies.* Portsmouth, NH: Heinemann.

Lindsay, G., & McLennan, D. (1983). Lined paper: Its effects on the legibility and creativity of young children's writing. *British Journal of Educational Psychology, 53,* 364–368.

Litman, M., Anderson, C., Anderson, L., Buria, B., Christy, C., Koski, B. & Renton, P. (1999). Curriculum comes from the child! A Head Start family child care program. *Young Children, 54*(3), 4–9.

Lock, J. (1993). *The child's path to spoken language.* Cambridge, MA: Harvard Press.

Lomax, R., & McGee, L. (1987). Young children's concepts about print and reading: Toward a model of word reading acquisition. *Reading Research Quarterly, 22,* 237–256.

Londergan, G. (1988). *Helping parents understand the stages of their child's reading development.* Bloomington, IN: ERIC Clearinghouse on Reading and Communication Skills.

Lonigan, C., & Whitehurst, G. (1998). Relative efficacy of parent and teacher involvement in a shared-reading intervention for preschool children from low-income backgrounds. *Early Childhood Research Quarterly, 23*(2) 263–290.

Luke, A., & Kale, J. (1997). Learning through difference: Cultural practices in early childhood language socialization. In E. Gregory (Ed.), *One child, many worlds: Early learning in multicultural communities* (pp. 11–29). New York: Teachers College Press.

Macias-Huerta, A., and Quintero, E. (1990). *All in the family: Bilingualism and biliteracy. The Reading Teacher, 44,* 306–314.

MacLean, P. (1978). A mind of three minds: Educating the triune brain. In J. Chall & A. Mirsky (Eds.), *Education and the brain: 77th yearbook of the National Society for the Study of Education.* Chicago: University of Chicago Press.

Mangiola, L., & Pease-Alvarez, L. (1993). Learning and teaching together. In S. Hudelson and J. Lindfors (Eds.), *Delicate balances: Collaborative research in language education.* Urbana, IL: National Council of Teachers of English.

Manning, M., Manning, G., & Long, R. (1994). *Theme immersion: Inquiry-based curriculum in elementary and middle schools.* Portsmouth, NH: Heinemann.

Manning-Kratcoski, A., & Bobkoff-Katz, K. (1998). Conversing with young language learners in the classroom. *Young Children, 53*(3), 30–33.

Manz, D. (1996). This is the House That Kindergarten Built. *Young Children,* 70–71.

Maras, L., & Brummett, B. (1995). Time for a change: Presidential elections in a grade 3–4 multi-age classroom. In P. Cordeiro (Ed.), *Endless possibilities: Generating curriculum in social studies and literacy.* Portsmouth, NH: Heinemann.

Maring, G., & Magelky, J. (1990). Effective communication: Key to parent/community involvement. *The Reading Teacher, 43,* 606–607.

Martinez, M., & Roser, N. (1985). Read it again: The value of repeated readings during storytime. *The Reading Teacher, 38,* 782–786.

Martinez, M., & Teale, W. (1987). The ins and outs of a kindergarten writing program. *The Reading Teacher, 40,* 444–451.

Martinez, M., & Teale, W. (1988). Reading in a kindergarten classroom library. *The Reading Teacher, 41,* 568–572.

Marvin, C., & Mirenda, P. (1993). Home literacy experiences of preschoolers in Head Start and special education programs. *Journal of Early Intervention, 17*(4), 351–366.

Mason, J. (1980). When do children begin to read: An exploration of four-year-old children's letter and word reading competencies. *Reading Research Quarterly, 15,* 203–227.

Masonheimer, P., Drum, P., & Ehri, L. (1984). Does environmental print identification lead children into word reading? *Journal of Reading Behavior, 16,* 257–271.

Mathews, M. (1966). *Teaching to read: Historically considered.* Chicago: University of Chicago Press.

Mattick, I. (1981). The teacher's role in helping young children develop language competence. In C. Cazden (Ed.), *Language in early childhood education.* Washington, DC: National Association for the Education of Young Children.

McDougal Littell. (1993). *Handwriting connections.* Evanston, IL: McDougal Littell.

McGee, L., & Richgels, D. (1989). "K is Kristen's": Learning the alphabet from a child's perspective. *The Reading Teacher, 43,* 216–225.

McGee, L. & Richgels. D. (1996). *Literacy's beginnings: Supporting young readers and writers* (2nd ed.) Boston: Allyn & Bacon.

Mehan, H. (1979). *Learning lessons.* Cambridge, MA: Harvard University Press.

Mehler, J. (1985). Language related dispositions in early literacy. In J. Mehler & R. Fox (Eds.), *Neonate cognition: Beyond the blooming buzzing and confusion.* Hillsdale, NJ: Erlbaum.

Meisels, S., Dichtelmiller, M., Jablon, J., Dorfman, J., & Marsden, D. (1997). *Work samples in the classroom: A teacher's manual.* Ann Arbor, MI: Mt. Rebus.

Menyuk, P. (1988). *Language development: Knowledge and use.* Glenview, IL: Scott, Foresman.

Michaels, S. (1986). Narrative presentations: An oral preparation for literacy with first graders. In J. Cook-Gumperz (Ed.), *The social construction of literacy.* Cambridge, England: Cambridge University Press.

Miller, S. (1997). Family television viewing: How to gain control. *Childhood Education, 74*(1), 38–40.

Miller-Lachman, R. (Ed.). (1995). *Global voices, global visions: A core collection of multicultural books.* New Providence, NJ: R. R. Bowker.

Moffett, J., & Wagner, B. (1983). *Student-centered language arts and reading, K–13: A handbook for teachers* (3rd ed.). Boston: Houghton Mifflin.

Moir, A., & Jessel, D. (1991). *Brain sex: The real differences between men and women.* New York: Carol Publishing Group.

Moll, L., Amanti, C., Neff, D., & González, N. (1992). Funds of knowledge for teaching: Using a qualitative approach to connect homes and classrooms. *Theory into Practice, 31*(2), 132–141.

Morgan, A. (1987). The development of written language awareness in black preschool children. *Journal of Reading Behavior, 19,* 49–67.

Morisset, C. (1995). Language devlopment: Sex differences within social risk. *Developmental Psychology,* 851–865.

Morrow, L. (1982). Relationships between literature programs, library corner designs, and children's use of literature. *Journal of Educational Research, 75,* 339–344.

Morrow, L. (1983). Home and school correlates of early interest in literature. *Journal of Educational Research, 76,* 221–230.

Morrow, L. (1988). Young children's responses to one-to-one story readings in school settings. *Reading Research Quarterly, 23,* 89–107.

Morrow, L. (2001). *Literacy development in the early years: Helping children read and write* (4th ed.). Boston: Allyn and Bacon.

Morrow, L., & Rand, M. (1991). Preparing the classroom environment to promote literacy during play. In J. Christie (Ed.), *Play and early literacy development.* Albany, NY: State University of New York Press.

Morrow, L., & Tracey, D. (1997). Strategies used for phonics instruction in early childhood classrooms. *The Reading Teacher, 50,* 644–651.

Morrow, L., Tracey, D., Gee-Woo, D., & Pressley, M. (1999). Characteristics of exemplary first-grade literacy instruction. *The Reading Instructor, 52,* 462–476.

Morrow, L., & Weinstein, C. (1982). Increasing children's use of literature through program and physical changes. *Elementary School Journal, 83,* 131–137.

Morrow, L., & Weinstein, C. (1986). Encouraging voluntary reading: The importance of a literature program on children's use of library centers. *Reading Research Quarterly, 21,* 330–346.

Moss, R. (1989). Big pencils for small writers: A message from a mother. *Journal of Teaching Writing, 8,* 77–83.

Mowery, A. (1993). *Qualifying paper on early childhood parent education programs.* Unpublished manuscript, University of Delaware, Newark, DE.

Murray, B., Stahl, S., & Ivey, M. (1996). Developing phoneme awareness through alphabet books. *Reading and Writing: An Interdisciplinary Journal, 8,* 307–322.

NCTE. (1993). *Elementary school practices: Current research on language learning.* Urbana, IL: National Council of Teachers of English.

National Education Goals Panel. (1997). *Special early childhood report.* Washington D.C: Author.

National Research Council. (1998). *Preventing reading difficulties in young children.* Washington, DC: National Academy Press.

Neuman, S. (1988). The displacement effect: Assessing the relationship between television viewing and reading performance. *Reading Research Quarterly, 23,* 414–440.

Neuman, S. (1995). *Linking literacy and play.* Newark, DE: International Reading Association.

Neuman, S. (1998). How can we enable all children to achieve? In S. Neuman & K. Roskos (Eds.), *Children achieving: Best practices in early literacy* (pp. 5–19). Newark, DE: International Reading Association.

Neuman, S. (1999). Books make a difference: A study of access to literacy. *Reading Research Quarterly, 34*(3). 286–311.

Neuman, S., & Roskos, K. (1991a). Peers as literacy informants: A description of young children's literacy conversations in play. *Early Childhood Research Quarterly, 6,* 233–248.

Neuman, S., & Roskos, K. (1991b). The influence of literacy-enriched play centers on preschoolers' conceptions of the functions of print. In J. Christie (Ed.), *Play and early literacy development.* Albany, NY: State University of New York Press.

Neuman, S., & Roskos, K. (1992). Literacy objects as cultural tools: Effects on children's literacy behaviors during play. *Reading Research Quarterly, 27,* 203–223.

Neuman, S., & Roskos, K. (1993a). Access to print for children of poverty: Differential effects of adult mediation and literacy-enriched play settings on environmental and functional print tasks. *American Educational Research Journal, 30,* 95–122.

Neuman, S., & Roskos, K. (1993b). *Language and literacy learning in the early years: An integrated approach.* Fort Worth, TX: Harcourt Brace Jovanovich.

Neuman, S., & Roskos, K. (1997). Literacy knowledge in practice: Contexts of participation for young writers and readers. *Reading Research Quarterly, 32,* 10–32.

Neuman, S., & Roskos, K. (Eds.). (1998). *Children achieving: Best practices in early literacy.* Newark, DE: International Reading Association.

New Standards Project. (1994). *Elementary English language arts teacher portfolio handbook: Field trial version, 1994–1995.* Urbana, IL: New Standards Project.

Ninio, A. (1980). Picture-book reading in mother–infant dyads belonging to two subgroups in Israel. *Child Development, 51,* 587–590.

Norris, A., & Hoffman, P. (1990). Language intervention with naturalistic environments. *Language, Speech, and Hearing Services in the Schools, 21,* 72–84

Norton, D. (1993). *The effective teaching of language arts* (4th ed.). New York: Merrill/Macmillan.

Nurss, J. R. & Hough, R. A. (1992). Reading and the ESL student. In S. J. Samuels & A. E. Farstrup (Eds.), *What Research Has to Say About Reading Instruction.* Newark, DE: International Reading Association.

Nurss, J., & Rawlston, S. (1991). Family stories: Intergenerational literacy. *TESOL Journal, 1,* 29–30.

Ogle, D. (1986). KWL: A teaching model that develops active reading of expository text. *The Reading Teacher, 39,* 564–570.

Oken-Wright, P. (1998) Transition to writing: drawing as a scaffold for emergent writers. *Young Children, 53*(2), 76–81.

O'Neill, J. (1994). Making assessment meaningful: "Rubrics" clarify expectation, yield better feedback. *ASCD Update, 36*(1), 4–5.

Opitz, M. (1998). Children's books develop phonemic awareness—for you and parents, too! *The Reading Teacher, 51,* 526–528.

Orellana, M., & Hernández, A. (1999). Taking the walk: Children reading urban environmental print. *The Reading Teacher, 52,* 612–619.

Ourada, E. (1993). Legibility of third-grade handwriting: D'Nealian versus traditional Zaner-Bloser. In G. Coon & G. Palmer (Eds.), *Handwriting research and information: An administrators handbook.* Glenview, IL: Scott, Foresman.

Paley, V. (1981). *Wally's stories.* Cambridge, MA: Harvard University Press.

Paley, V. (1984). *Boys and girls: Superheroes in the doll corner.* Chicago: University of Chicago Press.

Paley, V. (1990). *The boy who would be a helicopter.* Cambridge, MA: Harvard University Press.

Pappas, C. (1993). Is narrative "primary"? Some insights from kindergartners' pretend readings of stories and information books. *Journal of Reading Behavior, 25,* 97–129.

Pappas, C., & Brown, E. (1987). Learning how to read by reading: Learning how to extend the functional potential of language. *Research in the Teaching of English, 21,* 160–177.

Paulson, F. L., Paulson, P. R., & Meyer, C. A. (1991). What makes a portfolio a portfolio? *Educational Leadership, 48,* 60–63.

Pease-Alvarez, L. (1991). Oral contexts for literacy development in a Mexican community. *The Quarterly Newsletter of the Laboratory of Comparative Human Cognition, 13,* 9–13.

Peck, S. (1978). Child–child discourse in second language acquisition. In E. Hatch (Ed.), *Second language acquisition: A book of readings.* Rowley, MA: Newbury House.

Piaget, J. (1970). *Structuralism.* New York: Basic Books.

Piper, T. (1993). *Language for all our children.* New York: Macmillan.

Power, B. (1998). Author! Author! *Scholastic Early Childhood Today, 12,* 30–37.

Raines, S., & Isbell, R. (1994). *Stories: Children's literature in early education.* Albany, NY: Delmar.

Rasinski, T., & Fredericks, A. (1991). Beyond parents and into the community. *The Reading Teacher, 44,* 698–699.

Read, C. (1971). Pre-school children's knowledge of English phonology. *Harvard Educational Review, 41,* 1–34.

Reyes, M., and Franquiz, M. (1998). Creating inclusive learning communities through English language arts: From chanclas to canicas. *Language Arts, 75,* 211–220.

Reyes, M., Laliberty, E., & Orbansky, J. (1993). Emerging biliteracy and cross-cultural sensitivity in a language arts classroom. *Language Arts, 70,* 659–668.

Rhodes, L. K., & Nathenson-Mejia, S. (1992). Anecdotal records: A powerful tool for ongoing literacy assessment. *The Reading Teacher, 45,* 502–509.

Rice, M., Huston, A., Truglio, R., and Wright, J. (1990) Words from *Sesame Street:* Learning vocabulary while viewing. *Development Psychology, 26,* 421–428.

Richgels, D., Poremba, K., & McGee, L. (1996). Kindergarteners talk about print: Phonemic awareness in meaningful contexts. *The Reading Teacher, 49,* 632–642

Richgels, D. & Wold, L. (1998). Literacy on the road: Backpacking partnerships between school and home. *The Reading Teacher, 52,* 18–29.

Rigg, P. (1989). Language experience approach: Reading naturally. In P. Rigg and V. Allen (Eds.), *When they don't all speak English.* Urbana, IL: National Council of Teachers of English.

Roe, M., & Vukelich, C. (1998). Literacy portfolios: Challenges that affect change. *Childhood Education, 74,* 148–153.

Rosenblatt, L. (1978). *The reader, the text, the poem: The transactional theory of the literary work.* Carbondale, IL: Southern Illinois University Press.

Roser, N. (1998, February). Young children as competent communicators. *Scholastic Early Childhood Today,* 45–47.

Roser, N., & Martinez, M. (1985). Roles adults play in preschoolers' response to literature. *Language Arts, 62,* 485–490.

Roskos, K. (Personal communication, October 9, 1995).

Roskos, K., & Christie, J. (Eds.). (2000). *Play and literacy in early childhood: Research from multiple perspectives.* Mahwah, NJ: Lawrence Erlbaum.

Roskos, K., & Neuman, S. (1993). Descriptive observations of adults' facilitation of literacy in play. *Early Childhood Research Quarterly, 8,* 77–97.

Rowe, D. (1994). *Preschoolers as authors: Literacy learning in the social world.* Cresskill, NJ: Hampton Press.

Rubin, K., Fein, G., & Vandenberg, B. (1983). Play. In P. Mussen (Ed.), *Handbook of child psychology: Vol. 4. Socialization, personality, and social development* (4th ed.). New York: Wiley.

Rudnick, B. (1995, October). Bridging the chasm between your English and ESL students. *Teaching PreK–8,* 48–49.

Samway, K., Whang, G., & Pippitt, M. (1995). *Buddy reading: Cross-age tutoring in a multicultural school.* Portsmouth, NH: Heinemann.

Saville-Troike, M. (1988). Private speech: Evidence for second language learning strategies in the "silent period." *Journal of Child Language, 15,* 567–90.

Schickedanz, J. (1986). *Literacy development in the preschool* [sound filmstrip]. Portsmouth, NH: Heinemann.

Schickedanz, J. (1998). What is developmentally appropriate practice in early literacy? Considering the alphabet. In S. Neuman & K. Roskos (Eds.), *Children achieving: Best practices in early literacy* (pp. 20–37). Newark, DE: International Reading Association.

Schieffelin, B., & Cochran-Smith, M. (1984). Learning to read culturally: Literacy before schooling. In H. Goelman, A. Oberg & F. Smith (Eds.), *Awakening to literacy.* Exeter, NH: Heinemann.

Schrader, C. (1989). Written language use within the context of young children's symbolic play. *Early Childhood Research Quarterly, 4,* 225–244.

Schwartz, J. (1983). Language play. In B. Busching & J. Schwartz (Eds.), *Integrating the language arts in the elementary school.* Newark, DE: International Reading Association.

Scott-Jones, D. (1993). Adolescent childbearing: Whose problem? What can we do? *Kappan, 75*(3), K1–K12.

Seawell, P. (1985). *A micro-ethnograpaphic study of a Spanish-English bilingual kindergarten in which literature and puppet play were used as a method of enhancing language growth.* Unpublished doctoral dissertation, University of Texas at Austin.

Segal, M., & Adcock, D. (1986). *Your child at play: Three to five years.* New York: Newmarket Press.

Serafini, F. (2001). Three paradigms of assessment: Measurement, procedure and inquiry. *The Reading Teacher, 54,* 384–393.

Serna, I., & Hudelson, S. (1993). Emergent literacy in a whole language bilingual program. In R. Donmoyer and R. Kos (Eds.), *At-risk students: Portraits, policies and programs.* Albany, NY: SUNY Press.

Shepard, L., Kagan, S., & Wurtz, E. (Eds.). (1998). *Principles and recommendations for early childhood assessments.* Washington, DC: National Education Goals Panel, 1998.

Shepard, L., Kagan, S., & Wurtz, E. (1998). Goal 1 early childhood assessments resource group recommends. *Young Children, 53,* 52–54.

Shore, R. (1997). *Rethinking the brain: New insights into early development.* New York: Families and Work Institute.

Silvaroli, N. (1990). *Classroom reading inventory* (6th ed.). Dubuque, IA: Brown.

Skinner, B. (1957). *Verbal behavior.* East Norwalk, CT: Appleton-Century-Crofts.

Slavin R. (1989). Students at risk of school failure: The problem and its dimensions. In R. Slavin, N. Karweit, & N. Madden (Eds.), *Effective programs for students at risk.* Boston: Allyn & Bacon.

Smilansky, S. (1968). *The effects of sociodramatic play on disadvantaged preschool children.* New York: Wiley.

Smith, F. (1981). Demonstrations, engagement, and sensitivity: A revised approach to language learning. *Language Arts, 58,* 103–112.

Smith, F. (1988). *Understanding reading* (4th ed.). Hillsdale, NJ: Erlbaum.

Smith, M., & Dickinson, D. (1994). Describing oral language opportunities and environments in Head Start and other preschool classrooms. *Early Childhood Research Quarterly, 9,* 345–366.

Snow, C. (1977). The development of conversations between mothers and babies. *Journal of Child Language, 4,* 1–22.

Snow, C., Burns, M., & Griffin, P. (1998). *Preventing reading difficulties in young children.* Washington, DC: National Academy Press.

Snow, C., Chandler, J., Lowry, H., Barnes, W., & Goodman, I. (1991). *Unfilled Expectations: Home and School Influences on Literacy.* Cambridge, Mass: Harvard University Press.

Snow, C., & Ninio, A. (1986). The contracts of literacy: What children learn from learning to read books. In W. Teale & E. Sulzby (Eds.), *Emergent literacy: Writing and reading.* Norwood, NJ: Ablex.

Sochurek, H. (1987, January). Medicine's new vision. *National Geographic, 171*(1), 2–41.

Spizman, R. (1997). *Kids on Board.* Minneapolis, MN: Fairview Press.

Spizman, R. (1997). *Kids on Board.* :Fairview Press.

Sporns, O., & Tononi, G. (1994). Selectionism and the brain. *International Review of Neurobiology, 37,* 4–23.

Sprenger, M. (1999). *Learning and memory: The brain in action.* Alexandria, VA: Association for Supervision and Curriculum Development.

Stahl, S. (1992). Saying the "p" word: Nine guidelines for exemplary phonics instruction. *The Reading Teacher, 45,* 618–625.

Stahl, S., Duffy-Hester, A., & Stahl, K. (1998). Everything you wanted to know about phonics (but were afraid to ask). *Reading Research Quarterly, 33,* 338–355.

Stahl, S., & Miller, P. (1989). Whole language and language experience approaches for beginning reading: A quantitative research synthesis. *Review of Educational Research, 59,* 87–116.

Stainback, S. & Stainback, W.(1992). *Curriculum considerations in inclusive classrooms.* Baltimore, MD: Brookes.

Stallman, A., & Pearson, P. D. (1990). Formal measures of early literacy. In L. Morrow & J. Smith (Eds.), *Assessment for instruction in early literacy.* Englewood Cliffs, NJ: Prentice Hall.

Stanovich, K. (1986). Matthew effects in reading: Some consequences of individual differences in the acquisition of literacy. *Reading Research Quarterly, 21,* 360–407.

Stewig, J., & Jett-Simpson, M. (1995). *Language arts in the early childhood classroom.* Belmont, CA: Wadsworth.

Strickland, D., & Morrow, L. (1990). Family literacy: Sharing good books. *The Reading Teacher, 43,* 518–519.

Strong, M. (1983). Social styles and the second language acquisition of Spanish-speaking kindergarteners. *TESOL Quarterly, 17,* 241–258.

Sulzby, E. (1985a). Children's emergent reading of favorite storybooks: A developmental study. *Reading Research Quarterly, 20,* 458–481.

Sulzby, E. (1985b). Kindergartners as writers and readers. In M. Farr (Ed.), *Advances in writing research, Vol. 1: Children's early writing development.* Norwood, NJ: Ablex.

Sulzby, E. (1990). Assessment of emergent writing and children's language while writing. In L. Morrow & J. Smith (Eds.), *Assessment for instruction in early literacy.* Englewood Cliffs, NJ: Prentice Hall.

Sulzby, E. (1992). Research directions: Transitions from emergent to conventional writing. *Language Arts, 69,* 290–297.

Sulzby, E., & Barnhart, J. (1990). The developing kindergartner: All of our children emerge as writers and readers. In J. McKee (Ed.), *The developing kindergarten: Programs, children, and teachers.* Ann Arbor, MI: Michigan Association for the Education of Young Children.

Sulzby, E., Barnhart, J., & Hieshima, J. (1989). Forms of writing and rereading from writing: A preliminary report. In J. Mason (Ed.), *Reading and writing connections.* Boston: Allyn and Bacon.

Sulzby, E., Barnhart, J., Hieshima, J. (1989). Forms of writing and rereading from writing: A preliminary report. In J. Mason (Ed.), *Reading and writing connections.* Boston: Allyn and Bacon.

Sulzby, E., & Teale, W. (1991). Emergent literacy. In R. Barr, M. Kamil, P. Mosenthal, & P. D. Pearson (Eds.), *Handbook of reading research* (Vol. 2). New York: Longman.

Swain, M. (1972). *Bilingualism as a native language.* Unpublished doctoral dissertation, University of California at Irvine.

Swanborn, M., & de Glopper, K. (1999). Incidental word learning while reading: A meta-analysis. *Review of Educational Research, 69,* 261–285.

Sylwester, R. (1995). *A celebration of neurons: An educator's guide to the human brain.* Alexandria, VA: Association for Supervision and Curriculum Development.

Tabors, P. (1997). *One child, two languages.* Baltimore, MD: Paul Brookes.

Tabors, P. (1998). What early childhood educators need to know: Developing effective programs for linguistically and culturally diverse children and families. *Young Children, 53*(6), 20–26.

Tabors, R., & Snow, C. (1994). English as a second language in preschool programs. In F. Genesee (Ed.), *Educating second language children: The whole child, the whole curriculum, the whole community.* New York: Cambridge University Press.

Tafolla, C. (1992). *Sonnets to human beings.* Santa Monica, CA: Lalo Press.

Taylor, D. (1983). *Family literacy.* Portsmouth, NH: Heinemann.

Taylor, D. (1986). Creating family story: "Matthew! We're going to have a ride." In W. Teale & E. Sulzby (Eds.), *Emergent literacy: Writing and reading.* Norwood, NJ: Ablex.

Taylor, D., & Dorsey-Gaines, C. (1988). *Growing up literate: Learning from inner-cities families.* Portsmouth, NH: Heinemann.

Taylor, D., & Strickland, D. (1986a). Family literacy: Myths and magic. In M. Sampson (Ed.), *The pursuit of literacy: Early reading and writing.* Dubuque, IA: Kendall Hunt.

Taylor, D., & Strickland, D. (1986b). *Family storybook reading.* Portsmouth, NH: Heinemann.

Taylor, N., Blum, I., & Logsdon, D. (1986). The development of written language awareness: Environmental aspects and program characteristics. *Reading Research Quarterly, 21,* 132–149.

Teale, W. (1978). Positive environments for learning to read: What studies of early readers tell us. *Language Arts, 55,* 922–932.

Teale, W. (1986a). The beginnings of reading and writing: Written language development during the preschool and kindergarten years. In M. Sampson (Ed.), *The pursuit of literacy: Early reading and writing.* Dubuque, IA: Kendall Hunt.

Teale, W. (1986b). Home background and young children's literacy development. In W. Teale & E. Sulzby (Eds.), *Emergent literacy: Writing and reading.* Norwood, NJ: Ablex.

Teale, W. (1987). Emergent literacy: Reading and writing development in early childhood. In J. E. Readence and R. S. Baldwin (Eds.), *Research in literacy: Merging perspectives.* Thirty-sixth yearbook of the National Reading Conference. Rochester, NY: National Reading Conference.

Teale, W. (1990). The promise and challenge of informal assessment in early literacy. In L. Morrow & J. Smith (Eds.), *Assessment for instruction in early literacy.* Englewood Cliffs, NJ: Prentice Hall.

Teale, W., & Martinez, M. (1988). Getting on the right road: Bringing books and children together in the classroom. *Young Children, 44*(1), 10–15.

Teale, W., & Sulzby, E. (1986). Emergent literacy as a perspective for examining how young children become writers and readers. In W. Teale & E. Sulzby (Eds.), *Emergent literacy: Writing and reading.* Norwood, NJ: Ablex.

Teale, W., & Sulzby, E. (1989). Emergent literacy: New perspectives. In D. Strickland, & L. Morrow (Eds.), *Emerging literacy: Young children learn to read and write.* Newark, DE: International Reading Association.

TESOL (1996). *Promising futures: ESL standards for prek–12 students.* Alexandria, VA: TESOL.

TESOL. (1997). *ESL standards for prek–12 students.* Alexandria, VA: TESOL.

Tharp, R., & Gallimore, R. (1988). *Rousing minds to life: Teaching, learning and school in a social context.* Cambridge, England: Cambridge University Press.

Thousand, J., & Villa, R. (1990). Sharing expertise and responsibilities through teacher teams. In W. Stainback & S. Stainback (Eds.), *Support networks for inclusive schooling: Interdependent integrated education* (pp. 151–166). Baltimore, MD: Brookes.

Thurber, D. (1993). *D'Nealian handwriting.* Glenview, IL: Scott, Foresman.

Torgesen, J. (1994). *Torgesen test of phonemic awareness.* Shoal Creek, TX: Pro-Ed.

Towell, J. (1998). Fun with vocabulary. *Reading Teacher, 51,* 356.

Trelease, J. (1989). *The new read-aloud handbook.* New York: Penguin.

Troia, G. (1999). Phonological awareness intervention research: A critical review of the experimental methodology. *Reading Research Quarterly, 34,* 28–52.

Turner, E. (1994). *Emerging bilingualism and biliteracy in a primary, multi-age bilingual classroom.* Unpublished honors thesis, Arizona State University, Tempe.

Urzúa, C. (1980). *Language input to second language learners.* Paper presented at the third Los Angeles Second Language Research Forum.

Valencia, S. (1990). A portfolio approach to classroom reading assessment: The whys, whats, and hows. *The Reading Teacher, 43,* 338–340.

Valencia, S., Hiebert, E., & Afflerbach, P. (1994). *Authentic reading assessment: Practices and possibilities.* Newark, DE: International Reading Association.

Vasquez, O. (1991). Reading the world in a multicultural setting: A Mexicano perspective. *The Quarterly Newsletter of the Laboratory of Comparative Human Cognition, 13,* 13–15.

Veatch, J. (1986). *Whole language in the kindergarten.* Tempe, AZ: Jan V Productions.

Veatch, J., Sawicki, F., Elliot, G., Flake, E., & Blakey, J. (1979). *Key words to reading: The language experience approach begins.* Columbus, OH: Merrill.

Ventriglia, L. (1982). *Conversations of Miguel and Maria.* Reading, MA: Addison-Wesley.

Vines, S., & Rosenthal-Tanzer, J. (1988). Otitis media and speech and language development. *Communication Skill Builders, 11,* 173–174.

Volk, D. (1997). Continuities and discontinuities: Teaching and learning in the home and school of a Puerto Rican five year old. In E. Gregory (Ed.), *One child, many worlds: Early learning in multicultural communities.* New York: Teachers College Press.

Vukelich, C. (1984). Parent's role in the reading process: A review of practical suggestions and ways to communicate with parents. *The Reading Teacher, 37,* 472–477.

Vukelich, C. (1992). Play and assessment: Young children's knowledge of the functions of writing. *Childhood Education, 68,* 202–207.

Vukelich, C. (1993). Play: A context for exploring the functions, features, and meaning of writing with peers. *Language Arts, 70,* 386–392.

Vukelich, C. (1994). Effects of play interventions on young children's reading of environmental print. *Early Childhood Research Quarterly, 9,* 153–170.

Vygotsky, L. (1962). *Thought and language.* Cambridge, MA: MIT Press.

Vygotsky, L. (1978). *Mind in society: The development of psychological processes.* Cambridge, MA: Harvard University Press.

Waggoner, D. (1993). 1993 census shows dramatic change in the foreign-born populations in the US. *NABE News, 16(7),* 18–20.

Wagstaff, J. (1997–1998). Building practical knowledge of letter–sound correspondences: A beginner's word wall and beyond. *The Reading Teacher, 51,* 298–304.

Walker, D., Greenwood, C., Hart, B., & Carta, J. (1994). Prediction of school outcomes based on early language production and socio-economic factors. *Child Development, 65,* 606–621.

Washington, G. (1982). Second-language learning strategies in the elementary school classroom. In M. Hines and W. Rutherford (Eds.), *On TESOL '81.* Washington, DC: Teachers of English to Speakers of Other Languages.

Watson, D. (1983). Bringing together reading and writing. In U. Hardt (Ed.), *Teaching reading with the other language arts.* Newark, DE: International Reading Association.

Weinstein-Shr, G., & Quintero, E. (1995). *Immigrant learners and their families.* McHenry, IL.: Delta Systems.

Weir, R. (1962). *Language in the crib.* The Hague, Netherlands: Mouton.

Weiss, C. E., Lillywhite, H. S., & Gordon, M. D. (1980). *Clinical management of articulation disorders.* St. Louis, MO: Mosby.

Wellhousen, K. (1996). Be ever so humble: Developing a study of homes for today's diverse society. *Young Children, 52*(1), 72–76.

Wells, G. (1985). *Language, learning, and education.* Windsor, England: Nfer-Nelson.

Wells, G. (1986). *The meaning makers: Children learning language and using language to learn.* Portsmouth, NH: Heinemann.

White, B. (1985). *The first three years of life.* Englewood Cliffs, NJ: Prentice-Hall.

Wien, C., & Kirby-Smith, S. (1998). Untiming the curriculum: A case study of removing clocks from the program. *Young Children, 53*(5), 8–13.

Wiggins, G. (1993). *Assessing student performance.* San Francisco: Jossey-Bass.

Wilcox, C. (1993). *Portfolios: Finding a focus.* Papers in Literacy Series. Durham, NH: The Writing Lab.

Wilde, S. (1997). *What's a schwa sound anyway? A holistic guide to phonetics, phonics, and spelling.* Westport, CT: Heinemann.

Wilensky, S. (1995). Social studies and literacy in the second grade. In P. Cordeiro (Ed.), *Endless possibilities.* Portsmouth, NH: Heinemann.

Willett, J. (1995). Becoming first graders in an L2: An ethnographic study of L2 socialization. *TESOL Quarterly, 29,* 573–503.

Wixson, K. (1992, May). *Anchoring assessment to curriculum goals.* Paper presented at the International Reading Association Conference, Los Angeles.

Wood, D., Bruner, J. S., & Ross, G. (1976). The role of tutoring in problem solving. *Journal of Child Psychology and Psychiatry, 17,* 89–100.

Woodard, C. (1984). Guidelines for facilitating sociodramatic play. *Childhood Education, 60,* 172–177.

The Wright Group. (1998). *Phonemic awareness handbook.* Bothell, WA: The Wright Group.

Yaden, D., Smolkin, L., & Conlon, A. (1989). Preschoolers' questions about pictures, print conventions, and story text during reading aloud at home. *Reading Research Quarterly, 24,* 188–214.

Yaden, D., Smolkin, L., & MacGillivray, L. (1993). A psychognetic perspective on children's understanding about letter associations during alphabet book readings. *Journal of Reading Behavior, 25,* 43–68.

Yopp, H. (1992). Developing phonemic awareness in young children. *The Reading Teacher, 45,* 696–703.

Yopp, H. & Yopp, R. (2000). *Supporting phonemic awareness development in the classroom. The Reading Teacher, 54,* 130–143.

Zaner-Bloser. (1993). *Handwriting: A way to self-expression.* Columbus, OH: Author.

Credits

Photo Credits

p. 24: Courtesy of Grace and Dan Bass; p. 51: Elizabeth Crews/Stock, Boston; p. 77: Elizabeth Crews/The Image Works; p. 93, courtesy of Angela Eiss; p. 95: Jeffry Myers/Stock, Boston; p. 122: Richard Hutchings/PhotoEdit; p. 143: PhotoDisc, Inc.; p. 178, courtesy of Carol Vukelich; p. 219: Bob Daemmrich/Bob Daemmrich Photography.

Text Credits

Figure 5.1: B. N. Kupetz & E. J. Green. 1997. Sharing books with infants and toddlers: Facing the challenges. *Young Children* 52 (2). Reprinted with permission from the National Association for the Education of Young Children; Trade Secrets 5.1: Courtesy of Lynn Cohen; Trade Secret 9.1: D. Manz. 1996. This is the house that kindergarten built. *Young Children*. Reprinted with permission from the National Association of Young Children.

Author Index

287

Subject Index